Setting Ceramic Tile

Setting Ceramic Tile
Michael Byrne

Cover photo: Tile courtesy of Walter Zanger, Houston, Texas, through Waterworks, Danbury, Connecticut.

Photo, p. 15: Tile courtesy of Waterworks, Danbury, Connecticut; Ceramic Tile Outlet, Danbury, Connecticut; American Olean Tile Company, Lansdale, Pennsylvania; and Ro.Tile, Inc., Lodi, California.

Publisher, Books: Leslie Carola

Managing Editor: Mark Feirer

Associate Editor: Christine Timmons

Design Director: Roger Barnes

Associate Art Director: Heather Brine Lambert

Assistant Art Director: Vickie Joy Stansberry

Copy/Production Editor: Nancy Stabile

Illustrations: Elizabeth Eaton

Pre-Press Manager: Austin E. Starbird

Coordinator of Production Services: Dave DeFeo

System Operators: Dinah George, Nancy-Lou Knapp

Scanner Systems Operator: Swapan Nandy

Production Assistants: Lisa Carlson, Mark Coleman, Deborah Cooper, Barbara Snyder

Pasteup: Marty Higham, Deb Rives-Skiles

Indexer: Harriet Hodges

Typeface: Caslon Book, 9 point

Paper: Warrenflo, 70 lb., neutral pH

Printer and Binder: Kingsport Press, Kingsport, Tennessee

First printing: September 1987
International Standard Book Number: 0-918804-55-8
Library of Congress Catalog Card Number: 86-51320

A FINE HOMEBUILDING Book

FINE HOMEBUILDING® is a trademark of The Taunton Press, Inc.,
registered in the U.S. Patent and Trademark Office.

The Taunton Press, Inc.
63 South Main Street
Newtown, Connecticut 06470

Acknowledgments

For Margo.

Although my name is on the cover, getting this book into print would have been impossible without the help of many people. Mike McCloskey, my first tile boss who now runs the Ceramic Tile Center in Sparks, Nevada, gave me a solid foundation in the basics and a real appreciation for mortar work. Joe and Dan Marsh of Joe Marsh Distributing in Concord, California, and their staff provided materials, information and patient answers to my countless questions over the course of 15 years. Don Ruskofsky of the Dallas Tile Company, also in Concord, California, was equally helpful in providing materials and information.

Bill Remmick, a San Francisco Bay Area architect who's partial to tile, presented me with challenging designs and the opportunity to work with a company of skilled craftsmen who made my job much easier. Dennis Hourany, owner of Elite Tile in Walnut Creek, California, was both a good boss and a good friend who offered unusual installations and the chance to try out new ideas. Bill Harvey, one of Dennis' setters, was gracious in sharing his skills and techniques, many of which can be found in this book.

From the first moment I expressed interest in the tile business, Henry Rothberg of Laticrete International, Inc., in Bethany, Connecticut, and Harvey Powell of The Noble Company in Grand Haven, Michigan, always made time to help me out. Their guidance through the maze of installation specifications was instrumental in developing the methods and techniques presented in the project chapters of this book. And to Jon Lopez of San Francisco, a very special thanks for the opportunity years ago to hold ceramic tile classes at his Bay Area craft school, where I explored ways of teaching novice tilesetters the tricks of the trade.

Apart from the technical help I've received over the years, I am indebted to numerous other people as well. Turning a tilesetter into what passes for a writer is a job I wouldn't wish on an enemy. But John Lively and Charles Miller of *Fine Homebuilding* magazine proved admirable teachers, who were always encouraging, understanding and patient.

My family and friends kept me afloat with good cheer and unflagging support. My wife, Margo, inspired and bolstered me in countless ways—all the while tolerating the role of tile widow. How I can thank her escapes me. Dr. George A. Foote, an old family friend from Baltimore, Maryland, offered encouragement for more than 20 years, during which time he helped me understand that the possibilities were endless.

And last, but not least, I owe thanks to all the names you find printed on the facing page—especially my editor, Chris Timmons. She and the entire staff at The Taunton Press made writing this book a pleasure.

Contents

Introduction

I was eight years old when I first saw ceramic tile. Not on a wall or a floor, but in pictures my mother showed me of the Church of the Sagrada Familia in Barcelona, Spain. The incredible creation of Spanish architect Antonio Gaudí, this church is partially cloaked in tile and sculpted stone. I was seized both by the colored tile on the church's many spires and by the strange, often abstract creatures that upheld pillars and meandered around the tops of columns. My mother found these bizarre shapes and use of tile appalling. I loved them.

I immediately set about sketching my own creatures and trying to unravel how the shapes and colors in the pictures had been produced. I sculpted crude figures from clay and created my first mosaic—a high-topped tennis shoe adorned with pasta, navy beans, stones and glitter. Years later real tile substituted for pasta, and during a stint in art school I fashioned outdoor mosaics inspired by Gaudí's work in Guell Park in Barcelona. To my great chagrin, however, I soon found my mosaics falling apart.

The local tilesetters, from whom I sought advice about my mosaics, were experiencing the same trouble with their bathroom tiles. One of them suggested that I go to California, the mecca of tilesetters, to find the Right Way to set tile. So off I went to San Francisco, where I took a job with a tile repairman. I thought this sojourn would last six months, but six months turned into 16 years—and I'm still learning more about tile and tilesetting every day.

      ❊   ❊   ❊

There is, in fact, a great deal to be learned about ceramic tile. It has decorated walls and floors for thousands of years, yet its origin remains a mystery. While sun-dried clay objects have been found at prehistoric sites, the earliest tiles found with colored glazes are those from ancient Egypt. These tiles, finished with blue copper glazes, date to around 4000 B.C.

Unlike in Egypt, where ceramic tile was reserved for temples and the residences of the pharaohs, tile in ancient Rome embellished the homes and businesses of the merchant class. So prevalent was the demand for tile

Detail (facing page) and partial view of Antonio Gaudí's serpentine, tiled mosaic bench in Guell Park in Barcelona, Spain. Color photo by Rogers, Monkmeyer Press; black-and-white by Peter Menzel, Stock, Boston.

in Rome that tilesetting became established as a flourishing trade in the first century A.D. The Roman tile industry was organized much as ours is today: quarry workers provided the clay for tile and raw materials for glaze; tile makers and glazers produced the tile; and designers, tilesetters and finishers planned out and executed the installation.

The Romans made mortar and grout by mixing ground marble with volcanic ash, and they used tree resins or asphalt from tar pits to produce adhesives. For the most part, their tiles were soft-bodied and low-fired, and, when used for ordinary floors, were set directly on a thick bed of mortar. The tiles were then tapped level with one another, causing the mortar to ooze up between and around them. Once this mortar had set up, it was compacted into the joints, which meant that the mortar served simultaneously as setting bed, adhesive and grout. For wall hangings or portable murals, which were displayed on special occasions, the Romans simply glued tiles to wooden boards and added grout after the adhesive had dried.

For almost 2,000 years the setting methods and materials of the Romans remained unchanged. Then, in the 19th century, the Industrial Revolution ushered in a significant change in the tile trade. Mass-production techniques replaced the traditional method of making tile by hand, enabling tile makers to speed up their production, lower their costs and expand their markets. Yet because tilesetters continued to install tile using the traditional, laborious process of floating mortar setting beds, the costs of installation remained beyond the reach of all but the wealthy.

After the Industrial Revolution, the tile trade remained essentially the same until the end of World War II. Then, with America's storage tanks

Eighteenth-century Portuguese tile made for the rebuilding of Lisbon after the earthquake of 1755. Photo courtesy of Country Floors, New York.

Mid-17th-century tin-glazed, earthenware Dutch tile panel. Photo courtesy of the Board of Trustees of the Victoria & Albert Museum, London, England.

filled with the by-products of the oil that had fueled the war machine, chemists scurried off to their labs to invent new uses for these materials. This experimentation produced a wealth of new consumer goods, ranging from nylon products to adhesives that allowed tile to be set directly over drywall or plaster. This latter development meant that, for the first time, tilesetters had a real alternative to the traditional floated mortar bed—and that the average homeowner would be able to afford a tile installation.

Bathrooms and kitchens across the country were soon transformed with tile, and for a few years the tile industry mushroomed. Then the problems began. The new materials, it seemed, allowed moisture to penetrate the setting bed, turning drywall and plaster walls into crumbly messes and even rotting out the framing below. Drywall manufacturers quickly developed moisture-resistant panels, but these only slowed down the damaging effects of water without really solving the problem.

By the 1950s, the tile-repair business was booming, and tilesetters nationwide were busily replacing the short-lived, new "thinset" installations with tiles set on the traditional thick mortar bed. What was needed if the industry was to keep growing was a real solution to the problems of waterproofing installations and new ideas for keeping the costs of installations affordable. In the late 1960s the tile industry introduced a host of new materials designed to reduce labor and increase performance. Among these products were waterproofing membranes, mortar and grout additives, and new kinds of drywall that were unaffected by water. At long last, anyone with the inclination, moderate skills and a little time could produce tile installations that would be long-lasting and trouble-free. For the novice tilesetter, the only things that stood in the way of getting right down to work were a lack of experience, the absence of readable information on tilesetting techniques and the bewildering array of new materials.

At the time, I was one of those novice setters, eager to learn about tile— and how to preserve my disintegrating mosaics—but dismayed by the mysterious maze of techniques and materials. It was then that I apprenticed

Glazed earthenware tile, titled "Persian Antelope," produced in 1937 for the Moravian Pottery and Tile Works in Doylestown, Pennsylvania. Photo courtesy of the Cooper-Hewitt Museum, Smithsonian Institution/Art Resource, New York.

Sixth-century mosaic of the port and city of Classe in the church of S. Apollinare Nuovo in Ravenna, Italy. Photo by Scala/Art Resource, New York.

Victorian English tile (above). Photo courtesy of Country Floors, New York. Mid-19th-century relief tile in the Golestan Palace in Teheran, Iran (at right). Photo by Art Resource, New York.

The Indian Treaty Room with English Minton tile floor in the Old Executive Office Building, completed in 1888, in Washington, D.C. Photo courtesy of The White House.

myself to the tile repairman and unwittingly began what would become a life-long pursuit. During the next 15 years, I worked for a variety of companies, tiling everything from 2-ft.-square entry halls to huge industrial plants. In 1976, I started my own company because I had developed my own ideas about setting tile, which my employer dismissed since they ran counter to the accepted methods. Then in 1981, when *Fine Homebuilding* magazine published its first issue, I was disgruntled to find that it contained no articles on tilesetting. I complained to the magazine's editor. He responded by asking me to submit an article for consideration. To gain insight into what the public wanted to know about setting tile, I taught classes in San Francisco. I soon realized that I had gleaned enough information from all those years of tilesetting not just for a few more articles but for a full book.

From the outset, I wanted to write a book that would really clarify the complexities of setting tile and demystify a trade that has long been veiled in secrecy. I wanted this to be an informative and valuable book for both novice and experienced setter alike, a book that would clearly instruct the beginner in the basics and also significantly expand the veteran's store of information. I wanted this to be a book not just about tilesetting but about setting tile with quality. I emphatically wanted readers to grasp the importance of the installation and to understand that the culprit in disintegrating tilework was not the tile but the installation itself. And I wanted to convey to readers a sound appreciation of tilesetting as essentially a process of analyzing and solving problems—a process in which thought and strategy are as crucial to the installation as its physical execution is.

To present this large body of material in the clearest, most accessible way, I've organized this book into two parts. The first contains a series of reference chapters introducing the principles and techniques of tilesetting. These chapters explore not only tile itself but also tilesetting tools, setting materials, surface preparation and laying out tile installations.

The second half of the book puts this theoretical information to practical use in a series of project chapters. These chapters represent a cross

"Ploughing" (above), English tile panel designed by Walter Crane (1845-1915) for Maw & Co. Photo courtesy of the Board of Trustees of the Victoria & Albert Museum, London, England. "Le vieux marcheur" (below right), a mosaic created by Jean-Louis Forain around 1900 in the Café Riche in Paris, now in the Musée de Meudon. Photo by Giraudon/Art Resource, New York.

section of typical home installations, and provide a step-by-step account of the all-important decision-making process and technical execution of six very different jobs. These project chapters—half of them thick-bed mortar jobs, the other half thinset work—considerably expand upon the basic information set forth in the first half of the book. Although no two tile installations are ever alike, readers will find in these pages the information needed to successfully negotiate most home tile installations. In addition to these six common projects, there is also a chapter on special installations (including guidelines for such things as setting tile in steamrooms and around fireplaces and stoves) with a concluding section on repairs.

Because this is a book about setting tile to last, throughout you'll find recommendations for the techniques and materials that I've found produce the best possible results. There may often be other techniques and materials that will work in a given installation, but the ones recommended yield, I think, superior results.

No single book, of course, can transform a novice into a journeyman tilesetter. Learning to expertly set tile requires patience and lots of hard work. It also helps to couple this work with an ongoing curiosity about the subject, and for this reason I encourage readers to explore all they can find written about tile. In addition to the works cited in the bibliography (see the Resource Guide at the back of the book), tile organizations involved with installation procedures are an important source of information. These groups (also listed in the Resource Guide) produce publications with a lot of valuable technical material, which they now make available to people outside the trade. Another resource is the manufacturers of tile and tilesetting products. Most of these companies have brochures about their wares, and some even have toll-free information hot lines.

I hope in the end that you draw from this book a detailed working knowledge of tile and an appreciation of the wide range of possible solutions a tiling problem may have. I hope, too, that this book enables you to produce the thoughtful, careful and trouble-free installations that ceramic tile richly deserves. ☐

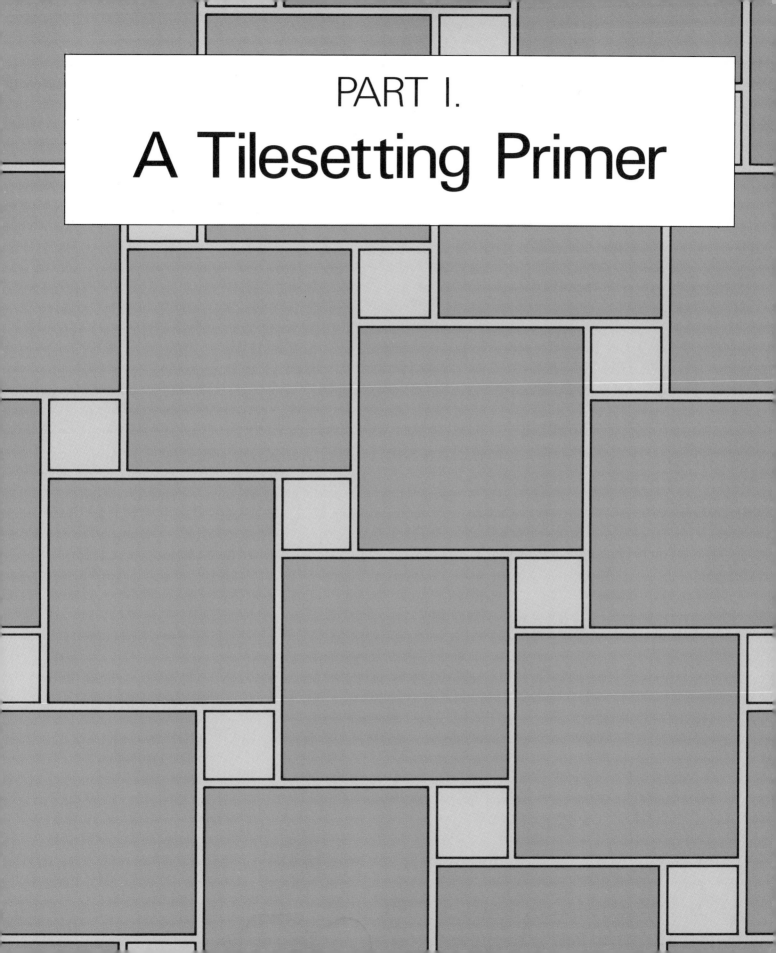

PART I.
A Tilesetting Primer

Tile

All tile was once made of pure clay from the bed of a stream or river. Tile makers gathered the wet clay, crudely processed it to eliminate stones and debris, formed individual tiles by hand, and let the pieces bake in the sun. Early in tile's history, which dates back at least 6,000 years, tile makers developed frames for shaping the body of the tile. And then, historians speculate, someone noticed that the fired clay inside the ovens used for baking bread was sturdier than sun-dried clay and was also unaffected by water. This significant observation led tile makers to try baking their tiles in these ovens and, in turn, to create special ovens, or kilns, for firing tile. These kilns were probably reserved for special tile, while ordinary tile continued to be baked in the sun.

After these advances—or perhaps before them—another important development took place that changed the laborious task of gathering clay, a process that involved moving the tile maker's household each time a source of clay was exhausted. At some point, a weary tile maker must have realized that it was possible to extend raw clay by mixing it with ground shards of pottery and broken tile. This practice probably took hold quickly and set a precedent for later extending clay even further by mixing it with ground shale and eventually ground gypsum.

Nowadays, while some commercially produced tile is made of pure clay or pure gypsum, the vast majority is made from a combination of clay, ground shale or gypsum, and other ingredients such as talc, vermiculite and sand. These latter materials serve both to extend the clay and to control shrinkage in the tile. After the clay has been refined and mixed with water and these additives, it's shaped into a bisque, or biscuit, which is the body of the tile. The green (unfired) bisque can be formed in several ways. It can be extruded through a die, like toothpaste squeezed from a tube, or it can be rammed into a die, in the same way that a piece of metal can be stamped. It can also be cut from a sheet, cookie-cutter style, or it can be formed by hand in a wooden or metal frame. Manufacturers who produce tile in great quantity form the bisque in a die, which yields uniformly shaped and sized tiles. (Most commercial tile today is made by the dust-press method, in which the moisture content of the ingredients is so low that they hold together only when rammed into a die.) Tile producers with smaller, less mechanized operations and makers who work by hand cut the bisque from sheets of clay or form the tiles in frames.

However the bisque is formed, it must leather-harden, or dry enough to lose its plasticity, before being fired in a kiln. Most tile, whether glazed or unglazed, is fired only once, though some tile is fired several times, and some highly decorated tile may even undergo five or more firings. The number of firings, as well as the purity of the clay, largely determines the eventual cost of the tile.

The temperature at which tile is fired ranges from as low as 900°F to as high as 2500°F, but, generally speaking, most tile is fired at temperatures between 1900°F and 2200°F. Low-temperature firing usually produces porous tile and soft glazes, while high-temperature firing yields dense, nonporous tile and hard glazes. The amount of time a tile remains in the kiln also contributes to the tile's porosity, and while some tile may be fired for only a few minutes, other tile may stay in the kiln for as long as a week.

Glazes

Although the bisque may be the backbone of the tile, it's the glaze that gets all the attention. The earliest examples found of tile finished with colored glaze date to ancient Egypt, where copper particles formed the base of this glaze. Today most glaze consists of a transparent or opaque coating of lead silicates and pigment, which is brushed or sprayed on the surface of the bisque and fired. The glaze can be applied to the tile's green bisque and be fired along with the tile itself, or it can be added after the tile has undergone one or more firings. Either way, it serves both to decorate the tile and to protect the surface of the tile. While much of the tile produced today is glazed, some, like quarry tile and many Mexican pavers, is left unglazed and derives its color only from the clay from which it's made.

In some cases, a glaze is intended not only to color and preserve the surface of the tile but also to give it texture. Sawdust is one of several substances added to the glaze of some tile for this purpose. As the temperature in the kiln rises, the sawdust burns, leaving behind a bumpy covering that's not as slick as the traditional, smooth glaze, making this a good tile for floors. For another type of tile, particles of silicon carbide are sprinkled on the wet glaze before firing to produce a similar, nonskid surface. (Some unglazed tile has carbide bits pressed into its surface before firing for the same purpose.)

When selecting tile for a particular installation, consider the use the tile will receive and how its glaze will hold up. Depending on the temperature at which it's fired and the amount of time spent in the kiln, a glaze may be soft, easily scratched and unable to withstand the wear a floor or kitchen countertop receives. Or the glaze may be hard, quite durable and serviceable for any installation. (For a discussion of the various types of tile available, see p. 13, and for suggestions on how to choose tile, see p. 19.)

Water absorption

The amount of water a tile absorbs depends on the number of air pockets in the tile's bisque. The presence and number of these air pockets depends not only on the temperature at which the tile was fired but also on the amount of time it spent in the kiln and the composition of the clay. (The glaze on tile absorbs no moisture, regardless of the firing temperature or

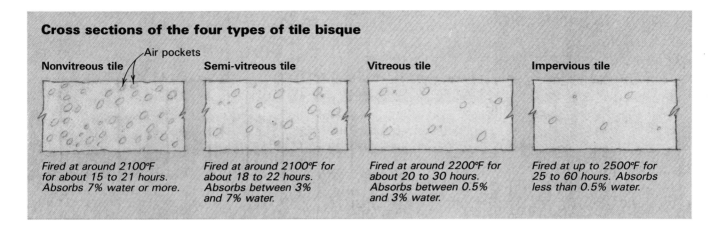

Cross sections of the four types of tile bisque

Air pockets

Nonvitreous tile

Fired at around 2100°F for about 15 to 21 hours. Absorbs 7% water or more.

Semi-vitreous tile

Fired at around 2100°F for about 18 to 22 hours. Absorbs between 3% and 7% water.

Vitreous tile

Fired at around 2200°F for about 20 to 30 hours. Absorbs between 0.5% and 3% water.

Impervious tile

Fired at up to 2500°F for 25 to 60 hours. Absorbs less than 0.5% water.

time in the kiln.) The American National Standards Institute (ANSI) measures the permeability of various types of tile by comparing the dry weight of a finished tile with its weight after it's been boiled in water for five hours. The four categories of tile established by ANSI, as presented in its handbook (see the Resource Guide at the back of the book), are nonvitreous, semi-vitreous, vitreous and impervious. Knowing how permeable a tile is is important in deciding which kind of tile to use for a particular installation. Tile that absorbs little or no water, for example, is more suitable for a wet installation (a shower stall, for instance) than tile that really soaks up a lot of water.

Nonvitreous tile readily absorbs water, about 7% of its weight, meaning that air pockets make up about 7% of this tile's bisque. The tile is fired at temperatures of around 2100°F for 15 to 21 hours, which produces its very porous bisque and, if it's glazed, soft glaze. Because this type of tile is fired at relatively low temperatures for a comparatively short time, it requires less energy to manufacture and is therefore less expensive than vitreous tile.

Since nonvitreous tile absorbs so much water, it's not a good choice for tiling wet areas or for exterior installations. In wet areas, this tile's porous bisque may not dry out completely between uses and may, in time, harbor bacteria. And because nonvitreous tile lacks what is termed freeze-thaw stability, when it's installed outdoors in cold climates, the water it absorbs in winter will expand as it freezes, causing the tile to crack.

That said, the fact is that setters install nonvitreous tile all the time in wet and exterior installations. And in areas with few tile stores nearby, nonvitreous tile may be all that's readily available. Nonetheless, I don't recommend using this tile in these potentially problematic locations. For this reason I would urge people without access to a fully stocked tile store to order the tile they need from a source listed in the Resource Guide. If you choose to use nonvitreous tile in these situations for whatever reason, at least upgrade the installation to minimize the problems. In addition to properly waterproofing the wet interior installation (see p. 89), install the tile with a thinset adhesive and mix a latex additive with the adhesive as well as with the grout. (To decipher this mysterious advice on adhesives, and for a full discussion on choosing and using setting materials, see Chapter 3.)

For setting nonvitreous tile in any installation, several adjustments should be made to accommodate this tile's high water-absorption rate. In ordinary installations, low-fired tile can be set with any of the four available adhesives—organic mastics, and water-mixed, latex or acrylic, and epoxy thinset adhesives. While mastics come ready to use, a thinset used with this tile should be mixed slightly wetter than it would be for tile that absorbs little or no water. And before any nonvitreous installation is grouted, the unglazed portions of the tile should be misted with water to prevent the porous bisque from sucking liquid out of the grout and causing the grout to cure prematurely.

Semi-vitreous tile is fired at about the same temperature as nonvitreous tile but usually for a little longer time, which produces a somewhat porous bisque. This tile has an absorption rate of from 3% to 7% of its weight and is, in effect, a transition tile between very porous nonvitreous tile and essentially nonporous vitreous tile. With proper waterproofing, semi-vitreous tile can be used for wet interior installations, but because it's not really freeze-thaw stable, it should not be used outdoors in cold climates. Like nonvitreous tile, it can be set with an organic mastic or a thinset adhesive, though a thinset should be used for a wet installation. When a thinset is used, it should be mixed slightly drier than for nonvitreous tile but wetter than for vitreous tile. To ensure good results, semi-vitreous tile should also be misted with water before grouting to prevent its somewhat porous bisque from sucking water from the grout.

Vitreous tile is fired at temperatures of around 2200°F for about 20 to 30 hours, which causes the ingredients in the bisque to fuse together like glass. Due to its very dense body, vitreous tile absorbs only from 0.5% to 3% water and is therefore an excellent choice for any installation, including those that will get wet or that will freeze. This tile's dense bisque also accounts for its high compressive strength (that is, it can withstand the compression of a heavy load without fracturing). Since it's able to bear considerable weight, vitreous tile is generally more suitable for floors than soft-bodied, nonvitreous tile. Because some vitreous tiles have relatively soft glazes, however, and because a few manufacturers of vitreous tile state that their products are unsuitable for floors, despite high-temperature firing, it's a good idea to always check the tile maker's specifications when selecting tiles for a particular installation.

For setting vitreous tile in dry installations, either an organic mastic or a thinset can be used. In wet installations, only a thinset adhesive should be used, and it should be mixed to suit the particular vitreous tile being set. Before grouting, vitreous tile needs only to be sponged down rather than misted with water.

Impervious tile is fired at temperatures of up to 2500°F for 25 to 60 hours. This treatment produces a tile that, as its name suggests, is almost waterproof. This tile absorbs less than 0.5% water and for this reason is frequently used for sanitary installations in hospitals and pharmaceutical plants. Impervious tile is easily sterilized and can withstand repeated cleaning and disinfecting. And since this tile absorbs practically no water, germs have little chance of finding a home in an impervious installation.

Like other tile, this, too, can be installed with either an organic mastic or a thinset adhesive, though a thinset should be used for wet installations, mixed to suit the particular tile being set. Unless the weather is hot when the tile is installed, impervious tile does not need to be misted or sponged down before grouting.

None of these four types of tile is any more difficult to work with than another. With regard to cutting, all can be trimmed with the snap cutter, biters and wet saw (for a description of these tools, see Chapter 2), though because of their density, vitreous and impervious tiles are likely to require a bit more pressure and time to cut than soft-bodied tiles.

Ceramic tile and specialty tile

This book is generally devoted to ceramic tile. Yet because there are several types of nonceramic tile installed with ceramic methods, they, too, are included in the listing below. Not included in this list is linoleum or vinyl tile, whose installation needs are quite different from those of ceramic tile. Before looking at the various types of tile available, however, let's consider the several formats in which tile is sold and a side of tile that usually goes unnoticed—its back.

Perhaps the most striking thing about visiting a tile store is the vast array of tile available. Produced in a wide spectrum of colors, sizes and shapes, tile is sold mainly as separate, loose tiles, all of which share a common requirement in setting: they must be consistently spaced. Setters installing loose tiles have used any number of devices to evenly space them—sticks, nails, string or rope, a finger (this takes patience!) and, since their development in the late 1950s, tile spacers. The latter are small plastic devices sold in varying shapes and widths (from ⅓₂ in. to ½ in.) that establish consistent grout joints between tiles. Some manufacturers resolve the problem of spacing by building spacing lugs into the sides of the tile or by packaging tile in sheet format.

Sheet-mounted tiles are individual tiles evenly spaced and mounted on a backing sheet, approximately 12 in. square or larger. Various kinds of tiles are packaged in sheet format, but most are vitreous, no larger than 4 in. square and mounted on paper, plastic mesh or a grid of rubber dots. The placement of the mounting material distinguishes the several types of sheet-mounted tile. As its name suggests, face-mounted tile has its mounting, a sheet of paper, adhered to the face of the tile. This paper is left in place during setting and is dampened and removed after the adhesive has dried. Back-mounted tile is held together by plastic or paper mesh applied to the back of the tile, which is left in place when the tile is set. Dot-mounted tile is joined by small rubber or plastic dots between the joints, which are not removed for setting. Wherever the mounting is positioned, it can be easily trimmed to approximate size with a sharp utility knife, a razor knife or an X-acto blade.

The obvious advantage of placing the mounting material on the back of the tile is that the face is then visible during setting, making it easier to align the tile and grout joints. The disadvantage of this arrangement is that the backing material interferes with the bond of the tile and adhesive. In the case of dot-mounted tile, some setters also report installation problems caused by a thin film of oil deposited on the back of the tile when the dots were applied. (For a full discussion of how to handle the installation problems with sheet-mounted tile, see p. 204.)

Another type of sheet-mounted tile goes a step further in resolving the question of spacing and considerably speeds up installation. Pregrouted tile sheets consist of large panels of tile held together with flexible silicone caulk. The tile in these sheets is usually 4¼-in.-square glazed wall tile, and the size of the sheets varies from 2 sq. ft. to about 6 sq. ft. These sheets are subject to the same bonding problems as ordinary sheet-mounted tile, but once installed need only some caulking between the sheets.

Pregrouted tile sheets are designed for tiling tract housing or large-scale commercial jobs, but they're also available in kit form for the do-it-yourselfer. I advise steering clear of these sheets for small residential jobs, though, for several reasons. First, this kind of tile is available only in a limited range of colors, and the caulk (used because it's easier to clean than grout) is shiny, looks very little like real grout and comes only in white. Second, these sheets are designed to save setters money on large

Pregrouted tile sheets are actually misnamed, since the "grout" is in reality silicone caulk. Developed to save labor costs on large-scale commercial tiling contracts, they're a poor choice for small residential jobs because they're more expensive than regular tile.

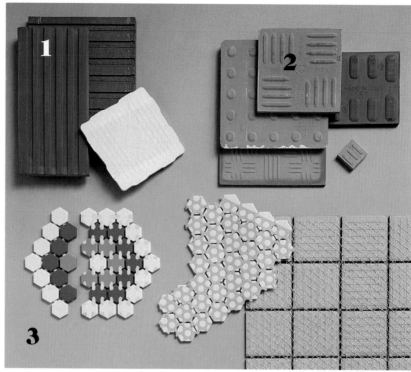

(1) Ridge-backed tiles alongside tile (at right) with spacing lugs and modified ridges; (2) button-backed tiles in a variety of configurations; and (3) sheet-mounted tiles, including (from left) dot-mounted tile and back-mounted tile with paper and plastic mesh backings.

commercial jobs since they eliminate the labor of grouting. On small jobs the savings is questionable, as the tile itself is more expensive than regular tile. Assuming that the do-it-yourselfer's labor is free, the only real savings would be, at best, a few dollars for the grout itself.

Although a tile's face gets most of the attention, its back deserves note, too, since it's oftentimes intentionally covered with raised ridges, dots or squares. The configuration of a tile back varies greatly from tile to tile, yet it's consistently designed to either expand the surface area of the back (and thus increase the adhesive's bond strength), aid in the firing process or denote manufacturing information. Ridge-backed tile is extruded tile whose back bears a series of elevations, which can effectively double, and in some cases even triple, the flat surface area of the back. Button-backed tile, most of which is produced by the dust-press method, has raised dots or squares on the back, which separate the individual tiles when they're stacked in a kiln, allowing heat to pass evenly among them and ensuring a uniform firing. Finally, many tiles are embossed with identifying marks to denote a particular production run of tile or to record color and other manufacturing specifications. All of these various markings can be helpful when you need to find replacement tiles for restoration or remodeling work.

Glazed wall tile Generally speaking, glazed wall tile is nonvitreous tile with a white gypsum or terra-cotta-colored bisque and a soft glaze, which makes it unsuitable for floor use. In contrast, floor tile is any nonvitreous, semi-vitreous, vitreous or impervious tile, whether glazed or unglazed,

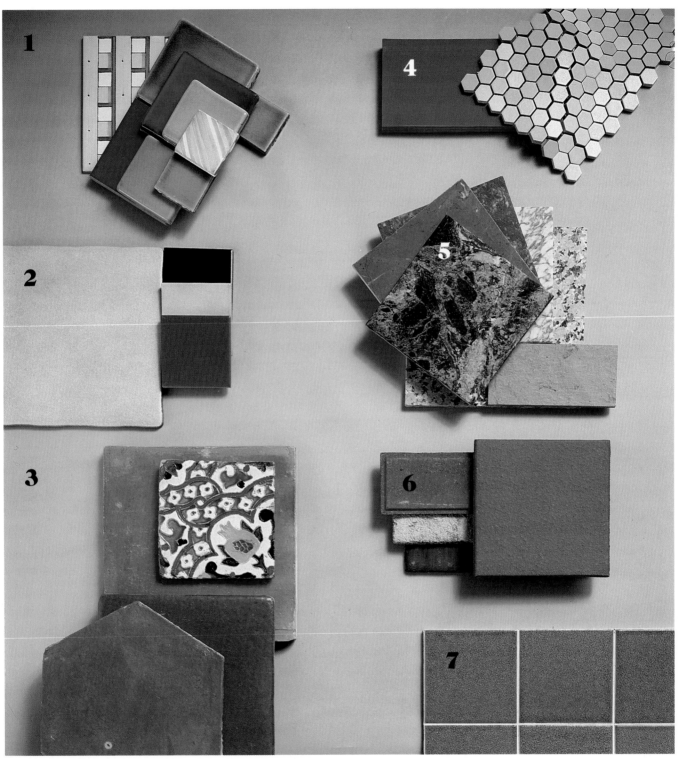

(1) Glazed wall tile; (2) glazed floor tile; (3) handmade, patterned Portuguese wall tile atop handmade, sealed Mexican pavers; (4) quarry tile beneath mosaic hexagons; (5) stone tile, including (from top, clockwise) green aosta marble, red alicante marble, French gray marble, green destours marble, granite and slate; (6) square cement-bodied tile on top of brick-veneer tile; and (7) pregrouted tile sheet.

that is considered sturdy enough to be used for floors. This tile could, of course, also be used for walls, as perhaps some of it should be—some tiles officially classified as floor tiles are not particularly durable, or they may have a tough vitreous bisque finished with a fragile glaze.

Most glazed wall tile sold in the United States is produced in this country by the dust-press method. Usually about ¼ in. thick, these tiles are most commonly made in 4-in. and 6-in. squares, though larger tiles up to 12 in. square are available. With a few exceptions, these tiles are intended for wall use, rather than for floor and countertop installations. With proper waterproofing, they can be used for wet installations, but they should be limited to interior use, as they are not freeze-thaw stable. Glazed wall tile requires no special setting bed and can be installed with either an organic mastic or a thinset adhesive for dry installations, but should be used only with a thinset adhesive for wet installations.

Paver tile Pavers are clay, shale or porcelain tile, made by hand or machine, which are at least ½ in. thick, sometimes glazed, and intended for use on floors. Machine-made pavers are produced both in the United States and in Europe. Sometimes they are extruded, but more often they are made by the dust-press method. Generally speaking, machine-made pavers are fired at high enough temperatures to produce semi-vitreous or vitreous tile. These tiles usually range in size from 4 in. by 6 in. to 12 in. square and are up to ⅝ in. thick. The large pavers are sometimes paired with 1-in.-square glazed pavers called spots. These accent tiles have been around for quite a while and were originally colored with various stains rather than glaze.

Whether used on floors or walls, machine-made pavers should be paired with a thinset adhesive. Because they are vitreous and thus freeze-thaw stable, these pavers can be used in both wet and exterior installations. They require no special setting bed, but due to their uneven surface, they may need to be back-buttered with adhesive (see p. 60) to ensure complete contact with the setting bed.

Unglazed handmade pavers are generally produced in Mexico and in the Mediterranean. Those from Mexico are usually terra-cotta-colored, yellow or brown, while Mediterranean pavers are traditionally doe-colored. Glazed handmade pavers are produced mainly in Mexico, Portugal, Italy and France. All handmade pavers are nonvitreous tiles fired at low temperatures. (Sometimes in remote regions of Mexico these tiles are fired in jury-rigged kilns made from the bodies of automobiles, with the heat supplied by burning discarded tires!) About ½ in. to 2 in. thick, these pavers range in size from 4 in. square to 24 in. square. Because these tiles are often crudely made, a run of a particular dimension can vary widely in size from tile to tile, and individual tiles may bear fingerprints, animal tracks or other such "signatures."

Like machine-made pavers, these tiles are produced primarily for floors, though they are sometimes used for walls, especially when glazed. They are unsuitable for countertops, though, because they are not flat and because, to be kept clean, they need to be finished with sealers that shouldn't be used around food. If you really want handmade pavers on a kitchen countertop, I suggest that you use them on the backsplash to accent a more practical choice of tile for the work surface. Finally, because handmade pavers are porous, they should not be used in wet interior locations or in exterior installations in freezing climates.

Before setting, the backs of handmade pavers should be cleaned of any debris and loose particles. They can be scraped or brushed and vacuumed,

These handmade Mexican pavers exhibit the individuality and texture inherent in the manufacturing process. Because they're non-vitreous, however, they shouldn't be used for wet or exterior installations in cold climates.

or, if time permits, submerged in water, scraped clean with a knife or a margin trowel, rinsed with clean water and turned on edge to dry. Any handmade pavers that need to be cut for the installation should be trimmed on the wet saw rather than on the snap cutter. Like machine-made pavers, they should be installed with a thinset adhesive for floor or wall use. Since handmade pavers aren't flat, they too should be back-buttered with adhesive to ensure complete contact with the setting bed. Finally, unglazed pavers should be sealed to protect them and slow down the wearing process.

Traditionally, these pavers were sealed with hot oil and beeswax, but now they are often sent untreated to the tile retailer, who stains and seals them. If the pavers you select are unsealed, seal them *before* grouting with at least two coats of top-coat sealer made especially for tile, or two coats of a penetrating oil such as Flecto urethane or Watco oil (see the Resource Guide). Both of these sealers will need to be reapplied about once a year. If a top-coat sealer is used, the floor will need to be stripped and completely resealed each time the sealer is reapplied. With a penetrating oil, the worn spots alone can be refinished.

Quarry tile   Originally quarry tile was quarried stone, cut, ground and polished to uniform dimensions. Now the term generally applies to semi-vitreous or vitreous clay tile, extruded and fired unglazed, which resembles the original quarry tile. The bisque of these hard-bodied tiles is usually a deep red color throughout, but black and tan quarry tiles are also available.

Quarry tile is manufactured in 4-in. to 12-in. squares and hexagons as well as in rectangles, most commonly 3 in. by 6 in. or 4 in. by 8 in. The pieces range in thickness from ½ in. to ¾ in. Because of their density, these tiles are excellent for floor and countertop use and could also serve for wall installations.

Quarry tile used for floors can be finished with a sealer or left unsealed. If you want to seal quarry tile after installing it, do so *before* grouting with a top-coat sealer especially made for tile (quarry tile is too dense for a penetrating oil). The floor will need to be entirely stripped and the sealer reapplied about once a year. Because tile sealer should not be used around food, a quarry-tile countertop must be left unsealed. This may mean that the countertop will become stained with use and that another tile would make a more practical choice for this installation.

Because they are vitreous, quarry tiles are excellent for wet installations and can also be used outdoors. They need no special setting bed or unusual installation treatment. Whether used for floors or walls, they should be paired with a thinset adhesive.

Mosaic tile   The tile industry considers any tile 2 in. square or smaller to be mosaic tile. This tile can be made of either glass or vitreous porcelain or clay. When made of the latter, it is usually unglazed but colored by pigment added to the bisque. Most ceramic mosaic tile is produced by the dust-press method and is almost always packaged in sheet-mounted format to make it easier to handle. Some can be bought loose on special order.

Sold in a wide variety of colors, ceramic mosaic tile comes in squares ¼ in. to 1 in. in size, 1-in. by 2-in. rectangles, or small hexagons. Glass mosaic tile usually comes only in 1-in. squares, and both types of mosaic tile range in thickness from 3/32 in. to ¼ in. Because of its density, mosaic tile is very tough and excellent for use on floors as well as countertops and walls. Since it's vitreous and freeze-thaw stable, it can be used for both wet and exterior installations. As with other back-mounted tile, the mounting material on mosaic tile may interfere with the bond of the adhesive. For

Hard-bodied quarry tile (at left) comes in a wide variety of shapes and sizes, and is suitable for a range of installations. Most ceramic mosaic tile (at right) is sheet-mounted for convenience; it, too, is durable and versatile.

Stone tile, such as marble, granite and slate tile (at top), can be used for floors, walls and countertops, but should be sealed in wet installations. Other types of nonceramic tile include brick-veneer, cement-bodied brick-veneer, and cement-bodied tiles (at bottom).

this reason, mosaic tile should be installed with a thinset adhesive for extra grip. (For a full discussion of the problems involved in installing mosaic tile, see p. 204.)

Marble and other stone tile An increasing number of stones are being cut for use as floor, wall and countertop tiles, among them marble, granite, slate, flagstone and onyx. Another stone that's occasionally used for tile is lapis lazuli, though at $500 per square foot, this is a bit expensive for most installations!

When made into tile, these stones are either cleft and left unpolished, or gauged (cut to consistent dimensions) and sometimes polished. Stone tile can be used for floors, walls and countertops, but some installations are more practical than others. Cleft stone, for example, makes an impractical choice for countertops since it's not flat. Nor is it a good choice for wet installations like showers, since it's difficult to seal and soap film is hard to clean off. To prevent similar cleaning problems, any gauged stone tile used for showers should be sealed, despite some people's preference for the tile's natural dull finish over the sheen a sealer gives it. Whether cleft or gauged, most of these natural stone products can be used outdoors, though I wouldn't recommend onyx or lapis lazuli for exterior installations. Some onyx tiles may be streaked with veins of porous stone and thus may not be freeze-thaw stable, and lapis lazuli is just too expensive to chance it.

Because of their dense structure, any stone tiles that need to be trimmed for installation should be cut with the wet saw rather than with the snap cutter in order to get a clean cut. I admit that this process may become tedious, so you may want to try initially scoring the tiles on the wet saw, cutting only about one-third of the way through, and breaking them in the snap cutter. If this technique produces ragged cuts, however, use it only for tiles whose cut edges will be hidden when set, and gather patience for cutting the other tiles on the wet saw.

Gauged stone tiles are generally installed like ceramic tiles, with the exception of onyx, which needs special treatment. Cleft stone also requires special treatment, and a full description of both these problem installations can be found on p. 211. Before setting any gauged tile, whether polished or not, wipe the back of the tile clean with a wet cloth or sponge to remove dust or any residue from the manufacturing process, which would interfere with the bond of the adhesive. Then let the tiles dry before installing them. Because of their weight, stone tiles should always be paired with a thinset adhesive.

After installation, polished stone tiles should be sealed with a product especially made for stone (see the Resource Guide). Unpolished stone can be left unsealed for dry installations, but it may get stained with use. (If you're unsure whether you'll like the look of the sealed tile, try sealing a sample.) Although cleft stone might be more versatile if sealed, this tile is difficult to seal properly, especially with a top-coat sealer. All stone tile, gauged or cleft, requires extra maintenance after installation, but it should be cleaned only with a product specifically designed for stone.

Brick-veneer tile There are several types of brick-veneer tile, all of which simulate the appearance of real brick. Some of this tile is actually brick produced in thin cross section. Other brick-veneer tile is imitation brick, low-fired and made from ingredients similar to tile but with a coarser texture. A third type is made from colored mortar that is extruded like tile and dried, but not fired, in a kiln. Sometimes additional mortar is applied to this unfired tile to simulate antique brick.

Real brick-veneer tile can generally be installed wherever regular brick is used, both indoors and outdoors and in wet and dry installations. Remember, however, that brick is very porous, and if used for shower walls or tub surrounds, it will harbor bacteria and will be difficult to clean.

Most imitation brick-veneer tile should be reserved for wall installations because it's too soft to wear well under floor traffic. Some manufacturers do specify that their tile can be used for floors, however, so check the manufacturer's specifications. Similarly, before settling on this tile for exterior use, make sure that the tile you want to use is freeze-thaw stable.

No special setting bed is required for brick-veneer tile. If installed outdoors, it should be set with a thinset adhesive. An organic mastic can be used for an interior, decorative installation.

Cement-bodied tile This tile is made of mortar rather than clay and is either extruded or cut from sheets. Because cement-bodied tile is only dried in a kiln, not fired at high temperatures, it is less expensive to produce than regular tile. Various surface textures are often stamped into the wet tile before it is dried, and instead of being glazed, the tile is stained after hardening with a colorant in one of a handful of earth tones. To improve wear, the manufacturer coats this tile with a protective sealer. Another coat of sealer may need to be applied after the tile is set and grouted, and will need to be occasionally reapplied as the tile wears.

Cement-bodied tile weighs no more than regular tile, has the look of stone or paver tiles and even develops a patina as it ages. Because its surface is very tough, this tile is excellent for floor installations and gives years of service when properly installed and maintained. This tile is not the best choice for wet installations, nor is it generally recommended for exterior installations in cold climates, as some brands may not be freeze-thaw stable (check the manufacturer's specifications). Since a selvage edge produced in the manufacturing process is occasionally left on the tile, this edge should be trimmed with the biters or a grindstone before cutting, and all cuts should be made on the wet saw rather than the snap cutter. This tile needs no special setting bed and can be installed on walls with an organic mastic adhesive and on floors with a thinset adhesive.

Choosing tile

Whenever I'm asked how to choose tile, I always tell customers to first determine the kind of use the tile will get, and next to draw a sketch of the proposed installation, showing the outline of the area to be tiled, its dimensions and any special features to be taken into account. I then advise them to go to a tile showroom and simply pick a tile they like. This tile may not be the one they select in the end, but it provides a place to start.

The tile in showrooms is organized in any number of ways, from color to intended use to pure whimsy on the part of the store manager. The one way tile is unlikely to be organized, however, is by density and porosity, that is, by nonvitreous, semi-vitreous, vitreous or impervious groupings. While it's important to know how permeable a tile is when making a selection for a given installation, the salesperson may or may not be able to tell you if a particular tile is vitreous or nonvitreous—some may not themselves be clear on the distinction. Nonetheless, the salesperson should have manufacturer's specifications on all tile in the showroom and should at least be able to tell you whether a given tile is rated for use on floors, walls or countertops. If the tile you like is not rated for the use you have in mind, the salesperson should be able to direct you to a similar-looking tile that's better suited to your needs.

You may also hear a tile retailer mention a tile's grade. This refers to the grading system established by ANSI for tile sold in the United States, whether made in this country or elsewhere. This somewhat arbitrary grading system classifies tile as standard grade, second grade or decorative thin wall tile. So-called standard-grade tile, which accounts for about 75% of all tile sold in the United States, is that which meets all the minimum requirements for tile established by ANSI. Second-grade tile is tile that is structurally equivalent to standard-grade tile, except that its glaze may have minor imperfections or its sizing may be slightly off from the specifications for that tile. Second-grade tile is less expensive than standard-grade tile, with much of it created as a manufacturer starts up production on a new run or changes equipment in the plant. Decorative thin wall tile is tile whose bisque and glaze are so fragile that it should not be put to any functional use, but should rather be reserved for decorating walls.

In addition to graded tile, there is a broad spectrum of ungraded tile whose production standards don't match those established for standard-grade tile. This tile includes products of genuinely inferior quality as well as crudely made Mexican pavers and even Japanese tile of high quality. Simply because a tile is ungraded, it should not be rejected out of hand.

I tell my customers in the end that, no matter what grade of tile they select, they can be the best judge of a tile's suitability by taking home samples of the tile they like and putting them through a few tests of their own to see how they hold up. It's only fair to tell the retailer of your plans first, though. Knowing this, the salesperson may or may not charge you for the samples, but will in any case be able to steer you away from tile that is fragile or inappropriate for your purposes.

To put a sample tile through its paces, I suggest first rubbing it with a favorite pot or frying pan to see how easily it's marked up and, in turn, cleaned off. I also recommend scuffing it up with junior's hiking boots and grinding your own heel into the glaze. If the tile resists marks, you're in business. If it scuffs easily, you may want to think twice—especially if the marks are difficult to clean off.

If you want to test the tile's permeability, turn it over and sprinkle a few drops of water on the back. If the water is absorbed, the tile is nonvitreous. If the water sits on the surface of the bisque, you have a vitreous tile. Alternatively, you can do as many setters do: touch your tongue to the back of the tile. If your tongue momentarily sticks to the tile, it is nonvitreous. If it doesn't, the tile is vitreous.

One important factor in selecting tile is obviously its cost. Most commercial tile ranges in price from about $1 to $60 or $70 per square foot, with a wide selection available for under about $5 per square foot. If cost is not an issue, exquisite art tile can be had for about $500 to $2,000 per square foot. While this is beyond most budgets, it sounds like a bargain compared to the tile used in a recent installation, which is the most expensive tile ever set. This was the heat-resistant tile used on the nose and underbelly of the space shuttle *Challenger*, which cost, including installation, $1,500 per tile!

Once you've established a price range, your choice of tile revolves around the questions of size, color and style. Although these decisions are highly subjective, a few guidelines may be helpful. With regard to size, begin by considering the dimensions of the entire installation. Generally speaking, small tiles look better in small installations, and large tiles in large installations. Yet this rule of thumb does not always hold true. One of the most attractive installations I've ever seen, for example, is the vast floor in the California State Capitol Building in Sacramento that is covered with more than a million 1-in.-square tiles. And similarly, while I would generally advise reserving tiles 12 in. square and larger for sizable floors, I have tiled several countertops with 24-in.-square tiles, with results that were streamlined and elegant. The point is to consider this size guideline sound but not sacrosanct. Disregard it if you want to, but plan your design carefully.

While considering size, it's important to point out that there is no standard sizing system in the tile industry and that most imported tiles will be sized in centimeters rather than inches. What is called an 8-in.-square tile by various tile manufacturers may actually turn out to be anything from 7½ in. square to 8½ in. square, and similarly a tile specified by a foreign manufacturer as a 20-cm-square tile may be a centimeter or two more or less along each edge. Sometimes a manufacturer's specifications are meant to allow room for a specific grout-joint width, but often this is not made clear. Because of the wide discrepancy in sizing, never begin planning a layout or ordering tile until you have actually measured a sample tile or have been assured by the retailer that a tile's stated dimension is correct.

Since tile is available in such a wide array of colors, selecting among them can be difficult. Generally speaking, a dark color used extensively in a room tends to make the room look smaller, while a light color opens up the space. Some designers I've worked with like to use thin stripes of boldly colored tile to accent the perimeter of a floor or to highlight an otherwise subdued decor. I'd be wary of such a treatment, however, or of using bold colors in general, unless you're a seasoned designer or decorator. And even then, I would suggest trying out your ideas first in a watercolor drawing. If you're planning a very complex installation, you might consider an even more direct approach: painting the full-scale design on the wall or floor. For a floor like one I tiled with an intricate 12-color pattern, there really was no way to work out the bugs in the design other than to paint—and repaint—it directly on the floor. Experimentation of this sort is far preferable to installing tile and finding out too late that you don't like it. Precisely because tile is so permanent and expensive to replace, I suggest choosing a color that's easy to live with and reserving the accent colors for the accessories in the room rather than the tile. On a very practical level, remember, too, when selecting floor or countertop tile that the lighter the tile, the more work it will take to keep it clean.

Tile comes not only in a range of colors but also in a large variety of styles. Perhaps the most prevalent style is square or rectangular tile with square corners and square edges. Other tile combines these same shapes with soft, rounded corners and traditional, square edges, or with edges that are "cushioned" (rounded over) and which may be straight or gently serpentine. Still other tile departs from the traditional square or rectangle in favor of such shapes as hexagons, diamonds and ogees. Depending on a tile's shape, composition, glaze, and edge and corner treatment, it can produce effects that range from the simple and classic to high-tech to rustic. And combining several types of tile in a single installation may yield anything from a streamlined, Art Deco look to a Gaudí-like carnival effect. The obvious place to begin selecting a style of tile is with the installation itself. Are you tiling a formal entry foyer in your home or a utilitarian mudroom at the back of the house? A cozy kitchen or a large restaurant facility? Each installation suggests a different style of tile, and it must be a style which not only you but the other people using the installation are comfortable with.

In the end, it may be the practical needs of the installation that dictate the selection of one tile over another. But choosing tile is a funny business, and I've seen even the most practical of people throw caution to the wind and select an exquisite but thoroughly impractical tile for their installation. The tiles selected for the project in Chapter 10, for example, were sturdy vitreous tiles, quite suitable for a kitchen countertop in all but one respect. Their lovely but delicate black glaze scratched far too easily for a kitchen work surface. Yet the customer had made up his mind, and nothing but these tiles would do. So we reached a compromise: I set his black tile countertop, and he made some wooden cutting boards to place over the countertop whenever using it.

Although this might seem an example of how *not* to choose tile, it points up a consideration as powerful as any: how you feel about the tile. In the end, almost every choice of tile will involve some compromise. But, provided that choice doesn't invite disaster (as would, for example, non-vitreous tile used outdoors in a freezing climate), I would urge you to compromise last of all on the look of a tile you really like.

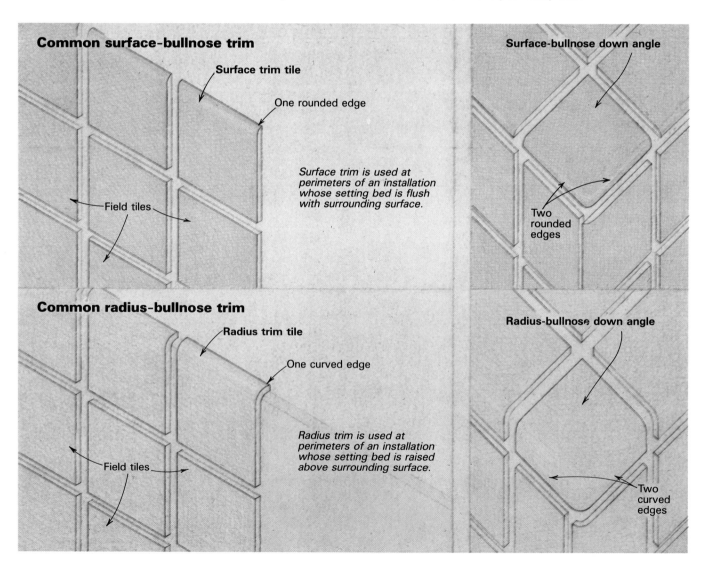

Common surface-bullnose trim

Surface trim tile

One rounded edge

Surface trim is used at perimeters of an installation whose setting bed is flush with surrounding surface.

Field tiles

Surface-bullnose down angle

Two rounded edges

Common radius-bullnose trim

Radius trim tile

One curved edge

Radius trim is used at perimeters of an installation whose setting bed is raised above surrounding surface.

Field tiles

Radius-bullnose down angle

Two curved edges

Trim tile

In use, all tile is either field tile or trim tile. Field tile is that set in the main field of an installation, which, if glazed, is glazed on the top surface only. Trim tile is glazed on one or more edges and is specially shaped to border and complete the main field of most installations. (No trim tile is used for floors tiled right to the walls, unless there are baseboard tiles around the perimeter.) Trim tile comes in a variety of shapes, sizes and colors to match many, though not all, lines of field tile. In general, this trim tile falls into two broad categories: surface trim and radius trim.

Surface trim, also called surface bullnose, is essentially flat tile with one edge rounded over. In general, this tile is used at the margins of an installation whose setting bed is flush with the surrounding surface—for example, at the front edge of many countertops, around door jambs, on windowsills, and on the top row of backsplashes or tile wainscoting. Sometimes a second rounded edge is added to surface bullnose to make a trim piece called a down angle, which serves to finish off an outside corner. If only a single corner on the tile has been rounded or curved, the trim piece is called an up angle and is used to finish off an inside corner. If a line of bullnose trim does not include a down angle or a sink corner, regular surface bullnose can be mitered to form this configuration.

Radius trim, also called radius bullnose, is curved trim tile that can be used to complete the same installations as those mentioned for surface bullnose, except that it is designed for installations whose setting bed sits above the surrounding surface. Like surface bullnose, radius trim is usually available in a variety of shapes, including down and up angles as well as

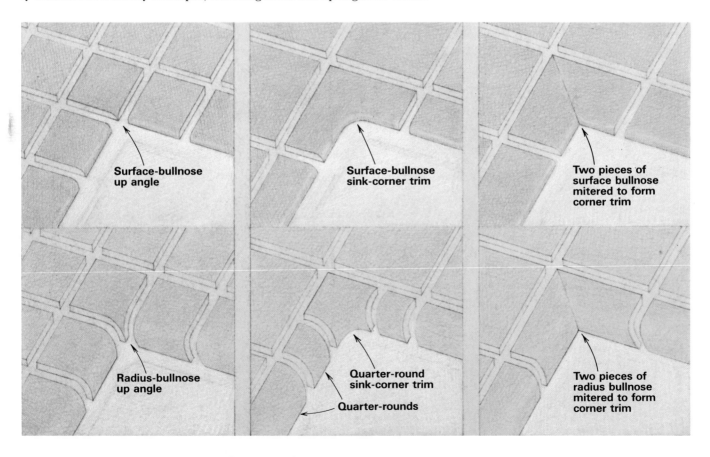

Surface-bullnose up angle

Surface-bullnose sink-corner trim

Two pieces of surface bullnose mitered to form corner trim

Radius-bullnose up angle

Quarter-round sink-corner trim

Quarter-rounds

Two pieces of radius bullnose mitered to form corner trim

Other common trim pieces

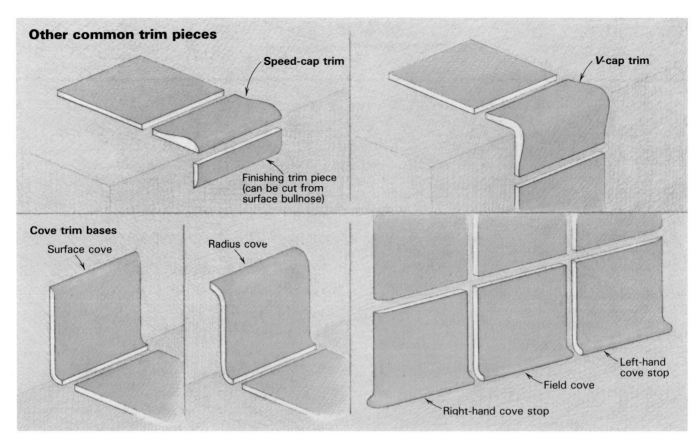

Speed-cap trim

V-cap trim

Finishing trim piece
(can be cut from
surface bullnose)

Cove trim bases

Surface cove

Radius cove

Left-hand
cove stop

Field cove

Right-hand cove stop

Making trim

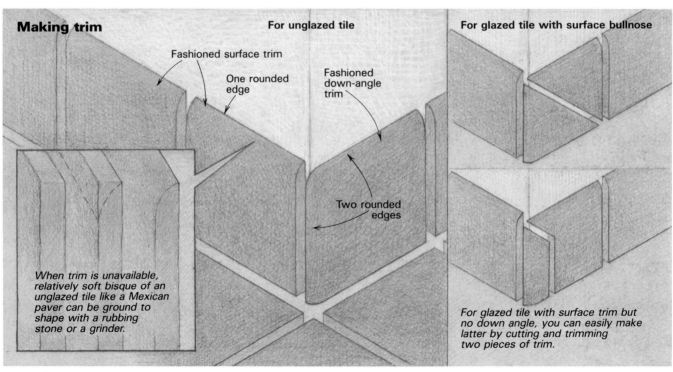

For unglazed tile

For glazed tile with surface bullnose

Fashioned surface trim

One rounded
edge

Fashioned
down-angle
trim

Two rounded
edges

*When trim is unavailable,
relatively soft bisque of an
unglazed tile like a Mexican
paver can be ground to
shape with a rubbing
stone or a grinder.*

*For glazed tile with surface trim but
no down angle, you can easily make
latter by cutting and trimming
two pieces of trim.*

quarter-round pieces called beaks, which finish off quarter-round trim. In addition to surface and radius bullnose, complementary pieces like *V*-cap, speed cap and cove trim are also often available, enabling a setter to neatly finish off almost any imaginable installation.

If a line of tile lacks a coordinated array of trim, some manufacturers produce pieces of field tile with one or two glazed edges, which can serve as finishing trim. If no trim at all is available for the tile you select, look at that produced for another line of tile. Sometimes a very similar trim can be found, or a contrasting color may look good. If the trim pieces are larger than the tile you're working with, they can be cut to size.

In the case of unglazed, soft-bodied tiles like Mexican pavers, for which there is usually no trim tile, a substitute can be made by rounding the edge of a flat tile with a masonry rubbing stone or a small hand grinder. Rounding two of the tile's edges produces a down angle, while rounding one of its corners creates an up angle. If the trim is needed for outside angles, for example on a staircase, it may speed up the process and make for a neater finished appearance if the tiles are rounded after being set. The sealer used for the surface of this tile will, of course, need to be reapplied to the newly rounded edges.

Finally, an alternative to trim tile that's gaining popularity for finishing the edges of countertops is wood trim. Although this trim may be much less expensive than ceramic trim, combining these two materials in a wet installation raises problems. The wood expands when it gets wet, while the tile does not. For this reason, the joint between the tile and trim must be caulked to prevent the inevitable cracking that would befall a grouted joint there. (For a full discussion of using wood trim, see p. 216.)

Tile in context

While the surface of the tile is the most visible part of any installation, what lies unseen beneath is perhaps the most important element of all. For tilework to be effective and durable, the choice of tile must be backed up with equally thoughtful decisions about the setting bed, adhesive and grout, and with a carefully executed installation.

The remainder of this book provides all the informational tools needed for producing quality tile installations that will give years of service. A full discussion of setting materials, including grout, is presented in Chapter 3, and a complete overview of setting beds and the surface preparation they need is found in Chapter 4. In Chapter 5, you'll find the all-important subject of laying out tile discussed in detail, and in Chapters 6 through 11 the principles and techniques of tiling are put into concrete practice. If you're new to tiling, I would urge you to look through these chapters carefully before launching into an installation. And before beginning any work, please take time to look through Chapter 2 on tools and safety.   □

Tools and Safety

Like any other trade, tilesetting requires a number of special tools. Some of these can make the job easier; some are necessary for professional-looking results. Many of these tools can be found in the average home kit, while others can be readily adapted from tools you have on hand. Several highly specialized tools are needed for tiling, but unless you plan on doing extensive work, generally you can rent these at a tool rental shop or a tile retail store rather than invest in them.

For convenience, I've grouped the tools presented in this chapter according to function and arranged them in the general order in which they're used on the job—though, of course, some of these tools will be used at several stages of the installation. While the many tools shown here are essential for the professional tilesetter, they are not all required for every installation. The novice or occasional setter can, in fact, do many small home projects with a minimum of tools. With one exception, the tools necessary for the various stages of the job are listed at the outset of the tool sections below. Because the surface-preparation tools needed vary greatly from installation to installation, this section contains no such listing.

Keeping tools sharp and clean is always a good idea, no matter what they're being used for, but in the case of tilesetting tools, careful and prompt cleanup is crucial unless you can afford to constantly replace them! Left to harden on tools, tile adhesive, mortar and grout become downright stubborn to remove. It's also wise to test any tiling tools you're unfamiliar with on scrap material, and to get acquainted with them before starting a project. This is especially true of both power and manual tools used for cutting tile.

Because some tilesetting tools can be dangerous to use, the discussion of the individual tools contains necessary warnings and suggested precautions. The chapter concludes with a look at the general health hazards involved in tilesetting and the safety measures that can be taken to avoid or minimize these hazards.

Surface-preparation tools

As you'll see in Chapter 4, tile can be set on a number of surfaces, and most will need some sort of preparation. The preparation of the setting bed may involve nothing more than cleaning off a little dirt and grime, or it may mean grinding a nice, flat surface on a slightly uneven concrete slab, or perhaps building a new subfloor. To ready a surface for tiling, you'll probably need either cutting tools; sanding, scraping and grinding tools; or cleaning tools. Or you may need them all!

Cutting tools   While professional union tilesetters only set tile, leaving the surface preparation to others, the do-it-yourselfer is obliged to handle all aspects of tiling, which in many cases includes some basic carpentry to build or rebuild floors, countertops and walls. For such work, handsaws and power saws are obviously essential. When precision cuts are not critical, a reciprocating saw can be used for cutting out old wooden floors or walls, or doing other demolition work. When greater accuracy is required—for example, when cutting contours in plywood for floors or cutting sink holes in countertops—use a saber saw. If you want to speed up the tedious process of making numerous straight cuts, switch to a circular saw.

Although handsaws could certainly be used in place of these power saws, the job will take far more time. But if you don't have access to power saws, straight cuts could be made with a crosscut handsaw, which cuts across the grain, or with a ripping handsaw, which cuts with the grain; a keyhole saw could be used to make curved cuts. One task for which a handsaw is better than a power saw is trimming door casings and molding around which tile is to be set. It takes far less time to trim the casing or molding to the height of the tile rather than to trim the tile itself. The best saw for this job is an offset dovetail saw with a reversible handle.

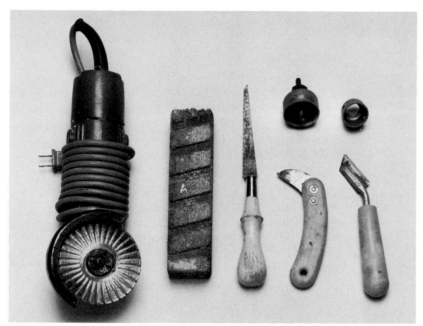

In addition to the general carpentry tools often used to prepare setting beds for tiling, there are some other tools that come in handy, including (from left) a dry-cutting diamond blade mounted in an electric grinder (this cutting tool serves both for ripping out old tilework and for trimming new tiles); masonry rubbing stone; keyhole saw; backer-board scoring tool, also called a carbide scriber; grout saw; and (above) two hole saws.

Surface preparation may occasionally involve ripping out old tilework set on a concrete slab or on plywood. A wide-blade masonry chisel and a hammer or hand maul are handy for this. A grout saw is also needed to cut away the hardened grout. If the tile being removed is set on a mortar bed, use a dry-cutting diamond blade (see the photo above) mounted in either an electric grinder or a circular saw. This speeds up the process and also prevents damaging any neighboring drywall and the framing below. (For more information on removing old tilework, see p. 217, and for a full discussion of tile-cutting tools, see p. 36.)

If you need to cut backer board to prepare the new setting bed, you can use either the dry-cutting diamond blade or a backer-board scoring tool, also called a carbide scriber. The latter is a hand tool, which usually has a wooden handle affixed to a slender metal shank shaped like a hawk's bill. The end of the shank holds a small, sharpened chunk of carbide, which will score the fiberglass covering on backer board so that the board can be broken along the scribed line. The edges of the cut won't be as clean as those produced by the diamond blade, but they are suitable for most tile-setting projects. This tool is relatively inexpensive, can be bought at a tile or building-materials supply house and is easy to use. One disadvantage is that it can be used only for straight cuts.

To cut backer board with a carbide scriber, mark the board for cutting, then run the scriber's carbide tip along the line, pressing firmly and guiding the scriber with a straightedge for a more even cut. Several passes may be needed to score the fiberglass. That done, snap the backer board over your knee so that it shears along the scored line and fold it back on itself to crease the fiberglass on the other side of the board. To complete the cut, turn the board and cut the remaining fiberglass on the other side.

Whenever you're using power saws for preparing setting surfaces, use caution and common sense. The obvious danger in working with these tools is increased if you give in to temptation and remove the blade guard from a power saw. *Don't* do it! These tools can slice bone just as easily as tile. Make sure, too, when working with these tools that you wear goggles or safety glasses to protect your eyes from flying debris, and hearing protectors to combat the noise.

Sanding, grinding and scraping tools Whether you're tiling new construction or doing a remodeling job, it's easy to get globs of construction adhesive, tar and taping compound on the setting surface. To remove these, you can use a stiff putty knife, paint scraper, trowel or inexpensive wide-blade wood chisel. These same tools can be used to remove old resilient tiles or foam-backed carpeting stuck to the floor. For thin, dried deposits of construction goo that resist the scraper, use a power sander or just a hand-held block sander. Remember when using the power sander to wear safety glasses and a filter mask. The mask is a good idea when hand-sanding, too.

Use a hand-held masonry rubbing stone or a hand-held power grinder with an abrasive wheel to flatten a hardened mortar bed or an uneven concrete slab. And for a slab whose surface is slick (which means it was finished with a steel trowel rather than a wood float), rough it up with hand or power grinders so that the tilesetting adhesive will grip it properly. Again, safety glasses are essential when power-grinding.

Cleaning tools and materials You can clean a surface to be tiled by scraping or grinding it or by some other mechanical means. Avoid using cleaning solutions at the outset, as their residues may prevent a good bond between the tile adhesive and the setting bed. If you have trouble removing oil or grease by mechanical means, try a detergent-and-water solution. Use degreasers, wax removers and other cleaning solutions only as a last resort.

To clean tilesetting tools, also begin with mechanical means. The fewer chemical agents you and your tools come in contact with, the better. Scrape as much residue off as possible and clean off what's left with a rag soaked in paint thinner or a piece of steel wool dipped in thinner. Never use gasoline to remove solvent-based residues from tools or construction surfaces. H.B. Fuller Co. (see the Resource Guide) makes a product called Adhesive Remover, which is specifically designed for cleaning solvent-based adhesive and which is safe to skin and rinses off with water.

Another cleaning tool that's imperative on any tile job is a good vacuum cleaner. I have an industrial-strength model, which I keep on the site until I've finished an installation. For small jobs, a home vacuum cleaner will be adequate. In addition to the vacuum's obvious merits, I use it during demolition work to draw excess dust from the air by waving the nozzle overhead. It's also good for cleaning a floor just before the tile is set, vacuuming up scraped-out grout joints, and cleaning up tile chips, sand and chunks of mortar that might get tracked into other areas of the work site.

To help keep finished floors clean elsewhere in the house or building, I spread waterproof kraft paper over them and cover the paper with tarps. The tarps cushion and protect the flooring from scratching, and the paper prevents water, adhesives, wet mortar and grout from seeping onto and staining finished surfaces. After the job is finished, I roll up the tarps and paper together and shake out the debris at the dump. I protect finished countertops, walls and the fronts of cabinets by taping waterproof kraft paper or plastic sheeting over them with masking tape.

Measuring and marking tools

Accuracy is crucial when setting ceramic tiles. Setting surfaces should be flat, square and plumb, and grout joints must be straight and evenly spaced. To properly install tile, you need accurate measuring tools. Some of these tools can be found in the average home shop, and many of them can be rented.

The minimum measuring and marking tools required for the average home tile installation are a 10-ft. tape measure; 32-in. and 48-in. straightedges; a 32-in. spirit level; a 12-in. combination square or, alternatively, a carpenter's square; a chalk line; and, of course, a marking pen or pencil. For larger jobs, the setter's tool kit obviously needs to grow. When I'm doing a very large commercial job, I may even call in a surveyor to measure and mark out the job with surveying tools.

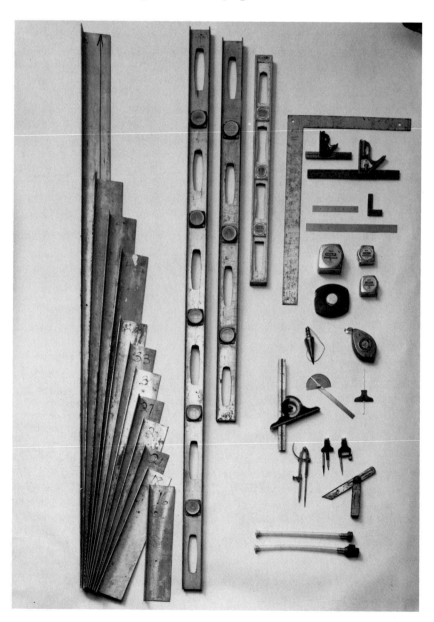

Measuring and marking tools used in tilesetting include, at left and center, a set of graduated straightedges and spirit levels. At right (from top to bottom, starting at left) are a carpenter's square; combination squares; steel scales and machinist's square; measuring tapes; plumb bob and chalk line; protractors and depth gauge; compass, trammel points and sliding T-bevel; and water levels.

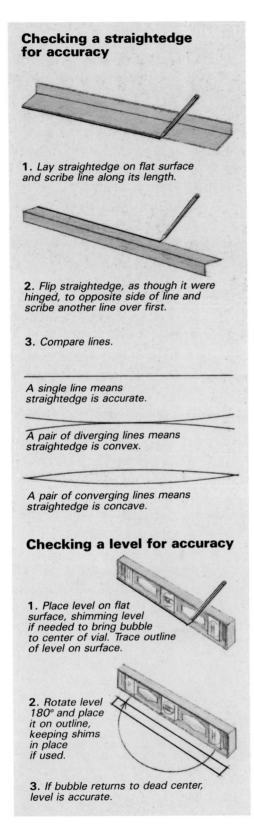

Checking a straightedge for accuracy

1. Lay straightedge on flat surface and scribe line along its length.

2. Flip straightedge, as though it were hinged, to opposite side of line and scribe another line over first.

3. Compare lines.

A single line means straightedge is accurate.

A pair of diverging lines means straightedge is convex.

A pair of converging lines means straightedge is concave.

Checking a level for accuracy

1. Place level on flat surface, shimming level if needed to bring bubble to center of vial. Trace outline of level on surface.

2. Rotate level 180° and place it on outline, keeping shims in place if used.

3. If bubble returns to dead center, level is accurate.

The tape measure I use on the job is a steel tape with a hooked end, graduated in sixteenths of an inch. When buying a new tape, I check both its inside and outside measure for accuracy against a 12-in.-long flat steel scale made by L.S. Starrett (see the Resource Guide). A tape measure is easily damaged when dropped and the hook slide gets worn in the abrasive environment of tilesetting, so I recheck it from time to time. Once the hook slide is worn out, I invest in a new tape. When using the tape, I also make sure to clean off any adhesive, mortar or grout that gets on the hook before it has a chance to harden on the slide, which would give imprecise readings.

Straightedges serve as a guide in marking underlayment, laying out installations and adjusting rows of tile, as well as in innumerable other tilesetting tasks. A serious setter should buy a set of nesting aluminum straightedges in graduated sizes. If you have access to a jointer, you can make a wooden set, but it won't be as sturdy or as accurate as an aluminum one. I think a pair of 32-in. and 48-in. straightedges are essential for most installations, but if you're tiling a smaller area, you'll obviously need a shorter straightedge. A spirit level can also be substituted for a straightedge, as can a narrow strip of plywood with a true edge cut on a tablesaw, or a straight piece of aluminum or steel stock. In a pinch, a piece of string stretched tightly on the work surface can even take the place of a straightedge.

The important thing about a straightedge is that it be straight! Provided you have good eyesight, you can sight along the edge to make sure that it's not bowed. Alternatively, lay the straightedge on a flat surface (such as a subfloor) and scribe a line from end to end; then flip the straightedge over to the opposite side of the line and scribe another line directly over the first. If the straightedge is straight, you will have drawn a single line with no bulge in the center and no split tails on the ends. If you do a lot of setting, you should periodically check your straightedges for accuracy and, if need be, adjust them. Because my aluminum straightedges see lots of duty and wear down at the ends, I take them to a machine shop about once a year for truing up.

Other staples in the tilesetter's tool kit include a graduated set of spirit levels and a plumb bob, the latter for checking the accuracy of the levels. I keep a 12-in., 24-in., 32-in., 48-in. and 72-in. level handy, although, if need be, I could combine a 12-in. level with my graduated straightedges to plumb or level a surface of any length. If you do a lot of setting, you'll probably need to buy a new level about every 18 months, as they get fairly banged up with regular use and the accumulation of minor, unavoidable damage can impair the level's functioning. In choosing a new spirit level, look for an aluminum one with adjustable vials. Although mahogany levels with brass inlay are beautiful, they're impractical for tilesetting because they frequently get wet and can warp out of shape.

Since I give my levels a steady workout, I check them before beginning every new job to make sure that the vials read correctly. I also check every new level I buy. Interestingly, many tilesetting shops keep a plumb-bob jig and a leveling flat permanently set up so that setters can quickly check their levels. No matter what the extent or frequency of your tilesetting, I suggest that you, too, check your level before beginning a job.

To check a level for plumb, compare it to a plumb line—gravity never fails. To check it for level, place the tool on a flat surface and check that the bubble is dead center in the vial. (If the surface itself is out of level, shim up the level with paper or wooden strips.) Scribe the outline of the level, then rotate the tool 180° and place it within the outline. If the leveling bubble is dead center again, the level is true. In the event that there are several leveling vials, repeat this process to check that each one is true.

On the job, make sure to clean off any fresh mortar, adhesive or grout from the edges of the tool. And when tapping a level to adjust the float strip or other surface beneath, strike only the areas of the tool that have reinforcing webs. If you strike over the open areas on the level, you risk banging it out of shape. (Carpenters reading this will no doubt have heart failure at the suggestion that a level might be struck with anything more than a light tap, but I know from experience that tilesetters and brick masons have a heavier hand! For the record, the correct technique is to tap the object being leveled, not the level itself. The object should then be checked with the level and tapped again if it's not yet correctly positioned.)

For plotting angles on setting beds and for marking out tiles, I use a combination of squares and protractors, as well as a sliding *T*-bevel. I measure depth with a depth gauge and, on very large jobs, a pair of water levels connected by a tube or even a garden hose. I sometimes use a set of trammel points for scribing a 3-4-5 triangle to check a room for square (see p. 114) and for plotting large arcs. For small arcs, a regular compass is fine. When I'm marking tiles that butt up against irregular surfaces, I use a contour gauge.

A carpenter's square is frequently used in tilesetting for checking and marking off 90° angles. Like other measuring tools, this one must be checked for accuracy from time to time. To do this, butt the square's short edge against a straightedge and scribe a line down the outside of the square's long edge. Then flip the square to the opposite side of the line, align its long edge with the line and scribe a second line. If the two lines form a single, straight line, the square is accurate. If, instead, the lines begin to diverge or converge, the square needs to be adjusted or, if it's so inaccurate that it defies correction, replaced.

A square is an invaluable tool, so it's worth some effort to fix one that isn't doing its job. To adjust the square, scribe a line on the square connecting its inside and outside corners. For a square that's reading less than 90°, use a center punch and a hammer to bang in a couple of dimples on the upper half of this diagonal line, which will ease the angle of the inside corner back toward 90°. Then check this angle by the method just described. You may need to hammer in a few more dimples if the angle still needs to be increased a bit more. For a square whose angle reads greater than 90°, hammer the dimples in the lower half of the line. Again check the angle and repeat this step if necessary.

To scribe layout lines on wet mortar beds, I use the edge of a trowel. And for laying out lines or connecting points on a dry setting surface, I either draw a pencil line or snap chalk lines, using a reel-type chalk line. To avoid confusion on floors that may already be criss-crossed with someone else's lines or that may have a number of my own measuring lines, I keep two chalk lines—one red, one blue. I mark any initial measurements on the setting bed with one color and chalk in the final layout lines with the other. This eliminates any second-guessing.

For marking tile to be cut dry, I generally use just a fine-point, felt-tipped pen, which seems to work better for me than a pencil. When I'm marking tile to be cut on the wet saw (see p. 39), I may put a piece of masking tape on the tile and make my marks on the tape rather than on the tile. I learned early on that the water jet on a wet saw will quickly erase a pen or pencil mark on tile!

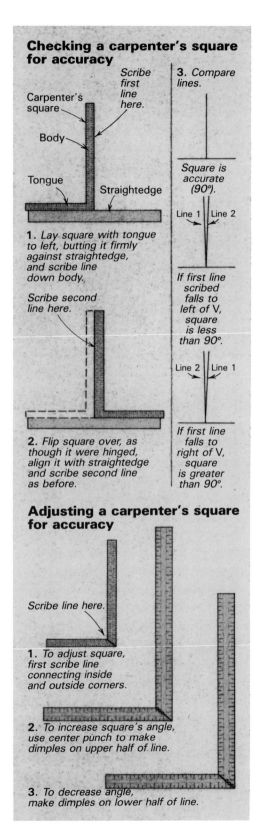

Checking a carpenter's square for accuracy

Carpenter's square

Body

Tongue

Straightedge

Scribe first line here.

1. Lay square with tongue to left, butting it firmly against straightedge, and scribe line down body.

Scribe second line here.

2. Flip square over, as though it were hinged, align it with straightedge and scribe second line as before.

3. Compare lines.

Square is accurate (90°).

Line 1   Line 2

If first line scribed falls to left of V, square is less than 90°.

Line 2   Line 1

If first line falls to right of V, square is greater than 90°.

Adjusting a carpenter's square for accuracy

Scribe line here.

1. To adjust square, first scribe line connecting inside and outside corners.

2. To increase square's angle, use center punch to make dimples on upper half of line.

3. To decrease angle, make dimples on lower half of line.

Mixing and floating tools

For preparing less than two gallons of thinset or grout, I mix by hand with a margin trowel. Although it's possible to do larger quantities this way, it's pretty tiring work and often produces lumpy results. Instead, I use a mixing paddle chucked in a ½-in., heavy-duty drill. (For important safety information on working with power tools around water, see p. 45.) Most home drills are light-duty drills and will burn out if used to mix 10 or 12 buckets of adhesive or grout. If you plan to do more than a very small installation (for which you'll probably need to mix only a single 5-gallon bucket of each material), I suggest renting a variable-speed heavy-duty drill that can be run at around 150 rpm. It's important to use the drill with a mortar mixing paddle (which can also be rented) rather than with a paint paddle. The latter should revolve at speeds too high for mixing grout and adhesives, and can whip air bubbles into the material being mixed and weaken it.

Mixing and floating tools include, at left and center, a mason's hoe and mortar mixing paddle chucked in a hand drill. At right (from top to bottom, starting at left) are a flat trowel, swimming-pool trowel and hawk; edging trowel, margin trowels and pointers; and wood floats.

To prepare mortar for floating floors, walls and countertops (professional setters often call this mortar "mud"), I mix the ingredients by hand in a mixing box with a mason's hoe, which I find is the best and easiest method to use. Mixing boxes come in a wide variety of sizes and materials, from 1-cu.-ft. plastic trays to 1-cu.-yd. sheet-metal barges. For installing tile on practically all residential work, I rely on a ⅓-cu.-yd. box. For larger jobs, I use a bigger box, but I also have a helper available to tend to the mixing. At times when I haven't had a mixing box handy, I've pressed into service, with surprisingly good results, a wheelbarrow, a sheet of plywood and once even 30-lb. tar paper spread over the ground.

A mason's hoe has a broad blade pierced with a couple of holes to aid in mixing. I prefer it to a rotary mixer because it agitates the ingredients less and because I can get exactly the consistency of mortar I want. Hoes are sold in several sizes, and I generally work with a 9-incher. If you don't want to invest in a mason's hoe, a regular garden hoe can be used. It's also possible to substitute a shovel or a large trowel. (For information on properly mixing and floating mortar for floors, see Chapter 7; for the procedure for floating a mortar wall, see Chapter 9.)

The minimum tools needed to float a mortar bed are a flat trowel, a margin trowel, a hawk (when floating walls), a wood float, a pair of wooden float strips (their size depends on the depth and dimension of the mortar bed) and a straightedge. Don't mix any mortar or begin work on the bed unless you have these tools on hand and are ready to float the bed.

Flat trowels are rectangular trowels used to apply and level a mortar bed. Available in a variety of lengths and widths, the flat trowel most commonly used for tiling is about 12 in. by 4 in. A swimming-pool trowel is an oblong trowel with rounded corners, which is used for spreading mortar in pools and other curved areas.

Margin trowels are long, thin, rectangular-shaped tools that look a bit like flapjack turners. These trowels are used for a number of tiling jobs, including mixing small batches of mortar, applying or leveling mortar in places too small for flat trowels, back-buttering tiles with adhesive, finishing grouted surfaces, repointing or packing joints, and cleaning other trowels. Margin trowels usually have 4-in.- to 6-in.-long blades that range in width from ⅛ in. to 2 in. or 3 in.

Pointers are trowels whose blade, as their name suggests, is pointed. Most often seen in brick mason's kits, these tools aren't essential in a basic tilesetter's kit, but are favored by some setters for back-buttering tiles with adhesive and for spreading or leveling mortar in tight corners.

Wood floats are rectangular wooden trowels used to finish the surface of a mortar bed. They produce a coarse, open-grained surface on the bed rather than the slick surface created by the steel trowel. Because the coarser surface is more easily gripped by the adhesive, a wood-troweled mortar bed is better for tiling than a steel-troweled bed. In addition to finishing mortar beds, wood floats are also used in shaping sloped mortar floors. These tools are preferable for this purpose to a steel trowel, whose sharp biting edge can easily cut into the mortar.

A hawk is a small square of aluminum with a protruding handle, which is used when floating a wall. While the mortar for a floated floor or countertop is dumped directly on the substrate, that for a floated wall must be applied in thin layers. The hawk serves to carry small amounts of mortar from the mud board (the plywood square holding the mortar brought into the room from the mixing box) to the wall. The setter then loads up the flat trowel with mortar from the hawk. A substitute for this tool can readily be made from a scrap of plywood and a dowel.

Setting and cutting tools

Tiles must be set with precision if the installation is to be handsome and long-lasting. The adhesive should be applied uniformly and the tiles trimmed and placed accurately. To achieve precise results—and to do so during the critical period before the freshly spread adhesive "skins" over—the setter needs special tools for applying the adhesive and for cutting tiles. The minimum setting tools required are a notched trowel, whose size depends on the type and dimensions of tile being set; a margin trowel; a snap cutter and biters for trimming tile; a level; a straightedge; tile spacers or wedges (folded paper or cardboard could also be used); and a bucket and sponge.

A snap cutter and biters are the basic cutting tools needed (more on these in a moment), since very few tile installations can be completed without some tiles having to be cut or shaped. I use a snap cutter for most straight cuts and the biters for simple, curved cuts. For very small jobs, you may be able to get by with just these cutting tools, but for jobs where more complex, curved or angled cuts need to be made, you'll probably need to use the biters in combination with a wet saw or a dry-cutting diamond-blade saw. All of these cutting tools can usually be rented from a tile retailer or a tool rental shop for a nominal charge.

Notched trowels Notched trowels look like flat trowels, except that they have at least two sides cut or ground with V- or square-shaped notches. The trowel's unnotched sides are used to initially spread the adhesive on the setting bed. Then the adhesive is "combed" with the trowel's notched sides to produce a series of uniform ridges. (For a full description of applying adhesive, see p. 57.)

Tools needed for spreading adhesive and setting tile include, from top right, clockwise, notched trowels, margin trowels, pointer, snap cutter, biters, brick hammer and chisel (used for cleaving stone tile), tile grindstones, and tile spacers and wedges. At center are a beating block and rubber mallet.

In the process of combing the adhesive, the trowel's notches are kept in contact with the setting bed and thus gauge the thickness of the layer of adhesive. The depth of the notch—and that of the adhesive—should equal about two-thirds the thickness of the tile being set. To determine if the trowel used is the right size, first spread and comb a small area of adhesive, making sure there's enough material to produce fully formed ridges. Next firmly press a tile into the adhesive and then remove it. If the tile back is not completely covered with adhesive, the layer of adhesive is still not deep enough and a trowel with a larger-size notch is needed (see photos, p. 59). Conversely, if the adhesive oozes up around the sides of the tile when you press it down, the layer of adhesive is too deep and a trowel with a smaller-size notch should be used. If you are using irregular-backed tiles, sheet-mounted tiles, stone tiles or tiles like Mexican pavers that are not completely flat, you may need to both comb adhesive on the setting bed and back-butter the tiles in order to ensure a strong bond of the adhesive.

If you're a novice setter and don't want to invest in a lot of tools, you may be interested in the disposable notched trowel, which is available at tile supply stores. This trowel—simply a piece of stamped metal with notches on one side—is inexpensive and can be thrown away at the end of the job, eliminating cleanup. Though this tool may not be as sturdy as a regular notched trowel, it should be used in exactly the same fashion.

Biters Biters, or nippers, are the least sophisticated of the cutting tools and are generally used to cut irregular shapes of tile to fit around faucet valves, toilet flanges, door casings and any other obstruction. Because biters tend to produce cuts with sharp, jagged edges, this tool is not used to make straight cuts. In a pinch a pair of pliers could be substituted for biters, but the cut produced by pliers is even more ragged than that of the biters.

Biters come in several sizes with different jaw configurations. The pair I prefer has two carbide-tipped jaws—the upper jaw ground straight across to contact the glazed face of the tile and the lower jaw curved to grip the rougher texture of the bisque.

Biters work by nibbling small bits of tile, and biting hard, vitreous tiles takes more patience than cutting soft-bodied tiles. The tricks to biting both types of tile are finding and maintaining the correct jaw position, and knowing how much tile to bite off.

I start each bite by marking the cut on the face of the tile with a pencil or a felt-tipped pen. The position the jaws take when in contact with the tile determines where the glaze will be fractured and how each bite will be shaped. I try to keep the jaws parallel to the mark, and, to keep control of the cut, I also position the biters so that only part of the full spread of the jaws contacts the mark. I find that if the jaws fully contact the tile, the bite sometimes goes wild, fracturing the tile beyond the actual grasp of the jaws. The idea is not to try to make the cut in one bite, but to gradually nibble away the unwanted area, working from the sides of the cut toward the center. It may take a little practice to get the hang of using this tool.

Snap cutter For repetitive, relatively straight cuts, the snap cutter does the quickest, most efficient job. Some tile stores, particularly the chain stores, will lend out these cutters with the purchase of tile. There are several different types of snap cutters, but all incorporate the same basic features: a frame for holding the tile, and a housing mounted on a guide bar that's comprised of a handle, a tiny wheel for scoring the face of the tile and a device (often "wings" at the base of the handle) for snapping the tile apart at the scored line.

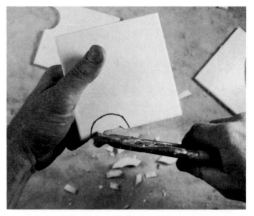

The biters are used to nibble away a waste area of tile, working from the outside toward the center of the cut. To produce a clean break, I use a prying motion rather than attempting to cut entirely through the tile with each bite.

Before using the snap cutter, put a few drops of oil on the guide bar and the scoring wheel. Check to make sure that the wheel is secured properly (it's usually held in place by a small bolt) and that it doesn't meander from side to side, which would crookedly score the tile. Also check to see if the scoring wheel is worn, and, if need be, get a replacement wheel, which is readily available at a tile store.

Begin by marking a cutting line on the tile with a fine-point, felt-tipped pen. Position the tile against the snap cutter's bottom edge, aligning the cutting line with the scoring wheel. (If you're making multiple cuts of a given size, screw the cutting fence in place to act as a stop.) Hold the tile in place with one hand and the wheel's handle in the other. Lift the handle so that the wheel is pressed against the top edge of the tile's surface and pull the handle toward you. Use only enough pressure to lightly and evenly score the tile in one pass. Making several passes usually produces a bad break, but remember that a misscored tile can be used for a smaller cut.

To snap the scored tile apart, position the wings at the base of the handle along the lower third of the tile. I hold the tile in position by putting light pressure on the handle with my left thumb, then I lightly strike the handle with the heel of my right hand. If the tile doesn't break, I hit the handle harder. If the tile still refuses to break, it means the scoring line was too light or not continuous, so I begin again with a new tile.

Depending on the composition of the tile you're working with, you can use the snap cutter to produce cut tile as narrow as ½ in. Usually the denser the tile, the easier it is to cut on the snap cutter and hence the likelier it is that close cuts can be made. Since this isn't always the case, however, experiment before making the actual cuts. If you're unable to

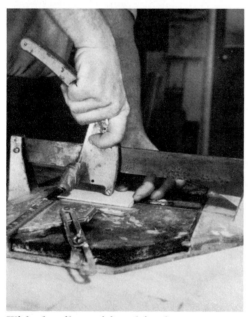

With the tile positioned in the snap cutter (top), I raise the handle and draw the scoring wheel lightly across the tile's surface (bottom). To break the scored tile, I hold it in place with the wings at the base of the handle and strike the handle with the heel of my hand (right). (I wrap the wings with duct tape to prevent them from marking the tile.)

use the snap cutter to make narrow cuts, either use the wet saw or score the tile with the snap cutter and pry off the thin waste with the biters.

In a pinch, a glass cutter and a 16d nail could be pressed into service in place of a snap cutter. Score the tile with the glass cutter and then place it over the nail, aligning the nail with the scored line and pressing down on both sides of the tile with your thumbs. You might also cut tile with a carbide-grit rod handsaw, but the procedure will take five to ten minutes, compared to five to ten seconds on the snap cutter. Neither of these alternatives gives as clean a cut as a snap cutter, though.

Wet saw The diamond-blade wet saw makes a perfectly straight cut, which, unlike that produced by either the snap cutter or the biters, is smooth and slightly rounded over. I use this saw to make cuts whose edges will be prominently exposed when set, and cuts that are less than ½ in. wide. I also combine the wet saw with the biters to simplify complicated cuts. And because the wet saw leaves a 1/16-in.-wide kerf when a partial cut is made, I find it handy for removing large, curved waste areas. By making a series of parallel cuts that end along the curved waste line, I can break away the pieces with my fingers. Then I trim the cut clean with the biters.

Both soft- and hard-bodied tiles and even paving stones can be cut on the wet saw, with a different blade required for the soft tiles than for the hard tiles and paving stones. The one tile that should never be cut on this saw is quarry tile with carbide chips on its face for a nonskid surface. These chips will quickly chew up the sawblade. Quarry tile should instead be cut on the snap cutter, and any rough edges smoothed down with a tile grindstone if the cut edge will be visible.

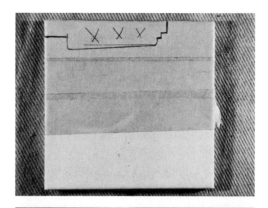

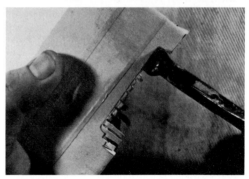

To make a complex cut on the wet saw, I first put masking tape on the tile and mark the cutting line (top right). Then I make a series of parallel cuts ending at the line (above) and break away the waste with my fingers (right, second from top). To complete the cut, I trim it with the biters (right, second from bottom).

Wet saws run on regular household current, and most are constructed with a stationary cutting blade and a sliding table. The blade, untoothed and usually 8 in. to 10 in. in diameter, is bathed in water while in operation to keep it cool. Commercial saws generally use a drip pan and a recirculating pump. Because these saws don't have a filter to separate the abrasive tile and glaze particles from the water that cools the sawblade, however, the blade is actually cooled by abrasive water, which shortens its life. For this reason, I have my saw connected to a hose. The blade is bathed in fresh water, which I think will extend its life two or three times. (This modification is easily done by simply changing a couple of fittings.) Because this saw is messy to use, I usually set it up outdoors or in a garage.

Whatever the wet saw's construction, its cutting action is the same. The amount of pressure needed when holding the tile against the blade depends in part on the blade's condition and the density of the tile. Nonetheless, generally speaking, this pressure should be light when the tile first contacts the blade, increase as the blade cuts through the tile and decrease as the end of the cut nears.

Throughout the cutting procedure, the tile should be kept in contact with the table to prevent vibration and to keep the blade from sticking in the middle of a cut. Many experienced setters, however, make the entire cut or finish a cut by holding the tile off the table in both hands. This technique allows the tile stock to be removed right up to the line, but it's dangerous. If the tile cocks to one side, the blade can knock off tile chips and send them flying, or it can grab the entire tile from your hands and fling it away. Since this tool routinely throws off tile chips whatever cutting method you choose, I strongly recommend wearing safety glasses whenever working with it. Because of the noise of the saw, I also suggest wearing hearing protectors.

A wet-saw blade generally lasts for thousands of cuts. Occasionally the blade will clog up with ceramic material and need cleaning. One way of doing this is to cut through an old sand-mold brick or to make several cuts in a tile grindstone. Another method is to remove the blade, flip it over and let it rotate in the opposite direction. Replacement blades are available when the blade becomes too worn.

Unlike the dry-cutting diamond blade discussed next and most power saws used for woodworking, the wet saw's untoothed blade cuts only very hard materials easily. This means that the wet saw will not readily cut through skin. But because this is not a complete impossibility, the wet saw should be treated with the same respect given to any other power saw. You need not, however, be afraid of the wet saw.

Dry-cutting diamond-blade saw   Another cutting tool that's helpful to have for some installations is a dry-cutting diamond blade mounted in a small electric grinder (see photo, p. 29). This tool can be used both to rip out old tilework, as you'll see in Chapter 12, and to cut new tiles. One advantage it has over the wet saw is that it requires no extensive set-up—just plug it into an electrical outlet. Like the wet saw, this blade can be used to make straight cuts and, by making a series of parallel kerfs, curved cuts. Because this tool is hand-held, however, it cuts with less accuracy than the wet saw and leaves a jagged edge. For this reason, the dry-cutting diamond-blade saw should be considered a "roughing-in" tool, though it certainly speeds up making cuts whose edges will be hidden, among them, enlarged sink and cooktop holes in tile countertops, and trimmed Mexican pavers. Another task for which this blade is very handy and quick is cutting tile backer boards to size.

The only drawbacks to using this saw are its speed and the chips and dust it generates. Safety glasses, a dust mask and extreme care are essential when using this tool. Unlike the wet saw, the dry saw will quickly cut through skin and bone and should be handled with the utmost caution. I always firmly hold the grinder in which the blade is mounted and make sure the work space where I'm cutting is completely clear. To combat the dust, I wear a dust mask and also get a helper to follow the cutting action with a vacuum cleaner.

Other cutting and grinding tools In addition to the saws already mentioned, a carbide-tipped hole saw is a very useful tilesetting tool. As its name suggests, this saw serves to cut holes, and it's indispensable for getting a finished look when tiling around faucets and supply lines and also for cutting sink corners. It cuts both soft- and hard-bodied tile, although cutting vitreous tile is pretty slow-going.

Chucked in a power drill, the hole saw and its ¼-in., carbide-tipped pilot drill bit are mounted on a mandrel. The saw can be used dry, but I've found that, when drilling a hole in a single, unset tile, it tends to break the tile. The reason for this is that the hole saw cuts rather slowly and heat builds up from the tile chips and dust trapped around the cutting edge. For this reason, I developed a way of using the hole saw to reduce the heat shock that cracks the tile. (Heat shock is not a problem with the other saws mentioned above. The wet saw is cooled by water, and the dry-cutting diamond blade not only has a toothed edge, which allows the hot dust to escape, but also cuts rapidly enough to prevent any damaging heat buildup.)

A carbide-tipped hole saw chucked in a power drill (top left) is indispensable for drilling holes in tiles to be set around faucets and supply lines. This tool is also essential for cutting sink corners and enlarging an existing hole for a new sink (top right and bottom).

To keep a tile cool during drilling, I immerse it in a bath of water. Because of the danger involved in working with a power tool around water, I chuck the hole saw in a cordless drill whenever using this method. I also make sure that the battery pack is fully charged, since drilling the hole draws a lot of power. Because an inexpensive cordless drill is usually not powerful enough for the hole saw, you may need to obtain a heavy-duty cordless drill for this operation.

To support the tile while it's being cut, I build a box of scrap ¾-in. plywood somewhat larger than the tile and caulk the box's corners. I fill the box with enough water to cover the tile by about ¼ in. Before submerging the tile, I use a center punch to break the glaze at the center of the cut so that the pilot bit won't slip. Then I submerge the tile, position the pilot bit and turn the drill to regular speed. As the pilot cuts through the tile, the hole saw will be drawn into the tile's surface and the drill's speed should be reduced. I don't put too much pressure on the hole saw as it's cutting, as that might cause the tile to split. Instead I let the saw feed itself into the tile. Because the hole saw operates best at a slow speed of about 100 rpm to 200 rpm, it's relatively safe to use. Nonetheless, it is capable of cutting through skin and bone and should be used with care.

Because cut tile often has sharp edges, especially when cut on a snap cutter, hand-held tile grindstones are needed to smooth these edges and round off corners, a job that could also be done by carbide sandpaper. I keep several stones in varying grades for soft and hard tiles. I also have a masonry rubbing stone, which is much coarser, for grinding down high spots and smoothing concrete slabs and mortar beds. In addition, I use it to grind the edges of unglazed Mexican pavers and shape them into trim pieces, since no ready-made trim is available for this type of tile (see drawing, p. 24).

Wedges and spacers Wedges and spacers are molded or extruded plastic pieces that facilitate the actual placement of tile. Wedges are used like shims to hold a vertically placed tile in position until the adhesive sets up. If time permits, I like to leave wedges in place overnight, but they can be removed as soon as the adhesive has cured enough to fully support the tiles. Spacers go between tiles, whether they're set horizontally or vertically, to ensure that the grout joint will be a consistent width. Spacers come in a variety of sizes and shapes so that they can be used with square, rectangular, hexagonal or octagonal tile. Although many setters leave spacers in place and grout over them, I recommend removing them before grouting because the thinner layer of grout over the spacers will dry to a lighter shade than that of the surrounding, deeper grout.

Beating block A beating block is a block of wood that's used to firmly seat tile in its setting bed. It's placed over the positioned tile and sharply tapped with a rubber hammer to both force the tile into the adhesive and ensure a level surface. This block can either be bought (and will then usually have a rubber face), or it can be made from a scrap piece of plywood about 6 in. by 10 in. Although only the rubber hammer is needed to beat in tile that's 8 in. square and larger, it's critical to use a beating block with the hammer for both smaller tile and sheet-mounted tile such as 1-in.-square mosaic tiles in order to produce a successful bond and a flat surface. One type of smaller tile on which a beating block is ineffective, however, is tile with an uneven surface—Mexican pavers, for example. These tiles should instead be firmly pressed into the adhesive by hand and then tapped individually with the mallet. The softer the tile's bisque, the gentler the mallet raps should be.

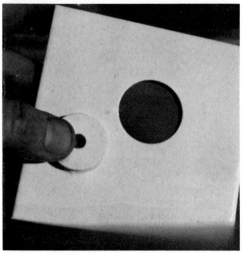

When drilling single tiles with the hole saw, I chuck the saw in a cordless drill and submerge the tile in water to prevent heat shock from cracking the tile.

Grouting and finishing tools

The minimum tools needed for grouting and completing a tile installation are a bucket for mixing and one for cleaning, a rounded sponge, a margin trowel, a grout trowel, and cheesecloth.

Grout trowels are rubber-faced trowels used for spreading grout over the surface of the tiles and packing it into the joints without scratching the tile's glaze. Grout trowels with stiff rubber faces are designed for grouting sturdy floor tiles, while those with a softer rubber face, sometimes backed with foam, are intended for grouting tile with more delicate glazes. After the grout is spread with the face of the trowel, the tool's edge is used to cut away excess grout from the surface of the tiles.

Once a small area of tile has been grouted with the grout trowel, cleanup can begin immediately. The key to successfully cleaning up grout is to do so before the grout hardens and to use a minimum of water. (For a full discussion of grout-cleaning techniques, see p. 65.) The principal cleaning tool needed is a good sponge with rounded corners, which will not gouge out the joints. It's also useful to have Scotch-Brite pads to gently scour any hardened grout that resists sponging, and steel-wool pads for really stubborn residue. To avoid marring glazed tiles, these pads should be slightly moistened with water. And once a steel-wool pad begins to deteriorate, it should be discarded to prevent the splintered strands from sticking in the joint where they will rust and discolor the grout. Finally, cheesecloth can be used to remove any haze left on the tiles after grouting. Since this filmy residue becomes very difficult to remove once it hardens, it should be removed quickly. Many setters use acid grout cleaners to remove grout haze, but I believe that these cause more problems than they solve. I suggest staying away from these cleaners and instead cleaning up promptly.

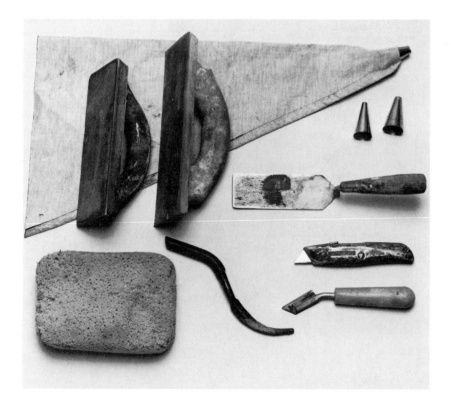

Grouting and finishing tools include (from top left, clockwise) grout trowels, grout bag and metal tips, margin trowel, razor knife, grout saw, striking tool, and sponge.

When grouting certain kinds of tile that would be particularly difficult to clean up—for example, those with a rough surface like antique brick-veneer tile—a grout bag should be used instead of a grout trowel. This bag looks like a cake-decorating bag and works the same way. A metal tip, sized to the width of the grout joint, is put on the end of the bag, which is then filled with grout and squeezed to lay a ribbon of grout in the joints. A striking tool is used to compact the grout into the joints, and very little, if any, grout gets on the surface of the tile, eliminating major cleaning problems. After striking, the mortar is allowed to harden a bit and a stiff brush is then used to remove any excess grout.

The disadvantage of this tool is that the grout must be mixed fairly wet to flow through the bag's tip and the extra water mixed into the grout weakens it. For this reason, a grout bag should be reserved for tile that cannot be grouted in the regular fashion. (For further discussion of how to use the grout bag, see p. 65.)

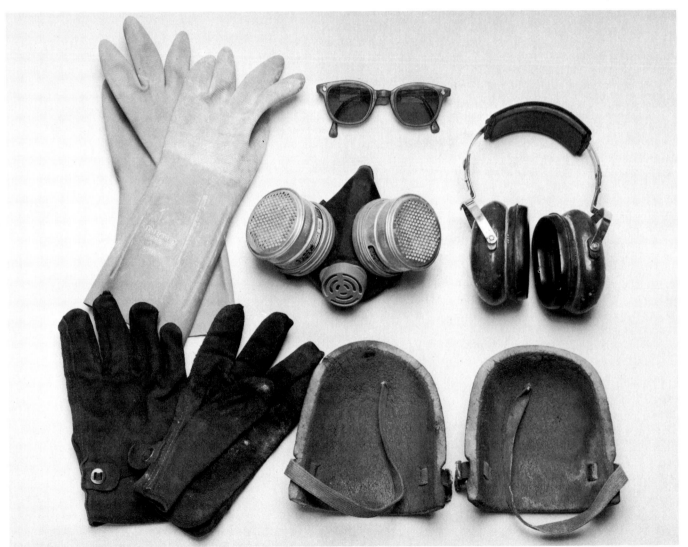

For safely setting tile, certain protective equipment is crucial, including (from left, top to bottom) both rubber and heavy leather gloves, safety glasses, charcoal-filter mask, knee pads, and hearing protectors.

Setting tile safely

Setting tile involves contact with some tools and materials that are potentially hazardous. If you set tile only occasionally, you're not likely to have a problem. But if you set tile frequently, prolonged contact with these materials is cause for concern. Unfortunately, no industry-wide safety standards exist, and there has been no real study of the long-term health problems associated with many tilesetting materials. For these reasons, I suggest minimizing potential problems, whether you set tile daily or only once a year, by using safety equipment, common sense and care as you work. The safety equipment recommended here is available at most hardware and building supply stores, and some of the more specialized equipment can be obtained from suppliers listed in the Resource Guide.

Because setting tile frequently involves working around water with power tools, extra caution is needed. Even a small amount of moisture can turn what would normally be a poor electrical conductor into a very good one, and it doesn't take much electricity to cause injury or death. For this reason, use double-insulated tools whenever possible and make sure that they are all plugged into a properly grounded outlet. In addition, using a portable ground-fault circuit interrupter (GFCI) provides considerable extra protection from electrical shock. A GFCI is a fast-acting circuit breaker designed to cut the flow of electricity to a tool in the event that the user accidentally becomes part of the electrical circuit. Permanent GFCIs are now required by code in bathrooms and kitchens, so if you're tiling in one of these rooms, look to see if an outlet is equipped with a GFCI. If not, you can buy a portable GFCI, which is about the size of a standard outlet box, and simply plug it into the nearest outlet. Then plug your tools into the GFCI and start work.

When using power cutting tools, whether to rip out old walls and floors or to cut new tile to size, *always* wear safety glasses or goggles and a fitted dust mask—these tools readily generate not only tile chips and other debris but also considerable dust. Make sure that the dust mask you buy has a rubber faceplate that fits snugly over your nose and mouth; a flimsy paper mask with a bendable metal noseclip affords little protection. Because of the noise produced by this machinery, I also suggest wearing hearing protectors. And for obvious reasons, wear heavy shoes or boots when doing rip-out or demolition work.

It's not only power tools that throw tile chips but the snap cutter and biters as well. Therefore it's a good idea to get in the habit of wearing safety glasses whenever you're cutting tile, whatever the method. And because floating mortar beds and grouting often both kick up sand and cement particles, I always try to wear safety glasses for these tasks, too.

Since it's easy to get cut when manually ripping out walls, floors and old tilework, I recommend wearing heavy leather gloves for demolition work. As I discovered early in my tilesetting career, gloves are especially important when ripping out tiled showers. Any cut I got doing this work seemed to take forever to heal, which, my family doctor explained, was due to the fact that the cuts were becoming infected by germs and bacteria harbored in some of the old tilework. Now I make it a habit to wear gloves when ripping out old tiles.

In addition to the mechanical hazards of tilesetting, the chemicals found in many setting materials are also cause for concern. Unfortunately, manufacturers are not required to list a product's ingredients on the label, only to indicate whether any of the ingredients is flammable. Thus you may unwittingly find yourself working, for example, with a solvent-based organic mastic that contains toluene, a petroleum by-product, or you may install a waterproofing membrane with a glue containing xylene, another petroleum by-product. As well, you may not realize that the cement particles in all thinsets, grout and mortar are toxic when in powdered form and caustic when wet. If you don't set tile often, you may not be bothered by any of these chemicals. Given the lack of thorough research on the long-term effects of contact with such chemicals, however, I suggest that you take precautions whenever you set tile.

To protect against the toxic fumes given off by solvent-based setting materials, I recommend wearing a charcoal-filter mask. Unlike a dust mask, a charcoal-filter mask protects not only against dust but also against fumes and vapors. These masks are available at building supply houses and paint stores—look for one with the seal of approval of either the Occupational Safety and Health Association (OSHA) or the National Institute of Occupational Safety and Health (NIOSH). (For specific information on toxic or otherwise hazardous substances, see the book *Artist Beware,* or contact the Art Hazards Information Center, both of which are listed in the Resource Guide.)

Since I have become sensitized over the years and now have severe reactions to fumes emitted by setting materials, I'm careful to wear a filter mask whenever working with these materials and to change the canisters the moment I smell any chemical odors within the mask. This mask is a little uncomfortable, but the protection it affords is more than worth it. Using this mask means freedom not only from worrying about the long-term health hazards of inhaling these fumes, but also from having my head spin with an unwanted industrial "high."

To protect against the toxic cement particles when mixing adhesives, mortar and grout, be certain to wear a fitted dust mask. Once these setting materials are mixed, the toxic particles are bound up in water and produce no dangerous vapors. Instead, the particles become caustic to the touch, and for this reason you'll need to wear rubber gloves when working with them. Although it's sometimes impossible to avoid handling these materials without gloves, continued exposure to them may cause skin sensitivity, severe rashes, blood poisoning and worse. I keep several pairs of rubber gloves on hand in case one breaks. At the end of the day when I've been working with setting materials, I rinse my hands and arms with an inexpensive apple-cider vinegar, which neutralizes these materials and helps condition my skin.

While on the subject of toxic materials in tilesetting, I should mention that U.S. tile manufacturers are now prohibited from including asbestos as a filler ingredient in tile. Foreign tile manufacturers, however, are free of such restrictions. If you purchase foreign tile, there is no way of knowing whether it contains asbestos without having it chemically tested. If it does contain asbestos, this ingredient will become problematic only when the tile is cut for installation and generates dust. Even then, the amount of asbestos dust that might be inhaled could be minimal. Nonetheless, given the unknowns and the general concern about asbestos, it's a good idea to get in the habit of wearing a fitted dust mask to protect against dust whenever cutting any tile with the snap cutter, biters or a dry-cutting power saw. If tile is cut on the wet saw, the water eliminates the problem of dust altogether.

Because solvent-based ingredients in some tilesetting materials are flammable as well as toxic, it's important to make sure that the room or area being tiled is well ventilated and that there are no sparks or open flames nearby. The latter includes pilot lights on the stove—remember to shut off the gas!

Finally, tilesetting is physically taxing work. Because a box of tile can weigh from 10 lb. to 50 lb. and a bucket of mortar may weigh more than 60 lb., it's very easy to pull or strain muscles. To avoid this, remember one cardinal rule: Keep your back straight when lifting. Lift with your leg and arm muscles, not your back. And always use knee pads when working on your knees—which happens often in tilesetting! I keep two pairs of knee pads handy: one for rough work and another clean pair for working on the positioned tiles. To further protect your knees, make sure to keep the job site clean. If you've forgotten to put on knee pads, kneeling on tile chips can cause bad bruises.

Several government agencies, for example, OSHA, NIOSH and the Environmental Protection Agency (EPA), are charged with responsibility for regulating and maintaining the health and safety of the nation's work place. In reality, however, these agencies do not protect all workers (the self-employed and, ironically, employees of federal, state and city governments are exempt, among others). Also, these agencies are often slow to act on job-site problems. And they understandably have trouble keeping pace with testing and evaluating the burgeoning number of setting materials on the market, which means that some products will get widely used before being tested. In the end, the individual tilesetter must take responsibility for protecting his or her own health. □

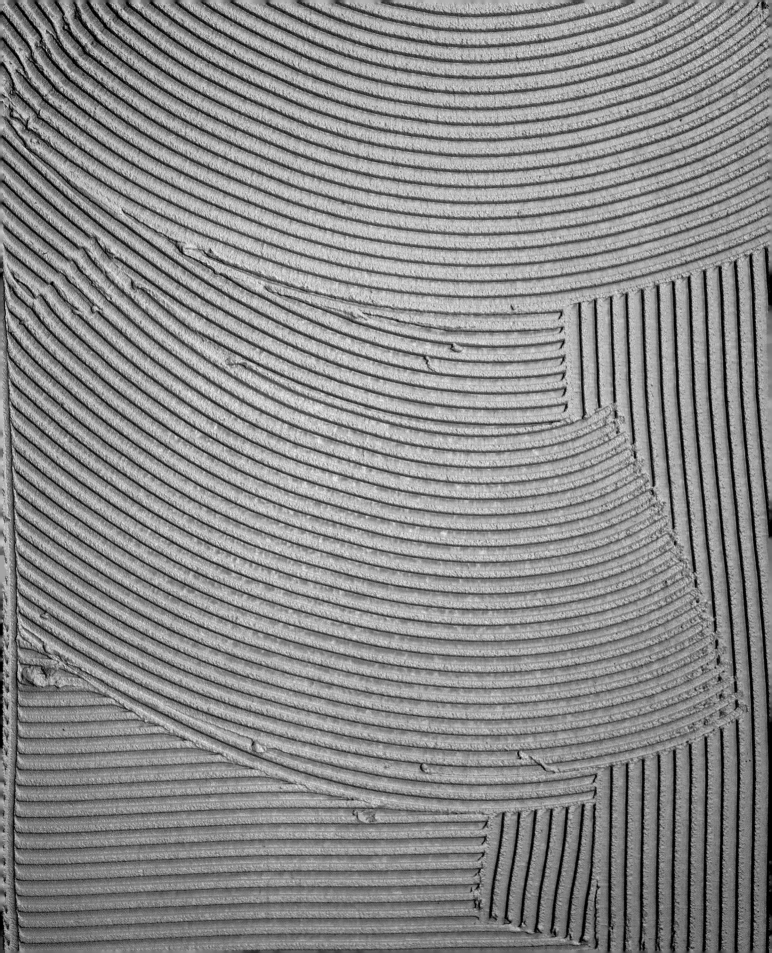

Setting Materials

Structurally, all tilework is like an open-faced sandwich: a layer of tile, surrounded by grout, sits atop a layer of adhesive and a setting bed. The setting materials—the adhesive and the grout—contribute to anchoring the tile to its bed, and these materials and the bed must be compatible for the bond to be strong and long-lasting.

Because many new setting materials are developed yearly, the range of choices has become enormous, and selecting among them may be perplexing for the novice or occasional tilesetter. Although many products on the market are excellent and consistently reliable, there are also many that are mediocre and some are markedly inferior. For this reason, it's a good idea to select name-brand adhesives and grout, particularly those with the seal of a major tile organization printed on the label (see the list of tile organizations in the Resource Guide). The presence of such a seal means that the product has been thoroughly tested and proven to have certain performance characteristics.

There are two basic types of adhesives on the market: organic mastics, which are ready-to-use, petroleum- or latex-based products; and thinset adhesives, which are powdered, cement-based products that must be mixed with liquid before use. (At this writing, a few ready-to-use thinsets had recently been introduced to the market, and there will doubtless be many more available in years to come. Since the vast majority of thinsets still require mixing, however, the discussion of thinsets here will be limited to this category.)

Whatever the setting bed, one of these two types of adhesives will be used. If that bed is a floated bed of mortar, the installation will be termed a thick-bed installation. If another type of setting bed is used, the installation will be called a thin-bed, or thinset (whichever adhesive is actually used), installation. While clarifying the tilesetter's vocabulary at the outset of this discussion of setting materials, I should mention the term *mortar*. Unless you're a veteran tilesetter, you probably associate the word with the material that adheres bricks and stones together in masonry walls. In

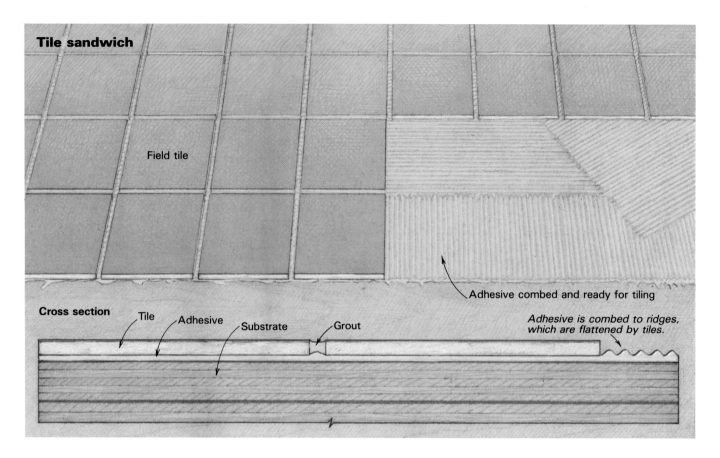

Tile sandwich

Field tile

Adhesive combed and ready for tiling

Cross section

Tile — Adhesive — Substrate — Grout

Adhesive is combed to ridges, which are flattened by tiles.

tilesetting, *mortar* refers to the sand-and-cement mixture used for floating mortar beds. *Thinset mortar* serves as a generic name for the adhesives that adhere tiles not to each other but to a substrate below. Since the terminology can get a bit confusing for those new to tilesetting, I've reserved the term *mortar* for the mortar in mortar beds and referred to adhesives by their specific names.

Organic mastics

The term sounds like something you buy in a health-food store. Actually, organic mastics are made of either latex or petrochemical materials and have two components: a bonding agent and a vehicle for this adhesive. In the case of petroleum-based mastics, the vehicle is often a solvent called toluene, and in latex-based mastics, it's water. Ready to use right out of the can, mastics cure, or harden, when the toluene or water evaporates.

Of all the adhesives, mastics are the least expensive per square foot of coverage, though only by a couple of pennies. Because mastics need no preparation or mixing, they're also considerably easier and less time-consuming to use than thinset adhesives. And since they begin gripping firmly even before they're fully cured, they're good for setting wall tiles—there isn't as much tile slippage to deal with as with other adhesives. For these reasons, organic mastics are probably the most commonly used adhesives, but they're nonetheless generally inferior to other adhesives. For the most part, they don't have the bond strength or compressive strength of thinset adhesives, nor are they as flexible when cured as some of the thinsets (latex thinsets in particular).

Whether solvent- or water-based, mastics are used principally for setting tile over drywall and plywood, although some brands can also be used on concrete slabs and mortar beds. Whatever the setting surface, mastics are generally used to install tiles only in areas that will remain dry. Mastics should be avoided not only in wet installations but also in areas that will be exposed to heat—a fireplace hearth, for example. Packaging labels on the mastics themselves will provide information on the appropriate uses for a given product.

While discussing surfaces on which mastics can be used, I should mention that the setting bed for a mastic should be entirely flat (this is not critical with thinset adhesives). If the bed has any low spots, it's possible that the thicker areas in the layer of mastic won't thoroughly dry out and reach maximum bond strength.

Whenever used, solvent-based mastics demand caution. Their vapors are potentially explosive, and when inhaled are definitely hazardous. Before opening the can, put on a charcoal-filter mask and check to see that there are no open flames nearby (including pilot lights on a stove) and that the work area is well ventilated. Despite the fact that water-based mastics are considered safer to use than their solvent-based counterparts, I prefer not to take chances with any mastic and always observe these precautions.

When you first open a fresh can of mastic, you may notice, depending on the product's composition, an oily-looking or watery puddle floating on the surface. This puddle, which results from the mastic's lighter ingredients separating and rising, should be stirred back into the mixture with a stick. If you have a problem doing this, it may be because the mastic sat on the store shelf too long. This rarely happens, but if it does, return the can to the store for a replacement.

If you've used the can before and find that the mastic has begun to harden when you open it this time, throw it out. Never, under any circumstances, try to thin a mastic. I've found that leftover mastic will harden quickly in the can, even if it has been closed tightly. Keeping the can out of direct sunlight and in a cool place will help lengthen a mastic's life. You can also extend the life of a solvent-based mastic up to about three months (and in the case of a couple of mastics, up to six months) by covering the adhesive with a few inches of water before closing the lid. The water prevents air from reaching the mastic and the vapors in the mastic from evaporating. (Pour off this water before using the adhesive.) Note, however, that adding water to the top of latex-based mastic before closing the lid will only dilute the adhesive and render it useless.

With regard to using mastics, the individual product label will tell you the product's open time (how long the mastic takes to begin to "skin over," or lose its bonding ability, after being spread) and set-up time (how long the mastic takes to begin curing once applied to a surface). The label should also recommend the size of notched trowel to use in spreading the mastic. (For a full discussion of applying adhesives, see p. 57.)

Both solvent- and water-based mastics must be cleaned up promptly, using, in most cases, paint thinner or water, respectively. Since there are now some mastics with solvent ingredients that can be cleaned up with water, however, check the individual product label for instructions. If the mastic on tile and tools is still soft, it can be removed with a rag dipped in thinner or water. For partially dried mastic, use steel wool and thinner or water. Once the mastic has hardened, it must be scraped or sliced off with a razor blade or a paint scraper. Since it's difficult to get dried mastic out of the tiny grooves of a spreading trowel, I heartily recommend cleaning up while the mastic is still soft.

Thinset adhesives

Thinset adhesives are powdered sand-and-cement products that must be mixed before use, with either water, liquid latex or acrylic additives, or epoxy resin. These adhesives have much greater bond strength and compressive strength than organic mastics, and, because they can support a considerable amount of weight, are often used for floor installations. They generally set up more quickly than mastics do and tend to be more flexible. Also, unlike organic mastics, they can be used both for wet installations when paired with the right setting bed, and in areas where heat is a factor.

Water-mixed thinsets   These thinsets combine sand, cement and water with retarder additives (which slow down the curing process) to produce an adhesive with both high bond and high compressive strength. After they've cured, these thinsets are unaffected by water and can therefore be used for dry and wet installations alike. They're generally used over mortar setting beds or concrete slabs, although some can be used over plywood and tile backer boards (product labels will provide information on use). Packaged in 5-, 10-, 25- and 50-lb. sacks, these water-mixed thinsets cost about a penny more than organic mastics per square foot of coverage.

To prepare water-mixed thinset, clean, room-temperature water should be used. When making up two gallons or less, I prefer to mix it by hand with a long-blade margin trowel. For larger amounts, a mixing paddle chucked in a drill is more efficient (see photo, p. 34). As I mentioned in Chapter 2, be sure to use a paddle designed for mixing mortar rather than paint. While there are no fumes to worry about when mixing these or any other thinsets, dust is a problem, so a fitted dust mask is recommended when you're working with any thinset. Because thinset is both caustic and very difficult to clean off your skin once it has dried, it's also a good idea to wear gloves when mixing and working with thinsets. If you find that you must take the gloves off for precise work, make sure to have a bucket of clean water nearby and occasionally wash off your hands.

Mixing any thinset by hand is a straightforward process that simply requires a bit of care. I like to pour the liquid into the bucket first and then add the powder gradually. Once all the dry ingredients have been stirred into the liquid, about 90% of the lumps can be eliminated with the trowel or a stick. I let the mixture slake, or rest, for about 10 minutes to allow moisture to penetrate the remaining lumps and make them easier to remove. I restir the mixture just before use to make it lump-free and ready for spreading.

If you're mixing thinset with a paddle, be sure to keep the paddle submerged to prevent air from being whipped into the mixture. This is important, as air bubbles will reduce the number of solid particles per cubic inch and thus can weaken the adhesive's bond strength by as much as 50%. Once the thinset is thoroughly mixed, let it slake for 10 minutes and then remix it before using it. (For information on how to determine when the adhesive is the proper consistency, see p. 57.) If a prepared thinset begins to set up on the job, it should never be thinned with water. Instead, the old mix should be discarded and a new batch made.

Like any mortar product, water-mixed thinsets clean up easily with water while they're still plastic. Because some harden quickly, however, steel wool and water may be needed to remove dried residue. If you leave the thinset to harden overnight, you'll need a margin trowel or a paint scraper and considerable elbow grease to get at it. Don't wait to clean up mortar products!

Latex and acrylic thinsets These thinsets combine liquid latex or acrylic additives (that is, natural or synthetic rubber) with sand and cement or with prepared powdered ingredients to produce a tough yet flexible adhesive. Compared to thinsets mixed with water, latex and acrylic thinsets have both higher bond strength and higher compressive strength. And because their dry component particles are bound up in a pliable matrix, these adhesives are also more flexible than water-mixed thinsets.

Generally speaking, latex and acrylic thinsets can be used over any substrate, though some may not be recommended for tiling over plywood (check the product label). While these thinsets are not strictly waterproof, their plastic matrix makes them water-resistant, and, when combined with a properly waterproofed underlayment, they make excellent adhesives for wet as well as dry installations.

The liquid additives for these thinsets are packaged in quart, half-gallon and gallon jars, 5-gallon buckets, and 55-gallon drums. The dry ingredients mixed with these additives are usually purchased separately. Per square foot of coverage, these thinsets cost only a few cents more than organic mastics and water-mixed thinsets. While easy to mix and use, these thinsets must be cleaned up rapidly because once dry they're extremely difficult to remove from tiles, tools and hands. So when working with them, always wear rubber gloves and clean up quickly, using water and a sponge to prevent disturbing tiles that have begun to set up. Despite the extra care required in cleanup and their slightly higher cost, I recommend these adhesives over water-mixed thinsets because of their resilience and bond strength.

While some of these liquid thinset additives are intended to be mixed with sand and cement, others are designed, for increased strength, to be combined with the dry ingredients for a water-mixed thinset. Many professional setters often combine latex or acrylic additives, whether they're designed for this treatment or not, with these dry ingredients. This eliminates the time-consuming process of separately measuring the needed dry ingredients. And because these prepared dry ingredients themselves include several additives, which, among other things, increase bond strength, this mixing technique also yields a thinset with an extra-strong grip.

I often mix my favorite brand of liquid latex additive with the dry ingredients for two or three different water-mixed thinsets, depending on the particular performance characteristics I need for a job. The addition of the dry ingredients from one brand of water-mixed thinset, for example, produces exceptional bond strength. Another reduces set-up time, and a third increases open and set-up time. Like many professional tilesetters, I'm continually experimenting with different mixtures and comparing notes with other setters to expand my repertoire of adhesives.

Epoxy thinsets Most epoxy tile adhesives are composed of three parts: a liquid resin, a liquid hardener, and a filler powder of sand and cement. (A few epoxies are two-part mixes, with a liquid resin and a powder combination of hardener and sand-and-cement filler.) Like latex and acrylic thinsets, epoxy thinsets are quite flexible and have high compressive strength and high bond strength. They develop their bond strength quickly, and, in fact, many setters use epoxies on commercial jobs when an installation must be returned to service in a hurry.

Unlike other thinsets, epoxy thinsets can be used on any setting surface, including metal, but they're particularly effective when combined with a plywood substrate. Although these adhesives are not waterproof, hardened epoxy can be considered water-resistant. Thus, with proper waterproofing, epoxy thinsets can be used for wet as well as dry installations.

Epoxy liquids are packaged in a variety of sizes, from half-gallon and gallon jars to 55-gallon drums. The dry ingredients are usually packaged in factory-proportioned sacks and included with the purchase of the liquids. Per square foot of coverage, epoxies are about four times more expensive than other thinsets. But because they have very high bond strength and flexibility, and are unaffected by water, these are the thinsets to use when tiling over a substrate that's incompatible with other adhesives. Consequently, if you have any doubt about whether an adhesive recommended in this book for a particular setting surface will work on your given installation, use epoxy. (Note that, while the all-purpose epoxy adhesives used for small household repairs would certainly adhere tile to a substrate, they would be exhorbitantly expensive in the quantities needed for most installations. What you want is an epoxy tile adhesive.)

Cleanup with epoxies varies from product to product, depending on the ingredients. Some are water-soluble when still wet and easily cleaned up; others require a solvent and a bit more work (cleanup information for a particular product will be provided on the label). As with any adhesive, cleanup is considerably easier if it's begun before the adhesive dries.

When mixing epoxies, proportioning the liquid ingredients is critical. Those adhesives specifying equal parts of resin and hardener are simple enough to mix, but those requiring unequal amounts require real care in measuring. Coffee cans with the indented rings make good measuring cups, but if you're mixing more than a gallon or two, make a dip stick marked off in inches to measure the proportions. Before pouring either of the two liquids into a mixing bucket, stir each ingredient with a separate clean stick or margin trowel. (Be sure you don't contaminate the contents of one container with that of the other, or the liquids will begin irreversibly to harden.) Then pour the liquids into the mixing bucket and stir or paddle them until they're thoroughly combined. Next mix the filler powder into the liquid a little bit at a time. If the initial mix is too dry, thin it with a properly portioned mixture of the liquid ingredients, which you should prepare in a separate container. Under no circumstances should you add anything to the epoxy adhesive to thin it once it has begun to harden. As with any thinset that starts to cure before use, discard it and prepare a new batch.

All the usual precautions concerning vapors and dust should be observed when working with epoxy adhesives: wear a charcoal-filter mask, make sure that the work area is well ventilated and check the product label for any additional safety precautions. Anyone with sensitive skin may be particularly bothered by epoxy. And because the hardened stuff is extremely difficult to remove from skin, it's a good idea to wear rubber gloves while mixing and working with epoxies.

Choosing an adhesive

Deciding which type of adhesive to use for a particular job depends on a number of factors, most importantly, the kind of substrate on which the tiles will be set and whether the installation will be exposed to water or remain dry. Other things that will influence your decision include the cost of the adhesive, its availability and its ease of use. There are a few prepared adhesives on the market that claim to be suitable for any type of installation, but while these adhesives will doubtless adhere the tiles to the setting bed, the results are liable to be mediocre and short-lived. If you want the job to last and be of high quality, begin by choosing the setting bed best suited to the wear the installation will receive and then select an adhesive that's specifically matched to this type of bed.

Pairing substrates, adhesives and membranes

Substrates		Adhesives				Membranes			
		Organic mastic	Water-mixed thinset	Latex or acrylic thinset	Epoxy thinset	Tar-paper curing	Tar-paper water-proofing	CPE isolation and water-proofing	Trowel-applied water-proofing
Floors									
Dry	a) Mortar bed		√*	√		√			
	b) Backer board		√*	√					
	c) Plywood			√*	√				
	d) Plywood	√							
Occasionally wet	a) Mortar bed		√*	√			√		
	b) Backer board		√*	√				√*	√
	c) Plywood			√*	√			√*	√
Wet	a) Mortar bed		√*	√			√*	√	√
	b) Backer board		√*	√				√*	√
	c) Plywood			√				√*	√
Sloped	a) Mortar bed		√*	√			√*		√
Solar gain	a) Mortar bed		√*	√		√			
Walls									
Dry	a) Mortar bed		√*	√		√			
	b) Backer board		√*	√					
	c) Drywall		√*	√					
	d) Drywall	√							
Occasionally wet	a) Mortar bed		√*	√			√		
	b) Backer board		√*	√				√*	√
	c) Drywall			√				√*	√
Wet	a) Mortar bed		√*	√			√		
	b) Backer board		√*	√				√*	√
	c) Drywall			√				√*	√
Countertops									
Dry	a) Mortar bed		√*	√		√			
	b) Backer board		√*	√					
	c) Plywood			√*	√				
	d) Plywood	√							
Occasionally wet	a) Mortar bed		√*	√			√		
	b) Backer board		√*	√				√*	√
	c) Plywood			√				√*	√
Wet	a) Mortar bed		√*	√			√*	√	√
	b) Backer board		√*	√				√*	√
	c) Plywood			√				√*	√

Note: *This chart lists in order of preference the substrates I recommend for various tile installations as well as the adhesive and waterproofing or protective membrane with which each is best paired. While a mortar bed is always my first choice for a setting bed, it requires skill, and the inexperienced tilesetter is advised to stick with the alternative substrates listed. (For further information on choosing a setting surface, see p. 88; for information on membranes, see p. 89.)*
If two adhesives or two membranes are checked for a given substrate, it means that either is suitable.

If I'm planning tilework for new construction, I have the luxury of picking the ideal setting bed and adhesive for the given job. If, however, I'm setting tile on existing floors or walls, I'll probably be limited in my choice, since the ideal setting bed for the job may be out of the question due to the extensive surface preparation needed and hence the added expense.

Whatever the limiting factors on a given job, I always try to produce the most durable installation possible. To determine which setting bed and adhesive will give the best results, I begin by asking the customer whether the area being tiled will frequently get wet, occasionally get wet or essentially remain dry. A floor in a bathroom that gets used daily, for example, is likely to be wet more consistently than the floor in a guest bathroom or a half-bath. For this reason, tile set in the main bath should be considered a wet installation and should be fully waterproofed, while the tilework in the second bathroom and half-bath could be considered an installation that occasionally gets wet and which would thus require less waterproofing. If, however, the customer wants to provide for the possibility that the second bathroom may someday be used as much as the first, it, too, should be treated as a wet installation and be fully waterproofed.

Not only do you need to establish whether the installation will be wet or dry, you must also determine the kind and degree of use it will get. A tiled countertop in a large restaurant kitchen, for example, will get considerably heavier wear than would the same countertop in most home kitchens. Therefore the tilework in the former should be considered a heavy-duty wet installation, while that in the latter could be treated as a medium-duty wet installation. This means that the home installation, while needing waterproofing, could use both a lighter-duty substrate than that in the restaurant and, in turn, also a lighter-duty waterproofing membrane, adhesive and grout. (For detailed information on waterproofing, which is needed for all the wet installations mentioned below, see p. 89).

Once the requirements of the installation have been determined and the substrate chosen (see p. 88), the next step is to select an adhesive that is compatible with both the substrate and the needs of the installation. If the setting surface is to be a mortar bed, it's best paired, for both wet and dry installations, with a latex thinset adhesive or, as a second choice, with a water-mixed thinset. If backer boards are to be used, match them with either a latex thinset (the best choice) or a water-mixed thinset for both wet and dry installations. On dry jobs with backer board, a compatible organic mastic can also be used, although this is less effective than the thinsets.

For a wet or dry installation using plywood as the setting bed, select a latex thinset designed for use over plywood, or, if cost is not an issue, an epoxy thinset. Adhesives for dry installations on drywall (including painted walls) are, in order of preference, a latex thinset, water-mixed thinset and organic mastic. On a concrete slab, the best adhesive for wet or dry installations is a latex thinset; for dry jobs, the second choice would be a water-mixed thinset and the third choice an organic mastic. For dry installations over linoleum or synthetic sheet flooring, use an epoxy thinset or, as second choice, a compatible latex thinset. And when old tilework is the setting bed, the best adhesive for both wet and dry installations is an epoxy thinset, with the next best alternative a compatible latex thinset.

The setting surfaces listed above are those most commonly used for tiling. If the surface you're interested in doesn't appear in this list, or you're uncertain of which surface to select, consult Chapter 4, where you'll find a full discussion of setting surfaces, how to prepare them for tiling, and the adhesives with which they should be paired. The chart on p. 55 shows the substrates and adhesives I prefer for specific applications.

Spreading and cleaning up adhesives

Whenever you're working with any adhesive, the temperature at the job site should be between 65°F and 75°F. I've successfully installed tile in 50°F and in 95°F weather, but in more moderate temperatures there are fewer problems. For example, at 35°F to 50°F readings, the adhesive will take a long time to set up (from four to eight, or even more, hours), and in freezing weather, the water in thinset adhesives will turn to ice, rendering the adhesive useless. When the thermometer goes above 90°F and in the direct sun, no matter what the temperature, thinset adhesives will "cook," meaning that the moisture will be driven out of them too quickly for them to properly cure. The resulting adhesive will eventually turn to powder.

If you're working indoors in cold weather, adjust the heat or use supplemental heating to regulate the room's temperature throughout the installation until the tile is set and the adhesive has dried. In hot weather, however, avoid using an air conditioner to cool down the room, as the unit's dehumidifier may dry out the adhesive prematurely. If need be, wait to spread the adhesive and set tile until the evening or early morning when the temperature has fallen.

Before you begin applying adhesive, you should clean the setting bed a final time to ready it for the adhesive, and to eliminate any dust that has settled and that may interfere with the adhesive's bond. When working with a thinset or a water-based organic mastic, wipe the bed with a damp sponge. If you're using a solvent-based mastic, moisten a rag with paint thinner.

All adhesives are generally applied in the same way. They're first spread on the setting surface with the unnotched edge of a V- or a square-shaped notched trowel. Then they're "combed" with the notched side of the trowel, which produces ridges of uniform height. Since the V-notched trowel yields more ridges per inch as it combs the adhesive than a comparably sized square-notched trowel, it's usually used for spreading adhesive for setting small tile, including sheet-mounted tile. The square-notched trowel is the better choice for spreading adhesive for setting larger tile.

If you're working with a thinset, you need to make sure its consistency is correct before spreading a lot of it on the bed. (Since organic mastics are premixed to the correct consistency, they don't need to be checked.) To do this, spread and comb thinset on a small area of the setting bed. Next press a single tile firmly into the adhesive and then remove it. By "reading" the back of this tile, you can ascertain the adhesive's consistency, and you'll also be able to decide if the layer of adhesive is the correct thickness. Since this test involves correctly applying the adhesive to the setting bed, let's look first at the general principles of spreading and combing adhesive, and then return to this sample patch and reading the tile back.

The adhesive should be spread with the unnotched edge of the trowel held at an acute angle of about 30° to the setting bed, which helps force

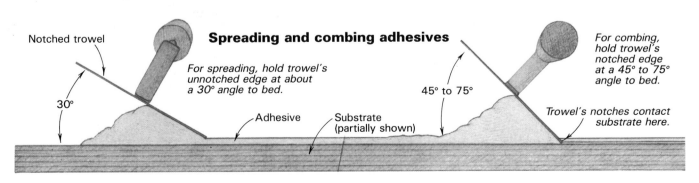

Notched trowel

Spreading and combing adhesives

For spreading, hold trowel's unnotched edge at about a 30° angle to bed.

30°

Adhesive

Substrate (partially shown)

45° to 75°

For combing, hold trowel's notched edge at a 45° to 75° angle to bed.

Trowel's notches contact substrate here.

the adhesive into the pores of the bed. Enough material should be applied to fully cover the immediate area being worked, and its depth should equal at least the height of the trowel's notches. The layer of adhesive between the tile and the setting bed should be at least 3/32 in. thick for the adhesive to reach its full bond strength. If the layer is too thin, it cannot be combed to produce fully formed, uniform ridges. The area you choose to work with can be anything from 4 sq. ft. to 20 sq. ft., depending on the size of the installation and the temperature at the job site (the hotter the temperature, the faster the adhesive will begin to set up). If you try to cover the entire area being tiled, chances are the adhesive will set up faster than you can set all the tile.

To comb out the adhesive, hold the notched side of the trowel at an acute angle of from 45° to 75° to the bed—the larger the angle, the higher the ridges will be. While combing, it's crucial to keep the angle of the trowel consistent. This will produce uniform ridges, and thus a level setting surface. It doesn't matter whether you make sweeping strokes or parallel passes as you comb, provided you maintain the trowel's angle *and* you leave no stray globs of adhesive anywhere on the surface. Precise workmanship at this stage will reward you later with a nice, flat bed of tiles.

Dump enough adhesive on the setting bed to cover only the area in which you're immediately working (above). Spread the adhesive with the unnotched edge of the trowel held at about a 30° angle (above right). Then comb the adhesive with the trowel's notched side held at an angle of from 45° to 75° (right).

Now back to the test tile. When it's removed from the setting bed, its entire back should be covered with adhesive. If the adhesive was mixed to the correct consistency and spread to the right thickness, half of its depth will remain on the setting bed and half will have adhered to the tile back. If the adhesive was mixed too wet, you would have noticed that the ridges produced by combing would not hold peaks. If the adhesive was mixed too dry, it will have formed full ridges, but will not have properly wet the tile and very little will have adhered to the tile. Should you need to adjust a thinset's consistency, add more dry or wet ingredients to the mix very gradually and test it after each adjustment until its consistency is right.

If you find only parallel lines of adhesive lifted from the tops of the combed ridges, the thinset's consistency is correct, but the layer of adhesive is combed too thin. In this case, apply more adhesive and comb it with a larger-notched trowel. Conversely, if the tile's back is so filled with adhesive that it has oozed up the sides into what will be the grout joint, the layer is too thick and needs to be combed with the angle of the trowel reduced or with a smaller-notched trowel. As a rule of thumb, pick a notch size equal to about two-thirds the thickness of the tile being set.

With regard to the adhesive's consistency, remember that heat and humidity can affect the mixture, as can the type of tile being set. Heat or low humidity requires that a thinset be mixed slightly wetter than it would be in cold weather or high humidity. As well, when setting nonvitreous tile, which readily absorbs water, mix a thinset adhesive a bit wetter than for vitreous tile, which absorbs little water.

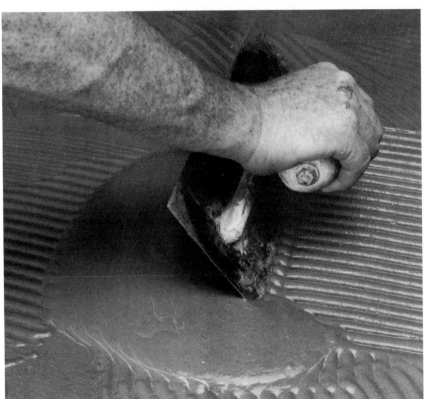

When using a thinset adhesive, you must mix it to the right consistency so that it can be combed into fully formed ridges and will completely cover the back of the tile (top right). If mixed too wet, thinset will not hold combed ridges (above left). If too dry, it will not adhere to the tile (above right).

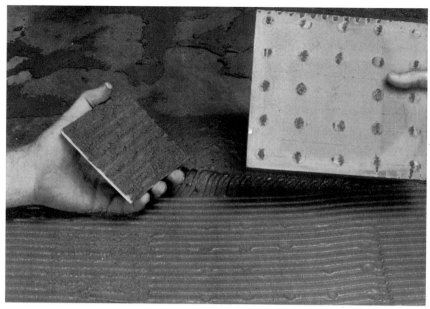

For spreading adhesive, the trowel's notch size must be paired to the size of the tile. The deep ridges produced by a large-notched trowel appropriately cover the back of large and button-backed tiles, but cause adhesive to ooze up into the joints between small tiles (above). Conversely, a small-notched trowel yields ridges suitable for small tiles but too shallow to fully cover large or button-backed tiles (right).

Button-backed tiles, handmade tiles with very uneven backs, sheet-mounted mosaic tiles and some small cut tiles may need additional adhesive buttered on the back with a margin trowel to ensure full adhesive contact between the tile and setting bed. Back-buttering should supplement, not replace, spreading adhesive on the bed. Insufficient or unevenly applied adhesive produces a poor bond, and leads to cracked tiles and grout joints.

The amount of adhesive needed to cover a given area can vary considerably from job to job, due not only to the differing physical properties of the four types of adhesive but also to the choice of setting bed and tile, the force used to spread the adhesive, and the weather. More adhesive is absorbed by a plywood setting bed, for example, than by a concrete slab, and by porous nonvitreous tile than by vitreous tile. Similarly, the more you force adhesive into the bed when spreading it, the more you will need to cover a constant area. And, finally, the hotter the day and the drier the climate, the more the adhesive absorbed by the tile and bed. Because these variables preclude a reliable adhesive coverage table, I recommend consulting your tile retailer to estimate your needs for a particular installation.

After the tiles have been positioned, it's imperative to clean up both excess adhesive on the face of the tile and any that has oozed up into the grout joints. Adhesive left in the joints will cause problems in grouting. First, grout applied over uncleaned joints may eventually crack, since it's thinner there than at other places. Second, globs of adhesive protruding through the grout are unsightly. And third, if colored grout is used in a joint clogged with adhesive, the thinner grout over the adhesive will take a slightly different cure than the surrounding material and become a different shade as it dries. The grout will, in effect, appear spotted.

A grout saw can be used to cut away excess adhesive, but I prefer a razor knife. If you opt for the knife, slide the blade along the edge of each tile and flick out adhesive between the tiles with its tip. Try to clean the joints while the adhesive is still plastic. If you have to remove hardened adhesive, use the grout saw to cut it from the joint and the knife to scrape or slice any remaining dried debris from the edges of the tile, then clean the tile with steel wool. Finally, vacuum the joints to pick up loose particles.

Allow the adhesive to cure at least overnight before grouting (check the label of the product you're using for instructions on precisely how long to wait). If you grout over wet or damp adhesive, it may discolor the grout.

Grout

Grouting is the final step in any tile installation. Tile grout, another form of mortar, is a powder mixed with liquid that's used to fill the joints between the tiles, protecting, supporting and framing their edges. Because of its high density, grout also helps retard water penetration into the joint. No grout, however, can ever be considered completely waterproof.

There are several types of grout used in other areas of the building trades, but these are not to be confused with tile grout. The former are usually applied in a wetter state than tile grout, and the most common of them is shot through a hose under pressure to repair cracked foundations or replace eroding soil around foundations.

Grout used for tiling comes in two forms: plain and sanded. Plain grout is essentially cement mixed with additives to give it certain performance characteristics—easy spreadability or a slow curing time, for example. Plain grout is used for joints less than $\frac{1}{16}$ in. wide. Sanded grout—simply plain grout to which sand has been added for strength—is preferable for joints larger than $\frac{1}{16}$ in. and may come in different grades to accommodate a range of joint widths. Some brands of these two grouts can be used with both vitreous and nonvitreous tile. Others are designed specifically for one kind of tile.

If you want to make your own grout, you can do so economically. If the joint is to be less than $\frac{1}{16}$ in. wide, use portland cement mixed with a liquid. If the joint is to be wider than $\frac{1}{16}$ in., you'll need a mixture of one part portland cement to one part sand. For joints $\frac{1}{8}$ in. to $\frac{1}{2}$ in. wide, get 30-mesh sand. For joints $\frac{3}{8}$ in. to 1 in. wide, all-purpose sand is the best choice. If a grout additive is to be used (see p. 71), follow the additive manufacturer's recommendations on proportions. For some guidelines on the amount of grout needed to cover a given area, see the grout coverage table on p. 63.

Commercial sanded and unsanded grouts are available in an assortment of premixed colors, and combining two premixed colored grouts can produce even more rich shades. It is possible to mix your own grout colors by adding cement colors to white grout—or to portland cement if you make your own grout—but I've found that the colors obtained are generally flat and uninteresting. Nonetheless, if you want to experiment, see p. 63 for mixing information.

Choosing a grout color is largely a matter of personal taste, but keep in mind that the color and shade of grout used with tile can greatly affect the look of the installation. Generally, a combination of dark-colored grout with light tiles—or light grout with dark tiles—emphasizes the geometry of the installation, while grout similar in color to the tiles de-emphasizes the geometry. If you want a color other than white but are unsure of what to select, cement-colored grout is also a good choice. And when setting irregular tiles like Mexican pavers, you'll find that they look better with cement-colored grout or with a grout that more or less matches the color of the tile. If you use grout that starkly contrasts with the color of such tiles, the viewer's eye will tend to be seized by the irregular grout lines. Whatever tile you're setting, if you choose a drastically contrasting color of grout, test it on a sample tile before grouting to see how well it cleans up. To do this, mix a small batch of grout slightly thinner than normal and smear it on the face of the tile. If you have difficulty cleaning the surface, use a sealer (see the Resource Guide) on the installed tiles before grouting.

The size of the grout joint is also in part a matter of personal taste, and I tend to favor narrow joints. Joints that are too wide will visually overpower the tile. With 4-, 6-, 8-, 10-, 12- and even 24-in.-square tiles, I think a ⅛-in.-wide grout joint looks crisp and clean. Irregular tiles are set off better with a wider joint, but I would never make it more than ½ in. Remember that as the width of the joint increases, so too does the possibility of cracking. Unless you increase the particle size of the sand in the grout, joints larger than ½ in. wide can be troublesome—although this doesn't always prevent cracking either. (Another factor that contributes to the problem is using too much liquid when mixing grout.)

Though grouting is not a particularly difficult job, it does take time, a bit of skill and some patience. It's worth the effort to become an adept grouter, however, since a sloppy grout job can ruin the appearance of an otherwise commendable tile installation.

Before you begin to grout, the grout materials should be brought to job-site temperature, which, as for adhesives, should ideally be between 65°F and 75°F. All the same temperature considerations for adhesives apply to grout as well, and the same recommendations should be followed (see p. 57).

To ready the tile for grouting, remove any plastic spacers used to align the tiles. The manufacturers of some spacers state that they can be left in the joint and covered with grout. But the thinner layer of grout above the spacers will cure to a different color, and ghosting will mar the appearance of the grout.

If you're working with vitreous tile, grouting can now begin. If you're setting nonvitreous tile, sponge the tiles with water, dampening the surface and the sides of each tile to prevent the bisque from sucking too much moisture from the grout. Some commercial tile crews use a garden sprayer to mist the tiles with water. Whichever method you choose, don't overdo it. Puddles of water left on the tile or in the joint will ruin the grout.

Mixing and applying grout   Grouting involves several steps. At each step, as the grout is mixed, allowed to slake, remixed, spread and cleaned up, it changes slightly in consistency, and these changes signal when the next step should begin. Briefly, when first mixed, the grout should be wet enough so that it could be spread with a grout trowel but not so wet that it runs. After slaking for 10 minutes, the grout will be slightly stiffer. Before you add any more liquid to the mixture, however, restir the grout, which will "loosen" it up a little. If it's still too stiff—if it won't stick to the sides of the tile—add a little more of the grout's liquid ingredient, mix thoroughly, and then slake and remix again. Grout that's ready to use will not pour out of the bucket but rather needs a slight shove, and it should be stiff enough to hold peaks when spread. After the grout is applied, cleanup should begin when the grout residue on the tile's surface is firm but not completely dry. And once the grout in the joints is firm enough so that it's not deformed by the cleaning sponge, cleanup of the joints should begin.

All grout can be mixed either with water or with liquid additives as a replacement for the water. Whatever liquid you use, add only enough to render the mixture plastic and spreadable. This is very important, since too much liquid will weaken the grout. The mixing bucket should be clean and dry, and if water is used as the liquid element, it should be clean and pure enough to drink.

I mix grout by gradually adding the dry ingredients to the liquid, beginning with only about three-quarters of the liquid I think is needed. Then after all the dry ingredients have been mixed into this liquid, I very gradually pour in the remaining liquid, checking the grout's consistency with

Grout coverage table					
Joint width	Tile size				
	1 x 1 x $\frac{3}{16}$	2 x 2 x $\frac{3}{16}$	4 x 4 x $\frac{1}{4}$	6 x 6 x $\frac{1}{2}$	8 x 8 x $\frac{3}{8}$
$\frac{1}{8}$	30	17	15	25	13
$\frac{1}{4}$		34	30	50	25
$\frac{3}{8}$			45	75	38
$\frac{1}{2}$			60	100	50

Note: *The amount of grout needed to cover a given area depends on the size of the tile and the width and depth of the grout joint (which are given here in inches). The table above shows the approximate number of pounds of grout powder needed to cover 100 sq. ft.*

each addition. As with any mortar, many factors affect the amount of liquid required, including temperature, humidity, the product used, and, in the case of grout, whether it's colored. Hence, I may find for a given batch that the amount of water prescribed in the label's mixing instructions is too much or not enough. Mixing grout or any mortar requires care, patience, and a bit of trial and error. But with experience, you'll begin to know instinctively when the grout is the right consistency.

If you choose to mix a custom color of grout, the dye should be added to the dry ingredients first, which will give you an idea of the color the cured grout will have. To check the color, mix up a small batch of the grout, test it on a sample board of the tile to be used, making the grout joint the same width and depth as that planned for the installation, and let the grout dry. Make sure to keep track of the proportions of grout and cement color used for the test sample, so that if you like the color you can reproduce it in quantity for the job. If the color needs to be changed, start the process over again.

Use a margin trowel or a mixing paddle to mix the grout. If you use a paddle, make sure to keep it submerged, as you would for mixing adhesives, to prevent air from being whipped into the grout and weakening it. After the ingredients have been initially mixed and most of the lumps eliminated, let the grout slake for 10 minutes. Then restir it to get out all the lumps.

If you need to mix several batches of grout for a job, make sure they're all identical. (When buying more than one package of grout, check to see that the lot numbers are the same.) Not only should the proportions of the ingredients be consistent from batch to batch, but also the order in which they are mixed and the mixing time should be the same.

Instead of grouting an entire installation all at once, spread only a small section at first—about 10 sq. ft. to 20 sq. ft.—until you see how quickly the grout sets up. This way, if you happen to be working with a grout that sets up fast, you won't get ahead of yourself and end up with a tough cleaning job. Sometimes it is possible to grout 100 sq. ft. of tile before cleanup must begin; at other times only a small area can be covered. A trial patch will tell you how to pace your work.

After dumping enough grout on the tile to work a small section (above), begin spreading it with a grout trowel held at a 30° angle (above right). When you've forcefully packed the joints in this area, cut away the excess grout with the trowel held at almost a right angle (right).

When you're ready to begin grouting, dump a pile of grout on the surface of the tile (tip the bucket if you're doing floor work, scoop out the grout with a margin trowel for wall tiles). To spread the grout, use a grout trowel rather than a steel trowel. Hold it, as you would to spread an adhesive, at an angle of about 30° to the tile. Grout over the entire area you're working two or three times, not just dabbing the grout into the joints but pushing and pressing it between the tiles so that you feel resistance as each joint is packed. The greater the resistance, the more densely packed and stronger the joints will be. The idea is to cram grout into all the nooks at the tiles' edges and into voids left by insufficient adhesive. The process also forces some of the liquid out of the grout, so that the joints are as fully packed as possible with sand and cement particles.

When all the joints are filled, hold the trowel at almost a right angle to the surface of the tile and cut the excess grout off the surface. As you do this, make sure to also move the trowel diagonally across the joints to prevent the tool's edge from dipping into the joints and raking out grout. Once the excess has been removed, let the grout begin to set up before you start cleaning. As you're grouting and cleaning up, of course, the grout in the bucket will also be setting up. For this reason, occasionally restir the grout in the bucket to loosen it up before applying it in a new area.

If the area being tiled has had expansion joints installed (see p. 95), these will need special treatment. They should not be filled with grout, but it may be impossible to prevent this. Don't worry, though, if grout does stray into these joints; it can be cut from the sides of the tile with a trowel or a razor knife while it's still wet and vacuumed away after the grout has been cleaned up.

If the tile you're working with has a surface that will be particularly difficult to clean up after grouting, for example antique brick-veneer tile, use a grout bag to fill the joints. This bag looks and works much like a cake-decorating bag (see photo, p. 43). A metal tip the approximate width of the grout joint is placed on the end of the bag. The bag is filled, and then folded and squeezed to force grout into the joints. In order to flow through the tip, the grout usually must be mixed slightly wetter than it normally would be, which tends to weaken it. For this reason, the grout bag should be used only where really necessary.

When working with a grout bag, hold the tip of the bag at the top edge of each joint and move the bag along the joint as it's filled. Without over-doing it, squeeze more grout into the joint than appears to be needed. After letting the grout harden slightly, compact the excess into the joint with a striking tool (see photo, p. 43) or simply a piece of metal tubing slightly wider than the joint. Let the packed grout harden for half an hour, and then whisk away any extraneous material with a stiff brush.

As a final note on the grout bag, I should mention that it's also very handy for filling in cracks in foundations, for repointing bricks, and for sealing between metal window frames and masonry walls. When filling in cracks or sealing window frames, I fill the bag with an epoxy thinset, which flows beautifully through the bag and adheres well to metal.

Cleaning and finishing grout joints   The time grout needs to set up before cleaning varies from job to job. It may set up within five minutes, or it may take as long as 20 minutes. The weather as well as the type of setting bed, adhesive and tile used all affect the rate at which moisture evaporates from the grout. Keep in mind that the grout residue on the surface of the tile can harden fairly quickly, while the grout in the joints may take considerably more time. The sponge will tell you when the surface of the tile and the grout joints are ready to be cleaned. Having wrung out as much moisture from the sponge as possible, test a small area by sponging over the surface of the tile. The grout in the joints should be resilient and firm but not hard. If the grout has set up too much, the tiles will need to be heavily scrubbed, which can harm the joints. On the other hand, if the sponge pulls grout out of the joints, the grout hasn't sufficiently set up. Wait a few minutes and test again. When grout is no longer pulled from the joints, cleanup can begin.

If you've waited too long to begin cleanup and the grout has dried on the surface of the tile, scrub each tile with a Scotch-Brite pad. (Unlike some other scouring pads, this brand will not scratch the surface of the tiles.) After scrubbing, go over the entire area once or twice with a thoroughly wrung-out sponge.

There are many techniques for cleaning grout, some of them rather unusual. Some setters, for example, sprinkle dry grout powder over the joints, while others use sawdust to collect moisture and excess grout particles. Many of these methods weaken or otherwise affect the grout joint, however, so I don't recommend them. I use a combination of approaches, which share one feature with all other grout-cleaning techniques: an absolute minimum of water is used during cleanup to prevent weakening the grout.

To clean up grout by my method, you'll need only a sponge and a bucket of clean water. (The sponge I use is 5½ in. by 7½ in. by 2⅜ in. and has rounded rather than square edges, which are less likely to gouge the joints.) Work only a section at a time, rinsing the sponge often to wash out the grout particles that collect in the pores. When rinsing the sponge, always wring as much water from it as possible, and remember to shake the excess water from your hands. Surprisingly, it's not necessary to keep changing the water in the rinse bucket. It's the way you use the sponge, not the cleanliness of the water, that determines how well the tiles are cleaned.

My process of cleaning grout involves several steps. An initial, quick sponging takes up most of the unwanted grout from the surface of the tiles; a second going-over neatens the grout joints themselves; and a third, careful cleaning removes any grout residue from the surface of the tiles. After these steps, the grout is left briefly to harden in the joints. Then any remaining grout haze on the tiles is wiped off with cheesecloth, and at the same time, while the grout is still plastic, the joints at the inside corners and margin of the installation are shaped with the margin trowel.

Begin cleaning up the grout on the surface of the tiles by gently sponging in a circular fashion to loosen the sand and cement particles. Be careful not to gouge grout out of the joints. Turn the sponge as soon as its pores fill with grout and rinse it often, remembering to wring it out well. If you haven't waited too long before starting to clean up, you should be able to remove the excess grout from the surface of the tiles in two or three separate passes.

Begin cleaning up the grout by sponging the tiles with a circular motion. Remember to rinse the sponge often and wring out all the excess water from it.

Turn next to cleaning and shaping the joints themselves, focusing your attention at this point only on the joints in the main field of tile. Make passes with the sponge that are parallel to the joint, gently shaving down any high spots and stopping to fill any voids with a fingerful of grout. The joint's actual shaping depends on the type of tile used and the treatment the factory or tilemaker has given the top edge. If that edge is sharply squared off, the grout should be flat and flush with the top of the tiles. If the top edge is rounded, the setter must decide how high to make the joint. Whatever height is selected, ideally the joint should be flat on top, not convex, although most will end up being slightly concave, which is fine. The important thing is to give all the joints a consistent shape and depth.

Once the joints in the field of tile have been shaped, the surface of the tiles should be carefully cleaned again. First rinse and wring out the sponge. Then make a straight, vertical pass of about 3 ft. with one side of the sponge, pulling it toward you slowly—more slowly than you think you need to—and without stopping. (If you pull the sponge quickly toward you or move it in stages, grout will streak across the surface of the tiles.) Turn the sponge to the clean side, make a similar pass parallel to the first, and then stop and rinse the sponge. Continue this procedure throughout the full area being cleaned, being careful again not to dig into the joints with the sponge. At the same time, watch to see if the sponge pulls color from the joints. If it does, the grout is either too high in the joints and needs to be shaved down farther, or there's too much water in the sponge. This cleaning should remove almost all of the grout residue from the face of the tiles, and they should be left alone for about 15 minutes.

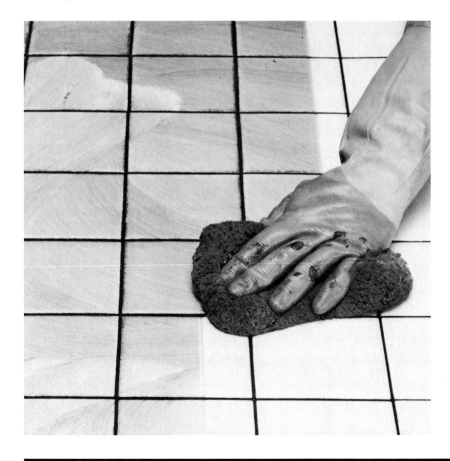

Next make slow, short, parallel passes with the sponge, pulling it toward you, to further clean the surface of the tiles and shape the grout joints. Again, rinse the sponge frequently and thoroughly.

After the initial cleaning, a grout haze may appear on the tiles as the moisture on the surface dries. If you don't wait too long, you can usually clean off this haze by rubbing the tiles with cheesecloth.

During this pause, the moisture left on the tiles from cleaning will evaporate and any cement particles suspended in the water will be deposited on the surface of the tiles. If the tiles are immediately rubbed with cheesecloth or a soft, clean rag, this grout haze should be easily removed. If the residue has bonded tightly to the surface of the tiles, you may need to scrub it away with a damp Scotch-Brite pad, allowing the surface to dry afterward and rubbing it again with the cheesecloth. If the grout haze still resists cleaning, you may not have adequately cleaned the surface of the tiles the first time, or, if you've used an additive with the grout, this additive may be the culprit. If you have no luck cleaning the haze with the above methods, try using a special grout-haze cleaning solution. Laticrete International (see the Resource Guide) makes one that's excellent, nonacidic and nontoxic. If all these attempts fail, you may have no choice but to use an acid cleaner. Before discussing these cleaners, however, let's assume that you successfully cleaned the grout haze and that you're ready to shape the grout joints at the inside corners and margin of the installation. Whether or not you completely cleaned away the grout haze, these joints must be shaped before the grout completely hardens.

After the grout has dried for about half an hour, it will still be slightly plastic and can easily be carved with a margin trowel. The finished joint at an inside corner (for example, a corner at the back wall of a tub shower) and at a margin should be, generally speaking, the same height and shape as that in the field of tile—flat or slightly concave on top, not convex. If cut tiles are used at these corners or margins, the joint should be flush with the surface of the tile. Similarly, if the margin of the tile borders painted or papered surfaces, the joint should also be squared off flush with the surface of the tile. Paint or paper can be cut in much more easily when these margins have sharp shoulders.

Shaping grout joints at various points in an installation

Shape joints in a field of tile with a sponge, and at corners and margin with a margin trowel.

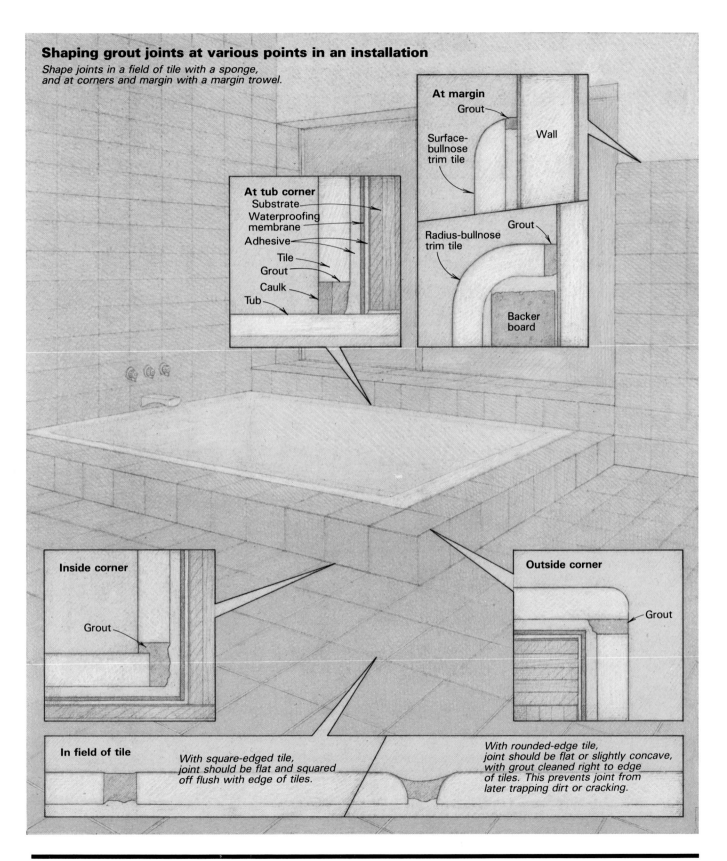

At margin

Grout

Surface-bullnose trim tile

Wall

Radius-bullnose trim tile

Grout

Backer board

At tub corner

Substrate

Waterproofing membrane

Adhesive

Tile

Grout

Caulk

Tub

Inside corner

Grout

Outside corner

Grout

In field of tile

With square-edged tile, joint should be flat and squared off flush with edge of tiles.

With rounded-edge tile, joint should be flat or slightly concave, with grout cleaned right to edge of tiles. This prevents joint from later trapping dirt or cracking.

Around tiled-in sinks or other fixtures, as well as around kitchen or bathroom countertops edged with wood or any nonceramic material, the joint should be treated differently. In part because grout does not adhere well to porcelain or stainless steel, and also because grout commonly cracks at these spots (due to the differing expansion rates of the grout and fixtures), the joint should be caulked with an elastic sealant to waterproof the setting bed. Since caulk laid over grout looks thick and unattractive, I like to excavate the grout around these fixtures to a uniform depth before caulking. If you're working with colored grout, use clear silicone caulk, which will transmit a tint of the colored grout below. Whatever the color of the caulk, it should not be applied until the grout beneath has thoroughly dried. Moisture sealed in the joint by the caulk will cause mildew, which is especially unsightly with clear caulk. (If the sink or other fixture has been removed before tiling and then reinstalled, there will not be a grout joint between the tile and the fixture. Nonetheless, the juncture at which the tile and fixture meet should be sealed with silicone caulk to prevent water from getting under the fixture.)

Once you've shaped the grout joints at the inside corners and margin of the installation, it's time to address any grout haze that resisted cleaning before. For really stubborn grout hazes, many tilesetters use full-strength acid cleaners, but I urge you to avoid these acids. They can damage the tile by "burning" the glaze, which produces a scaly-looking deposit on the tile's surface that cannot be removed. Acid can also eat drywall and porcelain and can stain wood.

Before resorting to acids, first allow the grout to harden for four or five days and then try a stiff brush or a wet steel-wool pad, a mild scouring powder like Bon-Ami, minimal water and a lot of elbow grease. If the haze still resists these mild cleaning methods, acid may be the only solution. But use an acid cleaner *only* as a last resort and *only* after the grout has completely cured for 28 days. Because the less acid used the better, begin with full-strength vinegar and a Scotch-Brite pad. If this doesn't work, try one of the less potent acid cleaners on the market. I like those sold by H.B. Fuller Co. (see the Resource Guide).

If you use an acid cleaner, whatever its strength, take safety precautions while working. In addition to the gloves, goggles and charcoal-filter mask needed for protection from acid spills and fumes, keep a bucket of clean water or a running hose nearby to flush your skin or eyes in case of an accident. Since most acids need to be diluted with water before use, the mixing should be done outdoors to dissipate fumes, and the acid should be poured into the water. (Pouring water into acid produces heat and fumes, in direct proportion to the strength of the undiluted acid.) Finally, be sure to follow all instructions on the label.

If there are any painted metal surfaces such as railings in the area where you'll be applying the acid, they should be given a protective coating of petroleum jelly. Since many acids will remove the polish from porcelain fixtures, they, too, should be coated.

Before putting the acid solution on the tiles, flood the entire surface with water. Allow the water to soak in for a few mintues to reduce the amount of acid that will penetrate the tile. (Remember from Chapter 1 that most tiles are not 100% impervious to liquids.) Work the solution into the grout residue with a stiff brush or steel wool. To keep the surface from drying out and allowing more acid to penetrate, rinse it often with water.

Once the area has been cleaned, it must be flushed at least three times with water to remove all traces of the acid. If you're working indoors, you'll have to figure out a way to dam and flood the tiled surface and at the same time protect any surrounding carpeting, wood floors or walls (this is no easy feat and another reason to avoid using acid cleaners). Finally, use hot, soapy water to remove the petroleum-jelly shield on the metal and porcelain fixtures. Having now explained how to work with an acid cleaner, I repeat what I said at the outset: acid cleaners should be avoided, which is easily done if you clean up while the grout is still plastic.

Adhesive and grout additives

Additives of one sort or another have been a part of the tile trade for a long time. The Romans, for example, added shredded hair from horses and other livestock to strengthen mortar and plaster. Nowadays there are countless additives on the market for adhesives, grout and mortar, which produce a wide range of results. Most of these additives are made of latex or acrylic compounds. Their cost is relatively low when weighed against the many advantages they offer for tilework, and, whether for the do-it-yourselfer or the professional tile contractor, the initial investment will pay off many times over. Since I started combining additives with all the adhesives, grout and mortar I use on a job, I have never once been called back to repair loose tiles or cracked joints.

Additives impart certain performance characteristics to the material with which they are mixed. While some of these products are designed especially to provide or enhance one property, most yield a number of beneficial traits to the mixture, among them:

1. Flexibility Think back to the structure of the open-faced tile sandwich, and you'll see why flexibility is desirable in setting materials. The adhesive, grout and any mortar used for a setting bed in the sandwich each form a layer, which is bonded to the neighboring layer. All these strata expand and contract at different rates, and once they've hardened, they tend to crack when flexed or stretched. Certain additives can increase the layers' ability to move without cracking, and because these additives also increase bond strength, the multilayered sandwich becomes a more physically unified whole, which is buffered against differing structural movement within.

2. Increased bond strength All additives act to retard the evaporation of water from adhesive, grout and mortar. Slowing down this curing process enables the setting material or the mortar to achieve a much higher bond strength and, ironically, to do so more quickly than it would have without the additive. For example, mortar mixed with additives achieves within seven days the bond strength that conventional, "undoctored" mortar requires 28 days to obtain. (Both mortars still require 28 days to fully cure, but when additives are used, the chemical process that binds the mortar particles together is considerably speeded up.) In both cases, this bond strength is only about 95% of the mortar's full strength, which will be attained several decades down the road.

3. Increased water resistance All cement-based adhesive, grout and mortar is filled with air pockets once the material has dried. These pockets, however minute, allow water to pass through the setting material or the mortar. But if the adhesive, grout or mortar is mixed with a liquid latex or acrylic additive rather than with water, the sand and cement particles are essentially encased in latex or acrylic (the water needed by cement to effect the curing process is provided by the water partially making up any latex or acrylic additive). For this reason, the pockets are filled principally with latex or acrylic rather than with air, making the adhesive, grout or mortar far more water-resistant than it would otherwise be.

A side effect of this increased water resistance is the elimination of efflorescence, or the whitish deposit of salts on the surface of grout or mortar. These salts can come from a variety of sources: the water and/or lime used in mixing the cement, the tiles themselves, the grout, or any salt-bearing water originating outside the installation that seeps into the setting bed. As the cement cures, the water evaporating from it transports and deposits these salts on the surface. If the efflorescence stops after the 28-day curing period for cement, the source of the salts is the cement itself. If efflorescence continues after 28 days, the salts are coming from an outside source of water, or are present in the body of the tiles and transported to the surface by this water. To eliminate the efflorescence in either case, the water must be stopped at the source. Adding a liquid sealer, as many people do to try to resolve the problem, doesn't work and may in fact cause more headaches than it cures. Making sure to use a latex additive with adhesive, grout and mortar, however, will virtually eliminate the possibility of the problem, since any salts present will be bound up in the latex matrix and be less able to migrate to the surface. (If you are faced with efflorescent deposits, wait 28 days for the curing process to be completed, then use a stiff scrub brush and a solution of one cup vinegar to a gallon of water to remove them.)

4. Improved freeze-thaw stability   Another side effect of the increased water resistance just discussed is the improved freeze-thaw stability of the setting materials and mortar. Since adhesive, grout and mortar mixed with latex or acrylic additives can absorb only residual amounts of water (around 4% of their volume), there is less water to expand as the material freezes in cold weather and thus much less likelihood that it will crack under these conditions.

5. Improved color retention   The fine pigments in colored grout can, over time and with normal wear, be washed or bleached out. Additives that encase these pigments in latex or acrylic prevent this from happening and enable the grout to maintain its true color throughout the life of the job.

6. Hardened grout joints   Latex or acrylic additives lubricate grout's mortar particles, which allows grout to be applied in a drier state than it could be without additives. In turn, with the amount of water needed for mixing the grout decreased, the grout joint will be made denser and hence stronger, which is always desirable.

7. Increased stain resistance   In adhesive, grout and mortar without additives, dirt and moisture on the surface is wicked to the interior by the tiny air pockets filling these materials when they have dried. And once embedded, these stains are difficult to remove. When additives are used, the latex or acrylic matrix formed around the sand and cement particles slows down the penetration of water into the material and, in turn, largely prevents the penetration of stains. In addition, latex grouts are more easily disinfected than untreated grout, and for this reason are used in most hospital installations.

For the most part, additives are enormously helpful to the tilesetter. But grout additives can potentially present problems. Because they combine with the fine pigment in grout, they sometimes transport this pigment into hairline cracks and tiny surface imperfections in the glaze, where it is almost impossible to remove. To prevent ruining the tiles, always test those you're using by smearing a runny mixture of additive and grout on the surface. Be sure to treat a sample from each box of tiles being used, as the glaze can vary from box to box. While hairline cracks and crazing may be attractive in some tile, they may look awful in other tile when highlighted by grout pigment. If you find that this is a problem with tile for a particular job, don't eliminate the additive; instead, use a grout sealer on the surface of the tile before applying the grout.

As I emphasized earlier, whenever you're working with adhesive, grout and mortar, cleanup should be prompt. But using additives with these materials increases the need for both extra care and speed in cleanup. I usually keep a steel-wool pad in a bucket of water close by to take care of the tools, and a damp sponge to use on tiles or other surfaces.

Finally, it's important to mention that not all additives have been thoroughly tested for reliability. For this reason, I heartily recommend avoiding off-brands of additives, which could easily lead to trouble. Instead, stick with brands that bear the seal of approval of one of the major tile organizations or a statement that the product meets the minimum requirements of ANSI. Since many of these products are sold worldwide, the seal of approval found on a product sold in another country will be that of one of the local professional tile organizations. □

Surface Preparation

T ile can be set on a wide variety of surfaces, among them, concrete slabs, floated mortar beds, drywall, plywood, tile backer board, plastic laminate and even old tilework. While these different surfaces may have little else in common, they all share the same requirements when used for tiling: all should be clean and flat, walls should be plumb (vertically straight), and floors and countertops should be level (horizontally even).

Before cleaning and preparing any surface for tiling, check to make sure that it's flat, plumb or level, and square. It must be flat in order for tile to be properly installed, and it should be plumb, level or square for the installation to look good. Technically, tile will adhere to a wall out of plumb or a floor out of level as easily as it will to a plumb or level surface, but I doubt you'll like the visual effect of such an installation. For example, if you're tiling a floor and the walls are out of square, the tiles around the perimeter of the floor will need to be cut on an angle to follow the wall. Particularly if the wall is long, the grout lines will accentuate the out-of-square condition. If you're tiling an entire wall and either the floor or the ceiling isn't level, you'll have the same problem, and the grout joints will again point out the error.

You may be lucky enough, whether working with new or old construction, to find walls and floors that are perfectly constructed and need only cleaning before they are tiled. If not—and this is usually the case—you'll need to do some surface preparation, the extent of which can range from simply scraping peeling paint off a wall to rebuilding a subfloor.

If you have the luxury of working with new construction or with a complete remodeling job, make sure in advance that the framing is done correctly, as it provides the foundation for the tilework. Be certain that the person in charge of the construction knows which areas are to be tiled and how the walls and floors in these areas should be prepared. You may want to look at the framing carpenter's layout before construction begins and check progress as the framing is installed. The goal is to make sure not only that the walls are plumb and square but also that hallway walls are parallel, rooms are square to one another, and the tops of the joists are installed on the same plane (otherwise the subflooring will not be flat).

Most of the time tilesetters find themselves faced with imperfect framing, which must be "corrected" by tiling rather than by carpentry. When framing problems can't be repaired, for whatever reasons, the tilesetter must either adjust the layout of the tile (see Chapter 5) or change the installation method. In the end, however, since tiling is finish work, it can mask only so many framing and carpentry problems. This means that sometimes compromises in the installation will need to be made, for example, tiling over an out-of-level floor (see Chapter 6). And in a few extreme cases, it may be better not to tile at all and instead select another finishing surface. Since there are usually several ways to approach every tile job, though, don't decide prematurely not to tile. Make sure that you've looked at all the possible options before settling for wall-to-wall carpeting or AstroTurf!

Plumb, level and square

Checking for plumb, level and square is quite simple, and few tools are needed. To determine if a wall is plumb, use a plumb bob or a long spirit level. Both allow the distance out of plumb to be measured with a tape measure, and each should be used at several points along the wall, since the wall may actually be twisted (plumb at one end and out of plumb at the other) or bowed (plumb at both ends but not in the middle).

A vertical surface out of plumb ⅛ in. over a length of 8 ft. (the height of the average ceiling) can be tiled and the discrepancy will probably go unnoticed. If the tile is to be bordered by a boldly patterned wallpaper or by some other starkly contrasting material on an adjoining wall, however, the discrepancy may become apparent. If you suspect that this will be a problem, float a layer of mortar on the wall to plumb it up (see Chapter 9 for instructions on floating a wall). If you're tiling two walls that meet in an outside corner, it's especially important that both be plumb, as tapering cut tiles on this projecting corner would be very unattractive. Were that corner an inside corner, though, the tolerance for out of plumb becomes a bit less exacting—½ in. in 8 ft.—since the cut field tiles on one wall can be partially hidden by the field tiles on the adjoining wall.

Use the spirit level also to determine if floors and countertops to be tiled are level. Check these surfaces in various directions and at a couple of different spots. In the case of floors and countertops, a surface out of level by no more than ⅛ in. in 10 ft. can be tiled and will probably look fine. But if you suspect that the surface adjoining the tile will unattractively point up the out-of-level condition, the pitch of the floor or countertop should be corrected. Likewise, the floor or countertop should be leveled when it's more than ⅛ in. out of level in 10 ft., whether by floating a mortar bed (see Chapter 7 for directions on floating a floor and Chapter 11 for information on floating a countertop) or by calling in a carpenter.

To determine if the inside and outside corners of the walls are square, check them with a carpenter's square. Unfortunately, it's possible for the corners to be square without the entire wall being square to adjoining walls. So to check if this is the case, set up what is called a 3-4-5 triangle (see p. 114 for a full discussion of 3-4-5 triangles). The base and height of this triangle are projected off the base of two connecting walls in the room (since you'll need to remove the baseboards before tiling, go ahead and do so before setting up the triangle). If these walls are square to each other, a triangle with a 3-ft. base and a 4-ft. height will have a hypotenuse exactly 5 ft. long. These walls can then be used as references to verify if the other walls in the room are square.

If the triangle's hypotenuse proves longer or shorter than 5 ft., the walls are out of square. If the walls are off no more than ⅛ in. in 10 ft., the perimeter rows of floor tile can be trimmed as needed. If the walls are more than ⅛ in. out of square in 10 ft., you really should square them up, either by rebuilding them or by floating a mortar bed over them to compensate for the problem. Yet both of these solutions are costly and time-consuming, and sometimes, if the condition isn't too serious, the walls will simply recede visually once the room is again filled with furniture. The decision of when to correct an out-of-square wall is in part subjective and, of course, depends on the degree of the problem. Whether or not you decide to correct such a situation, however, the tile itself *must* be set square. Setting floor tiles to follow an out-of-square wall, for example, will only lead to headaches and an unattractive job. If you decide not to correct the problem, a square set of reference lines must be established within the out-of-square area, and these should be the basis for projecting layout lines to position the tiles. (For further discussion of adjusting a 3-4-5 triangle to produce square reference lines, see p. 115; for information on adjusting a layout when a room is out of square, see p. 116.)

Preparing surfaces for installing tile

Below is a description of setting surfaces commonly used for dry installations, that is, those that will not get soaking wet. This listing includes a discussion of how suitable each surface is for tiling and how it should be prepared to receive tile. In each section, I've mentioned not only the preparations the given surface requires but also the type of adhesive with which it should be paired and whether it can be used for wet installations when properly waterproofed. (For a complete discussion of the adhesives recommended, see Chapter 3.) Because when properly waterproofed, most of these same surfaces are suitable for setting beds in wet installations, I've provided detailed information on waterproofing an installation, beginning on p. 89. Whenever a specific product is recommended for use in preparing a given surface, please consult the Resource Guide at the back of the book for information on the manufacturer.

Plywood Plywood was developed in Eugene, Oregon, in 1905 and until recently was a consistently sturdy material of good quality that made a fine substrate for tile. Within the last five years, however, some manufacturers seem to have started using inferior glues and relaxing quality control, which leads me to generally prefer backer board (see p. 85) to plywood as a substrate for tiling.

If you do opt to use plywood, select CDX or a better grade—for example, marine-grade, which is quite expensive, or AC exterior plywood, which is the most commonly available high-quality grade. Tilesetting does not require that the surface of a plywood setting bed be smooth, as it would be with AC exterior, which is designed to be painted; in fact, a coarser surface is preferable, since the adhesive will better grip it. But the construction of the plywood used for a setting bed for tile must be of good quality. Therefore, when buying plywood select only better-grade material and carefully examine each sheet, whatever its grade. Reject those that are warped or that have visible voids between the plies. Also be sure to avoid any sheets with beads of wood resin on the surface, as this will prevent some thinset adhesives from bonding properly.

Unlike the grades of plywood mentioned above, interior-grade plywood and particleboard (including flake board) are unsuitable setting surfaces for floors and countertops. Interior-grade plywood uses glues that are not waterproof, and, in my opinion, this plywood is not strong enough to support the weight a floor or countertop must bear. Particleboard, on the other hand, expands when wet and fails to contract when dry. If one of these surfaces is already on your floor or countertop (the grade stamp on plywood should tell you), add an overlayment of a more appropriate material before tiling.

Since walls bear far less weight than floors and countertops, interior-grade plywood and plywood paneling can both be used as a setting surface for wall installations that won't get wet. However, the material must be at least ⅝ in. thick and adequately secured to the studs. If you are inclined to remove the existing plywood, replace it with drywall or backer board, both of which make much better setting beds for tile.

Even if you have a plywood subfloor or countertop that meets the above criteria, it may need strengthening to serve as a base for setting tile. A single-layer, ¾-in.-thick plywood subfloor or countertop, if supported according to standard construction procedures, may flex and damage any tile installed directly on it. And although a setting bed may be well supported below, the American National Standards Institute (ANSI) recommends that a plywood setting bed for a floor or countertop be a minimum thickness of 1⅛ in. Instead of putting down a single-layer, 1⅛-in.-thick setting bed (which can still flex and cause tiles or grout joints to crack), I strongly urge building up the proper thickness by combining a plywood substrate with at least one more layer of plywood (or backer board or a mortar bed). The layers should be at least ½ in. thick.

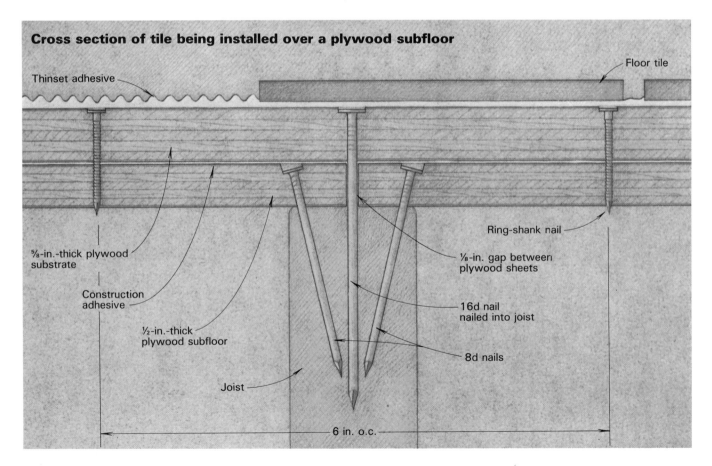

Cross section of tile being installed over a plywood subfloor

Floor tile

Thinset adhesive

⅝-in.-thick plywood substrate

Construction adhesive

½-in.-thick plywood subfloor

Joist

Ring-shank nail

⅛-in. gap between plywood sheets

16d nail nailed into joist

8d nails

6 in. o.c.

When installing plywood over subflooring, stagger the sheets so that no joint falls over a joint in the subfloor. Also position the sheets to leave a gap between them of no less than ⅛ in. and no greater than ¼ in. These gaps, which should later be filled with tilesetting adhesive to edge-glue the plywood, will allow for seasonal expansion in the wood. Laminate the sheets to the subfloor with construction adhesive rated for floor use. Then, with drywall screws or with ring-shank or underlayment nails, fasten the sheets every 6 in., making sure you hit the joists wherever you can. The length of these fasteners should equal about three times the combined thickness of the subfloor and underlayment. The nails or screws that won't hit the joists need only be slightly longer than the combined thickness of the subfloor and underlayment.

When fastening plywood to subfloors or countertops, make sure that the nail or screw heads are sunk below the top surface of the plywood to prevent any tile set over them from cracking under load. If the plywood surface veneer is crushed by the fasteners and wood fibers protude above the surface, trim them down with a chisel or sandpaper. Once you've vacuumed away any dust, the plywood is ready for tiling.

If you're setting tile over existing plywood, sand off any waxes, oils, or flaking varnish or paint on the surface before tiling, then vacuum away the dust. I find that an epoxy thinset is the best adhesive to use with a plywood setting bed for a dry installation. My second choice of adhesive would be a latex or acrylic thinset, and my third choice an organic mastic. If the plywood bed is to serve for a wet installation, the bed should be properly waterproofed and either an epoxy thinset or a latex or acrylic thinset should be used as the tile adhesive.

1x or 2x subflooring Although many people try to set tile directly on material such as 1x4s or 2x6s, this is not a suitable setting bed. As the lumber expands and contracts with seasonal changes in humidity, the numerous joints in this subfloor will become points of stress for the tile set over them. If you have this type of subflooring, cover it with plywood or backer board, fastened securely in place. The combined thickness of the subfloor and underlayment should be at least 1⅛ in., and the adhesive used should be compatible with the setting surface selected. When properly waterproofed, this subfloor can be used for a wet installation.

Composition paneling Composition paneling, or Masonite sheets covered with wood-grain veneer, should not be used for tiling. This paneling is both too thin and too flexible, and using it as a setting bed is only asking for trouble and lots of cracked grout joints. If your walls are covered with this paneling, it should be removed and replaced with backer board, plywood or drywall.

Wainscoted walls Wooden wainscoting makes a very poor base for tiles. Because the numerous boards making up traditional wainscoting expand and contract considerably, the grout joints of any tile set on this surface will probably crack. If you have wainscoting on walls, whether the traditional sort or made from grooved plywood, remove and replace it with drywall, ungrooved plywood or backer board. Wainscoting made of tile, however, is an acceptable surface for setting tile, provided the old tile is in good shape and uncracked. (For information on how to prepare a ceramic-tile setting surface, see p. 84). Use an adhesive that is compatible with the setting surface selected, and properly waterproof the bed if this is to be a wet installation.

Cover the ⅛-in. gap between adjoining backer boards with fiberglass mesh tape. Then trowel on thinset adhesive over the tape to fill and "edge-glue" the boards, feathering the thinset out to create a smooth, flat setting surface. (For more on backer board, see p. 85.)

Drywall Unpainted drywall makes a good setting surface for tile in dry areas and, if properly waterproofed, in wet areas, too. If radius trim tile is to be used (see p. 23), which requires a thicker setting bed, the drywall can be covered with another layer of drywall or with ½-in.-thick plywood or backer board. Doubling up the wallboard also offers a quick and economical way to cover drywall that has serious surface flaws, for example, any deep holes left when electrical outlet boxes were removed. If a second layer of drywall is used, install it as you would the first, keeping in mind that longer drywall nails or screws will be needed and that, though optional, laminating the two layers with thinset adhesive will strengthen the installation.

Whether you're using a single or double layer of drywall, leave a ⅛-in. gap between the sheets and cover the resulting joints with open-weave, fiberglass mesh tape instead of conventional paper joint tape, which isn't very strong. There are both sticky and nonsticky fiberglass tapes on the market. Because the latter must be stapled or glued in place, I find the sticky tape easier to work with (I like the 2-in.-wide Imperial Type P tape from U.S. Gypsum Industries). After taping, fill the joints with tile adhesive to embed the tape, seal the joint and help minimize cracking. The preparation needed for painting—filling the hammer dimples with joint compound and sanding them—is unnecessary when tiling drywall. Instead, merely dust the surface with a damp rag or vacuum it off and you're ready to go. For dry installations, use as the tile adhesive a latex or acrylic thinset (the best choice), a water-mixed thinset, or an organic mastic. For wet installations, add a waterproofing membrane and use a latex or acrylic thinset adhesive. Some building codes allow the use of water-resistant drywall for setting beds in wet areas, but read the "Waterproofing, curing and isolation membranes" section on p. 89 before you rely on this product.

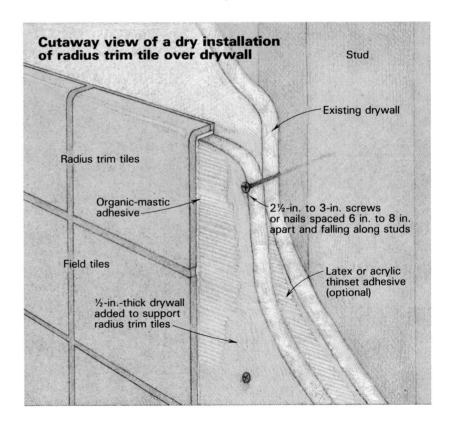

Cutaway view of a dry installation of radius trim tile over drywall

Stud

Existing drywall

Radius trim tiles

Organic-mastic adhesive

2½-in. to 3-in. screws or nails spaced 6 in. to 8 in. apart and falling along studs

Field tiles

Latex or acrylic thinset adhesive (optional)

½-in.-thick drywall added to support radius trim tiles

Masonry walls and concrete surfaces   Most masonry walls (including concrete block, brick and stucco walls), concrete walls and concrete slabs make an excellent base for tile, provided they are flat and free of major cracks. In the case of concrete slabs, a slab finished with a wood float has a coarse surface that works well for tiling, while the surface of a steel-troweled slab is too slick. If a new slab is to be poured, make sure that it will be finished with a wood float. Slabs and concrete walls should be reinforced with wire mesh or reinforcing bar to prevent cracking from seasonal movement (check local building codes for the type and amount of reinforcing necessary in your area). They should also be allowed to cure for 28 days before tile is set (although concrete continues to cure for years after placement, it gains most of its strength in the first 28 days). If your slab was finished with a steel trowel, you'll have to rough up its surface before tiling, either by grinding it with an abrasive wheel or by lightly bush-hammering it with special pneumatic or electric tools.

The one slab over which tile should never be set is that treated with a curing or acceleration compound, or a form-release agent. These chemicals will prevent tile adhesive from bonding. You can test the surface of the concrete for the presence of such chemicals by sprinkling it with water. If the water is not absorbed, a compound or release agent was probably used. While sandblasting may remove the offending material from the surface of the slab, that remaining below the surface may still interfere with the bond of the adhesive.

If the slab or wall is old, remove any wax or oil on the surface, using one of the cleaning preparations listed in the Resource Guide. Then check the slab or wall to make sure that its surface is no more than ⅛ in. out of level or plumb in 10 ft. Be sure to examine the surface of a new slab or wall, too, since new doesn't guarantee perfect. If the surface is not plumb or level, it will need a layer of mortar floated to correct it, which will additionally cover up any irregularities in an uneven surface.

Once you've determined that a slab is level or a wall plumb, check to see that the surface is flat. Do this by moving a long straightedge over the floor or wall. Outline any low spots with a pencil. If the depressions are less than ¼ in. deep, they can be leveled with latex thinset adhesive and screeded flat with a straightedge. Any high spots can be ground down with

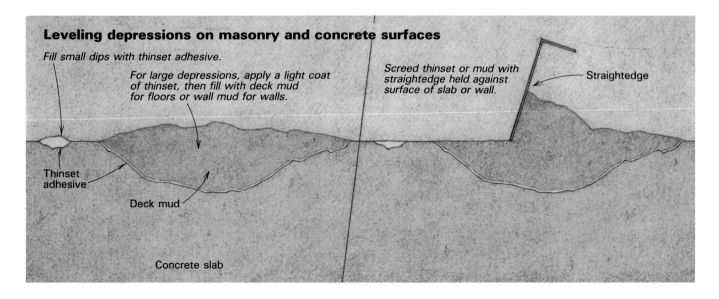

Leveling depressions on masonry and concrete surfaces

Fill small dips with thinset adhesive.

For large depressions, apply a light coat of thinset, then fill with deck mud for floors or wall mud for walls.

Screed thinset or mud with straightedge held against surface of slab or wall.

Straightedge

Thinset adhesive

Deck mud

Concrete slab

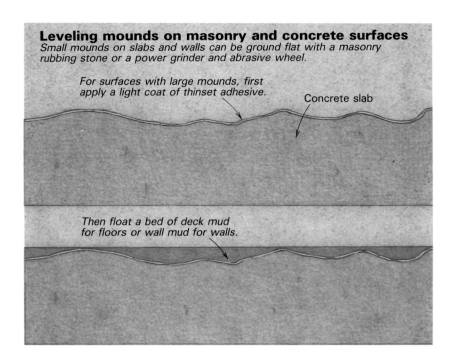

Leveling mounds on masonry and concrete surfaces
Small mounds on slabs and walls can be ground flat with a masonry rubbing stone or a power grinder and abrasive wheel.

For surfaces with large mounds, first apply a light coat of thinset adhesive.

Concrete slab

Then float a bed of deck mud for floors or wall mud for walls.

a rubbing stone or an electric grinder, or the tiles could be back-buttered with enough adhesive to allow them to lay on an even plane. Before making such adjustments, however, consider the size of the tile being set. A ¼-in. depression in a 2-sq.-ft. area may go unnoticed if covered with 12-in.-square tiles, but if 1-in.-square mosaic tiles are used, the depression is liable to be glaring and definitely needs to be filled and leveled.

If the depressions on a concrete slab are deeper than ¼ in., brush the surface of each one with water-mixed or latex thinset and then fill it with deck mud, or mortar prepared for floors (see p. 86), which has been combined with a latex additive. (The thinset, which should not dry before the mud is applied, helps the mortar grip the surface of the slab.) Then use a straightedge to screed any excess mud. If the slab's surface is marked with mounds larger than ¼ in., lightly coat the entire surface with thinset and float a thin bed of deck mud over the slab to even it out.

When a masonry wall has either dips or mounds greater than ¼ in., brush a thin coat of water-mixed or latex thinset, prepared to the consistency of thick paint, on the entire surface. With the thinset still wet, float a layer of wall mud—mortar especially prepared for walls, sometimes also called fat mud—to even out the surface. Use plumbed float strips to gauge the thickness of the float. (For information on mixing wall mud and for a discussion of how to float a wall, see Chapter 9.)

To prevent any small cracks in the surface of the slab or wall—or any future cracks that develop—from being transmitted to the tile, install an isolation membrane over the substrate before tiling (see p. 94). The cracks in question are those caused by seasonal movement in the slab or wall. Large cracks produced by expanding tree roots, shifting earthquake fault zones or shifting foundations are liable to telegraph to the tile, with or without an isolation membrane. Such cracks can be eliminated only by rebuilding and extensively reinforcing the slab or wall with rebar. If you detect active cracks of any size, you'll need to eliminate the source of the cracking before tiling.

For wet installations, a waterproofing membrane is also needed. Depending on your choice of materials, the isolation membrane itself may also serve to waterproof the installation (see p. 89). Use a water-mixed, latex or acrylic, or epoxy thinset for setting tile on these prepared surfaces.

Plaster walls   Plaster walls make good setting surfaces, provided they are composed of traditionally mixed plaster, and are in good condition, flat and uncracked. For the purposes of tiling, these walls can be treated just like masonry walls (see p. 81).

Walls composed of plaster made primarily of lime, however, are unsuitable for tiling. This recipe for plaster was commonly used for inexpensive construction about 30 years ago, but it is still occasionally used today. To determine if a wall is made of this type of plaster, poke it with a screwdriver. If the surface is hard, does not crumble and contains no lengthy cracks, it is traditional plaster and can be tiled. Lengthy cracks are those long enough to span two or more studs or wide enough to slip a knife blade into. Such fissures will telegraph to the face of the tiles. If the plaster is soft and crumbles or cracks under the screwdriver test, it should be replaced with drywall or backer board.

Painted and papered walls   Properly prepared, painted walls can be acceptable surfaces for tiling, provided the walls themselves are not composition paneling or any material that flexes more than ⅝-in. plywood does. Before tiling a painted wall, scrape or sand off any loose or peeling paint, rough up the surface with 80-grit sandpaper and remove any surface dust with a damp rag. Avoid using chemical paint removers, including paint etching compounds, since the residue may react with the tile adhesive.

Because wallpaper adhesives are too weak to support a heavy wall of tile, all wallpaper should be stripped before tiling. (Although some properly attached vinyl wallpapers could theoretically support this weight, I'd remove them, too, and not risk the need for later repairs.) After removing the wallpaper, wash, scrape or sand away any residual glue and remove any surface dust with a damp rag. With papered or painted walls (assuming this is to be a dry installation), I recommend using as the adhesive a latex thinset (first choice), a water-mixed thinset or an organic mastic.

Linoleum and synthetic sheet flooring   Floor tiles in a dry installation can be set over uncushioned linoleum or resilient vinyl or asphalt flooring, provided the existing flooring is firmly attached to the subfloor and is not cracking or peeling. Note, however, that tile should not be set over cushioned flooring or multiple layers of sheet flooring, because these layers can compress with the weight of the tile and cause the joints to crack. Instead, all the layers should be removed and a new plywood or backer-board underlayment attached to the subfloor. To find out if you have multiple layers of sheet flooring, cut into the flooring at an unobtrusive spot, such as under the refrigerator.

Before tiling over a single layer of linoleum or synthetic sheet flooring, rough up the surface with 80-grit or coarser sandpaper so the adhesive will grip. Use an epoxy thinset adhesive on this bed, or, as a second choice, a compatible latex thinset. Though I was skeptical when I first heard of tiling over linoleum, I have found that this flooring, when properly prepared and coupled with an epoxy adhesive, will give excellent service. If the installation is to be a wet one, however, the sheet flooring should be removed and replaced with another suitable, properly waterproofed setting bed.

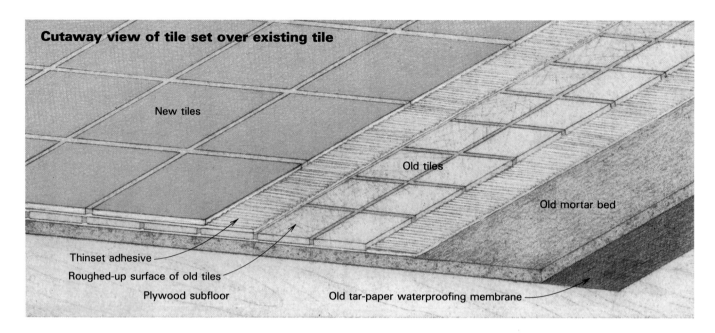

Cutaway view of tile set over existing tile

New tiles

Old tiles

Old mortar bed

Thinset adhesive

Roughed-up surface of old tiles

Plywood subfloor

Old tar-paper waterproofing membrane

Plastic laminate Plastic laminate makes an excellent surface for setting tile, as it's flat, solid, relatively stable and waterproof. To prepare laminate surfaces for tile, remove grease and any waxy film, then rough up the surface with coarse sandpaper. Epoxy adhesive should be used over plastic-laminate surfaces. Since these surfaces will usually be countertops, no waterproofing membrane is needed, unless this is to be a commercial installation that will get heavy-duty wet use.

Ceramic tile Old tilework in good condition and without cracks may serve as a base for setting new tile. Using an electric grinder or a masonry rubbing stone, cover the surface with scratches to enable the adhesive to grip it. Although most types of adhesive can be used with a tile substrate, an epoxy thinset is my recommendation because of its grip. Check the label of the product you want to use to make sure that it's suitable.

If the old tiles have a cushioned, that is, rounded, edge, the old grout joints may be about 1/16 in. lower than the surface of the tiles. To ensure an even application of thinset on this type of bed, you may want to fill in and level the grout joints before spreading adhesive over the full bed. Before doing this, however, consider the size of the tile being set. Large tiles can be set over this slightly uneven surface without a problem, but small tiles, such as 1-in. mosaics, will conspicuously highlight the unevenness of the bed.

Since seasonal movement in the old tile installation can develop cracks that may telegraph to the new tile, I recommend adding an isolation membrane to the substrate before tiling (see p. 94). If the installation is to be wet, it must also be waterproofed unless you're certain that the old tilework was installed with a waterproofing membrane.

Sheet metal The sheet metal found on most manufactured fireboxes can be used as a setting surface, provided it does not flex. Sand away any paint on the surface down to the metal, rough up any porcelain coating and grind away rust with an abrasive wheel. If the metal does flex, laminate a piece of backer board with epoxy adhesive to the paint-stripped metal, then set tiles.

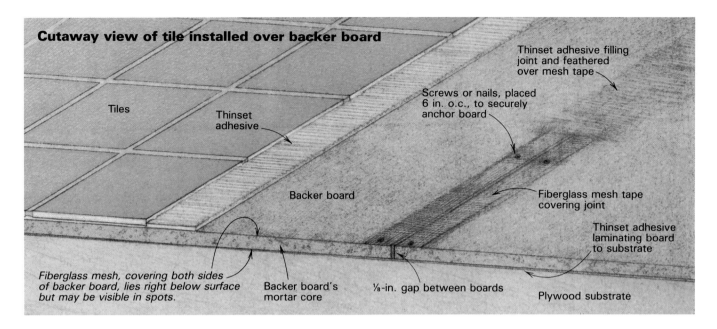

Cutaway view of tile installed over backer board

Tiles

Thinset adhesive

Backer board

Fiberglass mesh, covering both sides of backer board, lies right below surface but may be visible in spots.

Backer board's mortar core

⅛-in. gap between boards

Thinset adhesive filling joint and feathered over mesh tape

Screws or nails, placed 6 in. o.c., to securely anchor board

Fiberglass mesh tape covering joint

Thinset adhesive laminating board to substrate

Plywood substrate

Use a heat-resistant epoxy thinset, such as Laticrete's Latapoxy 100 AAR-II-HT, as the adhesive. And to cope with the metal's expansion from the heat, mix a latex additive in the grout.

Backer board   Specially designed as a substrate for tile, these sheets are composed of a mortar core covered on both sides with reinforcing fiberglass mesh. Because backer board is rigid and strong, it provides an ideal surface for tiling. And since the board itself is unaffected by water, it can be used for both dry and wet installations—although, of course, the installation itself must still be properly waterproofed to protect from water seepage at the joints around the backer board. Until recently, backer board was restricted to interior use, but now U.S. Gypsum Industries produces a special ½-in.-thick backer board in 4-ft. by 8-ft. sheets that is intended specifically for exterior use (see the Resource Guide).

Regular backer board for interior use is manufactured in ½-in.- and ⁷⁄₁₆-in.-thick sheets, whose dimensions range from 3 ft. by 4 ft. to 4 ft. by 8 ft. The weight of the board varies, depending upon the brand, from 2.6 lb. to 3.8 lb. per square foot.

When used for walls, backer board can be screwed or nailed directly to the studs, using drywall screws or 1½-in. galvanized nails, spaced 6 in. on center. (When placing backer board over drywall, use 3-in. screws or nails to connect with the studs below.) I prefer screws because their threaded shanks anchor them more securely in the backer board (or any other surface, for that matter) than do nails. On floors, the board should be both laminated, and nailed or screwed to plywood or lumber. To laminate it to plywood, use a latex thinset compatible with wood (check the label) and spread the adhesive with a ¼-in. square-notched trowel.

When more than one backer board is needed to cover an installation area, position the sheets with a ⅛-in. gap between them. (When used on floors, also leave a ¼-in. gap between the backer board and the wall or baseboard to accommodate seasonal movement in the floor and walls.) The resulting joints between the boards should be covered with fiberglass mesh tape (see photo, p. 80) and filled with thinset adhesive.

Once the board is installed, you can set tile immediately, though if you're working on a floor, I recommend waiting a full day to protect the bond of the laminating adhesive. Use a latex thinset as the adhesive for tiling (or, as a second choice, a water-mixed thinset), and, if the installation is to be a wet one, install a waterproofing membrane with the backer board.

Mortar bed   A bed of mortar makes an excellent surface for setting tiles. When set over a bed of mortar, the installation is called a thick-bed installation. When set over any other kind of setting bed, it is called a thin-bed, or thinset, installation. Both thick-bed and thinset installations use an adhesive, which is similarly applied to the bed (see p. 57).

Mortar can be floated over any type of surface and used for both dry and, if properly waterproofed (see p. 90), wet installations. This substrate is long-lasting and has a high compressive strength, meaning that it can bear considerable weight. A mortar-bed floor is also quiet to walk on and feels solid under foot. But perhaps most important, a mortar bed can mask and "correct" a setting surface that's badly flawed or out of level or plumb.

Mortar is made of sand, cement and water. Varying the proportions of these ingredients and sometimes adding other materials produces different kinds of mortar. The two types of mortar that can be floated to produce a substrate for tiling are deck mud, used for floors and countertops, and wall mud, which, as its name suggests, is applied to walls.

Deck mud is made, according to the Tile Council of America (TCA), by mixing roughly one part portland cement to six parts sand and approximately one part water (many factors may cause these proportions to change somewhat, including the weather and the use of additives). There are various recipes for deck mud, but all generally produce a strong mortar that can support the heavy loads a floor will bear. Deck mud should be rather dry and crumbly in consistency and should not spread like plaster. (For specific information on mixing deck mud, see p. 145.)

Wall mud is made by combining cement, sand and water with lime to make a mix that's plastic enough to spread on walls. The TCA recommends making wall mud with roughly one part cement, five parts sand, one-half part lime and enough water to produce a smooth, spreadable mixture. The lime, sold in powdered form in large sacks at building and masonry supply houses, makes this mortar sticky and enables it to grip the

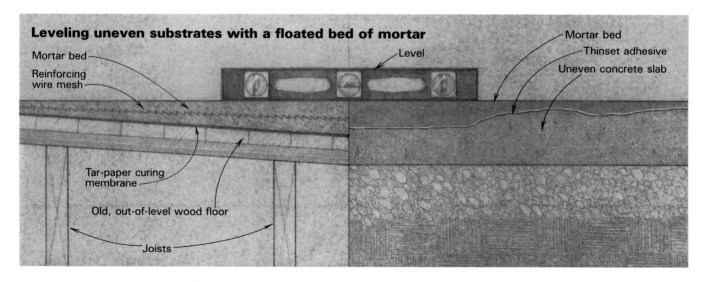

Leveling uneven substrates with a floated bed of mortar

Mortar bed

Reinforcing wire mesh

Level

Mortar bed

Thinset adhesive

Uneven concrete slab

Tar-paper curing membrane

Old, out-of-level wood floor

Joists

reinforcing mesh added to the surface before floating. Because more water is added to wall mud than to deck mud to make it spreadable, the grains of sand in wall mud are spaced farther apart. The resulting mortar is therefore weaker than deck mud and should not be used on floors. (For specific information on mixing wall mud, see p. 172.)

The basic process of floating a mortar bed, whether for a floor, countertop or wall, is simple. On the surface being floated, two strips of wood, called float strips (or sometimes screeds or grounds), are positioned parallel to each other and several feet apart (the distance depends on the size of the area being floated). The strips are securely anchored in columns of mud, with their top surfaces leveled at the intended height of the bed. Mortar is then distributed and compacted between the float strips. Next a third piece of wood or aluminum, called a screed, is positioned to straddle the float strips. This screed is moved side to side and at the same time pulled forward in a sawing motion to scrape away the excess mortar. Next any voids left in the surface are filled with mud and leveled with a wood float. The float strips are then pulled into the next area to be floated, and the empty channels are "backfilled" with mortar, compacted and leveled with the wood float. This sequence continues until the entire area being floated has been compacted and screeded. (See Chapter 7 for a full discussion of how to float a mortar floor, Chapter 9 for more information on floating a wall, and Chapter 11 for more on floating a countertop.)

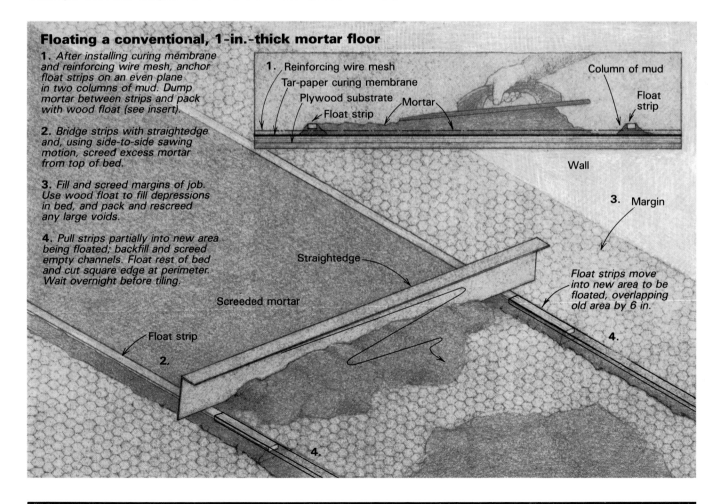

Floating a conventional, 1-in.-thick mortar floor

1. After installing curing membrane and reinforcing wire mesh, anchor float strips on an even plane in two columns of mud. Dump mortar between strips and pack with wood float (see insert).

2. Bridge strips with straightedge and, using side-to-side sawing motion, screed excess mortar from top of bed.

3. Fill and screed margins of job. Use wood float to fill depressions in bed, and pack and rescreed any large voids.

4. Pull strips partially into new area being floated; backfill and screed empty channels. Float rest of bed and cut square edge at perimeter. Wait overnight before tiling.

1. Reinforcing wire mesh
Tar-paper curing membrane
Plywood substrate   Mortar
Float strip

Column of mud
Float strip

Wall

3. Margin

Float strips move into new area to be floated, overlapping old area by 6 in.

4.

Straightedge

Screeded mortar

Float strip

2.

4.

If you want to float mortar over a portion of a floor or wall, I suggest nailing 2x4s to the surface to stop the float at the desired point. Alternatively, you could float slightly beyond the planned limit of the bed and trim back the float, using a straightedge as a fence and a margin trowel to cut the mortar. However you choose to float the surface, any membrane used below the bed should extend to the limit of the floor or wall.

Once the bed has been floated, it should be allowed to cure, or harden, before tile is set on it. The reason for this is that mud shrinks very slightly for about a week after floating, with most of the shrinkage occurring within the first 24 hours. If you're working in 70°F weather, wait overnight before tiling. If the temperature is closer to 50°F, you may need to wait longer for the bed to harden, perhaps two full days. By waiting, you not only avoid the difficulties involved in setting tile on a wet bed, but also have time to properly prepare the setting bed for tiling.

Preparing the surface for tiling involves making sure that the bed is entirely flat (that is, checking to see that all voids on the surface have been filled and high spots have been knocked down) and trimming a perfectly square corner at the perimeter of the installation. This work should proceed shortly after the bed has begun to set up, but before it has become too hard. In 70°F weather, this means between half an hour and an hour after floating. In 50°F weather, you'll need to wait longer, but no longer than two hours. The timing is important, since by beginning sooner you risk disturbing the chemical process at work as the mortar sets up. Also, if you wait too long to finish the bed, the hardened, uneven surface will require extensive grinding.

The mortar's actual set-up time varies with each batch mixed and will be affected by numerous factors, including the brand of ingredients used and the weather. When the surface of the mortar is ready to be prepared, it will not be as soft as it was when first floated, but rather will feel firm and resilient, though not hard.

When used for dry or wet installations, the mortar bed must have a curing membrane beneath it, but it may also need to be protected by an isolation membrane on top of it. For wet installations, the mortar bed must be properly waterproofed. Whatever the type of installation, the bed must be reinforced with a layer of wire mesh, theoretically placed in the middle of the bed. In practice, I reserve the tedious process of floating the bed in two layers for extra-thick mortar beds, and for conventional, 1-in.-thick beds, I place the wire mesh immediately over the curing membrane. I always use a latex thinset adhesive with a mortar bed, although a water-mixed thinset is also suitable.

Choosing a substrate

While the range of surfaces on which tile can be set is large, some are better than others for tiling, and some are appropriate only for dry installations or areas that will receive minimal wear. Given all the factors involved in choosing a substrate, there is no single setting surface that is right for every job. Nonetheless, a mortar bed is always an excellent substrate and is consistently my first choice, unless factors on a particular job dictate otherwise. But because floating a mortar bed is a difficult, time-consuming process that requires skill, I wouldn't recommend this setting surface to the inexperienced tilesetter. While on certain jobs mortar is the only substrate I would consider using (for example, when creating a sloped floor in a shower stall), for most home installations there are alternative substrates that are as effective as mortar and less costly since they require less skill and labor. If a mortar bed is the only substrate that will work for your particular installation and you don't feel qualified to undertake the job, do the obvious: call in a professional tilesetter or mason to properly float the bed. Then lay the tile and complete the job yourself.

The particular dry installations for which mortar is an especially effective substrate include: (1) Floors in commercial, public or private spaces that get constant, heavy wear (the mortar bed in this case should be at least 1 in. thick and, as with all the other installations listed below, paired with a latex or acrylic thinset). (2) Floors in solar-heated buildings where the mortar bed's thick mass is ideal for storing solar heat (the mortar bed should again be at least 1 in. thick). (3) Walls that must be especially sturdy, built up, or, if masonry or plaster, called upon to hide deep scars or defects (in all these cases, the mortar bed should be ½ in. to ¾ in. thick). (4) Countertops in restaurants or homes that get constant, heavy wear (the traditional setting bed for this installation is a ¾-in.- to 1-in.-thick mortar bed floated over a ¾-in.-thick plywood substrate).

For floors, walls and countertops subject to water and heavy use, a properly waterproofed mortar bed makes an excellent setting surface. In each case the mortar bed should be paired with a latex or water-mixed thinset.

As alternatives to a mortar bed, plywood and tile backer board are excellent substrates for dry installations. The minimum requirement for floors is ½-in.-thick exterior-grade plywood laminated and nailed directly to 1x's or ⅝-in. plywood subflooring. (Use a construction adhesive to glue the plywood to the subfloor, spreading it in parallel strips on the wood's surface.) For floors that get regular use, a sturdier underlayment of ⅝-in.-thick plywood or ½-in.-thick backer board should be laminated and nailed to a subfloor that is at least ¾ in. thick, giving the substrate and subfloor a combined thickness of more than 1⅛ in. (While the plywood should again be glued with construction adhesive, the backer board can be adhered with a compatible thinset adhesive spread over its entire surface.)

For wall installations that will remain dry and get regular wear, tile can be set over backer board or drywall. Tile for wall installations can also be set over existing surfaces—provided they are properly prepared—including plywood paneling, masonry or plaster walls, painted or papered walls, plastic laminate, old ceramic tile, and sheet metal. Information on the necessary preparation of these surfaces and the adhesive to be used with each is found under the appropriate heading in the section beginning on p. 77.

Countertops should be treated much like floors. For dry installations that will get light use, exterior-grade plywood makes a good substrate. It should be anchored to the cabinets with screws and paired with an organic mastic rated for use with plywood.

For counters that see daily service but do not get wet, a sturdier substrate is needed, with a minimum thickness of 1⅛ in. Plywood or backer board can be used, and any thinset can be paired with this substrate, provided it's compatible with the backing selected.

As alternatives to a mortar bed for wet floor, wall and countertop installations, properly waterproofed backer board or plywood can be used and should be paired with a latex thinset (for floors, the backer board should be laminated to the subfloor). For walls, another alternative is drywall that has been waterproofed with a suitable membrane. This substrate, too, should be combined with a latex thinset.

Waterproofing, curing and isolation membranes

Membranes of one sort or another have long been part of the tile trade. They can be made from a variety of materials, but whether constructed of lowly tar paper or of some sophisticated petrochemical by-product, all

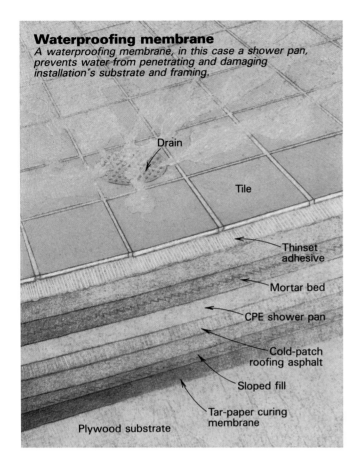

Waterproofing membrane

A waterproofing membrane, in this case a shower pan, prevents water from penetrating and damaging installation's substrate and framing.

Drain

Tile

Thinset adhesive

Mortar bed

CPE shower pan

Cold-patch roofing asphalt

Sloped fill

Tar-paper curing membrane

Plywood substrate

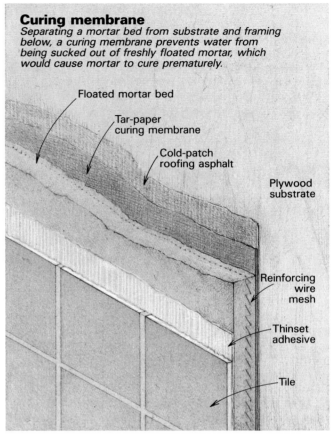

Curing membrane

Separating a mortar bed from substrate and framing below, a curing membrane prevents water from being sucked out of freshly floated mortar, which would cause mortar to cure prematurely.

Floated mortar bed

Tar-paper curing membrane

Cold-patch roofing asphalt

Plywood substrate

Reinforcing wire mesh

Thinset adhesive

Tile

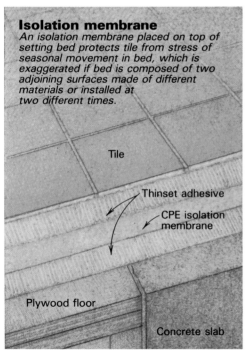

Isolation membrane

An isolation membrane placed on top of setting bed protects tile from stress of seasonal movement in bed, which is exaggerated if bed is composed of two adjoining surfaces made of different materials or installed at two different times.

Tile

Thinset adhesive

CPE isolation membrane

Plywood floor

Concrete slab

share the same purpose: they protect the tile installation from damage or deterioration. Membranes are used to combat the problems of water damage to the substrate (waterproofing membranes), premature curing of mortar beds (curing membranes) and unequal seasonal movement of dissimilar materials in the installation (isolation membranes, also called cleavage membranes). Sometimes a single membrane can do more than one job, and its function—or functions—depends largely on where it's located in the tile sandwich. For example, a curing membrane used beneath a freshly floated mortar bed is designed to keep water in the mortar as it cures (see p. 93). But by keeping water *in* one area of the installation, this membrane, by definition, simultaneously keeps water *out* of another area. Thus, this membrane can function at once as a curing membrane and as a waterproofing membrane. It's even possible, as you'll see below, for a single membrane to serve all three protective functions at the same time.

Waterproofing membranes For years consumers have thought of ceramic tiles as the ultimate protection against water damage to walls, floors and other surfaces. While it's true that ceramic tiles themselves are not harmed by water, they afford little or no waterproofing protection to what lies beneath them unless they are specifically installed to do so. It is the installation as a whole, not just the tiles, that provides, or fails to provide, the protection. And without some kind of waterproofing membrane installed on the setting bed, no tile job will fully protect against water, no matter how good the grout or the adhesive is.

Water that regularly penetrates an installation can cause serious problems. It can weaken the bond of the tile adhesive and eventually damage the substrate. Moisture seeping through a shower floor to a wood subfloor, for example, will promote rot and provide nourishment for wood-destroying organisms. Additionally, the weakened subfloor will not provide much support for the tile installation, and substantial cracking in the tiles or grout joints will inevitably result. These problems are easily prevented if a waterproofing membrane is incorporated into the installation.

There are several different materials that can be used for waterproofing membranes, and the choice depends largely on where the membrane is to be located in the installation. When used above the waterline (on shower walls, for example), the membrane is often dubbed an all-purpose waterproofing membrane and is traditionally made of tar-saturated felt paper, or tar paper, which is installed beneath or behind the setting bed. When the waterproofing membrane is used below the waterline (on sunken tubs or shower floors, for instance), it is called a shower or tub pan and must be made of a sturdier material. (See p. 93 for a full discussion of this type of membrane.)

Tar paper is sold in 1½-ft.-, 2-ft.-, 3-ft.- and 4-ft.-wide rolls in 50-ft., 100-ft. and 150-ft. lengths. Costing only pennies per square foot, this paper will last for about 30 years and requires minimal labor to install. It is stapled or nailed—or in the case of a concrete or stone surface, glued—directly to the substrate. While many setters use tar paper alone, I increase its protection against water by embedding it in cold-patch roofing asphalt spread over the entire substrate. Sheets should overlap at the seams by at least 2 in., and I always seal the joints with more asphalt. (For a full discussion of installing a tar-paper membrane, see p. 155.)

Despite tar paper's low cost, durability and ease of installation, however, this material has inherent limitations. When the setting surface is to be a floated bed of mortar, for example, the tar paper can warp between the fastening staples or nails when it gets wet from contact with the fresh mortar. As the paper bulges outward, it can leave an air space between the mortar bed and the substrate, and create a bulge in the mortar. While the mortar can be leveled over this high spot, it will be thin over the air pocket, producing a weak spot in the bed. Embedding the paper in cold-patch roofing asphalt minimizes the problem. And it also assuages my concern about depending on a membrane shot full of staple holes.

Another consideration with a tar-paper waterproofing membrane is that since it is placed beneath or behind the setting bed, the bed itself must be water-resistant. Thus only backer board or a mortar bed can safely be used as a setting surface. And if backer board is used, it can be combined with tar paper only for wall installations, since the board's manufacturers specify that, when used for floors, the board must be laminated directly to the subfloor. Backer board used for a wet floor installation must therefore be paired with a waterproofing membrane placed on top of, rather than below, the setting surface. All of this information makes waterproofing an installation sound a bit tricky, I know, but it points up the importance of considering the compatibility not only of adhesives and setting beds but also of membranes and setting beds.

Only in the last ten years or so have products been developed that could be used not only below the setting bed but also on top of it—directly under the tile—to waterproof the installation. Most of these new products are based on chlorinated polyethylene (CPE) in sheet form, synthetic fabrics and similar materials, and I've found the majority of them either unremarkable or unsatisfactory. However, NobleSeal T/S, recently developed by The Noble Company (see the Resource Guide), has proven excellent.

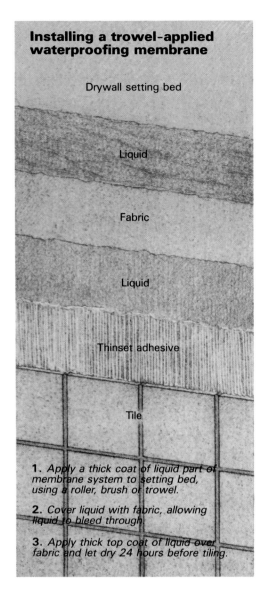

Drywall setting bed

Liquid

Fabric

Liquid

Thinset adhesive

Tile

1. Apply a thick coat of liquid part of membrane system to setting bed, using a roller, brush or trowel.

2. Cover liquid with fabric, allowing liquid to bleed through.

3. Apply thick top coat of liquid over fabric and let dry 24 hours before tiling.

NobleSeal is a 30-mil-thick sheet of CPE bonded between two layers of unwoven polyester fibers. Sold in rolls 100 ft. long by 60 in. wide, this material is considerably more expensive per square foot of coverage than the tar-paper membrane, but I'm convinced that its cost is offset by its effectiveness and versatility. It can be used to waterproof any substrate, including drywall, plywood, concrete slabs, mortar beds, metal surfaces and backer board, regardless of the amount of water or wear the installation will be subjected to. This means that, wherever local building codes permit, floors and countertops that must be waterproof can be constructed of plywood, and shower walls can be built from regular drywall. (Although some local codes allow the use of water-resistant drywall, or blueboard, as a setting bed for walls in wet installations, I urge you to avoid using this material. I feel that it's suitable for a wet installation only when paired with a waterproofing membrane and therefore has no advantage over less expensive, regular drywall.) Despite its expense, NobleSeal is unbeatable when maximum waterproofing is needed.

NobleSeal is installed by laminating it to the setting bed with latex thinset. Before the membrane is installed, however, the substrate should be prepared as it would be for tiling; that is, the surface should be flat, level or plumb, and clean. Once the surface has been prepared, a layer of latex thinset is combed on with a ⅛-in. or 3/16-in. notched trowel (the coarser the substrate's surface, the larger the notch size needed). Next the membrane is placed over the adhesive and smoothed out with a hand roller to eliminate air pockets and ensure complete contact with the thinset. After waiting about 24 hours for the thinset to harden, the setter can then spread another layer of thinset on the membrane and set the tiles.

If the job requires a membrane wider than 60 in., the edges of two or more sheets can be overlapped by 2 in. and glued with Nobleweld 100 or xylene. (Because the fumes from these bonding materials are toxic, wear a charcoal-filter mask when working with them, and keep the room well ventilated.) For further information on installing this membrane, see p. 206, and for detailed, step-by-step instructions, write the company for its literature. Note that whenever you're using a specialty material like this, it's a good idea to request a specification sheet or an installation pamphlet from the manufacturer in case there has been any change in the installation procedures.

Another type of material that can be used on top of a setting bed to waterproof it is what is called a trowel-applied membrane. These membranes are combinations of liquid latex and fabric. The liquid is first applied over the setting bed, and the fabric is then embedded in the liquid. A second coat of liquid is applied over the fabric, and the membrane is allowed to dry before tile is set. While useful over most setting surfaces, some trowel-applied membranes are not recommended for installation over wood (check the product label). And, when used over backer board, which already has a skin of reinforcing mesh, the liquid alone is used, except at the joints of the boards. For full instructions on how to install a trowel-applied membrane, write the manufacturer for an installation brochure (see the Resource Guide). Laticrete makes an excellent product in this category.

A trowel-applied membrane runs about the same cost per square foot as NobleSeal. Though I've found the former slightly less effective than NobleSeal, this type of membrane is more than adequate in most home installations. A properly prepared tar-paper membrane is also quite serviceable for home installations above the waterline, but these days I usually stick with a CPE membrane whenever possible.

Shower and tub pans Shower and tub pans are another variety of waterproofing membrane. To reiterate the distinction between these membranes and all-purpose waterproofing membranes, the former are used to waterproof installations below the waterline (for example, shower floors and sunken tubs), and the latter are employed for installations above the waterline (for instance, countertops and shower walls). This distinction means that while an all-purpose waterproofing membrane need only be able to shed water, a pan must be able to hold water. To perform its duties, a shower or tub pan is installed beneath the setting bed and should extend over the curb of the shower or tub. (For illustrations and full instructions on installing this type of membrane, see Chapter 9.)

Traditionally, pans have been made of copper, lead or galvanized sheet metal because they must be strong enough to bear the full weight of tiles, mortar and bathers. But electrolytic action quickly eats away these pans, usually where they connect with the drain, and they become useless scrap metal. (When I did repair work, in fact, I had a good side business selling the remains of these pans to scrap dealers!) Because of the problems with these pans, many local building codes now outlaw them.

Another type of pan, called a hot-mopped pan, has been around for quite a long time, but, mercifully, it too is heading toward extinction. Made of alternating layers of hot asphalt and tar paper, this pan is both a headache and very dangerous to install. After I accidentally spilled a bucket of steaming hot tar on a client's carpet, I decided to find a better way of waterproofing these installations. I soon came across something called Chloraloy 240, which is a CPE material like NobleSeal but without polyester fabric laminated to it. This product is thicker than NobleSeal (40 mil thick, compared to NobleSeal at 30 mil) and for this reason is my choice for pans, as building codes in many areas require additional thickness for pans made of CPE. This material forms a single-layer pan that needs no hot tar, and since I have been using it, I've had no failures in more than 600 pans.

Construction of a shower pan centers around the drain, which is alternately called a subdrain, split drain or clamping-ring drain (see drawing, p. 164). This type of drain is split in two sections, which clamp over the pan material. The upper section is designed to accommodate from 1½ in. to 2 in. of tile and mortar above the top clamping flange. This section also has several openings to allow residual moisture in the mortar bed to escape into the drain instead of lingering in the mortar, where germs and mold would be nourished.

With the Chloraloy sheet draped over the floor of the shower, folds are made at the corners to create a "pan." Upturned in this way, the pan covers the base of the shower walls. The pan is also folded over the top and outside face of the curb to protect it.

Curing membranes Every mortar or cement-based product in a tile installation requires protection as it cures to keep the water in it from being wicked to another layer of the tile sandwich. The reasons for this are twofold: First, because water is necessary for the chemical reaction that hardens mortar, wet mortar that loses water too quickly as it cures will fail to gain full strength. Second, while all mortar shrinks slightly as it dries, mortar that dries too quickly undergoes considerable shrinkage and is liable to crack. In the case of water-mixed or latex or acrylic thinset adhesives, the protection required is built into the mixture by the manufacturer, in the form of additives that minimize shrinking by slowing the loss of water. In the case of a mortar setting bed, the protection must be supplied by the tilesetter in the form of a curing membrane, which is placed beneath the bed to separate it from the substrate. Finally, freshly placed grout in an installation should be protected from curing too quickly on particularly hot, dry days by a temporary covering of lightweight plastic sheeting. This informal curing membrane is most useful when the grout has been mixed with just water, since grout additives minimize the need for cover. In the days before additives, I had to cover jobs for as long as a week to ensure a proper curing period for the grout.

If the only membrane needed for a particular installation is a curing membrane, the best material to use is the tar paper mentioned above in the discussion of waterproofing membranes. A sheet of CPE could also be used, of course, but its expense is unwarranted since tar paper is equally effective as a curing membrane. To minimize the paper's buckling beneath a newly floated mortar bed, cold-patch roofing asphalt should be spread over the entire setting bed and the tar paper embedded in it. The mortar bed is then floated over the membrane, and the tile is set with adhesive directly over the bed after it has hardened. Once the bed is dry, the curing membrane serves another function: it acts like an isolation membrane, protecting the tile from the stress of differing seasonal movement in the substrate and setting bed.

Isolation membranes All construction and tiling materials undergo a certain amount of internal movement, that is, expansion and contraction, as the climate and seasons change. Oftentimes the movement in one layer of the tile sandwich is slight and only negligibly affects the adjoining layers. At other times, however, the movement in the substrate or setting bed can be significant and produce enough stress in the installation to crack the tiles. To protect against this, an isolation membrane should be used whenever the setter suspects that seasonal movement within the setting bed may cause cracking in the tiles.

If you're tiling over an existing setting bed that seems structurally sound, has no visible cracks and is in a home or building that has fully settled, chances are that no isolation membrane is needed. If you see signs of cracking or you suspect structural weakness, however, an isolation membrane is called for. Similarly, if you are replacing a tile job because of cracks and you're unable, for whatever reasons, to improve the structure that will underlie the tile, an isolation membrane is a must. And if the setting bed consists of abutting sections installed at different times (a concrete floor with a later addition, for instance) or is made of different materials (a plywood floor, for example, adjoining a concrete slab), an isolation membrane is crucial. In short, any setting bed—whether mortar, concrete, masonry, plaster, drywall, old tiles or some combination thereof—that has uncorrectable structural problems or that may crack with seasonal movement should have an isolation membrane installed over it to separate it from the tile above.

Over the years I've experimented with a number of materials for isolation membranes, but until recently I'd found nothing that was really successful. Then I began using the same NobleSeal T/S mentioned above in the discussion of waterproofing membranes, and it has given me consistently good results. Because NobleSeal is a sheet of CPE bonded between two layers of unwoven polyester fibers, this material can stretch with the movement of the substrate without disturbing the bond of the tile adhesive and without allowing the movement in the bed to telegraph to the tiles above. (For information on installing a CPE isolation membrane, see pp. 92 and 206.)

Expansion joints

Expansion joints are intentional interruptions in a field of tile which, like isolation membranes, are designed to protect the tiles from the stress of regular seasonal movement in the setting bed. Because an expansion joint must interrupt the entire tile sandwich, it extends not only through the tile but also through the setting bed and, if the bed is mortar, any reinforcing wire. Any membrane used with the installation, however, should remain intact. Thus, if you're applying an isolation or waterproofing membrane on top of the bed, the joint must be made before the membrane is installed. In fact, these joints are always more easily installed before any tile is set. This requires some preliminary layout work, since the joints should coincide with a grout joint.

There are several different locations where expansion joints are typically used: at the margin of a tiled floor or wall (where the joint is called a perimeter joint); in the main field of a large tiled floor or wall; and in cove-tile installations, at the point where the walls and floor or countertop meet. While a cove-tile countertop installation always requires an expansion joint at the base of the backsplash, the countertop itself is too small an area to require either an expansion joint around the perimeter or one within the field.

A perimeter joint is simple to make and should be used for interior floors that are between 16 ft. square and 24 ft. square and for tiled walls 12 ft. to 24 ft. long. In these cases, the substrate and the tile are simply stopped ¼ in. from the base of the walls or from the neighboring wall. The resulting void is later filled with caulk, which allows the floor or wall to expand and contract without damaging either the tiles or the walls. When a mortar setting bed is floated, whether for a floor or wall, the void for the perimeter joint should be filled with a strip of compressible plastic foam, which is cut flush with the top of the setting bed and later capped with caulk. (For information on installing a perimeter joint, see p. 143.)

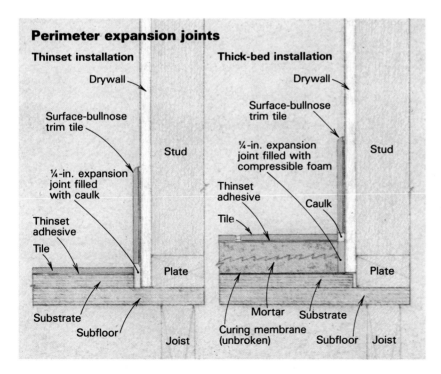

Perimeter expansion joints

Thinset installation

Drywall

Surface-bullnose trim tile

¼-in. expansion joint filled with caulk

Thinset adhesive

Tile

Stud

Plate

Substrate

Subfloor

Joist

Thick-bed installation

Drywall

Surface-bullnose trim tile

¼-in. expansion joint filled with compressible foam

Thinset adhesive

Tile

Caulk

Stud

Plate

Mortar   Substrate

Curing membrane (unbroken)

Subfloor   Joist

Multiroom layout with expansion joints

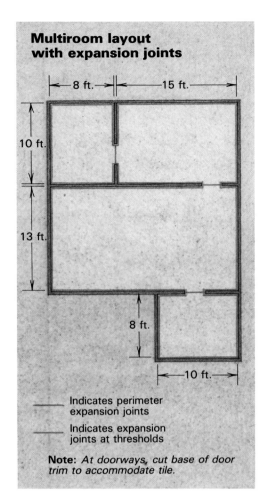

|← 8 ft. →|← 15 ft. →|

10 ft.

13 ft.

8 ft.

|← 10 ft. →|

—— Indicates perimeter expansion joints

—— Indicates expansion joints at thresholds

Note: *At doorways, cut base of door trim to accommodate tile.*

Expansion joint over an existing control joint

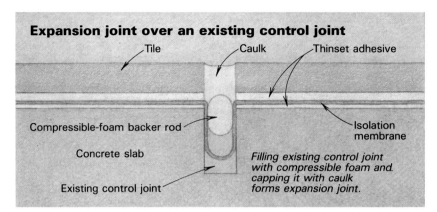

Tile   Caulk   Thinset adhesive

Compressible-foam backer rod

Concrete slab

Isolation membrane

Existing control joint

Filling existing control joint with compressible foam and capping it with caulk forms expansion joint.

Floors larger than 24 ft. square and walls longer than 24 ft., which are usually found only in commercial settings, require both perimeter joints and joints within the main field of tile. For exterior floors and walls, joints should be installed within the field every 16 ft. in both directions. For interior floors and walls, these joints should be created every 24 ft. to 36 ft. in both directions. And when tile is to be set over a concrete slab with existing expansion or control joints, the joints within the field should be positioned atop these joints. For very large, multiroom installations, there should also be expansion joints at every threshold.

Unlike perimeter joints, which are often hidden by baseboards, moldings or the presence of furniture, expansion joints within the field are likely to be visible and will look somewhat different from the grout joints. The caulk with which they are filled will be shinier and may, in time, get dirtier than grout. Also, if colored grout is used for the installation, it may be difficult to find a matching shade in the relatively small range of colored caulks available.

The traditional way of creating joints within a field for a mortar setting bed is begun by floating one side of the bed and stopping the float with a 2x4 wherever an expansion joint is required. The 2x4 is then removed, a foam strip is placed against the edge and the next section of the bed is floated. The resulting joint should be ¼ in. to ½ in. wide.

An alternative to this somewhat tedious process is to float the entire bed without interruption and later cut expansion joints into the cured bed with a dry-cutting diamond blade. If a power saw is used, this same method can be employed for creating joints in a thinset installation, although the expansion-joint gaps can, of course, be built into the setting bed as it's constructed.

The third type of expansion joint is that which should be used with all cove-tile installations. Cove tile can be set anywhere two perpendicular surfaces meet, regardless of what the setting surface is and whether the installation is thick-bed or thinset. Whatever the type of installation and whether for a floor, wall or countertop, a cove-tile joint should be located in the grout joint between the field and cove tiles. Without an expansion joint at this point, cove tile will invariably crack parallel to the grout joint, and no amount of replacing the cove tiles will resolve the problem.

The traditional method of forming this cove-tile expansion joint in a floated mortar setting bed is a laborious process. In the case of a floor, for example, rather than the floor being floated right to the base of the wall, a filler strip, equal in width to the thickness of the cove tile, its setting bed and the grout joint, is anchored next to the base of the wall, and the mortar is floated to this strip. Then the filler strip is removed, leaving a void at

Cove-tile installation with and without expansion joints

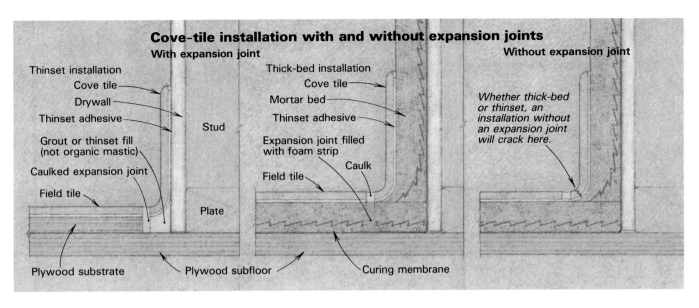

With expansion joint

Thinset installation
Cove tile
Drywall
Thinset adhesive
Grout or thinset fill (not organic mastic)
Caulked expansion joint
Field tile
Stud
Plate
Plywood substrate

Thick-bed installation

Cove tile
Mortar bed
Thinset adhesive
Expansion joint filled with foam strip
Caulk
Field tile
Plywood subfloor
Curing membrane

Without expansion joint

Whether thick-bed or thinset, an installation without an expansion joint will crack here.

Traditional method for installing a cove-tile expansion joint in a mortar floor

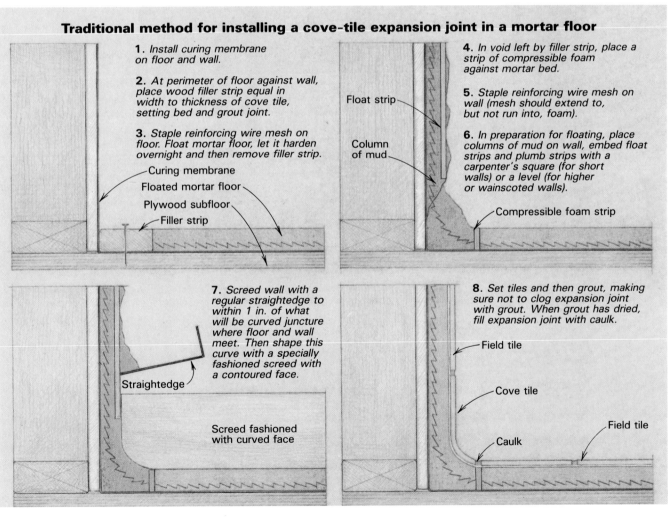

1. *Install curing membrane on floor and wall.*

2. *At perimeter of floor against wall, place wood filler strip equal in width to thickness of cove tile, setting bed and grout joint.*

3. *Staple reinforcing wire mesh on floor. Float mortar floor, let it harden overnight and then remove filler strip.*

Curing membrane
Floated mortar floor
Plywood subfloor
Filler strip

4. *In void left by filler strip, place a strip of compressible foam against mortar bed.*

5. *Staple reinforcing wire mesh on wall (mesh should extend to, but not run into, foam).*

6. *In preparation for floating, place columns of mud on wall, embed float strips and plumb strips with a carpenter's square (for short walls) or a level (for higher or wainscoted walls).*

Float strip
Column of mud
Compressible foam strip

7. *Screed wall with a regular straightedge to within 1 in. of what will be curved juncture where floor and wall meet. Then shape this curve with a specially fashioned screed with a contoured face.*

Straightedge
Screed fashioned with curved face

8. *Set tiles and then grout, making sure not to clog expansion joint with grout. When grout has dried, fill expansion joint with caulk.*

Field tile
Cove tile
Field tile
Caulk

the base of the wall. The void is filled with a compressible foam strip the width of the grout joint and the height of the mortar bed (a bit of thinset or organic mastic may be needed to hold the foam in place). If the neighboring wall is to be floated, reinforcing wire mesh is installed on it before floating and the mesh is bent outward at the base of the wall so that it touches the foam. The wall is then floated and screeded, with a specially contoured screed used to fashion the curved juncture where the floor and wall meet. Finally, the tiles are set, and the joint between the cove and floor tiles is filled with flexible caulk.

Once I added the dry-cutting diamond blade to my tool kit, I knew there had to be a faster way to complete a thick-bed cove-tile installation. So I developed the following method: First, I float the floor right up to the base of the wall. Then I screed the mortar floor as I would any floor. After the mortar bed has completely hardened, I float the wall. Then I scribe or chalk a line on the mortar floor representing the joint between the cove tile and the floor tile. I cut along this line with the dry-cutting diamond blade, mounted in my grinder, through the full depth of the mortar bed (making sure not to cut the curing membrane beneath the bed) until the cut equals the width of the grout joint. If you're using a diamond blade mounted in a portable circular saw, you may not have enough clearance to make the cut. If this is the case, float the floor first, make the cut, and then float the wall. After loosening the mortar at the bottom of the cut with a grout saw or margin trowel, I vacuum the cut joint. Next I slip a compressible foam strip into the joint and then set the tiles. When setting the cove tiles, I back-butter them to fill the curved area and support the tile, not worrying about fashioning a curved screed to shape the mortar. Once the tile has been grouted, I cut the foam strip back to the height of the mortar bed and cap the expansion joint with caulk.

General room preparations

Before you begin a tile installation, there may be things other than the surface of the area being tiled that need preparation. You may, for example, need to remove the plumbing fixtures in a bathroom or trim the bottom of a door to accommodate the added height of the tile. The following are general instructions for these preparations, but since each area is a complex subject unto itself and space is limited here, I recommend that you consult a good household-repair book with detailed information on plumbing and electrical work (see the Resource Guide).

Plumbing fixtures When tiling a bathroom floor, you must work around a toilet and often a sink support. Instead of leaving these fixtures in place and cutting tile to fit around them, I recommend removing them and tiling under them. The results will be much more attractive and professional-looking, and the job will be easier in the long run. By running the tile under these fixtures, you'll also reduce the number of exposed joints that will need to be maintained over the life of the installation.

To remove a conventional two-piece toilet, take out the tank and bowl together. Before removing the toilet, disinfect it by pouring a quart of liquid bleach into the tank and flushing. When the tank has refilled, locate the shutoff valve for the water supply line behind the toilet and turn off the water. Then flush again, this time holding the handle down until the tank empties. To remove as much of the water remaining in the bowl as possible, use either a small hand-operated bilge pump to pump the water into a nearby drain (like the tub, for example), or a plumber's helper to push the water through the trap. Stuff some old rags or paper towels into the bowl to keep any remaining water from sloshing around, but make sure you remove them when you replace the toilet!

Before removing the anchoring bolts, disconnect the water supply line from the wall or the toilet with an adjustable wrench. Then gently pry off any porcelain caps covering the two or four bolts holding down the bowl. If there are four bolts, the front two usually will be screwed directly to the floor, and the rear set will extend through the toilet base to connect with the closet flange, or connector between the toilet and waste pipe. Often the front bolts will be corroded and break off as you try to unscrew them, but replacement bolts can be bought at the plumbing supply store. The back bolts may also be corroded and snap off when unscrewed, or they may just spin when you try to undo the nuts. If they spin, try gently pushing the tank sideways, which will snug up the lower end of the bolt and allow the nut to unscrew. If you can't budge the bolts, try using Liquid Wrench to dissolve the corrosion, or, as a last resort, saw the bolt in two with a hacksaw blade.

After unbolting the toilet, remove the fixture and carry it to another room to get it out of your way. It's a good idea to get a helper, since the toilet will weigh between 30 lb. and 60 lb. and should be kept level to keep any remaining water in it from sloshing about. Next remove the old wax or plumber's putty ring, which seals the connection between the toilet and the flange. I suggest putting on gloves to do this job. Place a gloved hand into a plastic bag, grab hold of the ring, and, with your other hand, turn the bag inside out to enclose and remove the ring. Then clean and remove the flange below the ring, which connects the bowl to the waste pipe.

After preparing the surface of the setting bed, set tile to within ¼ in. to ⅛ in. of the flange. The top of the flange should be installed flush with or about ¼ in. higher than the finished height of the tile. If the flange is even ¼ in. lower than the tile, this may prevent the wax-ring gasket from sealing

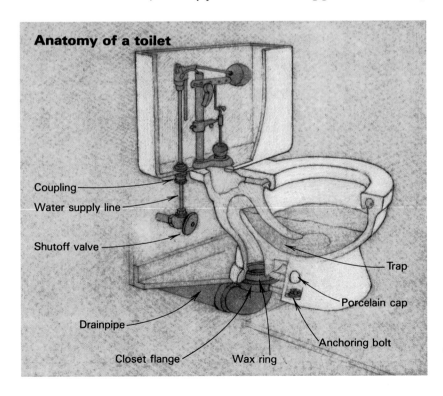

Anatomy of a toilet

Coupling
Water supply line
Shutoff valve
Trap
Porcelain cap
Drainpipe
Anchoring bolt
Closet flange
Wax ring

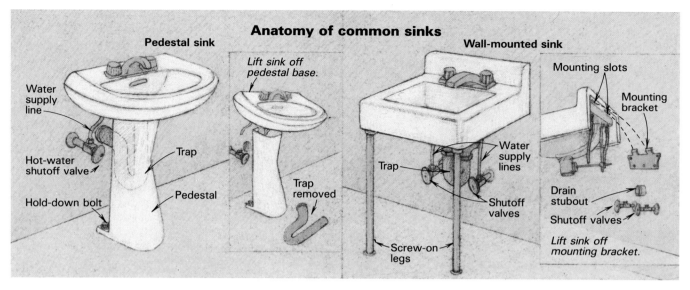

Anatomy of common sinks

Pedestal sink

Water supply line

Hot-water shutoff valve

Hold-down bolt

Trap

Pedestal

Lift sink off pedestal base.

Trap removed

Wall-mounted sink

Mounting slots

Mounting bracket

Trap

Water supply lines

Shutoff valves

Screw-on legs

Drain stubout

Shutoff valves

Lift sink off mounting bracket.

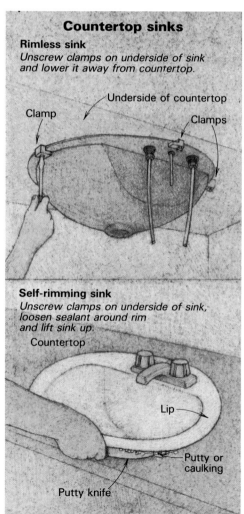

Countertop sinks

Rimless sink
Unscrew clamps on underside of sink and lower it away from countertop.

Underside of countertop

Clamp

Clamps

Self-rimming sink
Unscrew clamps on underside of sink, loosen sealant around rim and lift sink up.

Countertop

Lip

Putty or caulking

Putty knife

properly. In this case, replace the flange to accommodate the new floor height. Then install the new ring, which should be at room temperature when put in place in order for it to correctly seal the connection. Finally, replace the bowl and tank, simply reversing the dismantling process.

There are several basic types of sinks around which you might tile: pedestal sinks, wall-mounted sinks and countertop sinks. For purposes of tiling, pedestal and wall-mounted sinks (the kind with supporting "legs") should be treated just like toilets; that is, they should be removed and the entire floor beneath them tiled. A rimless countertop sink can either be removed before the counter is tiled and then be reinstalled, or it can be left in place and the tiles set over its lip. Tile is often set over self-rimming sinks, too, though it's far easier to remove the sink from the countertop and reposition it over the newly tiled surface. Almost any sink can be left in place, however, if the situation demands it.

The initial steps in removing any of these sinks are the same. First, cut the water off at the sink shutoff valves and then disconnect the water supply lines from the sink or the wall (there's no need to take off the faucet or control valves unless they need replacing). Finally, remove the trap from the sink with a pipe wrench.

To remove a two-piece pedestal sink, first unbolt the top and lift it off the base; then unbolt the pedestal and lift it from the floor (you may have to reach around the back of the pedestal to find the bolts). For a single-unit pedestal sink, simply unbolt it from the floor and wall. To dismantle a wall-mounted sink, first remove any legs supporting the front of the sink. Then dislodge the sink from the wall bracket in which it's mounted and lift it off the bracket. If you will be tiling the wall behind the sink, particularly if you plan to use thick tiles, you may have to remove the bracket and shim it out to compensate for the thickness of the new tile. One way to do this is to mount the bracket to the wall through a plywood "shim." If the bracket is designed to be installed on a finished surface, it will, of course, need to be removed from the wall and repositioned on top of the new tiles.

If you want to remove any of the several types of self-rimming countertop sinks, including the integral sink and countertop, first unscrew the pressure clips that secure the bowl on the underside of the sink rim or the full sink countertop to the vanity. Then, with a putty knife, cut the sealing material—usually caulk—between the sink and countertop or between the sink countertop and vanity, pry up the sink or countertop, and lift it out.

If the faucet and control valves are not attached directly to the bowl of the sink, they need to be removed for tiling the countertop. With the water shut off and the water supply lines disconnected, remove the nuts underneath the countertop that hold the valves in place. Then tile right to the edge of the mounting hole. If this is to be a thinset installation, the shanks on the valves should be long enough to accommodate the added height of the tile. If the tile is to be installed with a mortar setting bed, you may need to install valves with longer shanks. When reinstalling the valves, pack the area around the shanks with plumber's putty, not grout—grout would harden and make any future repairs very difficult.

If you're tiling around the water supply and drain lines in the wall behind a sink, the tile should be set to within ⅛ in. to ¼ in. of the pipes. These joints should later be caulked with silicone caulk, rather than grouted, because the expanding and contracting pipes will inevitably crack the grout.

Most shower heads are a three-part assembly consisting of a shower head, gooseneck and escutcheon plate. The gooseneck screws into a fitting located in the wall, and the escutcheon plate slips over the gooseneck to trim the hole in the wall. When tile is set around a shower head, the gooseneck should be treated just like any other pipe. That is, tiles should be set to within ⅛ in. to ¼ in. of the gooseneck and the void around it filled with silicone caulk.

If you won't be replacing the walls or adding backer board to install tile, and you don't have major demolition work to contend with, you don't have to remove the shower head before tiling. Simply slip a plastic bag over it (freezer bags work best because they're heavier than sandwich bags) and tape the end of the bag around the gooseneck. This will protect the shower head from stray globs of adhesive. Otherwise, though, I'd recommend removing the entire shower-head unit to prevent damaging its finish. To do this, pull the escutcheon plate away from the wall, and unscrew the gooseneck from the fitting in the wall, using a pipe wrench if necessary (protect the finish of the gooseneck by wrapping it with a rag or duct tape). When you're ready to install the backer board, screw a pipe nipple into the fitting. A nipple is simply a short length of water pipe, maybe 5 in. or 6 in. long, that's threaded on one end and capped at the other—you can borrow one from your plumber or buy one from any plumbing supply store. The nipple temporarily substitutes for the missing gooseneck and ensures that the hole cut into the backer board for the gooseneck ends up in the right place. It also keeps the fitting threads from getting fouled with adhesive as the tiles are being set. When you're ready to tile, the tiles should then be set to within ⅛ in. to ¼ in. of the nipple. After the tiles have been grouted, remove the nipple and replace it with the shower-head assembly. Before pressing the escutcheon plate back into place, fill the void around the gooseneck with plumber's putty.

If you're installing a new single-handle control valve in the shower, the unit will come with a plastic setting gauge that shows the exact mounting depth for the valve. This gauge usually will be positioned flush with the surface of the tile and removed after the tiles have been installed. The wall is then tiled to within ⅛ in. to ¼ in. of the gauge. After the tiles have been grouted, the gap around the valve is covered by a chrome or brass escutcheon plate. This plate often has a foam strip adhered to its underside to seal out water between the plate and the tiles. A second foam strip seals the valve handle from water. If the plate has no foam sealing strips, use silicone caulk to do the same job.

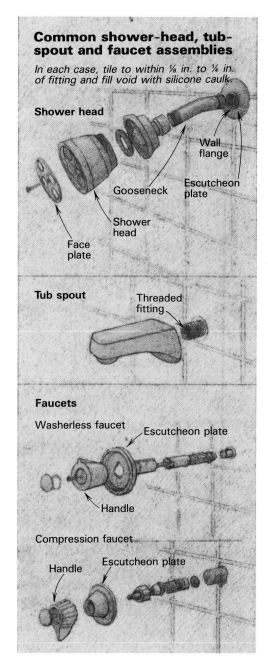

Common shower-head, tub-spout and faucet assemblies

In each case, tile to within ⅛ in. to ¼ in. of fitting and fill void with silicone caulk.

Shower head

Wall flange

Gooseneck

Escutcheon plate

Shower head

Face plate

Tub spout

Threaded fitting

Faucets

Washerless faucet

Escutcheon plate

Handle

Compression faucet

Handle

Escutcheon plate

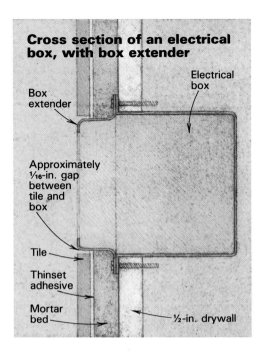

Cross section of an electrical box, with box extender

Box extender

Electrical box

Approximately ⅟₁₆-in. gap between tile and box

Tile

Thinset adhesive

Mortar bed

½-in. drywall

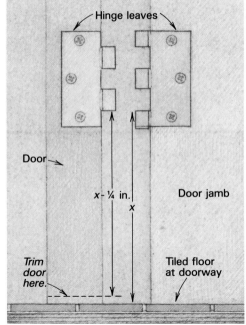

Trimming a door to clear a new tile floor

1. Measure distance from point on jamb hinge to newly tiled floor. Subtract ¼ in. from this distance for clearance.

2. Measure this distance from corresponding point on door hinge to bottom of door to determine where to trim door.

Hinge leaves

Door

Door jamb

x - ¼ in.

x

Trim door here.

Tiled floor at doorway

Many tub spouts use a threaded pipe to connect with the water supply line, while some newer spouts have a clamp that cinches the spout to a ½-in. copper pipe soldered to the supply line. Either way, remove the spout, and tile to within ⅛ in. to ¼ in. of the pipe. Before replacing the spout, pack the void between the threaded pipe or the copper pipe and the tile with plumber's putty or silicone caulk.

Appliances Before tiling a kitchen floor, check to make sure that the dishwasher and trash compactor will still fit under the countertop with the additional height of the tile. Tilework should always extend underneath these and any other kitchen appliances, though these are good places to use up cut waste pieces or tiles whose glaze is flawed. If the dishwasher or trash compactor will sit too high to fit under the countertop, either raise the height of the entire countertop, or, if the counter has a lip, notch out this lip to allow the appliances to be slipped in place.

Heat pipes Some baseboard heating elements and radiators have hot-water delivery pipes that protrude through the floor. When tiling floors with such pipes, tile only up to within ¼ in. of these pipes and fill the void with silicone caulk instead of grout. This treatment allows the pipes to move around without noisily scraping against the tiles.

Electrical outlets When tiles are set on a surface containing electrical outlets, the utility boxes must be made flush with the surface of the tiles. If you are setting directly on the existing floor or wall, that surface is likely to become only ¼ in. to ⅜ in. higher. In this case, before tiling, shut off the power, remove the outlet's faceplate and back out the screws holding the outlet or switch enough to fit the tiles under the mounting tabs. You may need to buy longer screws from an electrical supplier or hardware store.

If the installation increases the thickness of the floor, wall or countertop by more than ⅜ in., you will need to reposition the box to make it flush with the surface of the tiles. Alternatively, you may be able to purchase a box extender from an electrical supply house or hardware store.

If you need to change the position of an electrical box or eliminate it altogether, things get more complicated. In either case, consult a good electrical repair book (see the Resource Guide) or hire an electrician.

Trimming doors If you raise the height of an existing floor with tile, you may need to trim the bottom of any doors in the room to accommodate the new floor. There are several ways to trim off the bottom of a door, but the method I like is the following: Remove the doors before beginning the tilework. Once the tiles have been set and grouted, measure from the bottom edge of the lowest jamb hinge to the top of the tile and subtract ¼ in. from this figure for clearance. Then measure down this distance from the corresponding point on the door's hinge, mark a line along the bottom of the door and cut away the door's excess with a power or hand saw.

Thresholds To create a smooth transition between floors of unequal height or different materials, a threshold can be used. Oak makes a durable threshold that is easily cut on a tablesaw and installed by screwing it into the substrate. Marble makes an elegant threshold, and most marble dealers can supply one sized to your needs. Install the marble with thinset adhesive. Aluminum thresholds are becoming common at exterior openings because they allow for various weatherstripping details. If you have to install one yourself, screws sunk into the substrate will do the job.

Sometimes thresholds can be installed directly over the tile, for example, at a doorway between two rooms that will be tiled. Generally, however, thresholds will be installed directly on the substrate, and the tile will be brought up to the threshold. Thresholds can be installed either before or after tiling. When tiles are to be set up to an existing threshold, they should be kept ⅛ in. away from the threshold and the joint filled with silicone caulk. If you can, adjust the layout of the tiles so that you don't end up with a sliver of tile at the threshold.

When you're tiling up to a threshold over which a door will close, the last grout joint should be positioned so that more than just a thin edge of tile is visible when the door is closed. Again, this requires a careful layout before tiling. And if you're tiling between two rooms joined by a door and threshold, remove both fixtures before tiling. The door will, of course, need to be trimmed before it is replaced.

Be prepared!   Don't start any tile installation unless you're sure that you have all the materials needed. Gather all the tools required for the job and put them in a convenient spot. Keep a bucket of water and a sponge handy to clean up tools or spills quickly. Spread tarps or drop cloths over finished areas you want to protect, cover up kitchen cabinets with plastic or protective paper when tiling countertops, and use tape or other masking devices on wood, papered or painted surfaces to keep grout contained to the tiles. (Don't leave masking tape in place for too long, though—it can pull up the wallpaper, paint or finish on woods if it stays in place for a long time.) If you're tiling around other workers doing finish work, make sure you both know what to watch out for in each other's jobs.

Last but not least, don't tile yourself into a corner. Before you begin work, plan the sequence of areas to be tiled so that you will be positioned at or near the door to the room when you finish. If, however, you need to walk on a freshly tiled floor for whatever reason, keep handy some plywood squares, 2 ft. square by ¾ in. thick, to serve as a walkway over the floor. Make sure as you exit the room to remove each square, and check to see that you haven't disturbed the position of the tile below.   □

Layout

Tile catalogs were once filled with drawings of ceramic tile and trim in nearly infinite variety. Almost anything imaginable was available in tile, including ceramic window stools, ceramic rosettes and even ceramic crown molding. In an 80-year-old house I recently visited, our ancestors' passion for this material was evident everywhere: tile covered all the floors, special pieces finished all door and window openings, and sculptural ceramic trim adorned the baseboards.

Not only is tile no longer available in the variety it once was, something else has changed too. Nowadays, tilesetters have to fit tile to the building, whereas rooms were once frequently designed around the tile. Tilesetters were involved with the design of the building from an early stage, since it was, after all, tougher to make tile conform to a particular room dimension than it was to cut and shape plaster or wood to conform to the tile.

Sometimes I dream of those days. Contemporary setters rarely enjoy the luxury of having the other trades work around them, and layout of a tile job must account for the unexpected and out of square. Although I've never met another setter who lays out tile like I do (aside from those I've trained), my techniques have proven themselves over the course of many jobs.

Layout is the step in the tiling process that allows the setter to "see" and plan out the way an installation will look before any tile is actually set. In effect, layout is a dress rehearsal of the real thing, presented graphically with a set of lines marked on the setting bed. Each of these layout lines represents the center of the grout joint between two rows of tile, and together these lines guide the setter in positioning the field of tile. Like an architect's blueprint, the assembled body of layout lines constitutes the tilesetter's plan of action.

For any tile job, there are two basic layout problems to contend with: arranging the tiles accurately in relation to each other, and arranging the entire field of tiles accurately in relation to the surrounding building and its features. Many tilesetters sidestep layout altogether and simply begin setting tile along the longest edge of the installation. Sometimes the results of this approach are fine, but more often than not, using such an arbitrary starting point dictates an arbitrary look for the entire job. Small, trimmed pieces of tile, for example, may end up positioned at a doorway or another obvious spot, where full tiles would look much better. By carefully considering the size and shape of the area being tiled and the size and shape of the tile itself, you can easily avoid such problems and produce an installation with the tiles placed exactly where you want them. Since layout is crucial to the ultimate look of the job and it involves no expense other than time, I heartily urge that you begin any installation with this step.

I can't stress the importance of layout enough. Not only is it essential for producing a handsome installation, it's also necessary for accurately calculating the amount of tile needed for a particular job (see p. 112). As well, it's vital if you are to quickly and correctly set a field of tile on the first try, which is especially important if you're working with an adhesive that sets up in five minutes. Because layout entails carefully selecting and plotting out the best possible setting configuration *before* any tile is set, it eliminates last-minute surprises, including, in the worst-case scenario, the need to frantically reposition all the tiles on a wet bed. And because you know ahead of time the size and number of any trimmed tiles needed for the installation, you can make all these cuts before you start spreading adhesive, which considerably speeds up the actual setting process.

In addition, the steps involved in layout point out any surface preparation needed before tiling can begin, and they unveil any framing or structural problems that would complicate an installation. A deft layout can also mask structural problems that might otherwise be prohibitively expensive to repair—a tapering hallway, for example.

Layout is especially helpful when you're working on a large job with a helper or crew. With the lines snapped on the setting bed, you can divide the labor—one of you can cut and set trimmed tiles, which will be marked off by the layout grid, while the other sets full tiles. Moreover, a minimum of verbal instructions to your co-worker will be needed.

Principles of layout

Because tilework is actually a finishing process for floors, walls and countertops, it should, of course, be as attractive as possible. Many things affect the look of tilework, most obviously the color and shape of the tile selected and the pattern in which it is set. The visual impact of the finished job, however, is also greatly influenced by the physical placement of the individual tiles. Using a wide rather than a thin grout joint throughout a field of tile, for example, will considerably change the look of the installation (see p. 62 for more information on grout joints).

Perhaps first among the guidelines for laying out a handsome installation is to use as many full and as few cut tiles as possible. If a job requires that some tiles be cut, these trimmed tiles should be placed, if possible, away from the visual focal points—doorways, thresholds and in front of a fireplace. Only full tiles should be set in these areas. You may encounter situations when this guideline can be abandoned (I'll discuss them later), but the look of most jobs will improve if you minimize the number of cut tiles used.

When cut tile is necessary to fit a specific installation, no tile should be trimmed to less than half-size—a guideline that many architects, in fact, insist upon in their specifications for a job. It may be impossible to avoid small cuts in some *L*-shaped and multiroom layouts or when masking a particular structural problem, but careful adjustment of the layout will again downplay the visual impact.

When trimmed tile is called for, it should be positioned symmetrically if possible. That is to say, a job requiring a row of cut tile will be more attractive if that row is visually balanced by a second trimmed row on the other side of the field. If you find, for example, that 6 in. must be cut from a row of 12-in.-square floor tiles where they meet a wall, it's best to cut 3 in. from that row and 3 in. from the row on the opposite side of the room. The end result is the same, but the second option looks far better. Using two rows of cut tile means, of course, that the layout of the full tiles will shift, as shown in the drawing below.

Trimmed tile should also be positioned so that the cut edge is hidden from view wherever possible. On floor and wall installations, this is easily accomplished, since these unattractive edges are usually masked by baseboard trim and moldings. On countertops, where the surface of the tile is routinely touched, all cut edges should be hidden by trim or buried beneath backsplashes.

Positioning cut tile symmetrically

An installation will be more attractive if trimmed tiles are symmetrically placed wherever possible. For rows of cut tiles to be balanced, as in example 2, one full tile must be eliminated and size of cut tiles increased.

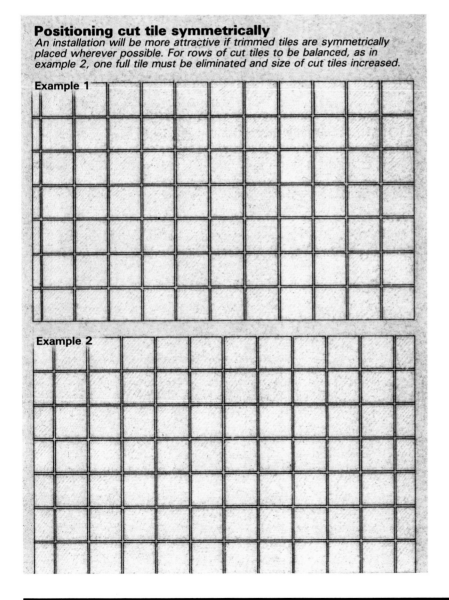

Example 1

Example 2

Hiding the edge of cut tiles

Cut edges of floor tiles can be hidden under baseboards.

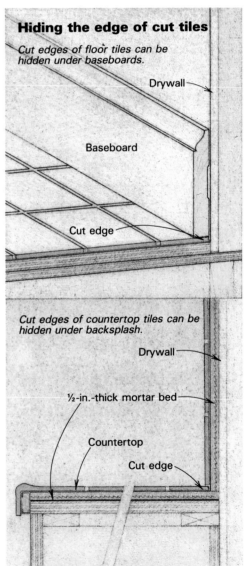

Drywall

Baseboard

Cut edge

Cut edges of countertop tiles can be hidden under backsplash.

Drywall

½-in.-thick mortar bed

Countertop

Cut edge

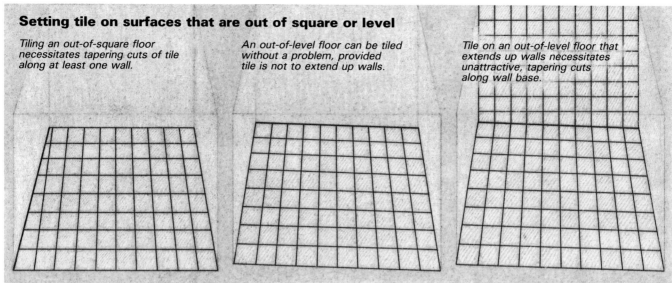

Setting tile on surfaces that are out of square or level

Tiling an out-of-square floor necessitates tapering cuts of tile along at least one wall.

An out-of-level floor can be tiled without a problem, provided tile is not to extend up walls.

Tile on an out-of-level floor that extends up walls necessitates unattractive, tapering cuts along wall base.

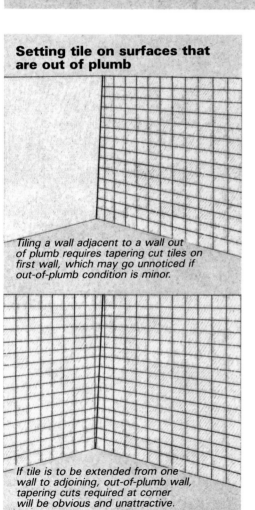

Setting tile on surfaces that are out of plumb

Tiling a wall adjacent to a wall out of plumb requires tapering cut tiles on first wall, which may go unnoticed if out-of-plumb condition is minor.

If tile is to be extended from one wall to adjoining, out-of-plumb wall, tapering cuts required at corner will be obvious and unattractive.

Preparing for layout

Layout is a process akin to solving a puzzle with a variety of solutions. Since each solution is likely to involve compromise, the goal of layout is to explore the various possibilities and pick the one that produces the most attractive installation with the fewest significant compromises.

The basic tools used for layout include an accurate, 10-ft. tape measure; a carpenter's square; a 32-in. spirit level; 32-in. and 48-in. straightedges; a chalk line; and a pencil. In a pinch, I have precisely laid out a job with nothing more than a tape measure and a pencil, but things are considerably easier if you have at least the tools listed above. A jury stick, sometimes called a story pole, is also an extremely useful tool to have. Easily made by the directions on p. 117, this pole provides a quick means of measuring the number of full tiles that will fit into a given area. As well, if your tool kit includes the following items, you might find them handy, too: a machinist's surface gauge for measuring heights, a depth gauge for measuring depth, and trammel points for extreme accuracy in projecting right triangles (needed to determine if a floor is square).

The area to be tiled should be checked to see if it's square (that is, if all its corners measure 90°) and plumb (vertically straight) or level (horizontally even). If the area is only slightly out of square, plumb or level and within the standard tolerance limits (explained on the facing page), minor changes in the layout can be made to accommodate these conditions. If the area is more significantly out of square, plumb or level, the process stops for any required structural repairs or surface preparations. If the framing problems are serious, it may not be possible to tile at all.

Checking for square The object of checking a floor, wall or countertop for square is to determine if the sides of the area being tiled are square to one another and can be used as reference points from which to plot the layout of the tiles. (In the case of a floor, this means figuring out if the walls enclosing it are square to each other.) If the surface being tiled is only slightly out of square, the effect on layout may be negligible. If that surface is more seriously out of square, however, the effect will be obvious (see the drawing above and, again, the discussion of tolerance limits).

Whether a floor or countertop is level or a wall plumb is of less concern than whether the surface's sides are square because the out-of-level or out-of-plumb condition does not necessarily affect layout to any significant degree. If the floor or countertop alone is being tiled and it's only slightly out of level, the effect on the job will probably be unnoticeable. Similarly, a single, slightly out-of-plumb wall can usually be tiled without a problem, provided the tile will not be bordered by a starkly contrasting material or a boldly patterned wallpaper. If tile is to extend from a considerably out-of-level floor or countertop up the walls, however, or from a seriously out-of-plumb wall to an adjoining wall, the whole installation will look askew. In such cases, the floor, countertop or wall will require repair before tiling, or the setter may want to rethink the decision to extend the tile over the adjacent surfaces.

More often than not, floors, walls and countertops are at least slightly out of square, level or plumb, so the tilesetter should be ready for imperfect conditions. Even the most competent carpenter won't always leave behind square, level and plumb surfaces, so I approach every job as if the structure were totally out of whack—that is, I check all the surfaces to determine the problems. While assessing the extent of the problems is largely a subjective judgment, the Tile Council of America (TCA) has established some guidelines that professional setters use in deciding when to repair walls and floors before tiling and when to forgo tiling altogether.

The tolerance limits established by the TCA state that when walls are no more than ⅛ in. out of square in 10 ft., the problems can be compensated for by minor adjustments in the layout. Likewise, walls no more than ⅛ in. out of plumb in 8 ft. (the height of the average ceiling) and floors or countertops no more than ⅛ in. out of level in 10 ft. can be tiled without the discrepancy being noticed. (While walls meeting at an outside corner should be almost perfectly plumb for tilework, the tolerance for plumb for walls meeting at an inside corner is less exacting, that is, ½ in. in 10 ft.) If the out-of-square, -level or -plumb condition exceeds these guidelines, however, the surface should be corrected, if possible, before tiling. This may entail either rebuilding it (in the worst case) or floating a mortar bed over it (see p. 86 and Chapter 7). If the surface is seriously out of square, level or plumb and cannot be corrected, it should not be tiled—period.

You can check walls for square in a small area like a bathroom by simply holding a carpenter's square in each corner. In a larger room, however, you'll get only a partial reading of the area if you check only the corners, since it's possible for them to be square even though the walls themselves are bowed along their length. To determine if a wall that's not too long is bowed, use a straightedge at least 6 ft. long, holding it against the wall and looking for gaps. For a longer wall, sight down the length of the wall as if you were eyeballing a stick of lumber for straightness. You can also stretch a string across the wall, keeping it about ½ in. from the surface, and compare the gap between wall and string at various points. Since I've checked a lot of walls, I can generally tell just by looking at them if they have a bow big enough to worry about.

If you're tiling a floor that's complex in shape or unusually large, or that extends into several rooms, you can plot a 3-4-5 triangle on the floor to help you check if the walls are square to each other. The 3-4-5 triangle is simply a triangle with a 90° angle at one corner whose proportions are easy to plot in any size (see p. 114). You'll soon see how to use the triangle as a guide to aligning tile, but as an aid to checking a room for square, it acts like a giant, imaginary carpenter's square. (Information on checking for level and plumb is found on p. 76.)

Making a preliminary drawing The layout process begins on paper, with a drawing of the surfaces to be tiled, showing all critical dimensions and features. Your preliminary drawing of a wall should note, for example, the exact location and size of any windows or doors, the location of electrical boxes, and the location and dimensions of any built-in furniture (particularly shelves and cabinets). Drawing a countertop may seem like a waste of time, but, particularly if you're a novice, the exercise is a valuable one. Note the location of sinks, abutting walls and any other feature that could affect the placement of tile. Effort spent on a preliminary drawing really pays off when you're tiling a floor. Floor plans generally require the most effort because the spaces to be tiled are larger, and there are many aspects of the room that can influence tile placement (see the drawing below). Your initial sketch should record the dimensions of the area being tiled, trace its perimeter, and note everything in the space that will affect the installation, including doorways, thresholds, any obstructions (such as water pipes) and any surfaces that will adjoin the tile. Sometimes it's impossible to repair problem walls, so you should also note on the floor plan whether the walls enclosing the area being tiled are square to each other. Once finished, the preliminary drawing becomes part of your "reference library" for the job, and you'll find that you'll consult it frequently during the layout process.

I like to use graph paper (usually ⅛-in. or ¼-in.) to do these drawings because I can quickly scale out a sketch and because, with the paper's printed grid, I don't need a T-square or drawing tools to create right angles. Although graph paper is not critical for a simple drawing, it is very helpful when the area being tiled is a complicated floor or wall that takes frequent turns or extends into other rooms.

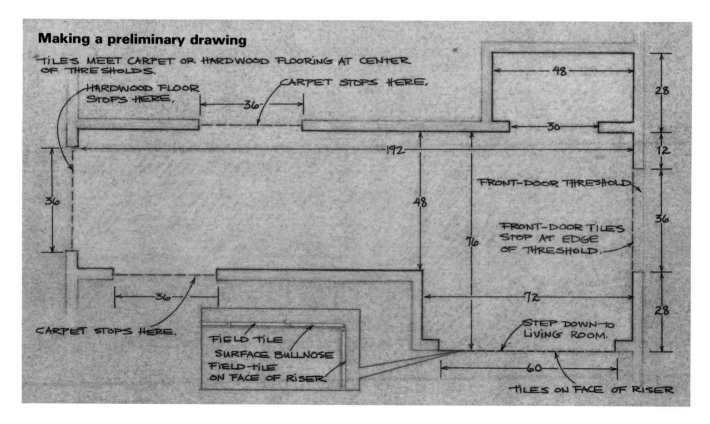

Making a preliminary drawing

Making a tile/grout-joint list and layout sketch Once the preliminary drawing has been done, you can begin figuring out how the tile will fit in the area. While it's possible to spread the actual tiles out on a floor or countertop (though not a wall) and move them around to try various layouts, this is physically tiring work, particularly on a large job. Besides, at this stage, you may not even have all the tile in hand. So in most cases you're better off figuring out on paper the layout of tile that best suits the space.

Working out a layout on paper involves calculations. Because the odds are good that the combined width of the selected tile and grout joint won't equal a nice, round number of inches, doing these computations in inches and feet can be difficult. Instead, I always compile a tile/grout-joint list, whose basic unit of measurement equals the width of a single tile and grout joint. I make the list long enough to compute the number of tiles needed to fit on the longest segment of the job. This list becomes an invaluable reference that's easy to use and far more reliable than juggling figures in my head. And by comparing this list with the dimensions on the floor plan, I can immediately determine if a possible layout will work.

Because tiles vary somewhat in dimension, the only way to make an accurate list is to measure at least a few of the tiles you'll be setting. Thus, ideally, samples of the tile should be in hand before a tile/grout-joint list is worked up. If the tiles are readily available locally, I just purchase or borrow some. But if sample tiles are difficult to obtain—perhaps the tiles are being custom-made—I do the best job I can of estimating the combined dimension of tile and grout joint. If the actual tile turns out to be slightly different in size from the dimension that I used to work up the tile/grout-joint list, I can make up the difference by running a larger or smaller grout joint. If the difference in size is appreciable and cannot be made up in varying the width of the joint, I prepare a new tile/grout-joint list.

To get a better idea of how a tile/grout-joint list is used, let's look at a very simple example, in which, for clarity's sake, I've purposely made the width of a single tile and grout joint equal a whole number of inches. (Later in this chapter, and in each of the project chapters in the second half of the book, I'll give examples of more complicated floor plans and tile/grout-joint dimensions.) Let's suppose a foyer floor measuring 12 ft. 2 in. square is to be tiled with 11⅞-in.-square tiles and that the grout joints are to be ⅛ in. wide. The basic unit of measure for the tile/grout-joint list is therefore 12 in. By simple multiplication, I arrived at the list shown at right. This list shows the space required for the width of from one to 13 tiles and grout joints. The list stops at 13 tiles because I wouldn't need more than this many to span the full length and width of the floor.

Tile/grout-joint list

Since the combined width of a single tile (11⅞ in.) and its grout joint (⅛ in.) equals 12 in., the combined width of additional tiles and joints can be calculated as follows:

1 = 12 in.	8 = 96 in.
2 = 24 in.	9 = 108 in.
3 = 36 in.	10 = 120 in.
4 = 48 in.	11 = 132 in.
5 = 60 in.	12 = 144 in.
6 = 72 in.	13 = 156 in.
7 = 84 in.	

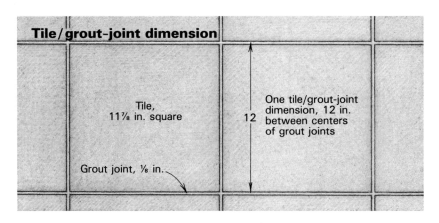

Tile/grout-joint dimension

Tile, 11⅞ in. square

One tile/grout-joint dimension, 12 in. between centers of grout joints — 12

Grout joint, ⅛ in.

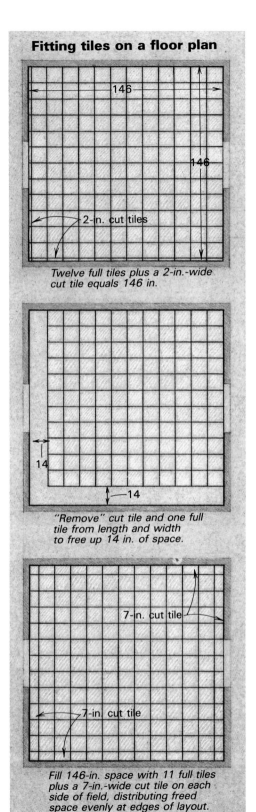

Fitting tiles on a floor plan

Twelve full tiles plus a 2-in.-wide cut tile equals 146 in.

"Remove" cut tile and one full tile from length and width to free up 14 in. of space.

Fill 146-in. space with 11 full tiles plus a 7-in.-wide cut tile on each side of field, distributing freed space evenly at edges of layout.

By looking at the simple floor plan at left and the tile/grout-joint list, I can see that 12 full tiles plus a 2-in.-wide cut tile will fit across the floor's 146-in. length and width. Since the imaginary specifications for this job call for no tile less than half-size and since an asymmetrical row of trimmed tiles would be unattractive anyway, I want to avoid having two rows of 2-in.-wide cuts (one row across the width of the foyer, and one across the length). To do this, I need to "remove" both a row of full tiles and the row of cut tiles, then calculate the amount of space freed up (14 in.) and divide this figure by two (7 in.). This becomes the size of the symmetrically placed trimmed tiles that will be set as the first and last rows across the width and length of the foyer. On a more complex tile job, such as a large L-shaped room, the tile/grout-joint list allows you to see how shifts in the layout will affect the look of the job. If you want to see how using a slightly different width of grout joint will change the layout, it's easy enough to do another tile/grout-joint list. Over small distances, even a major change in the width of the grout joint may not make much difference in the layout of the tile, but over, say, a living-room floor, the difference could be significant.

Estimating tile Once you've arrived at a layout on paper, you're ready to estimate the amount of tile needed for the job. Unless the planned layout uses full tiles only, there will be a certain amount of waste that must be accounted for when ordering the tile. This is where the layout sketch and tile/grout-joint list will prove particularly helpful.

The degree of accuracy needed for an estimate for tile depends partly on how complex the installation is and also on how easy the tile is to get—and return. When I'm dealing with a local supplier who has plenty of the tile I'll be using in stock, I can make an approximate estimate. If I under-order (something to be avoided if possible) I can quickly get more tile, though it's a nuisance to break setting stride to make a tile run. On the other hand, if I order too much tile I can return the excess. An approximate estimate can be made simply by figuring the square footage of the job, adding 8% to 10% to cover waste and unforeseen circumstances, and then ordering enough tile to cover that adjusted square footage.

If the tile is difficult to obtain quickly or costly to return, however, or if the spaces to be tiled are complex, I'll do a more precise estimate. The most accurate way to figure out how much tile you'll need is to actually count the individual tiles called for in the layout. Often the results of this method are surprisingly different from those obtained with the square-foot method of estimating, and it's the individual-tile method that's more accurate. The reason for this arises from the fact that manufacturers assign an arbitrary grout-joint width to tile sold by the square foot in order to calculate the area a given amount of tile will cover. Often the grout-joint size they figure on won't coincide with that planned for your installation, and hence the possible discrepancy between your calculations and the manufacturer's. Also, calculating by the square foot fails to take into account the number of full tiles that will be lost in making trimmed pieces, since each cut more than half-size must be cut from a full tile.

Let's look at these two methods of estimating the amount of tile needed, again using the foyer floor as an example. Since this floor is 12 ft. 2 in. square, the square footage to be covered is approximately 149 sq. ft. (12.17 ft. x 12.17 ft. = 148.1, or, rounded off to the next whole number, 149 sq. ft.). With the combined width of the tile and grout joint being 12 in., I would figure that 149 tiles will be needed to cover 149 sq. ft. If I went to a tile store, though, and bought tile by the square foot (which is how it is often sold), using the manufacturer's coverage recommendations, I might end up with a different number of tiles for this job. I might well find that the manufacturer packaged this imaginary tile 25 pieces to the box, stating that one box would cover 26.6 sq. ft. What this means is that each tile should cover a little more than one square foot, a calculation that assumes about a ½-in. grout joint. Thus, according to the manufacturer, I would need 140 tiles to cover the designated area.

Now let's see what the results are from actually counting the number of individual tiles called for in the layout. In checking my floor plan and tile/grout-joint list, I can see that the main area of the floor requires 121 full tiles, plus 44 tiles to make the rectangular cuts around the perimeter (only one 7-in. cut can be made from each 11⅞-in. tile) and 4 tiles to make the square cuts in each corner, or a total of 169 tiles, as shown in the drawing below. This figure takes into consideration the almost 20 sq. ft. of tile waste.

As you can see, it's much more accurate to compute the tile needed by actual count than by the square foot. And once you've arrived at the total number of tiles called for in the layout, add 5% to 10% to this figure to account for breakage in shipment or miscut tiles. For the foyer floor, then, I would probably order a total of 180 tiles. If any tiles remained after the job was completed, I could always store the leftovers in case future repairs were needed.

I find it best to wait until my order arrives before actually chalking layout lines on the setting bed. This way, I can measure a random selection of the tiles to make sure their dimensions conform to my expectations.

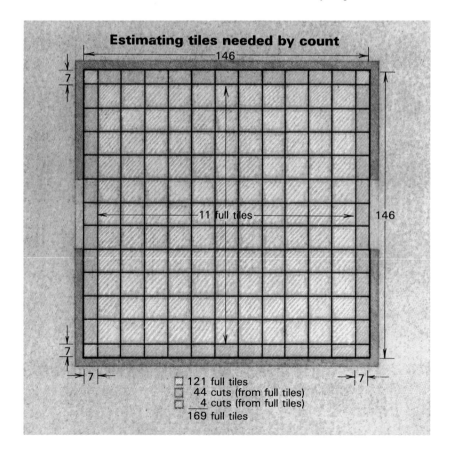

Estimating tiles needed by count

☐ 121 full tiles
☐ 44 cuts (from full tiles)
☐ 4 cuts (from full tiles)
169 full tiles

Establishing square reference lines with a 3-4-5 triangle

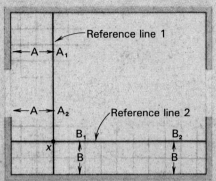

Consult layout sketch and tile/grout-joint list to determine where to place reference lines 1 and 2 so that they fall at what will become centers of grout joints.

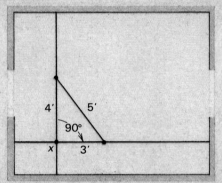

Plot a 3-4-5 triangle on reference lines to determine if walls from which lines are projected are square to one another. If triangle's hypotenuse equals exactly 5 ft., walls are square.

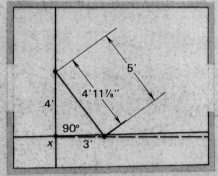

If hypotenuse does not equal exactly 5 ft., walls are out of square. To square up reference lines, pivot one line at point of intersection to correct length of hypotenuse.

Laying out floors

The general procedure for laying out floors, walls and countertops is basically the same. In effect, a wall is nothing more than a rectangular or square floor turned on edge, and a countertop is simply a floor made smaller. A floor can be both considerably larger than a wall or countertop, however, and more complex, sometimes extending into several rooms. As the floor's size and complexity increase, so too does the complexity of its layout. For this reason, let's begin with the most simply shaped floor, a square or rectangle, then move to floors with more complicated shapes and finally to multiroom installations. If you can lay out a floor, you'll have little problem laying out anything else.

Plotting reference lines   I've talked to a lot of novice tilesetters and heard a lot of stories about their first tiled floor. Just about every new setter ends up cussing the walls. A setter usually figures that the framing contractor has singled him or her out for some special punishment, because when the floor tiles reach the walls, the hitherto "perfect" layout begins to go awry. Tiles are, more or less, perfect little rectangles; floors and walls are not, and a competent layout minimizes or eliminates awkward results at the walls. Reference lines are the key to layout.

Tiles are rigidly geometric, and to ensure that they look correct in place, they must be aligned with a grid of lines oriented at 90° to each other. A single pair of lines, called reference lines, are first plotted directly on the setting surface, and these serve as the backbone of the grid. Although reference lines can also be used to check the room for square, their primary purpose is to establish the basic 90° relationship necessary for plotting the grid. Composed of what are called layout lines, this grid will later be plotted on the setting bed to guide the actual setting of the tile.

On a small setting surface, such as a bathroom floor or a countertop, a carpenter's square can be used to establish the basic right-angle intersection of the reference lines. But on larger and more complex surfaces, such as the floor of a patio, the carpenter's square isn't big enough to establish large, truly accurate right angles. This is where the 3-4-5 triangle comes in handy. The triangle isn't an actual tool; it's simply a method of establishing a pair of long lines that are perpendicular to each other—that is, reference lines. The method is based on the fact that a triangle with sides in the proportion of 3:4:5 will contain a right angle. That is to say, if the baseline of a triangle is three units, the triangle's height four units and its hypotenuse five units, the triangle is a right triangle. By projecting on the setting bed an accurate 3-4-5 triangle (or a larger triangle with unit measurements in the same proportional relationship—6-8-10, 12-16-20, and so on), the square reference lines needed for layout can be established, whatever the size or shape of the floor being tiled, and the walls can be checked for square.

To begin making a 3-4-5 triangle, you need one straight line. To establish this line, first consult the layout sketch and the tile/grout-joint list and pick a measurement for a grout joint that will fall several feet away from one of the walls. Then measure this distance from both ends of the wall, mark these points with a pencil and connect the points by snapping a chalk line. If possible, measure from an outside wall, since this wall was built over the foundation and is likelier to be straight than an inside wall. If there is no outside wall in the room, take the measurements off the longest wall. Also, if you can see that a baseboard is bowed or uneven, choose another wall from which to measure to avoid introducing error into later measurements.

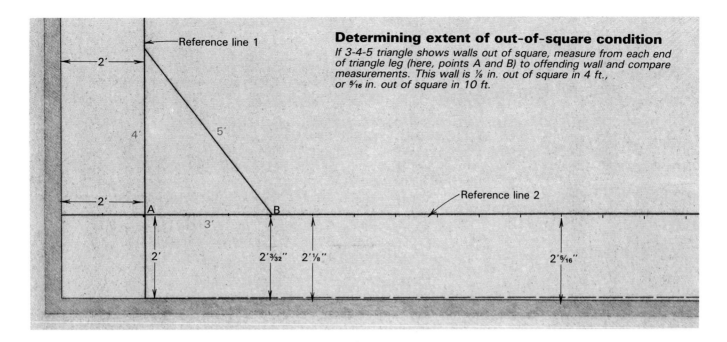

Determining extent of out-of-square condition

If 3-4-5 triangle shows walls out of square, measure from each end of triangle leg (here, points A and B) to offending wall and compare measurements. This wall is ⅛ in. out of square in 4 ft., or ⁵⁄₁₆ in. out of square in 10 ft.

Next, again consult the layout sketch and tile/grout-joint list to pick a second measurement for a grout joint that will fall several feet away from the adjoining wall. This time measure that distance out from the adjoining wall, first along the reference line you've just drawn and second at another point along the wall. Mark these points with a pencil and connect them by snapping a chalk line.

Then measuring from the point where the two lines intersect, make a mark *exactly* 3 ft. away on one of the lines. (If you're working on a large floor, you can enlarge this distance proportionately as long as you follow suit with subsequent dimensions.) Next measure along the other line a distance of *exactly* 4 ft. from the point of intersection and make a mark. Then measure the distance between these two marks. If it is exactly 5 ft., the two reference lines—and the two walls from which they were projected—are square to each other. This is *all* the 3-4-5 triangle tells you, although these square lines can in turn be used to determine if the other walls are square. (To do this, simply measure from both ends of one of the lines to the unchecked wall opposite it and compare the distance. If the measurements are the same at both ends, that wall is square to the neighboring wall, which you already determined was square to the first wall. Proceed in the same fashion to check the remaining walls in the room.)

If you find that the hypotenuse of the triangle is not exactly 5 ft., the walls from which you projected the lines are not square to one another. As shown in the drawing above, you can use the 3-4-5 triangle to determine the extent of the problem. If the walls are out of square less than ⅛ in. in 10 ft., they will not noticeably affect the layout. Nonetheless, you will need to adjust the reference lines to make sure that the triangle contains a right angle and hence that the reference lines intersect at a 90° angle. This will mean that the triangle will not be square to both walls, only to one wall. If you need to adjust the triangle, square it up to a wall containing the most obvious focal point—a fireplace, a threshold, maybe a bay window. This is a compromise, but if you can't align the tile perfectly with every wall, it should at least be aligned with the wall people will look at first.

After deciding which wall to square up the triangle with, make the adjustment by moving the reference line perpendicular to that wall. Note that the first snapping point for this line (point *B1* in the drawing on p. 114) remains unchanged, and the line is pivoted at that point until the hypotenuse equals exactly 5 ft. Once the hypotenuse is corrected and the reference lines are square to one another, the grid of layout lines can be chalked on the setting bed, as described on the facing page.

If the walls prove to be out of square by more than ⅛ in. in 10 ft., you'll have a decision to make, which, I'm afraid, is a judgment call. Either you'll have to fix the walls to make them square to each other, or you'll have to live with a tile layout that features obviously angled, cut tiles at one wall and maybe at other walls as well. This is when you'll need to draw on all the insight you can muster. Scrutinize the room for places where the angled tile will be least noticeable. Sometimes this means putting it along a wall that's broken into shorter lengths by built-in furniture, or a wall with windows covered by floor-length drapes.

The basic layout rule of using no tiles less than half-size will also minimize the visual problems associated with setting tile in problem rooms. Imagine a floor of 6-in.-square tiles in which the setter allowed a row of full tiles against one wall and a row of 1-in.-wide cuts along the opposite wall. If the latter wall happened to be ¾ in. out of square along its length, the tiles against one end of the wall might be a full inch wide, but against the other end of the wall they'd be only ¼ in. wide—making the out-of-square condition glaringly obvious. But if the layout were adjusted to use a 3½-in.-wide cut on both opposing walls, tiles on the one wall would taper from 3½ in. to 2¾ in. Even though the amount of taper is unchanged, it will be far less noticeable on the larger portion of tile. As a general rule, larger tiles will mask an out-of-square condition better than smaller tiles will. Given uncorrectable, out-of-square conditions, you'll have a better-looking job with larger tiles. Again, though, let me stress that the best-looking jobs are those where effort has been spent to correct problems, not disguise them.

If you're dealing with a real problem room in which no corner is really square and whose problems you can't correct—*and* you insist on setting tile—the reference lines will be particularly important. Even if nothing else in the room is square, the reference lines must be square to one another. They will serve as the benchmark from which to measure everything else. If you can visualize the entire tiled floor shifting every time you shift the reference lines, you'll understand how to use the lines to plan the tile job.

Another situation that points up the importance of reference lines is a multiroom installation where the tile needs to look continuous. In this case, reference lines plotted throughout the series of rooms enable the setter to position the tile so that, wherever possible, the grout lines run uninterrupted from one room through the doorway into the next room (see p. 120). For the layout of such an installation, reference lines are plotted first in one room—usually the largest or most complex in shape— and arranged so that one leg of the 3-4-5 triangle can be extended to pass through a doorway into the next room. This line will then serve as the basis for plotting another 3-4-5 triangle in the new room. Depending on the complexity of the job, you may need to plot a series of 3-4-5 triangles in this fashion. You may also find that you have to adjust the multi-triangle layout to correspond to differences in the squareness of each room. The important thing to remember in this case is that adjusting or moving one triangle means similarly altering the others as well.

Making a jury stick   Once reference lines have been established, the next step in layout is determining where to chalk layout lines on the setting bed to guide the actual placement of the tile. A jury stick will considerably speed up this task.

This tool is a sort of measuring stick that uses as its unit of measure the average width of a single tile and grout joint, rather than inches or centimeters. It eliminates the need for a tape measure and calculator at this stage of tiling, enabling the setter to quickly and accurately locate layout lines and determine exactly how many tiles will fit into a given area.

A jury stick is usually 6 ft. to 8 ft. long and can be made out of any dimension of wood stock, provided the board is straight. Because I do a lot of work with mortar setting beds, I usually make my jury stick from a float strip, but I will occasionally use pine lattice. When I'm working with a multiroom layout, I find it convenient to have two jury sticks, a short one for hallways and other narrow places and a long one for large rooms.

To establish the jury stick's basic unit of measure, line up 10 tiles against a straightedge. If the tiles are self-spacing, that is, if they have built-in spacing lugs, butt the lugs tightly against each other. If you plan to use tile spacers, be sure to include them when lining up the tiles. If the tiles don't have lugs and you're not using spacers, just space the tiles with a scrap of wood cut to the thickness of the planned grout joint. Next measure the overall width of the 10 tiles and grout joints. Divide this figure by 10, which will give you the average width of one tile and grout joint. Because individual tiles can vary in size—even as much as ¾ in. if they're handmade—it's better to establish the unit of measure as the average width of a tile and grout joint rather than simply using the measured width of one particular tile and joint.

After calculating the unit of measure, transfer this unit to the jury stick with a set of large dividers or a tape measure, and mark off the full stick with these units. The jury stick now provides a quick means of figuring out how many full-size tiles will fit into a given area. By starting at one side of the area and measuring with the jury stick across to the other side, you can determine what adjustments will be needed in layout to produce the visual results you want. You're doing basically the same thing as you did when you worked with the floor plan and the tile/grout-joint list to produce a layout sketch on paper, but this process is more accurate because it deals with the actual floor, rather than a representation of it. Using the jury stick accomplishes the same thing as physically laying out all the tiles on a floor to develop the correct layout—but, believe me, it's a lot easier.

Marking layout lines   With the reference lines marked on the floor and the jury stick made, you're ready to snap layout lines on the setting bed to guide the actual positioning of the tile. Again, you will need to consult the layout sketch and the tile/grout-joint list to figure out the exact distances from the reference lines at which layout lines should be plotted. Because the series of layout lines are projected off the reference lines, they, too, will be square to one another. And because the two reference lines were positioned to coincide with grout joints, they now become part of the grid of layout lines.

The purpose of layout lines is to prevent the grout joints—and tiles—from wandering off square and running at an angle. Imagine a large living-room floor, for example, and the problems you would have keeping tiles running straight across 15 ft. or 20 ft. of space without layout lines. Even self-spacing tiles can accumulate error over five or ten rows, so you can't depend on them to do the thinking for you. Layout lines provide a guide to work by, ensuring not only that the tiles run straight but also that each tile ends up exactly where you want it. If you want to avoid having to cut tiles at a threshhold, or if you want a particular grout joint to line up with, say, the edge of a built-in cabinet, layout lines are essential.

Layout lines also allow the setter to cut tiles to size where necessary *before* the actual setting begins. If you're setting tile on a large floor, for example, and you have a section of it spread with quick-setting adhesive, you don't want to spend time measuring the cuts and dashing back and forth to the wet saw. Instead, by using a layout line to separate cut tiles from full tiles, you can measure and make all the cuts at once ahead of time. That way, once it's time to set the tile, you can concentrate on this step alone.

And if you're not yet convinced of the importance of layout lines, consider another advantage they offer. By using layout lines to break up a large surface being tiled into smaller sections, you can spread adhesive and set tiles in the small areas one by one. Doing this divides the job into manageable segments, ensures that every portion of each small "box" is comfortably within your reach, and also reduces the possibility of spreading adhesive over a larger area than you can cover before the adhesive sets up. I like to divide the setting bed into small sections about 3 ft. square. Of course, the exact size of these areas depends on the size of the tile I'm working with.

The steps for establishing layout lines involve deciding the number and location of the lines needed; using the jury stick to project measurements from the square reference lines established on the setting bed; and, finally, snapping chalk lines (or using pencil and straightedge) to mark the layout lines on the bed.

The number and position of the layout lines depend on the size and complexity of the installation, the size and shape of the tiles, the speed with which the adhesive will set up, and the skill of the setter. Generally speaking, small, simply shaped installations need fewer layout lines than large, complex jobs, and large tiles necessitate fewer lines than small tiles do. As well, machine-made tiles of uniform size and shape, self-spacing tiles, and tiles to be set with spacers require fewer layout lines than irregularly shaped, handmade tiles do. Slow-setting adhesives allow you to work larger areas at any one time, so fewer layout lines are necessary. And, finally, an experienced setter will probably need fewer layout lines than the novice. But since it never hurts to put in more layout lines than you'll actually need, don't skimp on this step.

All of the above factors mean that a small, rectangular floor may require only a pair of intersecting lines for layout, while a large, complex floor extending into several rooms may need a dozen or more layout lines. And in a few rare instances—when you're working with very irregularly shaped, handmade tiles or unusual tiles, for example—it may be necessary to mark a layout line for every grout joint.

Rectangular floors and single-room layouts Let's look at some examples of floor layouts, the first being a bathroom floor, 5 ft. by 8 ft., set with self-spacing, 6-in.-square tiles, as shown in the drawing at left. Because of the floor's small size and simple shape, it's easy to check the room for square by putting a carpenter's square to the corners, rather than going to the trouble of chalking reference lines and a 3-4-5 triangle on the floor. Assuming that the room is square, a pair of layout lines will suffice to guide the placement of the tile. These two lines, which, of course, fall in the center of grout joints, divide the floor into four sections, in each of

Laying out a small floor
In a small space, to be set with self-spacing tile, a single pair of layout lines may suffice.

Toilet flange

96

Marble threshold

60

which all the tiles, both full and cut, are within easy reach. Because the floor is small and requires relatively few cut tiles, I wouldn't bother adding another layout line to separate the cut tile from the full tile—the time saved cutting the tiles in advance would be negligible. I would begin positioning full tiles at the point where the lines intersect, working from the center of the room outward and cutting the trimmed pieces as needed to complete the layout.

On a large floor being tiled with handmade Mexican pavers, which have a somewhat irregular shape, a layout line should be drawn to mark the rows of cut tiles around the perimeter, and a grid of layout lines should be plotted to enclose all the full tiles in sections no more than about 3 ft. square, as shown in the drawing below. With the rows of cut and full tiles separated, the cuts can be accurately measured and trimmed before setting actually begins. And the grid breaks the job into manageable segments.

After marking the joint separating the cut and full tiles on this floor, which is 11 ft. 2 in. by 15 ft. 8 in., I plotted additional layout lines every 36 in. across the floor's length and width. This produced a grid of twelve 36-in.-square boxes, each containing nine tiles, as well as one horizontal row of boxes, 24 in. by 36 in., which would accommodate six tiles, and one vertical row, 12 in. by 36 in., into which three tiles would fit. In each of the boxes, all of the tiles were easily within my reach.

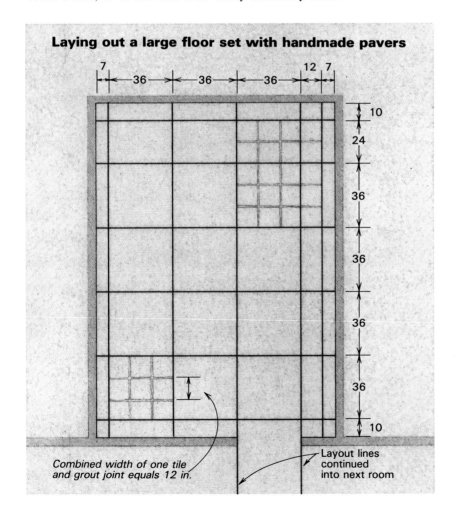

Laying out a large floor set with handmade pavers

Combined width of one tile and grout joint equals 12 in.

Layout lines continued into next room

Laying out an *L*-shaped floor

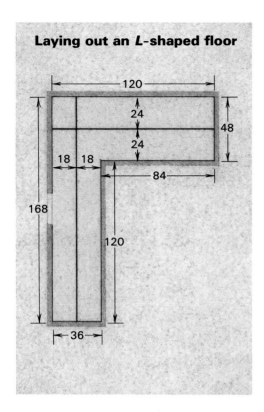

L-shaped floors and multiroom layouts *L*-shaped floors are simply composed of two parts, whether square or rectangular, and they are no more difficult to lay out than a simple square or rectangular floor. The trick in laying out this type of floor is to project the reference lines from the longest walls and to position the lines so that one falls in each leg of the *L,* as shown in the drawing at left.

In doing a multiroom layout, the key is not to lay out each room individually, but rather to connect the layout from room to room with one of the initial pair of reference lines. Additional reference lines can then be plotted in each room from the original pair, and the entire surface being tiled can then be treated as one continuous installation.

When plotting the original pair of reference lines for a multiroom installation, make sure, if possible, to project the lines off a wall that extends to the connecting rooms. In the case of the example shown below, *line 1,* plotted the full length of the installation, was projected off the west foundation wall that stretches along three rooms. *Line 2* was projected off the full width of the installation, and a 3-4-5 triangle was plotted to establish this pair of reference lines as square. *Line 3* was then projected off *line 1,* and *line 4,* the next longest line, off *line 2.* Then *line 5* was projected off *line 3* with a 3-4-5 triangle. *Line 6* was projected off *line 4,* and *line 7* off *line 1* with a 3-4-5 triangle. Once these reference lines were plotted throughout the installation, I could project layout lines to further divide the larger areas into manageable segments. Then, as with all the layouts shown, I began positioning tile in the center of the installation and worked outward toward the perimeter. (For further information on laying out and installing tile on floors, see Chapters 6 and 7.)

Laying out a multiroom floor

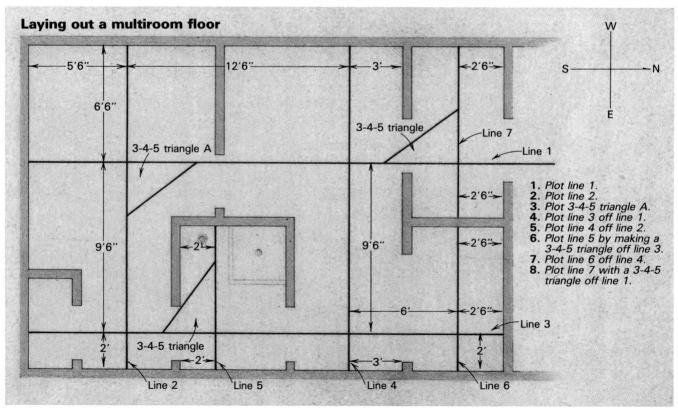

1. Plot line 1.
2. Plot line 2.
3. Plot 3-4-5 triangle A.
4. Plot line 3 off line 1.
5. Plot line 4 off line 2.
6. Plot line 5 by making a 3-4-5 triangle off line 3.
7. Plot line 6 off line 4.
8. Plot line 7 with a 3-4-5 triangle off line 1.

Laying out walls

Laying out walls is much easier than laying out floors. One reason is that to check a wall for plumb and square, you need only use a spirit level. Hold the level vertically against the wall to determine if it's plumb. Then place the level on the adjoining horizontal surface to be tiled—the floor or a countertop—to see if that surface is level. If the wall is plumb and the horizontal surface is level, the two surfaces are square to one another. Walls are set to the same tolerances as floors: if the surfaces are out of square more than ⅛ in. in 10 ft., corrective action should be considered. And as with floors, the kind and size of tile you plan to use will figure into your decision about correcting the problems or living with them. Crisp, rigidly uniform Italian tile might exaggerate the out-of-square conditions, but the natural irregularities of Mexican tile might disguise them.

Reference and layout lines should never be projected directly from adjoining walls or floors. Instead, use a level positioned on the wall first vertically and then horizontally to establish a pair of square reference lines, as shown in the drawing at right. As when laying out floors, place each of the reference lines in what will become the center of a grout joint. The two reference lines can then later serve as layout lines.

While setting tile on walls is in many ways like tiling floors, working on a vertical surface introduces the added concern of dealing with gravity. The inevitable pull of gravity on the tiles means that you must work quickly when tiling walls, and on large walls you can speed up the setting process by using plenty of layout lines. On most small walls, however, I usually divide the wall only into quadrants. In addition to these layout lines, I also add a line, if needed, to separate the field tile from any trim tile around windows, doors or other features. The drawing below shows a typical layout for a tub-shower surround with a window in the back wall, using 3-in.-square tiles. Let's look at each of the layout lines and what it denotes.

Scribing reference lines on walls

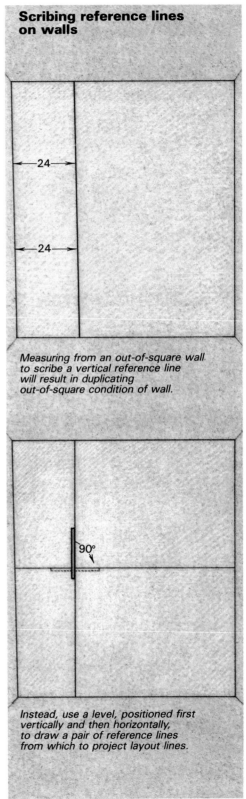

Measuring from an out-of-square wall to scribe a vertical reference line will result in duplicating out-of-square condition of wall.

Instead, use a level, positioned first vertically and then horizontally, to draw a pair of reference lines from which to project layout lines.

Laying out a tub surround with a window

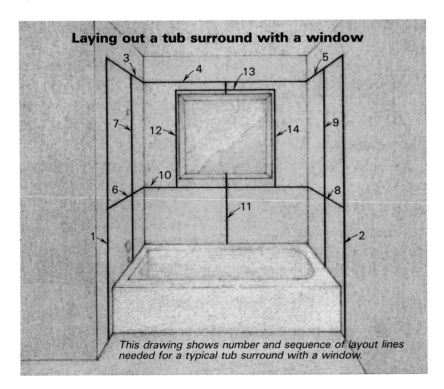

This drawing shows number and sequence of layout lines needed for a typical tub surround with a window.

Lines 1 and *2* mark the outer vertical limit of the field tiles and the grout joint between these and the trim tiles. *Lines 3, 4* and *5* mark the upper horizontal limit of the field tiles and the joint between these and the trim tiles. *Lines 6* and *7*, and *lines 8* and *9* split each of the side walls into four easily managed sections of field tiles. Note that *line 7* is positioned to clear the spout, shower-head and control-valve holes, and that *lines 6* and *8* are continuations of *line 10*.

Lines 10 and *11* divide the back wall into manageable quadrants. *Line 10* is located below the row of field tiles abutting the trim tiles on the window sill (in this case, there would be no room for the line between field and trim tiles). *Lines 12, 13* and *14* denote the grout joints between the field tiles on the header of the window and jambs and the trim tiles on the window's face. With all of these lines in place, I would not need to use a level during the actual setting of the tile, which eliminates the constant bother of having to clean adhesive off this tool.

Had a mortar setting bed been used for this tub surround, I would have also placed layout lines to note the outer limits of the mortar bed on the substrate (the other layout lines would, of course, have been chalked on top of the mortar bed once it was dry). This first set of lines would have facilitated the installation of the tar-paper curing membrane and the reinforcing wire mesh necessary with a mortar bed (see p. 169). For further information on laying out and tiling walls, see Chapters 8 and 9.

Laying out countertops

Countertops are the easiest installation of all to lay out. Because you're working with relatively small, narrow surfaces, there's less chance of positioning the tiles askew. Before beginning the layout, check the countertop for level and square. Then also make sure that the cabinets are securely fastened in place, since any wobbling might cause the countertop to move or flex, which will likely result in cracked tiles or grout joints.

The principal rule in laying out a countertop is to position full tiles at the front edge of the countertop and any required cut pieces at the base of the backsplash where they will be less noticeable and probably covered by the backsplash tiles. If you're installing a new plywood setting surface for a countertop, it's a good idea to cut a fresh edge on a tablesaw, as plywood's factory edge may not always be perfectly straight. Cut the other edge to accommodate any irregularities in the backsplash wall, and place the straight edge at the front of the counter. If you don't have a tablesaw, use the factory edge of the plywood at the front of the countertop.

Fitting a countertop to an uneven back wall

Cut tiles placed at back of countertop

Cut plywood to fit crooked backsplash wall.

Full tiles placed at front of countertop

Place factory or freshly cut edge of plywood here.

You needn't plot reference lines on a countertop—the front edge of the countertop *is* a reference line. But layout lines, projected from the edge of the countertop, can be helpful. If the countertop is a simple rectangle bordered on both ends by walls, the only layout line needed is one to separate the field tiles from the trim tiles used at the forward edge of the counter, as shown in the drawing below. If one end of the countertop is not bordered by a wall, or if the countertop is *L*-shaped or *U*-shaped, additional lines are needed to position the trim tiles on the counter's other exposed edges. And if the countertop contains a sink or stovetop, several lines are also needed to mark the position of the trim tiles around these fixtures. Finally, if the tiles are to continue up the wall as a backsplash, remember to plot the layout lines on the wall with a level to make sure that they're perfectly vertical. For a good-looking job, always line up the grout joints on the countertop with those on the wall. (For further information on laying out and installing countertop tiles, see Chapters 10 and 11.)

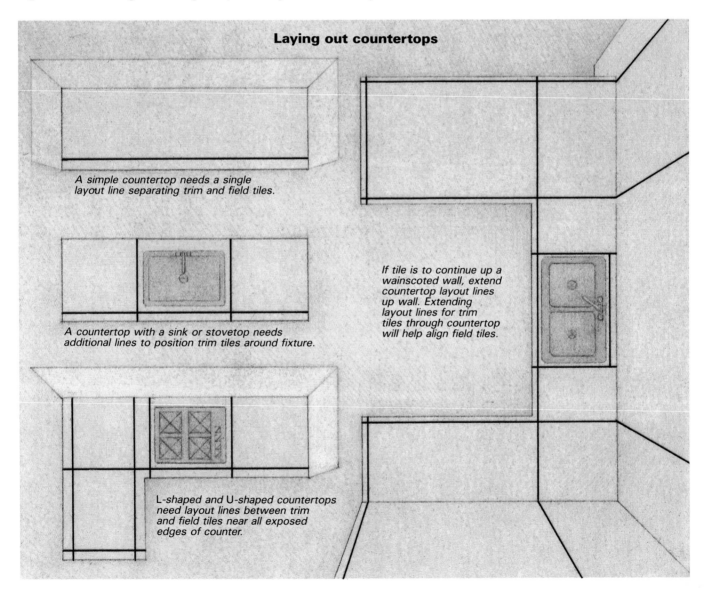

Laying out countertops

A simple countertop needs a single layout line separating trim and field tiles.

A countertop with a sink or stovetop needs additional lines to position trim tiles around fixture.

If tile is to continue up a wainscoted wall, extend countertop layout lines up wall. Extending layout lines for trim tiles through countertop will help align field tiles.

L-shaped and U-shaped countertops need layout lines between trim and field tiles near all exposed edges of counter.

Laying out tile set on the diagonal

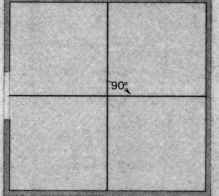

1. *Plot two reference lines, square to area being tiled.*

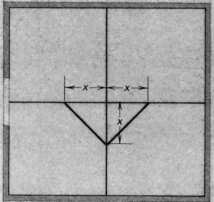

2. *Plot two neighboring isoceles triangles at point of intersection.*

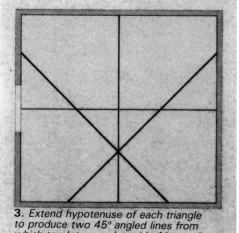

3. *Extend hypotenuse of each triangle to produce two 45° angled lines from which to plot a regular grid of layout lines.*

Laying out hexagonal and ogee tiles

Hexagonal tile

Ogee tile

Laying out irregular tiles and setting patterns

While it's a relatively simple task to lay out square or rectangular tiles in similarly shaped spaces, laying out irregularly shaped tiles or laying out standard tiles in unusually shaped spaces can present more of a challenge. Keep in mind, however, that all consistently shaped tiles, no matter what their contour, have points of reference that can be used to align them, and that any space can be inscribed with reference and layout lines to aid in setting these tiles.

In the case of hexagonal and octagonal tiles, the flat sides and pointed corners both offer places for alignment. Each of these tile shapes can be aligned to the same kind of layout lines described earlier, that is, a grid of layout lines intersecting at right angles. In fact, even penny-round tiles can be set to the 90° grid. When it comes time to set irregularly shaped tiles, however, the grid won't offer as perfect a guide for spreading adhesive. Because of their shape, the tiles won't butt up against the layout lines along their full length or width. This isn't a big problem, just something to bear in mind. Also keep in mind that tiles in any shape other than squares or rectangles will overlap the layout lines. If you have trouble following the layout lines, just lay a straightedge on top of the already set tiles to "bridge" parts of the lines covered by tile. While more complex in shape, ogee tiles nonetheless have repeating points that can be used for aligning them with layout lines formed into a 90° grid.

When setting floor, wall or countertop tiles on the diagonal, keep all the layout lines at a true 45° angle to the edge of the installation. There are various ways to do this, but I start by snapping a pair of intersecting reference lines to form a 90° angle, as I would for any installation. Then, starting from the intersection of the lines, I measure out equal distances in three directions, as shown in the drawing at left. Connecting the points and extending the lines forms a large *X* on the setting floor, and these lines become the new reference lines. Layout lines can then be projected as needed from the new reference lines.

Diagonally set tile, with and without a border

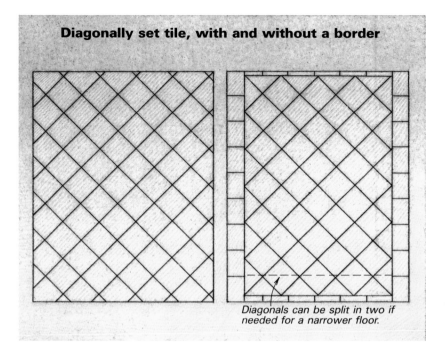

Diagonals can be split in two if needed for a narrower floor.

Setting tile on the diagonal has long been popular, especially for floors, but many setters shy away from this pattern because of the numerous cuts required at the perimeter of the installation and the often unattractive look of these cuts, as shown on the left side of the drawing above. To give this kind of installation a professional, finished look, try using the standard border treatment employed by old-time setters. After diagonally setting the full field, they cut enough tiles in half on the diagonal to fill in the remaining spaces around the perimeter. Finally, they bordered this square or rectangle of diagonally placed tile with a row of full or, if need be, cut tiles set square to the field. The border tiles can even be a different tile, as long as they are compatible in thickness and durability with the field tiles. To achieve this kind of layout, I usually plot a standard diagonal layout grid on the floor, wall or countertop. Once this is in place, it's not too hard to see how big the field should be in order to leave a single row of tiles between the field and the edge of the installation. A straightedge is generally all I need to guide the placement of the bordering trim tiles. It takes a bit of figuring, but the results are well worth the effort. Because the border serves as a decorative element in the installation, I don't mind using tiles here that are less than half-width. Chances are that in setting any other arrangement of tile you can imagine, a 90° grid of reference and layout lines will do the job. □

Sample tile layouts in irregular patterns

Tile is usually set in a simple grid layout, but many other layouts are also possible.

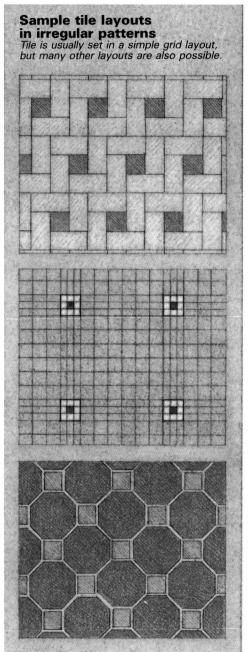

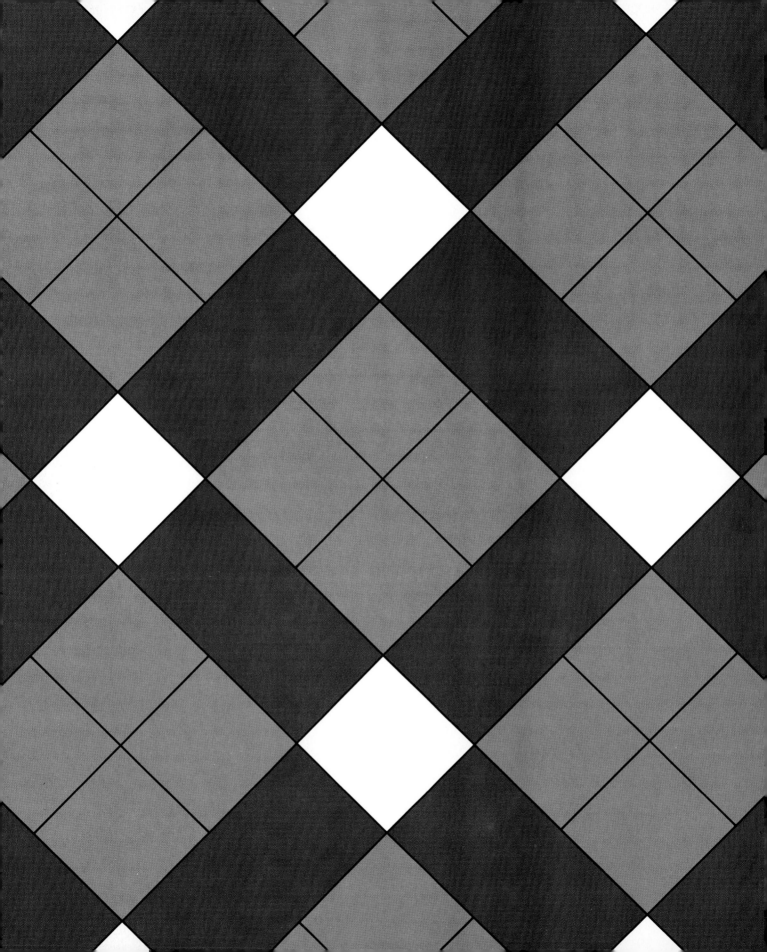

PART II.
Setting Tile: Projects, Special Installations and Repairs

Floor plan of kitchen

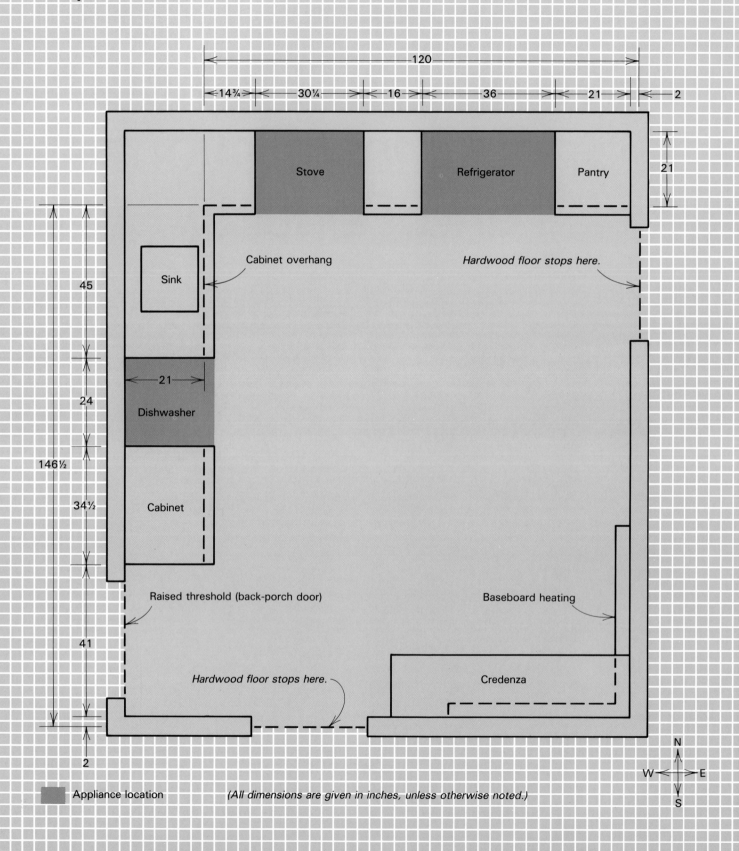

120

14¾   30¼   16   36   21   2

Stove   Refrigerator   Pantry

21

Cabinet overhang

Hardwood floor stops here.

45

Sink

21

24

Dishwasher

146½

34½

Cabinet

Raised threshold (back-porch door)

Baseboard heating

41

Hardwood floor stops here.

Credenza

2

N
W ← → E
S

■ Appliance location   (All dimensions are given in inches, unless otherwise noted.)

Thinset Floor

Tiling this floor was part of a kitchen remodeling job that was under way before I was called in. The owner had halted work on the floor after another contractor had nailed down, over two existing layers of vinyl flooring, a layer of ⅛-in.-thick lauan plywood as a setting bed for the tiles. The customer had noticed that the plywood was springy in places and that there was no clearance to install tiles below the dishwasher. She phoned the office and asked if I could take a look at the job.

Sizing up the job

When I went to the house to measure the job, the situation was worse than I thought. The whole first floor of the house sloped from west to east, leaving the kitchen floor out of level 2 in. in the space of 10 ft. Of the three doorways leading into the kitchen, two were located on the high side of the room and one was on the low side. New kitchen cabinets had already been installed on two walls and were perched on 2-in.-high shims on the room's downhill side. This arrangement meant that the cabinet's rough toe kick, which the customer wanted tiled, was suspended in midair at one end.

Normally, a condition like this could easily be remedied by floating a mortar bed to level up the floor. But in this case that would have left a 2-in.-high step down into the living room from the doorway on the low side of the kitchen. A step might not even be objectionable, except that since none was needed at the two doors on the high side, this solution would awkwardly point up the house's structural problems. (Some people might also find a step hazardous.) The only other way to even out the floor would be to correct the framing or the foundation, an expensive prospect that was beyond the customer's budget. Since she definitely wanted to tile the kitchen floor and decided she could live with it being out of level, I changed installation plans: we would rip up the lauan plywood (it was just too thin to support tiles), remove the two layers of vinyl flooring below (they contributed in part to the floor's springiness), and install a sturdy, suitable setting bed.

When I yanked a piece of the lauan plywood off and pried up a section of the two sheets of vinyl, I found that the first sheet was glued to a ½-in.-thick particleboard underlayment, which, in turn, was nailed to 1x8 subflooring. The subflooring was fine, but the particleboard, an inappropriate substrate for tiling, would need to be removed. I decided on ½-in.-thick, AC exterior plywood for the setting bed, which would strengthen the floor but would still leave room to tile underneath the dishwasher once the other underlayments had been removed. Because this installation would not get wet, other than an occasional washing, no waterproofing membrane was necessary, and the tile could be set directly over the plywood.

For a plywood setting bed like this, an organic mastic rated for use with plywood could be used, but I prefer a suitable latex thinset or an epoxy for floors because these adhesives are stronger than mastics. In this case, a strong adhesive was especially important because the floor had a crown, or hump, in the middle, produced by structural forces that might still be at play. After considering an epoxy adhesive, I opted for a latex thinset because of the client's budget and the extra expense she had already borne for the first contractor's efforts. While the compressive strength of the adhesive I wanted to use is not as high as that of an epoxy, its greater flexibility made it better suited than epoxy to the plywood underlayment. To strengthen the adhesive, I decided to combine the thinset's liquid latex component with the dry ingredients for a water-mixed thinset.

Despite the fact that this would not be a wet installation, I suggested that vitreous tiles be used because of their strength and durability. And because of the crown in the floor, I recommended that the tiles be 8 in. square or smaller—larger tiles would not sit flat over the hump without their corners sticking up. Knowing that the floor would undoubtedly be subject to slippery spills from time to time, the customer wanted a tile with a non-slick glaze. She selected four samples that she liked, and took them home to test their practicality by grinding her heel into each to see how well it would stand up and, in turn, clean up. In the end she picked a sand-colored, Italian floor tile 7$\frac{15}{16}$ in. square. She chose to pair the tile with a tan-colored, sanded grout, specially formulated for joints wider than $\frac{1}{8}$ in. Although I generally prefer a $\frac{1}{8}$-in.-wide joint, we had agreed on a $\frac{3}{16}$-in.-wide grout joint to help mask the presence of the floor's crown.

Estimating tile and materials

On my initial visit to the client's house, I had sketched in my notebook a floor plan of the kitchen, showing room dimensions with the baseboards removed and with indents for the dishwasher, stove and refrigerator, since each cutout was to be tiled (see drawing, p. 128). I also noted where the cabinets overhung the floor, where the baseboard heating elements were located, where the tiles met hardwood flooring in other rooms and where there was a raised threshold at the back door to the porch. All these factors would affect the eventual layout. Once I knew the size of the tile and grout joint selected, I could proceed to work out the layout on paper and to calculate the amount of tile needed for the job.

I used $\frac{1}{8}$-in. graph paper to do a detailed floor plan because it's easy to scale out a drawing on this paper and to fairly accurately lay out a floor. Each graph-paper square represents a 6-in.-square floor area (I didn't worry about fractions of an inch on this drawing). Although I usually have to make some adjustments on any job once I begin to check the room for square and to do the actual layout, working things out on paper beforehand helps speed up this process.

Next I made up a list of tile and grout-joint dimensions, which I would refer to when doing the layout. This list, shown on the facing page, begins with the combined width of a single tile and grout joint (8⅛ in.) and ends with the combined width of 18 tiles and grout joints (146¼ in.), as this measurement was nearest the room's longest dimension.

Since the door on the east wall led from the living room into the kitchen and the tiles abutting the hardwood floor at the doorway would be very visible, I wanted to use full tiles at this point. To calculate the number of rows that would fit from this doorway to the back of the toe kick under the cabinets on the west wall, I checked the room dimensions on the sketch and the tile/grout-joint list. The width of the room at this point was 120 in., which meant that 14 full tiles would fit, with a 6¼-in.-wide cut tile tucked under the overhanging cabinets. The cut tile was to be more than half-size, so it would not detract from the floor's appearance even if there were no overhang. Except for the tile at the doorway, the remaining tile in the first row along the east wall would have to be trimmed by 2 in. to accommodate the width of the wall. Since this cut, like that across the room, would be more than half-size, it would not be visually distracting.

Looking next at the length of the room from the toe kick on the north wall to the doorway on the south wall, I saw that the tile would again abut a hardwood floor at this door and I wanted to use full tiles here, too. Within the 146½-in. length, I found from my list that 18 full tiles would fit, with a ¼-in. space left over. This gap would be hidden at the back of the toe kick, but even if there were no toe kick, it would still be obscured by the overhanging cabinets.

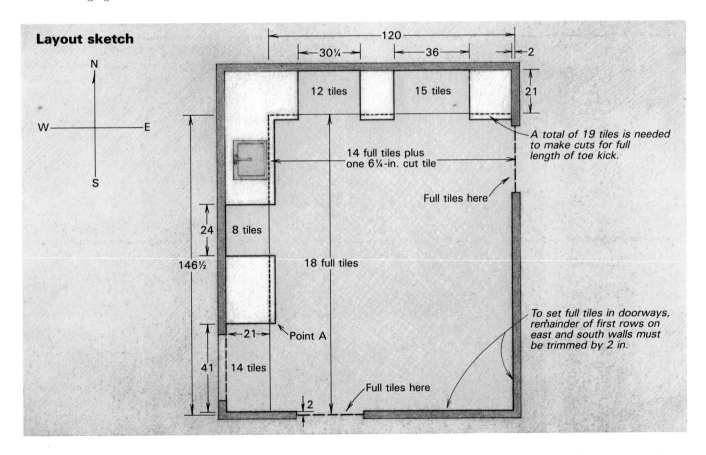

Layout sketch

12 tiles
15 tiles
A total of 19 tiles is needed to make cuts for full length of toe kick.

14 full tiles plus one 6¼-in. cut tile
Full tiles here

8 tiles
18 full tiles

21
Point A
14 tiles
To set full tiles in doorways, remainder of first rows on east and south walls must be trimmed by 2 in.

Full tiles here

Having established the crucial spots where full tiles had to be used, I wanted to check the rest of the room to see if the proposed layout would work. The one area that concerned me was the floor at the corner of the cabinet near the door to the back porch (point *A* in the drawing on p. 131). The distance from point *A* to the threshold at the south door was 43 in., into which I could fit 5 full tiles with a 2⅜-in. space left over. This meant that there would need to be a strip of cut tiles 2⅜ in. wide along the base of the cabinet. Shifting the layout 2⅜ in. north would eliminate the cut tiles at the cabinet, but would produce a gap of the same width at the threshold. Since there was no other alternative and a compromise had to be made, I chose to place the cuts along the base of the cabinet, where they would be far less obvious than at the threshold. This layout also meant that the first row of tiles along the south wall on either side of the threshold would need to be trimmed by 2 in.

The areas beneath the dishwasher, stove and refrigerater would be hidden once the appliances were repositioned, and I was therefore not too concerned with the layout there. In fact, these locations were just the place to make use of leftover cut tile and any tile with surface blemishes.

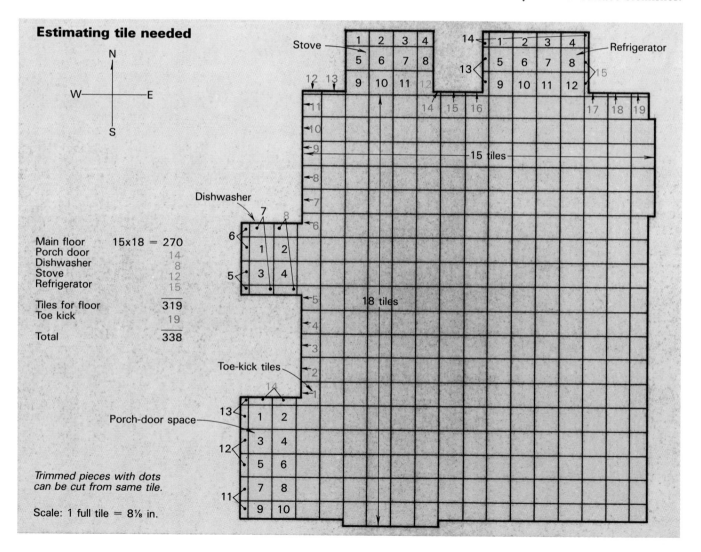

Estimating tile needed

Main floor	15x18 =	270
Porch door		14
Dishwasher		8
Stove		12
Refrigerator		15
Tiles for floor		319
Toe kick		19
Total		338

Trimmed pieces with dots can be cut from same tile.

Scale: 1 full tile = 8⅛ in.

Once I had settled on a layout, I could calculate the number of tiles needed. This can be done either by calculating the square footage covered and then ordering the tile by the square foot (it's usually sold this way), or by adding up the number of individual tiles called for by the layout. Since the latter method is more reliable (see p. 112), I referred to the floor plan and layout to do the count, as shown in the drawing on the facing page.

For each east-west row in the main portion of the floor, a total of 14 full tiles and a 6¼-in. tile cut from a full tile would be needed, that is, 15 tiles in all. Each north-south row here required 18 full tiles. The number of tiles needed for the main area of the floor was therefore 270 (15 x 18 = 270). The count of tiles needed for the other sections of the floor was as follows: 14 for the porch-door area, 8 for the space under the dishwasher, 12 for the stove recess, 15 for beneath the refrigerator, and 19 for the toe kick along all the cabinets. The total counted number of tiles needed for the floor was thus 338. To be on the safe side, in the event that some tiles arrive at the scene broken or I miscut one or two, I always order more than needed. On this job I added 10 tiles to the count and ordered 348 in all. The customer could store any leftovers in case any future repairs were required.

Installing the underlayment

I don't like to start work on any job until all the tiles and setting materials have arrived at the supplier's shop. Should any of the materials needed be unavailable or different than ordered, I may need to change the layout or installation plans. Once the materials have been delivered to the job site, I begin work.

The first step on this job was to disconnect the water supply and electrical lines to the appliances and move them out of the kitchen. Next I took the baseboards off the walls and then tore out the lauan plywood with a pry bar and hammer. To make it easier to remove the vinyl flooring and particleboard underlayment, I cut through the flooring along the toe kick with a small-diameter sawblade mounted in an electric hand grinder—it was a tight space, so I used extra care to avoid damaging the cabinets.

I also made several cuts with the saw a few feet away from the kick so that I could easily pry up the old layers of the floor. Because the sawblade is only 4 in. in diameter and the saw has no depth adjustment, it can cut only ¾ in. deep when mounted in my hand grinder. Thus I didn't have to worry about sawing into the joists. Once the flooring was removed, I extracted any nails sticking up on the subfloor.

When plywood underlayment is installed, the joints should be staggered over the joints in a plywood subfloor. But in this case, the existing subfloor was made of 1x8s, and so there wasn't much I could do to stagger the joints. After thoroughly vacuuming the entire floor, I installed the new underlayment by working in the following sequence: I started in one corner of the room and cut a piece of plywood to fit, with about a ⅛-in. gap planned between sheets. (These gaps would be filled with adhesive when the tile was set, effectively edge-gluing the sheets.) With the plywood laid in position, I snapped chalk lines on it to indicate the location of the floor joists, which I determined from the placement of the nails in the surrounding subfloor. Then I picked up the plywood sheet, turned it on edge, and caulked a bead of construction adhesive (rated for floor use) around the perimeter of the sheet and in parallel lines down its length about every 8 in. Once I had relaid the sheet, I secured it by hammering in a few 1½-in. ring-shank nails, starting in one corner and working toward the opposite corner. Next I nailed down the sheet every 6 in., then went back to

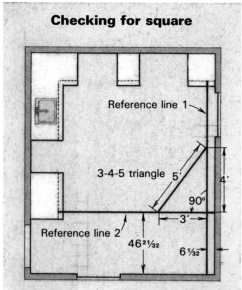
the chalk lines and used 3-in. nails every 6 in. to firmly anchor into the joists. Finally, I ran my hand over all the nails and hammered down any whose heads stuck up (these might crack the tile). I moved all my tools onto the first installed segment of underlayment, and proceeded sheet by sheet to cover the floor.

In the process of installing the plywood, I came across one sheet that was slightly warped. To counteract the warping, I turned the sheet concave-side-down before measuring and cutting it. I also added a little extra construction adhesive to this sheet and nailed in a few more nails once it was in position to ensure that it would lie flat.

Snapping layout lines

Doing the actual layout on this floor would be simple. In effect, I had already figured out the position of the layout lines when I did the layout on paper and calculated the number of tiles needed. Since the planned layout would work only if the walls and cabinets at the job site were square to each other, however, I needed to check this before chalking any layout lines. Two reference lines on the floor were required, from which I could measure the cabinets, toe kick and other areas to determine if the room was square.

Inasmuch as I had planned my layout with full tiles at the east and south thresholds, I decided to use these points to help me establish the reference lines. To begin, I measured out from the edge of the east threshold a distance of one tile and one grout joint, subtracted half the thickness of the grout joint, and made a mark. This would give me a point representing the center of a grout joint. From my earlier layout on paper I knew that tiles along the east wall would have 2 in. cut from them, so I measured out from the wall a distance identical to the one I had measured at the threshold, subtracted 2 in., and made another mark. Then I connected the two marks with a snapped chalk line to get a line parallel to the east wall, which represented the center of a grout joint between the first and second rows of tile. I would have repeated the process on the south wall for the second line, but because it would be difficult to work beneath the built-in credenza, I made my measurements so that they would put this reference line between the sixth and seventh rows of tile. By positioning the reference lines in the center of what would become grout joints, I could later use these lines, once established as square, as layout lines.

With these two lines in place, I could begin to check the room for square by plotting a 3-4-5 triangle on the reference lines. If the east and south walls were square to one another, a triangle plotted on the lines with a base of 3 ft. and a height of 4 ft. would have a hypotenuse of 5 ft. (For more information on 3-4-5 triangles, see p. 114.) If the hypotenuse were shorter or longer than 5 ft., I would know that these walls were out of square and I would have to adjust the reference lines. Unless the walls were drastically off, this adjustment would only slightly affect the outermost row of tiles along these two walls and would keep the tiles in the rest of the room properly in square.

To begin making the 3-4-5 triangle on the two reference lines, I measured north 4 ft. on the first line from the point where the two lines intersected and penciled a mark. Next I drew a mark on the second line 3 ft. west of the point of intersection. When I measured the distance between the two marks, completing the triangle, I found that it was exactly 5 ft. This meant that the east and south walls were square to one another. (For information on adjusting the reference lines if the walls prove not to be square, see p. 115.)

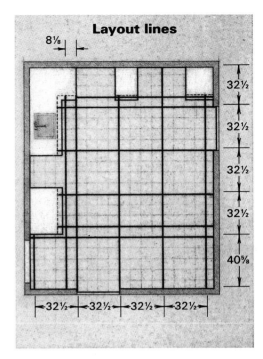

Layout lines

8⅛

32½
32½
32½
32½
40⅝

32½ 32½ 32½ 32½

After projecting a pair of reference lines off the east and south walls, I made a 3-4-5 triangle to see if the walls were square.

Next I wanted to check to see if the cabinets on the west and north walls were square to each other. If the toe kicks on these walls proved parallel to the first and second layout lines respectively, I would know that the cabinets were square. To check whether each kick was parallel to the opposing line, I simply measured the distance to the line from each end of the kick and then compared the measurements. In doing this, I knew that if I found the measurements to be the same, the kick would be parallel. The west toe kick turned out not to be parallel to the east reference line. Instead, it angled out from the line about ½ in. at the south end of the cabinets. This meant that the tiles along this kick would have to be cut to fit the angle. Since I had planned to cut these tiles anyway, however, and since the kick would largely hide the tapering cuts, this was not a problem.

If the north toe kick was not parallel to the south reference line, however, it would cause problems. If the kick angled away from the line, the ¼-in. space planned in the layout to fall between the last row of tiles and the kick would increase and need to be filled with slivers of tile. Since this would be an unattractive solution, I could instead solve the problem by shimming out the kick's depth with plywood equal in thickness to the width of the taper.

If, on the other hand, the toe kick angled toward the line, the tiles at the kick would need to be trimmed. Though this was not an ideal solution, it would not detract too much from the visual effect of the entire floor. After taking the necessary measurements, I was pleased to find that the north kick was parallel to the reference line.

With the room checked for square, I was ready to snap layout lines on the setting bed. Ordinarily in a room this size, I would probably need only two reference lines to keep the tiles straight, provided I could get tile spacers long enough to extend beyond the rounded corners of this tile. (I would want to use more layout lines with smaller tiles, regardless of whether spacers were available.) Unfortunately, I couldn't get the spacers I needed quickly because the local supplier had none in stock, so instead I added more layout lines.

For the sake of accuracy, I projected all the layout lines off the two reference lines. I wanted enough layout lines on the setting bed to quickly and accurately set the full tiles and also to separate these tiles from the cut tiles. First, I chalked lines that were parallel to the two reference lines and spaced 32½ in. apart. This produced a series of boxes, most of which would hold 16 tiles each, all of them comfortably within my reach. Then I snapped additional lines around the north, west and south walls to mark the grout joint between the full tiles and the cut tiles. While setting up this layout grid obviously takes time, I am firmly convinced that it saves time in the long run, as the actual setting goes much more quickly and efficiently than it would otherwise.

Setting the tiles

Because the thinset adhesive I would be using sets up in about 30 minutes, I gathered and arranged all the tools and materials needed on the job before starting to tile. I also took time to trim all the cut tiles so I wouldn't have to keep stopping once the tiling was under way. I figured the size of the cuts by subtracting 3/16 in. (the width of one grout joint) from the distance between the toe kick or wall and the nearest parallel layout line. This would give me some space between the tile and the toe kick, as well as some space at the layout line. The space between the tile and the kick or wall would be filled with caulk instead of grout to allow the floor to freely expand and contract. If this space were grouted, the floor would have no room in which to expand and, when it did, might cause the tiles to crack (and might also damage the walls and cabinets).

Once everything was ready and I had staged the cut tiles around the perimeter of the room, I had to decide where to start setting tile. Since I was working alone and there were a number of cuts to set, I decided to begin with these and then to move on to the full tiles. Given the many layout lines, I could start setting full tiles anywhere on the outermost row of one of the large layout squares, provided I could eventually work my way out one of the doors. Because I had set my tile saw up just outside the east doorway and I always like to have quick access to it when tiling, I decided to start in the southwest corner of the room and work toward the east door. The setting sequence is shown in the drawing at left.

Setting sequence

Margin tiles (shown in blue) were set first. After all cut tiles had been set, sections of full tiles were installed in above sequence.

A number of cut tiles had to be set around the perimeter of the installation, so I decided to stage and set these tiles first (left). After sponging down the perimeter of the installation, I spread and combed adhesive and then back-buttered each cut tile as I set it (center). With the cuts at the perimeter of the floor set, I installed the cuts on the face of the toe kick, using wedges to keep the tiles in position until the adhesive had set up (right).

I next hauled six boxes of tile into the kitchen, leaving the rest outside the door to keep them out of the way. I checked the coverage table on the adhesive's label and estimated how much thinset to mix to complete about a fourth of the floor. I didn't want to mix more than I could use in the half hour the thinset would take to set up. By starting out slowly, I could check the adhesive's actual set-up time under the conditions on this job and, if I wanted, adjust the amount I mixed for the rest of the floor.

After preparing the thinset, I sponged off any dust that had settled on the area of the setting bed I wanted to cover with adhesive. Then I spread the adhesive with the unnotched edge of a ¼-in. square-notched trowel, covering each area with a layer of adhesive that was ¼ in. to ⅜ in. thick. (For full instructions on applying adhesive, see p. 57.) I next combed the thinset with the notched edge of the trowel to produce ridges of uniform height. To make sure that the adhesive was the right consistency and the layer of adhesive the right depth, I set and removed one tile and checked it. Since the underside was correctly covered with thinset (to judge this, see photos, p. 59), I proceeded to back-butter and set the cut tiles around the perimeter of the room. Then I set tiles on the face of the toe kicks, using wedges to hold them ⅛ in. off the floor tiles until the adhesive had set up.

With the cut tiles set, I staged the full tiles around the room, sponged down the setting bed in the first square along the west wall, spread the adhesive in this square (making sure to spread it just up to the layout lines so that the lines would remain visible) and started setting the tile. I laid down all the tiles in one square and then began aligning them by butting the first vertical row snugly against a long straightedge, positioned half the width of a grout joint from the layout line. I worked my way across the square, adjusting each vertical row in relation to the first row and then aligning the rows horizontally in the same fashion. As I completed positioning the tiles in each square, I placed a beating block over each one and gave it a few light taps with the hammer to ensure full contact of the tile and thinset.

After beating in the tiles, I rinsed the sponge, wrung it out well and cleaned up spilled adhesive from the face of the tiles. At the same time, I readjusted any tiles that had been nudged out of position by the sponge or the beating block.

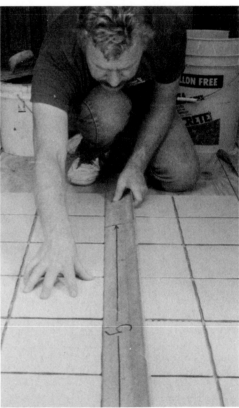

Working in one square of the layout grid at a time, I spread and combed adhesive (left), then set the full tiles (top). After initially positioning the tiles, I straightened each row horizontally and vertically by butting the tiles against a straightedge, which was long enough to reach into the neighboring section of tiles already aligned (above).

At the beginning I set the tile quickly to keep the thinset from setting up in the bucket. Then, as I approached the bottom of the bucket, I slowed down to look over the tiles set and make sure that they were all properly aligned and cleaned. Whenever I spotted a tile that sat a bit too high, I wiggled it down by hand or with a straightedge if it was out of reach. When I occasionally spied a tile that sat too low and needed repositioning but which was beyond my reach, I covered the path to it with plywood rectangles measuring 1 ft. by 2 ft. by ¾ in. so that I could walk over the newly tiled surface. I then back-buttered the offending tile with thinset, seated it properly and got off the floor quickly. Finally, I checked to see if any tiles under the plywood needed to be realigned with the straightedge.

I continued tiling until I had used up every bit of the thinset in the bucket, even though this meant that I had worked my way into the next tiling area. Before mixing any more thinset, I carefully cleaned all traces of it out of the bucket to prevent any old, hardening thinset from contaminating the next batch and causing it to set up prematurely. When I had finished setting the entire floor, I let the tiles sit overnight to allow the adhesive to set up sufficiently before grouting.

Grouting and finishing

Before I could start grouting, I had to do some preparation. First I went back over the full surface of the tilework with dampened steel wool to remove any excess adhesive. (For further discussion of my method for cleaning up adhesives, see p. 60.) Next I used a utility knife to pare down any adhesive that clogged the grout joints (a grout saw would also work). Ideally, the adhesive should be pared down to the underlayment, but this is a lot of work that's not absolutely necessary. Instead, I concentrated on removing any thinset in the joints that was higher than the ridges of adhesive. I also cleaned away any thinset clinging to the sides of the tiles and between the tiles and the walls and cabinets. The gap between the cut tiles and the walls and toe kicks would later be caulked to allow for expansion of the floor. Finally, I vacuumed the floor to remove any loose particles of adhesive from the joints.

The grout for this job was a sanded grout with which I mixed a latex additive to help prevent staining, which is likely in a kitchen. By consulting the grout manufacturer's coverage table, I estimated that the floor would need about 30 lb. of dry grout, which I mixed, allowed to slake and mixed again. (For more information on mixing and applying grout, see p. 62.)

To prevent kneeling on fresh grout, I wanted to grout the room in the same sequence that I had tiled it. So I began in the southwest corner, spreading grout over an area of about 10 sq. ft. To ensure that the density of each grout joint would be consistent, I followed the same grouting procedure throughout the room. As I worked each section of floor, I first dumped on more grout than I would actually need, since the weight of the grout mass would help fill the joints. I spread the grout, holding the grout trowel at about a 30° angle to the floor. To make sure that each joint was fully packed, I spread grout over the area twice, working the trowel from two different directions and firmly pushing the grout into each joint. When I felt that each joint was densely packed, I held the trowel at a 90° angle to the tiles to cut away the excess grout, scraping diagonally across the joints to keep the trowel from gouging them.

At this point I moved from the first 10-sq.-ft. area into the next and began grouting it. When I reached the same stage in the grouting sequence in the second section, I went back to the first to see if the grout had begun to set up. By working in this fashion, I was able to have the final cleaning

I let the adhesive harden overnight, then I began grouting the tile, spreading and cleaning up the grout in about a 10-sq.-ft. area at a time.

keep pace with the spreading. This was important because the additive I used with the grout made it very sticky and difficult to remove when dry. Since the temperature in the room was in the mid 70s this day, I found that I could spread quite a bit of grout before needing to clean up. In fact, I was able to pack a 3-ft.-wide strip of tiles from the southwest corner of the room along the full length of the west wall before cleaning.

Cleaning the grout residue from the surface of the tiles takes patience. The method I use, described in full on p. 65, keeps the work to a minimum. After I had cleaned the first 3-ft.-wide strip of tiles, I checked the grout in the bucket, which I found had begun to stiffen up. I stirred it with the margin trowel to loosen it up, and then grouted and cleaned another 3-ft.-wide strip next to the first. Then I changed direction, grouting a 3-ft.-wide strip east to west at the south wall, so that I could eventually grout my way out the door on the east wall. At the same time that I cleaned the joints, I shaped them with the sponge, making them slightly concave on top.

After the floor had been grouted and cleaned, I waited 15 minutes for the moisture on the surface of the tiles to dry and the grout to set up. At that point, a cement haze appeared on the tiles, which I rubbed away with a soft cloth. If the haze had not come off easily, I would have used a barely dampened sponge. The important point is to clean the grout haze as soon as possible, before it becomes extremely difficult to remove.

After the grout had dried and hardened for almost three days, I capped the joint at the walls and cabinet sides with a bead of clear silicone caulk (I could have also used butyl caulk). This cap prevents dirt from accumulating in the joint, which would interfere with the floor's free expansion. I also covered the grout joint between the base of the toe kick and the tiles with a thin bead of caulk. If there is any movement between the cabinets and the floor, the caulk will keep the joint clean if it cracks. Finally, I moved the appliances back into the kitchen. □

Layout sketch

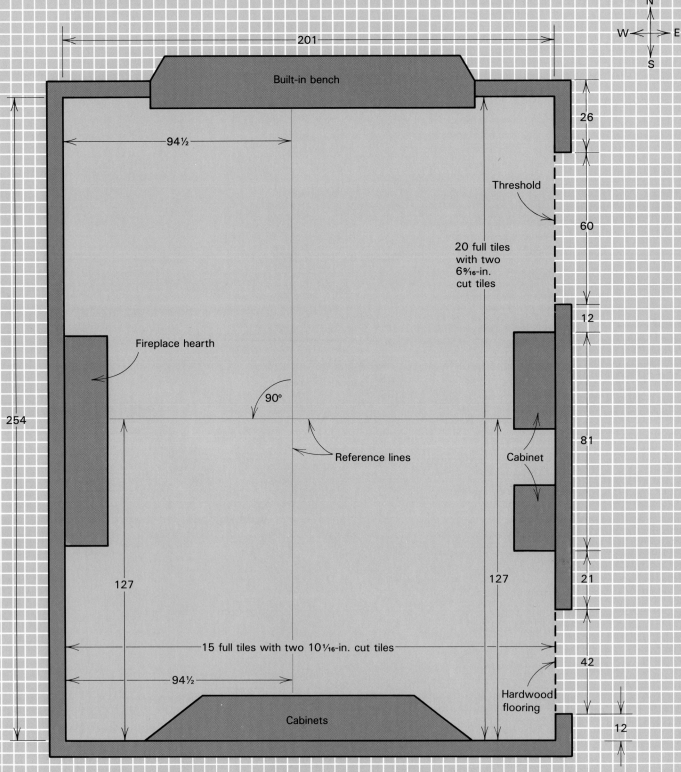

201

Built-in bench

N

W —←—→— E

S

94½

26

Threshold

60

20 full tiles
with two
6⁹⁄₁₆-in.
cut tiles

12

Fireplace hearth

254

90°

81

Reference lines

Cabinet

127

127

21

15 full tiles with two 10¹⁄₁₆-in. cut tiles

42

94½

Hardwood
flooring

Cabinets

12

(All dimensions are given in inches, unless otherwise noted.)

Mortar-Bed Floor

This job was designed by an architect with whom I had worked for several years and whose crews always provided me with carefully constructed substrates. The installation was to serve as a solar-gain floor for a heavily insulated family room, which was being added to the existing house. Because of its solar-gain function, the setting bed had to be a floated bed of mortar and would need to be thicker than a conventional mortar floor. Specified by the architect as a 2-in.-thick bed (about twice the thickness of most mortar beds), this floor would act like a heat sink, absorbing the heat of the California sun by day and releasing the warmth back into the house at night when the incoming fog chilled the air.

Sizing up the job

The room was basically rectangular, measuring overall 16 ft. 9 in. wide by 21 ft. 2 in. long. On the north wall was a built-in bench below a bay window; on the south wall was a cabinet with angled sides. On the east wall were French doors leading to a deck, two cabinets and the entryway to the rest of the house; on the west wall a fireplace hearth extended into the room.

The architect had planned for the extra-thick floor by making the subfloor in the addition 2¾ in. lower than normal. To support the weight of the mortar and tile, his crew had installed a 1-in.-thick plywood subfloor. Whereas tiles set directly on a plywood subfloor would normally require a double-layer bed at least 1⅜ in. thick to prevent flexing, a reinforced mortar floor can be set on plywood as thin as ¾ in. because the mortar itself provides some stiffness to the installation. In this subfloor, the crew had cut four small rectangular openings to house the combination heating/air-conditioning ducts. To prevent mortar from getting into the ducts while the floor was being floated, they had sealed the openings with scrapwood blocks that extended above the subfloor about 3 in. I was able to pack mortar tightly against the blocks, and later when they were removed, neat, rectangular openings sat ready to accept the heating registers.

Materials list

Subfloor:
1-in. AC exterior plywood

Curing membrane:
15-lb. tar-saturated felt
paper (tar paper)

Mortar bed:
3 parts mason's sand and 1 part
portland cement, mixed with liquid
latex mortar additive

Mortar-bed reinforcement:
20-gauge, 1-in. mesh poultry netting

Adhesive:
1 part 40-mesh sand and 1 part
portland cement, mixed with liquid
latex thinset additive

Tile:
Mexican paver, 11⅝ in. square,
355 pieces

Grout:
1 part mason's sand and 1 part
portland cement, mixed with liquid
latex mortar additive

Tile sealer:
Penetrating oil

Since normal expansion and contraction of a floor this size might cause the mortar bed and tile to crack, I decided to combine a liquid latex mortar additive with both the mortar and the grout to increase their flexibility (see p. 71). To protect the walls from damage by the floor's expansion, I also planned to install an expansion joint around the perimeter of the floor. While the expansion joint would be hidden by baseboard trim around the walls, it would be visible at the fireplace hearth and so was omitted there. I would simply grout this area.

The mortar bed was to be covered with 11⅝-in.-square Mexican pavers, which were ¾ in. thick and had been stained and sealed with two coats of sealer. Unlike many Mexican pavers, the tiles in this batch happened to be a remarkably consistent 11⅝ in. square. Because the customer wanted a grout joint narrower than the ½-in.-wide joint ordinarily used with irregular pavers, we agreed on ⅜ in. This width would additionally simplify the layout, since one tile and grout joint together would measure an even 12 in.

The architect had specified a cement-colored grout for the tiles, with which I would mix the latex additive. Consulting the grout coverage tables I've compiled for myself over the last several years, I found that if I used ready-mixed dry grout, I would need nine 25-lb. sacks of grout and about 4½ gallons of additive to cover the 355 sq. ft. of tile I calculated was needed. With that much grout required, this job was going to get expensive.

I decided to mix my own grout for several reasons: It would cost less (I would use as a base the same sand and cement that went into the deck mud for the mortar bed). I knew the color would satisfy both the architect and the client. And most important, the planned ⅜-in.-wide joints were large enough for me to question whether commercially prepared grout would eventually crack. The sand I would be using for the deck mud was much coarser than that in prepared grouts, and though it would probably be too coarse for a joint ¼ in. wide by ¼ in. deep, it would be ideal for these ⅜-in.-wide by ¾-in.-deep joints.

Estimating tile

Since the tile and grout joint together would measure 12 in., I didn't really need to make my usual tile/grout-joint list. I could simply rely on my tape measure or calculator.

The shape of this floor was relatively simple, but in doing the layout I had to allow for the thickness of the expansion joint around the perimeter. With my preliminary sketch and calculator in hand, I figured I could fit across the full 16-ft. 9-in. width of the room 15 full tiles and two 10¹⁄₁₆-in. cuts. (As shown in the drawing on the facing page, I had accounted for two ¼-in. expansion joints and an additional ⅜-in. grout joint in my calculations.) Across the floor's full 21-ft. 2-in. length, I found I could fit 20 full tiles and two 6⁹⁄₁₆-in. cuts, again subtracting the two expansion joints and the additional grout joint. I then computed where I would plot the pair of reference lines on the actual floor so that they would fall in the center of what would become grout joints and thus could later be used as layout lines.

With the layout established, I could calculate the amount of tile needed for the job. Normally, I would determine the precise number of tiles the layout required. But because pavers often get broken in transit, and some of the unbroken tiles would nonetheless be too convex or concave to use, I instead figured how many tiles would cover the overall dimensions of the floor. Considering the obstructions in the room that wouldn't be tiled, I guessed that everything would average out in the end. The floor measured slightly more than 354½ sq. ft., and thus I ordered 355 tiles.

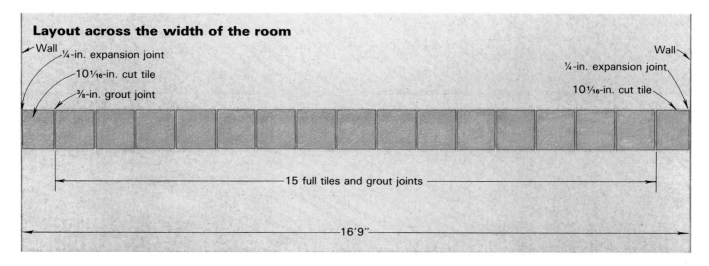

Layout across the width of the room

Wall
¼-in. expansion joint
10¹⁄₁₆-in. cut tile
⅜-in. grout joint

Wall
¼-in. expansion joint
10¹⁄₁₆-in. cut tile

15 full tiles and grout joints

16'9"

Installing the curing membrane and expansion joint

Like any floated mortar bed, this one would need a curing membrane placed beneath it to ensure that it cured properly (see p. 93). Unlike with 1-in.-thick mortar beds, however, I wouldn't need to laminate the curing membrane to the subfloor or seal its joints with cold-patch roofing asphalt for several reasons. It was unimportant if the subfloor in this family room got a little wet when the mortar bed was floated—the exterior-grade plywood would not delaminate. And since the absence of the asphalt would result in only a very small loss of moisture as the mortar bed cured, I wasn't concerned about the bed curing prematurely. Nor was I worried about the tar paper puckering, as it inevitably does when it comes in contact with wet mortar, because the additional weight of the extra-thick floor would keep it flat. I needed only to roll out the 15-lb. tar paper over the subfloor and staple it in place every 6 in., overlapping the seams by 2 in.

Next I installed the perimeter expansion joint. I ran the strip of compressible foam, ¼ in. thick by 4 in. wide, around the room's perimeter (except in front of the hearth), tacking it in place lightly to keep it against the wall. You can use dabs of construction adhesive or an occasional roofing nail for this, but try not to compress the foam. Once the floor has been floated, cut the strip flush with the top of the bed. Then after the tiles have been set, fill the remaining gap between the tiles and the wall with caulk.

Had this been a conventional 1-in.- to 1⅛-in.-thick mortar-bed floor, I would have next stapled chicken-wire mesh over the entire curing membrane to reinforce the bed, and then I would have floated the floor, as shown in the drawing on p. 87. But because this bed was to be 2 in. thick, the mesh needed to be sandwiched between two layers of mortar to be most effective as reinforcement. In theory, the reinforcing mesh should be placed in the middle of all mortar beds to prevent cracking. But in practice, I've found after hundreds of trouble-free installations that only the thicker beds really require this time-consuming treatment.

To position the mesh in the middle of the mortar bed and ensure that the bed was level on top, I needed to float the floor in two layers. The first layer, which would be about half the thickness of the final bed, needed to be level but not necessarily smooth. In fact, a somewhat coarse surface on this layer would enable the second layer to better grip it through the mesh. On floors smaller than 100 sq. ft., the entire first layer can be floated at once and covered with mesh before the top layer is begun. (On such floors, where you'll need to step on the first layer of mortar to float the second, use 2-ft. squares of ¾-in.-thick plywood to distribute your weight and protect the newly floated surface.) On larger floors, like this one, the bottom layer should be floated in stages, advancing only slightly ahead of the addition of the reinforcing mesh and the floating of the second layer of mortar. The area you cover in floating each section of the first layer isn't as important as getting all the layers laid down at the right time. If you float the entire first layer of mortar on a large floor before beginning the second layer, you risk having the lower layer dry out before the upper layer is complete. When this happens, a cold joint might form between the two batches because of their differing moisture content. When a cold joint is created, the two layers of mortar fail to marry, and later expansion in the cured bed may cause the two to separate at this point. Therefore, if this is your first mortar job, begin by working sections of only about 15 sq. ft. Then expand the area being floated as you get faster and more confident.

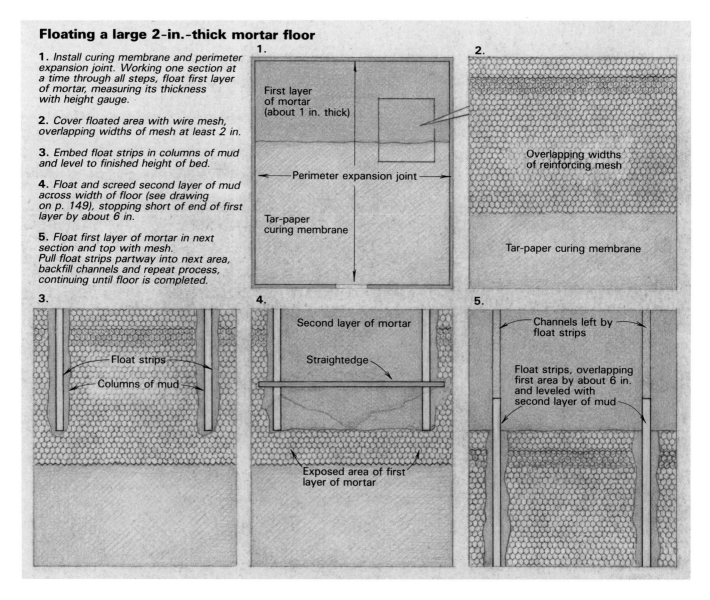

Floating a large 2-in.-thick mortar floor

1. Install curing membrane and perimeter expansion joint. Working one section at a time through all steps, float first layer of mortar, measuring its thickness with height gauge.

2. Cover floated area with wire mesh, overlapping widths of mesh at least 2 in.

3. Embed float strips in columns of mud and level to finished height of bed.

4. Float and screed second layer of mud across width of floor (see drawing on p. 149), stopping short of end of first layer by about 6 in.

5. Float first layer of mortar in next section and top with mesh. Pull float strips partway into next area, backfill channels and repeat process, continuing until floor is completed.

1.
First layer of mortar (about 1 in. thick)

Perimeter expansion joint

Tar-paper curing membrane

2.
Overlapping widths of reinforcing mesh

Tar-paper curing membrane

3.
Float strips
Columns of mud

4.
Second layer of mortar
Straightedge
Exposed area of first layer of mortar

5.
Channels left by float strips
Float strips, overlapping first area by about 6 in. and leveled with second layer of mud

Preparing mortar

With the curing membrane installed, I was ready to prepare the mortar. Ordinarily I like to work alone when floating a mortar bed, but on a floor this size a helper ensures that I'll have a continuous supply of mortar available throughout the floating process. If I had to occasionally stop floating the bed to mix more mud, the area of floor already floated would partially dry out and I'd increase the risk of forming a cold joint.

Ordering the sand and cement   With regard to the amount of mortar needed to cover a given area, you need only be concerned with the cubic amount of sand required to fill the space. The amount of cement and liquid needed for a given amount of mortar does not appreciably increase the volume of material used. Instead, the individual grains of cement mixed with the liquid form a paste that fills the spaces between the particles of sand. Once you've figured the amount of sand needed to fill the space, consult the label on the mortar additive that you'll be using (I urge you to use one) to determine the manufacturer's recipe for the mix.

For small jobs of 100 sq. ft. or less, buying bagged sand is fine. But for a job like this where 2½ cu. yd. of sand was needed, the only sensible thing to do was to order sand in bulk and have a dump truck deliver it to the site. Calculating the amount of sand needed was easy: I multiplied the square footage of the area to be covered by the thickness of the bed. Before doing the calculation, I subtracted a few square feet from the 355-sq.-ft. floor for the space occupied by the hearth and cabinets and arrived at about 350 sq. ft. of coverage. The 2-in. thickness of the mortar bed translated to about 0.17 ft. Thus, multiplying the square footage of the floor by the depth of the bed yielded 59.5 cu. ft. (0.17 ft. x 350 sq. ft. = 59.5 cu. ft.), or, rounded off, 60 cu. ft. of sand.

Since sand is usually ordered by the cubic yard, I divided 60 cu. ft. by 27 cu. ft. (the number of cubic feet in a cubic yard): 60 ÷ 27 = 2.2 cu. yd. Because a lot of sand gets lost from the pile on any job, I would need to order 2½ cu. yd.

To calculate the amount of cement needed, I consulted the label of the latex additive I wanted to use with the mortar. The label provided a mortar recipe calling for three parts sand to one part cement. Thus with a 94-lb. bag of cement equaling 1 cu. ft., I ordered 20 sacks (60 cu. ft. of sand ÷ 3 = 20 cu. ft. of cement needed). Actually, 23 sacks of cement would be needed if I used the full 2½ cu. yd. of sand ordered, but because cement is expensive and extra sand was ordered, I preferred not to have cement left over. If I needed more, I would get it at a nearby supplier.

When the sand was delivered, I had it dumped close to the area of the house I'd be working in to save steps. And to keep the cement and additive from overheating in the summer sun, I stored them in the garage. Because heat can cause mortar to set up prematurely, I also covered the sand pile with a tarp to keep it as cool as possible.

Mixing mortar   When mixing mortar, whether deck mud for floors or fat mud for walls, I never fool with mechanized mixing machines. Mortar should be mixed only enough to thoroughly combine the ingredients. A mixing machine tends to produce either improperly mixed mortar filled with globs of sand-covered cement, which is useless for floating, or mortar that is overmixed. Therefore I always mix mortar by hand with a slotted mason's hoe, making sure to completely integrate all the ingredients. This is important, since any unmixed pockets of sand or cement in the mortar will cause weak spots in the bed.

After thoroughly mixing the dry ingredients, I poked a series of holes in the mix and poured in three-quarters of the liquid needed (top). I then repeated the mixing procedure used for the dry ingredients. When properly mixed, deck mud neither crumbles nor oozes from your hand when squeezed but rather holds together firmly (bottom).

Additionally, when several batches of mud are required for a job, I make sure that the ingredients and proportions for each batch are identical. If the batches are dissimilar, they will expand and contract at different rates and the bed may crack. Not only must the ingredients and proportions be consistent, the procedure for mixing each batch should not vary. The ingredients for each batch should be mixed in the same order, for the same amount of time and with the same technique. Since the weather and temperature at the job site can greatly affect the mortar mixed, it's important to take these factors into account when preparing mortar. (For more on the effect of weather and temperature on mixing mortar, see p. 57.)

To begin mixing the mortar, layer the dry ingredients in the mixing box. I use 5-gallon buckets as measuring cups when I'm mixing mud for anything larger than the equivalent of about six linear feet of countertop. Start with a layer of sand, then add a layer of cement. Continue alternating layers until the box is about two-thirds full. Then with the mixing hoe, begin chopping through the layers, driving the hoe to the bottom of the box. The idea is to take small bites with the tool, not to chop off a big chunk of the dry stuff. Stand at one end of the box, and with each bite, pull the dry stuff toward you, piling it up at your end until all the layered material has been chopped. This completes the first mixing cycle. Repeat the process twice more, each time moving to the opposite end of the box. If you've taken small enough bites, the dry ingredients will be thoroughly mixed after three cycles.

While the routine for mixing mortar's dry ingredients remains the same for both deck and wall mud, the procedure for adding the liquid varies according to the type of mortar being mixed. Deck mud requires only enough liquid to precipitate the chemical reaction in the cement that causes it to harden. This mortar must be dense and strong enough to support considerable weight, and adding too much liquid will dilute the cement and weaken the mortar. The question, of course, is how much liquid is enough—a question that's difficult to answer, since the precise amount needed for any batch is affected by a number of factors ranging from the kind of sand used to the heat and humidity of the day. Generally, if dry sand is being used, the setter will need about 5 gallons of liquid for every 94-lb. bag of cement. I prefer to use damp sand, though, for two reasons. First, this reduces the amount of dust kicked up during mixing. Second, I've found that mixing dry sand directly with any kind of additive gives the wrong kind of texture to the mix. The ideal sand is moist enough for sand-castle work—it will hold its shape when dumped out of a bucket. With damp sand, you'll require less liquid for every bag of cement to get the right mortar consistency, which I'll discuss in a moment. If I have to, I'll mist the sand pile with a hose in order to get it the way I like it.

I began mixing the liquid into the dry ingredients for deck mud, as I always do, by spreading the combined dry ingredients in an even layer in the mixing box. Then I punched holes to the bottom of the layer every 8 in. to 10 in. with the handle of the hoe. Next I poured about 75% of the liquid required over the mix, distributing it equally among the holes. Using the same mixing pattern as for the dry stuff, I went through three mixing cycles and then tested the mortar to see if it was ready to float.

When I squeezed a handful of the deck mud, I found that it stuck together, which meant that it was ready for floating. If the ball had crumbled, I would have known that the mortar was too dry and that I needed to add a little more liquid and rechop the mixture. If the mix had oozed out the sides of my fist, it would have meant that it was too wet and in need of more sand and cement. (If you find that the latter is the case, be careful to avoid directly combining the extra, unmixed dry ingredients with partially mixed mortar. Instead, combine the additional dry ingredients in a separate container, then spread this newly mixed sand and cement on top of the wet stuff and chop it in, testing the new mix frequently to keep from overmixing.) For information on mixing wall mud, see p. 172.

Floating a mortar floor

I began floating this two-layer mortar bed at the northeast corner of the room and planned to end at the southeast corner. These were the two locations where the height of the floor would be the most critical. The architect had designed the floor so that the surface of the tiles was to be flush with the top of the threshold at both the doorways. The thresholds would be oak, but they were only about ⅞ in. thick, not nearly thick enough to match the combined thickness of mortar floor and tiles. So the carpentry crew ripped stock to lift the thresholds to the proper height. These spacers, or subthresholds, were cut ½ in. wider than the oak, and to the thickness of the mortar bed. They were attached to the subfloor, then the thresholds were attached to the spacers. The extra width of each spacer was placed toward the tile side of the door opening, creating a small lip on which I could later place my level to set float strips.

My helper and I began spreading the first layer of mortar across the width of the floor in a band that ended about 7 ft. out from the north wall. I used a wood float instead of a steel trowel to spread and compact the first layer because it would produce the coarser surface I wanted.

As I spread the first layer, I gauged its thickness by eye rather than with the usual pair of float strips. Then after compacting the area, I more accurately measured the layer's thickness with a tool I quickly made. I drove a 16d finishing nail into each end of a wooden straightedge so that each nail head protruded a distance equal to half the thickness of the full bed, that is, the height of the first layer of mortar. I positioned the tool over the bed, with the nail heads penetrating the mud and resting lightly on the tar paper below. By pulling the tool forward, keeping the nails touching the tar paper and perpendicular to the bed, I screeded away the excess mud and cut the first layer of mortar to the right height. I then filled the tiny channels left by the nails with mortar (to prevent the bed from cracking at these points as it cured) and cut away the excess with the wood float.

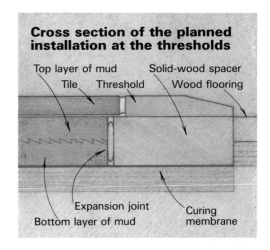

Cross section of the planned installation at the thresholds

Top layer of mud   Solid-wood spacer
Tile   Threshold   Wood flooring
Expansion joint   Curing membrane
Bottom layer of mud

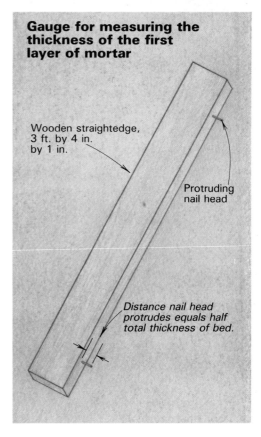

Gauge for measuring the thickness of the first layer of mortar

Wooden straightedge, 3 ft. by 4 in. by 1 in.

Protruding nail head

Distance nail head protrudes equals half total thickness of bed.

I spread and compacted the first layer of mortar with a wood float, gauging the layer's thickness with a tool I quickly made from a wooden straightedge (see drawing at right).

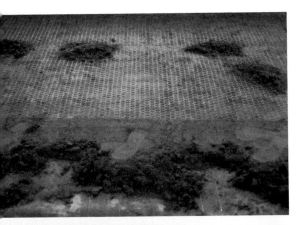

I laid wire mesh over the first layer of mortar and weighted it with handfuls of mortar (top). After leveling the first float strip with the wood spacer supporting the threshold, I positioned the level along the strip's length and lightly tapped it to adjust it evenly (bottom).

Next I placed the reinforcing mesh over the first layer, holding it flat against the bed with one hand and weighting it down every foot or so with a handful of mortar. As I positioned each new width of mesh, I overlapped the previous piece by 2 in.

Before continuing to float more of the first layer, I wanted to install the top layer on this section. Since this floor was almost 17 ft. wide and the longest straightedge I had was about 9 ft. long, I would have to place three float strips across the width of the floor and advance along the floor's length, alternately floating one side of the floor and then the other, as shown in the drawing below. By using a combination of various lengths of float strips, levels and straightedges, a floor of any dimension or shape can be floated. If you don't have some of the longer levels mentioned below, use a shorter one held against a straightedge of the required length.

Had this been an L-shaped floor, I would have completely floated one leg of the floor in stages before moving into the other leg. And if this had been a multiroom installation, I would have made sure that I didn't float myself into a corner. Concerning multiroom layouts, my advice to the novice is to start at the most critical part of the job. This may mean that you have to float one section of the job and let it set up before you can float another section. There are no hard-and-fast rules to follow—each job will require a different approach and a combination of skills and techniques.

The first step on this floor was to position the three 6-ft.-long float strips parallel to the northeast doorway. To anchor the strips on the mesh, I laid down three columns of mud, about 6 in. wide by 3 in. high by 6 ft. long. When compacted, the columns would fully support the float strips at the appropriate height and not get forced out of position when the bed was screeded. I positioned the two outside columns of mud parallel to the doors and about 20 in. out from each wall, and centered the third column between them. Then I wet down the float strips to prevent them from warping when they came in contact with the wet mortar. (If you place a dry float strip on a bed of mortar, it's mostly the bottom of the strip that will get wet from the mortar. As the bottom absorbs moisture, it will swell, curling the strip toward the dry side. But if you wet the float strip on all sides before placing it in the mortar, the swelling will be equalized and the float strip will stay straight.)

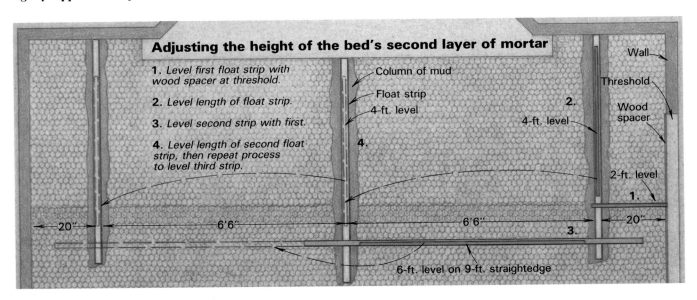

Adjusting the height of the bed's second layer of mortar

1. *Level first float strip with wood spacer at threshold.*

2. *Level length of float strip.*

3. *Level second strip with first.*

4. *Level length of second float strip, then repeat process to level third strip.*

Column of mud

Float strip

4-ft. level

Wall

Threshold

Wood spacer

4-ft. level

2-ft. level

20″   6′6″   6′6″   20″

6-ft. level on 9-ft. straightedge

I seated the first strip in the column nearest the doorway and placed my 2-ft. level with one end on the lip of the wood spacer supporting the threshold and the other end on the float strip. (The mortar grips the float strips well enough to hold them in place, so there's no need to nail them down.) By lightly tapping the float strip into the mortar until the bubble in the level's vial was dead center, I worked the first strip to the height of the wood spacer. Then I laid a 4-ft. level on the length of the strip to evenly adjust the entire strip. Next I got my 6-ft. level and sat it on the 9-ft. straightedge, spanning the first two float strips. I tapped the second strip level with the first and, with the 4-ft. level, adjusted the second strip along its length. Then I moved the 6-ft. level and 9-ft. straightedge to span the second and third strips and repeated the leveling procedure.

With all three strips leveled, I dumped deck mud in the area between the first two strips and compacted it with the wood float to eliminate any air pockets. This left the unscreeded mortar about ½ in. to 1 in. above the level of the float strips. I stopped the second layer of mortar about 6 in. short of the end of the first layer, which ensured that the chicken wire would run continuously into the next area being floated.

To cut the bed's top layer to the right height, I placed the blade of my long straightedge on the float strips and pulled it side to side and at the same time toward me. This sawing motion pared away the excess mud and left a flat, level surface. With properly mixed mud, a minimum of lumps will tear away from the surface during screeding. Small craters left by such lumps should be backfilled and the surface flattened with the wood float.

Before screeding any more, I wanted to check to see how firm the screeded section was. Since deck mud should be densely packed, I knew that I ought to be able to stand on the screeded section and leave a footprint only about ⅜ in. deep, and I found this to be the case. Had my foot sunk deeper, it would have meant that I had done a poor job of packing the mortar before screeding. In that event, I would have spread

I compacted the second layer with a wood float (top) and screeded the excess (bottom).

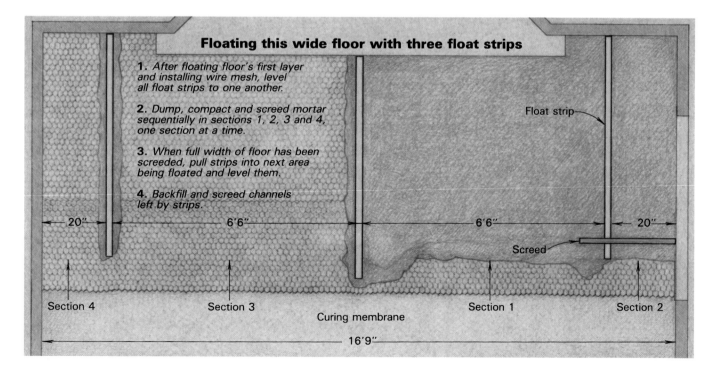

Floating this wide floor with three float strips

1. After floating floor's first layer and installing wire mesh, level all float strips to one another.

2. Dump, compact and screed mortar sequentially in sections 1, 2, 3 and 4, one section at a time.

3. When full width of floor has been screeded, pull strips into next area being floated and level them.

4. Backfill and screed channels left by strips.

Float strip

Screed

20"   6'6"   6'6"   20"

Section 4   Section 3   Curing membrane   Section 1   Section 2

16'9"

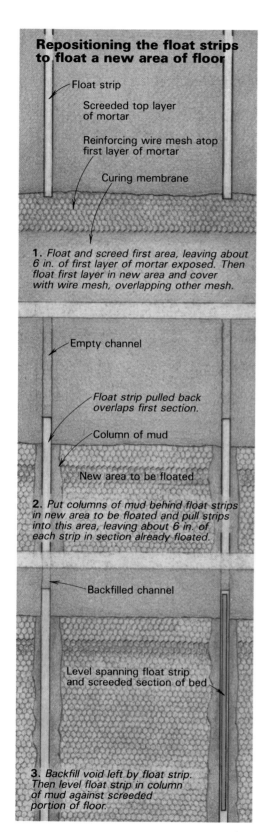

Float strip

Screeded top layer of mortar

Reinforcing wire mesh atop first layer of mortar

Curing membrane

1. Float and screed first area, leaving about 6 in. of first layer of mortar exposed. Then float first layer in new area and cover with wire mesh, overlapping other mesh.

Empty channel

Float strip pulled back overlaps first section.

Column of mud

New area to be floated

2. Put columns of mud behind float strips in new area to be floated and pull strips into this area, leaving about 6 in. of each strip in section already floated.

Backfilled channel

Level spanning float strip and screeded section of bed

3. Backfill void left by float strip. Then level float strip in column of mud against screeded portion of floor.

about an inch of fresh mud over the screeded section, packed it down hard and rescreeded.

Before moving on to float the next large area, I packed and screeded the narrow section between the first float strip and the wall. Where the protruding blocks of wood protecting the heat vent prevented screeding, I cut off the excess mortar with the wood float held firmly against the mud's surface.

I next packed and screeded the large area between the second and third float strips, and finally the narrow area between the third float strip and the wall. Having floated the full width of the floor, I cut the mortar at the margin with the margin trowel so that it butted the foam strip against the wall at a sharp 90° angle.

By this time, my helper had spread the first layer of mud for another area. I put reinforcing mesh over the new bottom layer, overlapping the exposed mesh by 2 in., and laid another column of mud behind each float strip. I pulled the float strips partway into the new section and leveled them to the height of the finished area. By leaving 6 in. of each strip in the finished area, I kept the floor from getting wavy at the juncture of the new and old sections and ensured that the floor's height would be uniform. Then I backfilled, packed and screeded the channels left by the float strips.

I continued repositioning the float strips and floating each new area until the entire floor was completed. Whenever I needed to get on the fresh mud—for example, to fill a depression—I protected the surface with plywood squares, which distributed my weight. After I had completely floated the floor, I let it harden overnight before continuing work.

Snapping layout lines

Even though I was familiar with the work of this construction crew and knew that they didn't sign off on a job unless it was plumb, level and square enough to warm a tilesetter's heart, it never hurts to check a site before snapping layout lines. So after trimming the perimeter expansion joint to the height of the mortar bed, I established two reference lines from which I could project a 3-4-5 triangle (see p. 114) and, subsequently, layout lines. For the first line, I measured out from both ends of the west wall a distance representing the center of the grout joint between the seventh and eighth horizontal rows of full tiles (this put the line conveniently well into the room). I marked each point and connected the marks with a snapped chalk line. Next I measured from two points on the south wall a distance representing the center of the grout joint between the tenth and eleventh vertical rows of full tiles, marked the points and snapped the second reference line. Then I plotted a 3-4-5 triangle and found that the west and south walls were square to each other. Finally, I measured out from two points on each of the reference lines to the respective opposite walls and found the measurements the same, which told me that these walls were square to the first two. With this done, I could snap layout lines.

My helper and I snapped a grid of lines 3 ft. apart in each direction, projecting them off the reference lines. Finally, we snapped layout lines for the cut tiles at the perimeter of the floor.

Mixing the thinset and tiling

One of the hallmarks of Mexican pavers is that each tile responds differently to the heat of the kiln: some emerge slightly concave, some convex, some fairly flat. Thus in addition to spreading thinset on the setting bed, I would have to back-butter any tiles that did not fully contact the thinset.

Convex and concave tiles require lots of thinset. For this job, I used a liquid latex thinset additive mixed with equal parts of portland cement and

40-mesh sand. Because Mexican pavers are quite porous and need a fairly wet adhesive, I mixed about one part liquid to three parts dry ingredients.

As with mortar, the sand and cement had to be mixed separately before the liquid was added. To save time in preparing the large quantity of thinset needed, I first dumped a sack of sand and one of cement into the mixing box and chopped them together with the hoe to make up a sizable amount of the dry component. Then I prepared small amounts of thinset as needed by shoveling the mixed dry ingredients into a 5-gallon bucket until it was about four-fifths full, adding about 1⅓ gallons of liquid and blending this with the mixing paddle. (For more on mixing adhesives, see p. 52.)

I planned to begin setting tile in the room's northwest corner and end at the door in the southeast corner, filling the squares in the grid one at a time with thinset and tiles. Because grid lines are very helpful when setting irregular tiles like Mexican pavers or other tiles unsuited for tile spacers, it's crucial to keep the lines visible as the thinset is combed out on the floor. Thus when spreading the adhesive, I made sure to keep it about ³⁄₁₆ in. from the grid lines. Remember that the empty area on either side of the lines represents part of a grout joint that will, of course, later be filled with grout.

Normally when I'm working with consistently sized tiles, I use a straightedge to align them along the layout lines. But with Mexican pavers, this method would produce a straight line on one side of a row of tiles and a jagged line on the other side. Thus on this job I depended on my eye to center the tiles between the grout joints to balance out the different sizes.

Usually when I install a floor, I make and set the cut tiles first, using the layout lines around the floor's perimeter as guides. On this job, however, because the floor was large and setting the full tiles would alone be a day's work, I began with these tiles and left the cuts for later.

When I had finished setting the full tiles, I cleaned stray globs of thinset from the joints and sponged off the surface of the tiles. (For a full description of cleaning up adhesive, see p. 60.) Then I waited overnight for the thinset to dry in order to measure, cut and set the trimmed pieces.

Grouting the tiles

Due to their porosity, unsealed Mexican pavers are almost impossible to grout. They will immediately suck the moisture from wet grout dumped on them, causing the grout to lose its plasticity and spreadability. The only way to prevent this is to give the tiles at least two coats of sealer before grouting. (On this job, the supplier had already sealed the tiles.) Also, wetting down the tiles and the joints with a damp sponge is absolutely essential for successfully grouting Mexican pavers. Thus, once I had mixed the first batch of grout, I let it slake for 10 minutes and meanwhile sponged over the floor, dribbling a little water in the joints (don't flood the joints with water, as this will weaken the grout).

After the grout had slaked, I remixed it and checked its consistency. It was just right—moist but still firm enough so that it didn't pour out of the bucket but rather required a firm shove to make it spill out. I then began grouting and cleaning up the floor, about 50 sq. ft. at a time. (For a full discussion of grouting tile, see p. 62.)

With the surface of the tiles cleaned, I saw that the sealer had taken quite a beating during grouting and needed to be reapplied. After waiting a few days for the grout to dry completely, I applied two light coats of sealer to both the tiles and the grout joints. (Avoid applying sealer in heavy layers, which will not dry properly and will chip. Thick layers will also give a yellowish cast to the surface of the tiles.) Finally, I caulked the expansion joint to complete the job. □

Working one square at a time, my helper applied adhesive while I set the tiles.

Aligning irregularly shaped tile

Straightedge

Using a straightedge to align a row of irregularly shaped tiles will produce a jagged grout joint on one side.

Centerline of tile

Instead, balance out irregular dimensions by positioning tiles by eye and centering them between grout joints.

Layout sketch

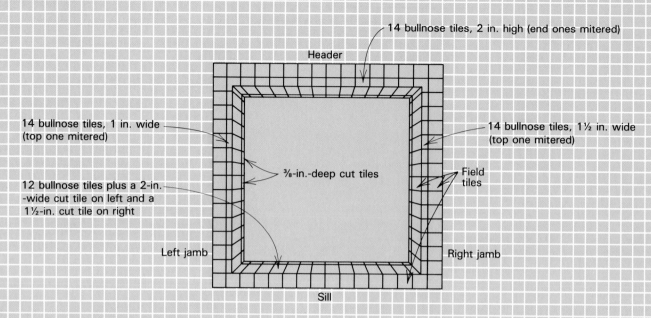

14 bullnose tiles, 2 in. high (end ones mitered)

Header

14 bullnose tiles, 1 in. wide (top one mitered)

14 bullnose tiles, 1½ in. wide (top one mitered)

12 bullnose tiles plus a 2-in.-wide cut tile on left and a 1½-in. cut tile on right

⅜-in.-deep cut tiles

Field tiles

Left jamb

Right jamb

Sill

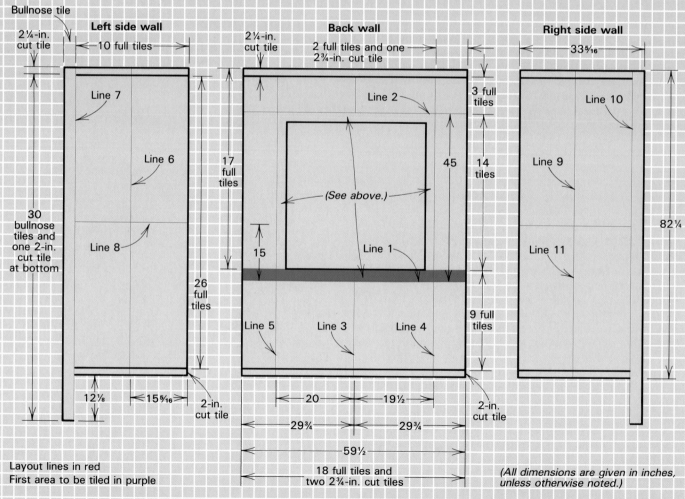

Bullnose tile

Left side wall

2¼-in. cut tile

10 full tiles

Line 7

Line 6

Line 8

30 bullnose tiles and one 2-in. cut tile at bottom

17 full tiles

26 full tiles

12⅛

15⁵⁄₁₆

2-in. cut tile

Back wall

2¼-in. cut tile

2 full tiles and one 2¾-in. cut tile

Line 2

3 full tiles

45

(See above.)

15

Line 1

14 tiles

Line 5

Line 3

Line 4

9 full tiles

2-in. cut tile

20

19½

29¾

29¾

59½

18 full tiles and two 2¾-in. cut tiles

Right side wall

33⁵⁄₁₆

Line 10

Line 9

Line 11

82¼

Layout lines in red
First area to be tiled in purple

(All dimensions are given in inches, unless otherwise noted.)

Thinset Tub Shower

This tub shower was part of a complete renovation of a bathroom that had been badly damaged by termites. The culprit had been the leaky walls in the original shower installation, which kept the wall studs constantly wet and the termites delighted. In the course of the repairs, almost every wall stud had been replaced and all new plumbing installed. The floor had been damaged as well, but since the new flooring was to be teak (salvaged from an old boat), it wouldn't be part of the tile job. After the tub and new subfloor were in place, I tackled the tile installation.

Sizing up the job

Ordinarily, when tiling a tub surround, I would float a mortar bed as the setting surface because I like the performance of a mortar job and the look of the radius trim tile it requires. This client, however, wanted the flatter, more streamlined look of surface-bullnose trim, applied directly to the wall (see p. 23). I thus decided to install backer board for the walls of the tub surround, applying it directly to the studs. This would ensure that the finished tiles would sit just slightly proud of the adjacent drywall surfaces.

Made of a mortar core with fiberglass-mesh reinforcing skin on either side, backer board itself is unaffected by water. Water can nonetheless penetrate the joints where two boards meet, even when these joints are "sealed" with thinset adhesive. Because water can also get through surface cracks and around nails or screws, a waterproofing membrane is necessary. Given this tub shower's history and the fact that it would get regular use by two exhuberant young boys, I wanted the most effective waterproofing possible and suggested a chlorinated polyethylene (CPE) membrane or a trowel-applied membrane (see p. 89) on top of the backer board. But because the client was concerned about cost, we agreed on a tar-paper waterproofing membrane, which is quite effective for residential jobs.

Installing the tar-paper membrane beneath the backer board would be the first step of the job. But before any work could start, I needed to do a layout sketch and estimate the amount of tile and other materials required.

Doing a layout sketch and estimating tile

The client had already chosen some handmade tile and placed an order before I became involved in the job. After I had quickly assessed the situation, I realized that he had not ordered enough. To calculate how much more tile would be needed, I had to first figure out the combined width of one tile and grout joint and then make a layout sketch.

The tile my client had chosen was sold as 3-in.-square tile, though it actually ranged in size from $2^{13}/_{16}$ in. square to $2^{15}/_{16}$ in. square. Since the tile maker recommended a ⅛-in.-wide grout joint, I figured that if I mixed the different sizes of tile and alternately set larger and smaller tiles, I could assume an average tile/grout-joint dimension of 3 in. This was a nice, whole number to work with, so I dispensed with making my usual tile/grout-joint list. I could also do the layout sketch on graph paper on which each square represented one tile and grout joint.

To start the layout, I measured and noted all the dimensions of the tub surround, figuring in the thickness of the backer board that would later be put in place. After determining the measurements of the three walls of the installation, I needed to locate its visual focal point. It was clear that the window was it and that, aesthetically, full tiles just beneath the sill were mandatory. I therefore began my layout here by dividing the wall's 82¼-in. height into two segments: the first one 29 in. from the top of the tub to the sill, and the second 53¼ in. from the sill to the ceiling. Vertically, 9 full tiles plus a 2-in. cut tile could fit in the first section, and in the second, 17 full tiles plus a 2¼-in. cut at the ceiling. Although the tiles at the ceiling and the tub would not be full tiles, the size of the cuts would be roughly the same, and visually the job would be fairly well balanced.

With regard to the horizontal alignment of tiles on the back wall, I wanted any cut tiles to be equally distributed at either corner. I could have centered all the tile on the slightly off-center window, but I decided that it wasn't worth the trouble in this case. Instead, I cut the bullnose tiles on either side of the window to different dimensions. Across the 59½-in. width of the back wall, I could fit 18 full tiles plus a 2¾-in. cut at each side.

I wanted the window sill set with surface-bullnose trim tiles that would overlap the top edge of the field tiles beneath the window. Arranging the tiles this way, rather than setting the bullnose on the face of the wall, eliminated a grout joint on the sill that might collect water. If I did the same thing on the jambs, however, the visual result would be a grout joint encircling the window opening. So instead, I would set the bullnose *around* the jambs rather than on them—outside the window opening, rather than inside.

The tiles on the sill would have to be aligned with those on the face of the wall to make the grout joints line up. This meant that I could fit 12 full bullnose tiles along the width of the sill, with a 2-in. cut tile on the left side and a 1½-in. cut tile on the right. The inside surface of the head jamb would require the same number of tiles as the sill, while the header's face would need fourteen 2-in. cut bullnose tiles, with the two tiles at each end cut diagonally to accommodate the corners. Given that the window was ⅜ in. off-center to the right, I decided to make up the difference at the bullnose tiles on the face of the side jambs by cutting them to slightly different sizes. The 14 bullnose tiles to be set on the face of the wall at the left jamb would need to be 1 in. wide, while those at the right jamb would be 1½ in. wide. On both jambs the top tile would be mitered to fit the corner. To cover the jambs' 3½-in. depth, I would need one full tile and a ⅜-in. cut tile (½ in. minus the thickness of the grout joint). Though I generally try to work with cut tiles larger than half-size, this would have visually "split" the jambs and sill with an unattractive grout line.

Totaling up the tiles required for the back wall, I calculated that the base of the wall would need 20 tiles across the width (18 full tiles, 2 cut tiles) x 10 tiles from the sill to the top of the tub (9 full tiles, 1 cut tile), or 200 tiles (remember that the rows of trimmed tiles on the bottom and top of the wall must be cut from full tiles). Each segment of the wall beside the window, from the sill to the ceiling, would require 18 full tiles (17 full tiles plus a 2¼-in. cut) x 3 full tiles across its width, or 108 tiles for both sides. Next, the portion of the wall above the head jamb would need 4 tiles along its height (3 full tiles plus a 2¼-in. cut) x 14 tiles across its width, or 56 tiles. Finally, I would need 31 full tiles to make the cuts around the inside of the jambs, plus 38 full tiles for the rest of the inside of the jambs. I would therefore need 433 full tiles for the back wall and 56 bullnose tiles.

With the layout on the back wall established, I could move to the side walls. Since the back wall would be the first surface set with tiles, I needed to subtract the ¼-in. thickness of the tile from the width of the side walls. This meant that the area to be laid out was 33⁵⁄₁₆ in. wide by 82¼ in. high. With a row of surface-bullnose tiles trimming the wall's outside edge, 10 field tiles would fit across the wall's width, while 26 full tiles would be needed along the height, with a 2-in. cut on the bottom and a 2¼-in. cut on the top. Finally, each wall would need 4 full bullnose tiles to fill the 12⅛-in.-long by 3-in.-wide area running alongside the tub to the floor. The two side walls would thus require a total of 560 field tiles and 64 surface-bullnose tiles.

All in all, then, I would need a total of 993 field tiles and 120 surface-bullnose tiles. Since the owner had ordered only 900 field tiles and 106 trim tiles, I would need another 93 field and 14 trim tiles. To be on the safe side, I added a few tiles to each count for a total of 1,000 field tiles and 130 surface-bullnose tiles.

Installing the waterproofing membrane

On this job, I planned to install the membrane in seven segments, wrapping each horizontally around the walls and overlapping the rows by at least 2 in. Each segment would be attached directly to the studs, and I would use cold-patch roofing asphalt to seal the overlaps and any other spot that might leak (neither silicone nor butyl caulk will stick to tar paper).

Installing the tar-paper membrane would require only a couple of tools: a utility knife, a putty knife or a margin trowel, and a staple gun. Since the asphalt is petroleum-based and not only sticky but also smelly, I would need my charcoal-filter mask and some rubber gloves.

I began installing the membrane by sealing the entire top edge of the tub where it fastened to the blocking with a layer of cold-patch roofing asphalt about ⅛ in. thick and 2 in. wide. This strip of asphalt would anchor the

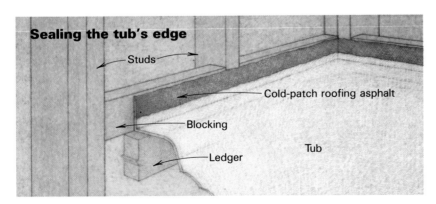

Sealing the tub's edge

Studs

Cold-patch roofing asphalt

Blocking

Ledger

Tub

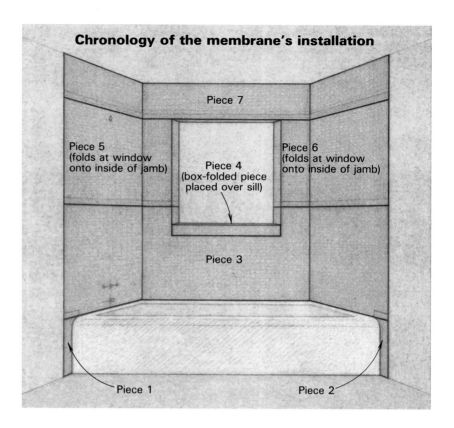

Chronology of the membrane's installation

Piece 7

Piece 5
(folds at window
onto inside of jamb)

Piece 6
(folds at window
onto inside of jamb)

Piece 4
(box-folded piece
placed over sill)

Piece 3

Piece 1

Piece 2

first band of tar paper. Then I proceeded to install each of the seven seg-ments in the order shown the drawing above. The box-folded piece at the window sill was required because the sill would be exposed to standing water, but the top of the window did not need this protection.

Because the tar paper should be sharply creased where it wraps the cor-ner of a job, it's a good idea to warm the paper before installing it to make it more pliable. Folding cold tar paper can cause it to split. To warm the tar paper, store the roll under room-temperature conditions the night be-fore you intend to use it, or put lengths of paper in direct sun just before installing it. In a pinch, a hand-held hair dryer can even work. In any case, make sure that the membrane lays flat against the studs.

After cutting the two pieces for the legs of the side walls (*pieces 1* and *2*), I pressed them into the asphalt sealing strip at the edge of the tub and stapled through them and into the asphalt to hold them in place. Each piece extended about 2 in. above the top of the tub, and I coated the upper lip of each with a ⅛-in.-thick layer of asphalt.

To install the first full horizontal band of the membrane (*piece 3*), I stapled it to the studs and pressed the base of the paper into the asphalt at the top edge of the tub, overlapping the lip of the tub by about 1 in. and overlapping the first two pieces of the membrane by about 2 in. Once the backer board was installed, I could trim any excess tar paper at the edge of the tub. Where the membrane was to pass over a faucet or a control valve, I cut a hole just large enough for the valve to pass through, and sealed the opening between the paper and the valve with asphalt. After *piece 3* was positioned, I cut it flush with the sill so that it could be lapped by the box-folded sill piece (*4*), but left tails at the right and left jambs, which would be folded over each end of *piece 4.*

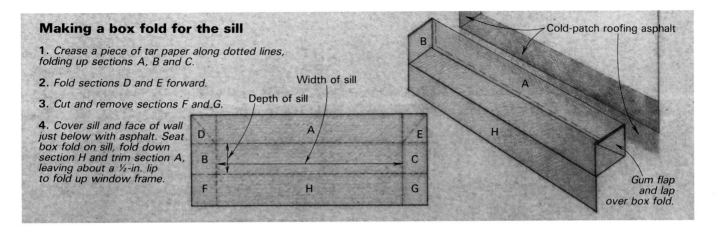

Making a box fold for the sill

1. *Crease a piece of tar paper along dotted lines, folding up sections A, B and C.*

2. *Fold sections D and E forward.*

3. *Cut and remove sections F and G.*

4. *Cover sill and face of wall just below with asphalt. Seat box fold on sill, fold down section H and trim section A, leaving about a ½-in. lip to fold up window frame.*

Width of sill

Depth of sill

D   A   E

B   C

F   H   G

Cold-patch roofing asphalt

B

A

H

Gum flap and lap over box fold.

Next I coated the top 2 in. of this band with a layer of asphalt, working carefully to avoid tearing the paper between studs. Then I made the box fold to fit on the window sill (*piece 4*), as shown in the drawing above. After coating the sill and inside of the jambs with asphalt as an additional precaution against water leakage, I positioned the box fold in the window opening and pressed it down into the asphalt all around—the box needn't be stapled to the sill because the asphalt will hold it in place. If the window is already in place, as it was in this case, the tar paper should run right up to the window frame. (If the finished window is not in place, simply run the paper out the opening and lap it down over the outside.) Next I cut the two sides of the box-folded piece flush with the jambs, covered a 2-in.-wide strip below the sill with asphalt, and folded the overhanging sill flap onto the face of the wall and into the asphalt. Then I covered the jamb sections of the box fold with asphalt right up to the window frame and folded the tails from *piece 3* over the bottom of each side. I made sure that any folds were crisp, not bulky, in order to avoid unnecessary lumps beneath the backer board. Finally, I trimmed the section of the box fold that fit against the window frame (section *A* in the drawing above).

With the lower portion of the window completed, I installed *pieces 5* and *6*. I folded each piece inward at the jamb (covering the top 2 in. of the box-folded piece), bedded them in the asphalt and trimmed them with a knife at the window frame. With the window sill and jambs covered, this left the head jamb and area above the window still exposed. This I covered with *piece 7*. I made this piece wide enough so that a flap could be folded inward, toward the window, and bedded in asphalt. I could, of course, have box-folded a single piece of tar paper to cover the head jamb, but I've never found it worth the time, since, again, this area will not be exposed to standing water.

Just before installing the backer board, I coated the membrane with asphalt along each stud. This sealed the staples and created a gasket between the board and the paper that would seal the fasteners used to attach the backer board. Exactly the same procedure can be used to install the waterproofing membrane beneath a mortar setting bed for a wall.

As far as I'm concerned, the basic technique for arranging and sealing the tar-paper membrane is the very heart of the tile installation. The proper positioning of the tar paper isn't really as complicated as it may sound. Basically, make sure that there's tar paper behind the entire area to be tiled, and install it as though you were planning to skip the tile and rely solely on the tar paper for waterproofing.

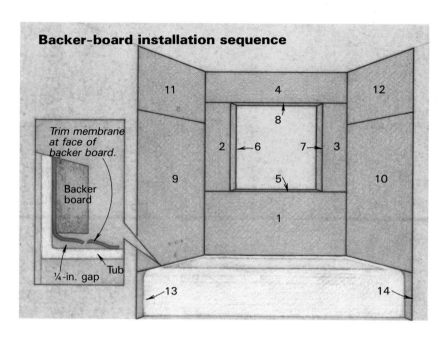

Backer-board installation sequence

Trim membrane at face of backer board.

Backer board

¼-in. gap

Tub

Installing the backer board

After measuring and marking the backer board, I cut it with a dry-cutting diamond blade mounted in a power grinder. This left a cut with smooth edges, which made it easy to fit the backer boards together. Backer board can also be scored with a carbide-tipped scriber and broken along the scribed line. The technique leaves a fairly rough edge, but because it's sometimes quicker than cutting with the saw, I use the scriber when rough edges won't be a problem. After cutting the sheets, I began to install them in the sequence shown in the drawing above.

While backer board used on floors must be laminated as well as screwed or nailed to the substrate, it's unnecessary to use an adhesive when fastening it to walls. Although 1½-in. galvanized roofing nails can be used to fasten the backer board, on vertical surfaces I prefer to use drywall screws, which won't loosen as nails might. Standard drywall screws resist corrosion, but extra-corrosion-resistant drywall screws are now available. I've never had any trouble with standard drywall screws, but you might want to consider using these new screws for wet installations.

Holes in the backer board for the valves and spouts can be made with a carbide-tipped hole saw, or by "punching" them out with a hammer. When using a hammer, first outline the position of the hole with a pencil and then cut through the backer board's reinforcing mesh on both sides with a utility knife. Support the back of the board with one hand and punch through the board at this point with a hammer.

To provide space for caulk and to keep the backer board from wicking water from the edges of the tub, I installed the board ¼ in. above the tub (it should not rest on the shoulder of the tub). Once all the boards had been fastened in place, I covered the joints between the boards with fiberglass mesh tape and sealed the joints with thinset (see p. 85). Sometimes I seal the joints as I'm setting tile—it really doesn't matter when it gets done.

While I had the thinset mixed for sealing the joints between the boards, I troweled enough on the top of the sill to create a slight pitch toward the tub. This would prevent shower water from collecting on the sill and possibly penetrating the grout into the backer boards.

After cutting the backer board to size and "punching out" holes for the shower valves and spouts, I started the drywall screws by "nailing" them partially into place.

Marking layout lines

If this shower had had no window and if the tiles being used had been uniformly sized, a pair of centered, intersecting layout lines would have probably sufficed for the entire installation. Given the presence of the off-center window in the back wall, however, and the irregularity of the tile, I needed 11 lines to ensure that everything was positioned squarely.

Rather than using the top of the tub or the ceiling as the starting points for the layout, I preferred to start from a line I knew would be level. Using a 4-ft. spirit level and a pencil, I first marked a horizontal line on the back wall 3 in. below the edge of the window sill. Then I drew a second line parallel to and 45 in. above the first, that is, 15 tiles and grout joints away.

The third line I made was a vertical line centered on the back wall. I measured to the center of the first horizontal line to establish the center of the wall and used the level to accurately scribe a line above and below the window. Then I scribed two other lines on the back wall to mark the grout joint between the field tiles and the surface-bullnose tiles on the window jambs. Again, instead of taking measurements off the existing walls or the window opening, I projected these lines off the centered vertical layout line, 21 in. to each side.

On the side walls, a pair of centered, intersecting lines would suffice. But to be safe I decided to add a third line to mark the grout joint between the field tile and the trim tile. To establish the first vertical line, I measured 15⁵⁄₁₆ in. from the corner where the side and back walls met. This point represented the center of the joint at the fifth of the side wall's 10 vertical rows of field tiles plus the ¼-in. thickness of the tile set on the back wall and the ¹⁄₁₆-in. layer of thinset under the tile.

Using the level, I accurately marked and drew in the first line. Then I measured out 15 in. from this line for the second vertical line, which represented the grout joint separating the field and trim tiles. Finally, to make a horizontal line, I measured 15 in. up from the sill line on the back wall, or the space of five tiles. Again using the level, I positioned this line essentially in the center of the wall where it would be the most helpful.

Setting the tiles

This job was done in the heat of the summer. With the temperature hovering around 95°F and with no relief in sight, I had to make some adjustments in the latex thinset adhesive I planned to use to keep it from setting up too quickly. Instead of the portland cement and fine sand I would normally mix with Laticrete 4237 liquid latex mortar additive, I used Bon-Don thinset powder. Because this thinset powder contains an additive that slows the curing of the thinset, this mixture would give me some extra time on each section to deal both with positioning the irregularly shaped tiles and with gravity's pull on the tiles. I could expect to have about 15 minutes in all before the adhesive began to set up at this temperature.

I began setting tile on the window sill, since the grout joints here would locate those for the field tiles below. I spread thinset on the sill and on a small portion of the wall just below it, figuring I would set all these "related" tiles. After I had carefully positioned the bullnose trim tiles on the sill, I started setting the tiles on the wall (I planned to butter and install the ⅜-in. cuts later). It was then that I discovered that I had a problem.

When mixing an adhesive to get certain qualities, there are usually a few tradeoffs for the advantages gained. Unexpectedly in this case, the adhesive I mixed to be slow-setting also turned out to have less "hang." ("Grip" is the holding power of an adhesive once it has cured; "hang" is its ability to hold tile on a vertical surface before it has cured. Mastics generally have low grip and high hang, while epoxy thinsets have tremendous grip but very low hang.) This was surprising, since I knew that each of the component thinsets alone would tenaciously hold freshly set tile. But the evidence was easy to spot—the first few tiles I put up on the wall just wouldn't stay up. Tile spacing wedges might have helped matters, but fiddling with them would take too much time. And I didn't want to mix up my normal recipe of thinset because I still needed the slow-curing characteristics of the Bon-Don. To solve the problem, I pulled out an old standby—masking tape. The sill tiles weren't going anywhere, so I stuck a length of tape to each one and let the tape cascade down the wall. Then all I had to do was stick the tiles to the wall and stick the tape to the tiles. Elsewhere on the walls, I supported the topmost row of tiles with small nails partially driven into the backer board. Each of the tiles in this row then served to anchor the tape that would hold the tiles below.

Although the special adhesive I mixed had the slower curing time I wanted, it also failed to hold the tiles in place while curing. To resolve the problem, I used strips of masking tape, anchoring each vertical row either to a sill tile (right) or to a tile supported in place by nails (above).

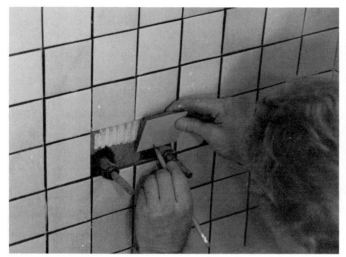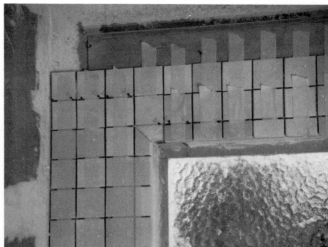

To set the tiles above the window, I nailed a straightedge in place at the ceiling and anchored on it the strips of masking tape that would hold the tiles (above left). Once the adhesive had begun to set up, I could remove the straightedge and set the topmost rows, using spacing wedges to hold the tiles in place. The last tiles to be set were those that needed to be cut to accommodate the shower's faucets and valves (above).

To begin the upper portion of the wall, I first positioned three tiles on each side of the window, 3 in. above the header layout line. Once supported by nails, these tiles would serve to support a 54-in. straightedge, which was held against the wall by nails. The remaining rows of tile on the upper half of the wall could then be aligned with the straightedge and secured with masking tape hung from it. By using a straightedge, I eliminated the time-consuming task of supporting every tile in the top row with nails. After letting the adhesive set up for an hour and a half, I carefully removed the straightedge above the window and set the last row of full tiles and the row of cut tiles at the ceiling, using spacing wedges to hold the cuts in place.

Once I had set the field tiles on the upper wall, I cut the bullnose trim to size and cut the tile for the jambs. Whenever setting bullnose tile at a corner, as in this case, it's a good idea not to begin setting until the tiles for both locations are ready. That outside corner is critical and has to be a nice, smooth transition. If I set one part of the corner ahead of time and let the thinset harden, I wouldn't be able to adjust it when the second part was installed. So once the cuts were complete, I set the bullnose trim around the window and immediately began setting tile on the jambs.

To speed up the setting process on the side walls, I went back to using nails to support the entire top row of cut tiles, suspending the rows below with masking tape. While this procedure took time, I didn't have to wait 90 minutes, as I had had to do using the straightedge-bridge system, for the adhesive to harden before setting the top row. When setting the main fields of tile, I had left out those that would require cuts to accommodate the faucets. These I carefully marked, cut and installed last.

The next day I returned to grout the job. Considering the effort I'd spent preparing the walls and setting the tiles, grouting was uneventful. Then, after waiting three days to allow the grout to harden, I caulked the joint between the tub and tiles and the one between the tiles on the inside of the window and the window frame. Once my work was complete, the owner caulked around the faucets and valves to finish off the job. □

Shower, preliminary sketch

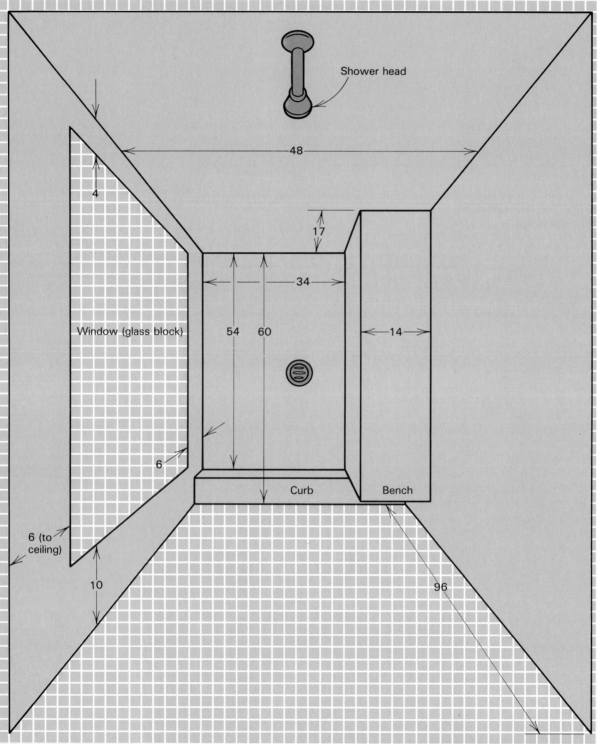

Shower head

48

4

Window (glass block)

17

34

54   60

14

6

6 (to ceiling)

10

Curb

Bench

96

(All dimensions are given in inches, unless otherwise noted.)

Mortar-Bed Shower

Once a standard installation for tilesetters, the tiled mortar-bed shower shows up less and less in residential construction. Nowadays you'll often see one-piece fiberglass tub-shower units instead of tile. These units must be installed before the surrounding walls, however, so they're not always suitable for remodeling projects. And, to me, none of them offers the durability, beauty or versatility of a mortar-bed tiled shower. If walls are out of plumb, or if the surfaces are uneven, floating new mortar surfaces over them is a great way to make corrections.

I didn't set the tile on this project. The client, who was relatively new to tilesetting, wanted to install the tile himself, but since he was reluctant to float the mortar setting bed, he called me to do all the work prior to tiling. The job came along at a time when I was still using tar paper to waterproof shower walls, and I've since changed to using chlorinated polyethylene, or CPE, for that purpose. Nevertheless, the project offers an excellent opportunity to discuss mortar-bed showers, and an inexpensive tar-paper waterproofing membrane can still provide leak-free service if installed properly.

Sizing up the job

This shower was in a new addition to an existing house. The customer and I agreed that the setting bed on the walls and floor should be floated mortar and that the bed on the ceiling should be backer board. To ensure the proper curing of the mortar and to help waterproof the installation, a curing membrane (see p. 93) would be needed beneath the bed on both the floor and the walls; and to fully waterproof the floor, a shower pan would be installed over a sloped floor. This pan could also serve as the curing membrane on the floor. The ceiling would occasionally get wet, but I felt that the backer board there would be sufficient to stop any water that managed to get past the tiles. If, however, I had been concerned about rambunctious bathers, I would have installed a waterproofing membrane behind the backer board.

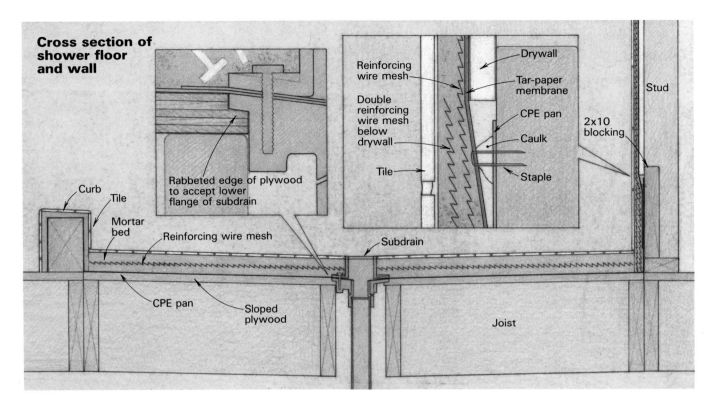

Cross section of shower floor and wall

Reinforcing wire mesh

Double reinforcing wire mesh below drywall

Tile

Drywall

Tar-paper membrane

CPE pan

Caulk

Staple

Stud

2x10 blocking

Curb

Tile

Mortar bed

Rabbeted edge of plywood to accept lower flange of subdrain

Reinforcing wire mesh

Subdrain

CPE pan

Sloped plywood

Joist

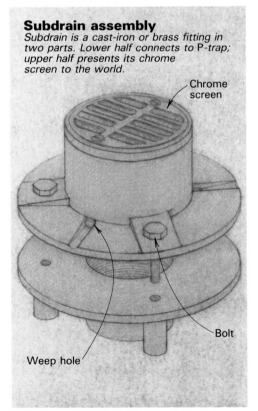

Subdrain assembly

Subdrain is a cast-iron or brass fitting in two parts. Lower half connects to P-trap; upper half presents its chrome screen to the world.

Chrome screen

Bolt

Weep hole

Anatomy of a mortar-bed shower

Before addressing the actual installation procedure, let's look first at the anatomy of a mortar-bed shower. At the center of the mortar-bed shower installation is the subdrain, a two-piece, cast-iron or brass fitting. The upper half of the subdrain is a hat-shaped casting with an open top that's fitted with a chrome screen. The lower half is similar, but it's threaded to secure it to a nipple extending from the shower's *P*-trap (the portion of the drain beneath the floor). Around the circumference of the top half are six small holes. Three of them accommodate the bolts that clamp the drain halves together, with the shower-pan membrane sandwiched between. The other three are weep holes to let any moisture that gets into the mortar bed escape into the drain. If this residual moisture were trapped, it might promote the growth of fungus and bacteria in the bed.

In any tiled shower, the floor must be sloped toward the subdrain to ensure that water on the surface of the tiles (as well as any water penetrating the mortar) runs to the subdrain. I know three basic methods for creating the required slope, and there are situations where each is appropriate.

The first method, floating a sloped mortar bed on top of a level subfloor, takes some practice, but it's the approach many tilesetters prefer. While I've seen quite a few mortar floors sloped using either sand fill or cedar shingles fanned out around the drain, with the mortar floated on top, I wouldn't recommend either of these materials. The sand can sift through the cracks in the subfloor, eliminating the support for the pan, and the shingles aren't strong enough to support the weight of the mortar bed, tiles and occupant of the shower. With either of these materials, the shower pan is sure to fail. The best method is to use a solid base of mortar and work the slope into this base. (For information on how to float a sloped floor, see the sidebar on p. 178.)

The second method involves cutting long, wooden 2x4 wedges to support pie-shaped ¾-in. plywood panels which pitch toward the drain. A relatively uniform thickness of mortar is then floated over this "subpan" to achieve the required slope. For avid carpenters who prefer this technique, the only counsel really necessary is to make sure that the plywood is adequately supported by the wooden wedges and that the subdrain is likewise supported to prevent it from punching through the shower pan when the shower is used.

The third method involves considerably more carpentry. Basically, floor joists beneath the floor are boxed off and replaced with joists at the proper slope for good drainage. These are then covered with plywood, and a mortar floor of uniform thickness is applied, which forms the base for the pan. This was the method used on this project.

In either of the latter two methods, preparing a base and setting the tile are done exactly the same, and with both, the plywood must be covered with a shower pan. As explained in the basic discussion of pans in Chapter 4 (see p. 93), numerous materials have been used for pans over the years, but until recently I'd found none that was particularly successful. Now I always use a CPE (chlorinated polyethylene) material called Chloraloy 240 from The Noble Company (see the Resource Guide, and see p. 206 for detailed instructions on installing a CPE membrane). An important element in the first method is that a curing membrane must separate the mortar from the subfloor. The membrane must be located beneath any mortar, so it should cover not only the floor but also the curb and the walls. On the floor and curb, the Chloraloy does the job, while on the walls I used tar paper on this job.

Beginning the installation

Once the carpenters were gone, I started the installation. The first order of business was to measure and fit water-resistant drywall to the ceiling framing. Since the backer board would be the same size as the drywall, I didn't measure it—I simply used the cut piece of drywall as a template for marking the backer board. After spreading construction adhesive (the kind that comes in a caulking tube) on the framing, I screwed the drywall in place. To install the backer board, I combed epoxy thinset over the back side of the board, then hefted it into place and screwed it securely. The combined weight of drywall, backer board and tile is considerable, so I never scrimp in securing the assembly to the ceiling framing. Though the backer board could have been installed later on, I like to get it up before drywall is placed on the walls. That way, the drywall will support the edges of the ceiling. I also don't have to worry about damaging the drywall on the walls while juggling a heavy sheet of backer board above my head.

With the ceiling up, I checked to make sure that the shower seat was solid and fastened securely to the wall framing. I also checked to see that along its length the plywood seat top was pitched slightly away from the wall to aid drainage. The slope in any horizontal surface intended to drain water should equal at least ¼ in. for every foot, whether it's a walkway, a seat or a shower floor. For example, a shower floor that measures 3 ft. from the center of the drain to the farthest point away should slope a total of ¾ in. over that distance. In a square shower, the slope must be measured from the corners, which means that the sides are actually at a steeper slope. For practical and aesthetic reasons, the shower should be designed so that the subdrain is centered in the floor. Not only does this positioning look better, it also makes floating the mortar bed far easier than if the drain were off-center.

Materials list

Subpan:
¾-in. exterior-grade plywood

Shower pan:
40-mil-thick CPE material

Wall waterproofing membrane:
15-lb. tar-saturated felt paper (tar paper), laminated and sealed with cold-patch roofing asphalt

Mortar bed:
3 parts mason's sand and 1 part portland cement, mixed with approximately ¼ part lime and 1 part liquid latex mortar additive for wall mud and slightly less than 1 part liquid latex mortar additive for deck mud

Mortar-bed reinforcement:
20-gauge, 1-in. mesh poultry netting

Adhesive:
Portland cement mixed with liquid latex thinset additive for floor and wall tiles; epoxy thinset for ceiling tiles and backer board

Tile:
Nonvitreous, 8 in. square, for back wall and ceiling; vitreous, 2¼ in. square, sheet-mounted, for floor and side walls

Grout:
White sanded, mixed with liquid latex mortar additive

Before beginning the installation, I checked to see that the carpenters had properly sloped the plywood subfloor (above), which ensures that water in the shower will run to the subdrain. Then to support the sides of the shower pan that would extend up the base of the walls and the built-in seat, I nailed blocking between the studs (above right).

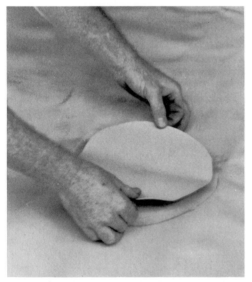

To reinforce the area around the subdrain, I cut a circle of CPE slightly larger than the flange on the subdrain and glued it to the shower pan.

To install the subdrain, I cut a hole in the subfloor for the lower half of the fitting. To support the subdrain, I made this hole ½ in. smaller in diameter than the drain flange and routed a ¼-in. rabbet around the top edge of the hole. This allowed the flange to bear on solid material, which would prevent the upper drain casting from punching through the shower pan when someone stepped on it. I checked both halves of the casting for burrs and filed off any I found. With the lower drain half bearing on the rabbet, the top surface of its lower flange was flush with the subfloor.

Next I turned to creating some support for the section of the shower pan that would extend up the base of the shower walls and the built-in seat. Without support, the pan would simply sag between the studs, so to provide it I installed blocking between the lower end of the studs. The pan must extend at least 2 in. higher than the shower curb, according to the plumbing inspectors I've worked with, so I install blocking accordingly. I like to use 2x10s for blocking, but on this project I used what was handy: a combination of 2x4s and 2x6s. When nailing in the blocking, I made sure that it was secure and that its outer face was flush with the edge of the studs, because it would also offer a place to which the drywall's lower edge could be attached.

Making and installing the pan Square shower pans are the easiest to make. To determine the size of the piece of CPE I needed to cut, I first measured the dimensions of the floor and then added 9 in. for each wall and about 14 in. to 16 in. for the curb. The curb had to be covered completely—inside face, top and outer face—and the CPE would be cut so that it lapped over the curb. After sweeping off a section of floor to ensure that I didn't damage the CPE with construction debris, I unrolled the material (I buy it by the roll for economy) and cut off a piece that best matched one of my overall dimensions. Because this material is rather expensive, I didn't want many scraps left over.

The pan material I use comes in 4-ft.- and 5-ft.-wide rolls. If this hadn't been wide enough to make the pan in one piece, I could have cut another section from the roll and bonded it to the first piece with either xylene or Nobleweld 100 (see the Resource Guide). Because these and the other materials used in pan-making can give off fumes and are messy to work with, it's a good idea to wear a charcoal filter mask and rubber gloves.

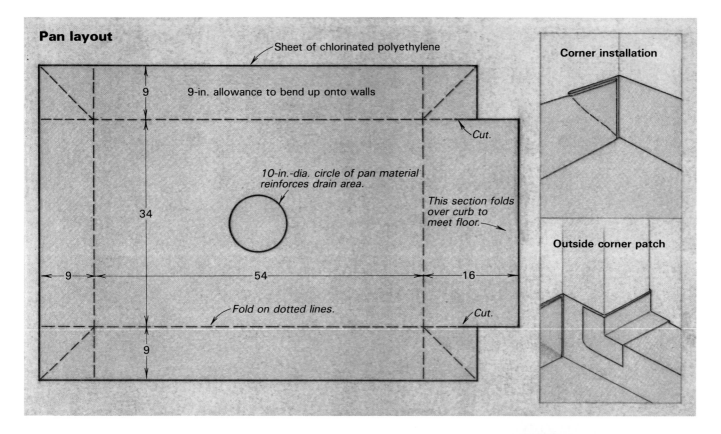

Pan layout

Sheet of chlorinated polyethylene

9-in. allowance to bend up onto walls

9

Cut.

10-in.-dia. circle of pan material
reinforces drain area.

This section folds
over curb to
meet floor.

34

9 | 54 | 16

Fold on dotted lines.

Cut.

9

Corner installation

Outside corner patch

I next drew the layout of the pan on the CPE with a felt-tipped marker, as shown in the drawing above. The dotted lines show where the material was to lap up the walls and how the corners were creased. At this point I glued a circle of pan material about 10 in. in diameter to the area that would end up between the drain halves. This made a thicker gasket for the drain to grip at this potential point of abrasion. Then I cut the pan to proper dimension with a utility knife guided by a straightedge. Next I creased the material along the four lines representing the perimeter of the floor and folded the diagonal corner lines away from the center of the pan so that the triangular tabs would end up between the pan and the blocking (see the detail at right in the drawing above).

Since only the top inch of the pan should be fastened with staples, the rest of the pan would be free to droop away from the wall during installation. To counter this tendency and to keep the pan tight against the floor, I coated the blocking, floor and curb with a thin layer of cold-patch roofing asphalt, spreading it evenly with a ⅛-in. notched trowel. Although some companies make special adhesives for this purpose, the asphalt is compatible with CPE and is also economical.

To ensure a watertight seal between the pan and the drain, I laid down two circles of butyl caulk (I use Chloraloy 150 or Bostik 2000) on the bottom half of the drain, one inside and one outside the bolt circle. Then I partially screwed the bolts into the lower half of the drain. Later, I would be able to feel where the bolt heads were so I would know where to cut holes for them, but I wanted to wait until the pan had been positioned and fastened to the blocking before actually cutting the holes, since a mistake in positioning them would waste an expensive piece of material.

After cutting and marking the pan layout on the CPE, I creased the material along the various fold lines.

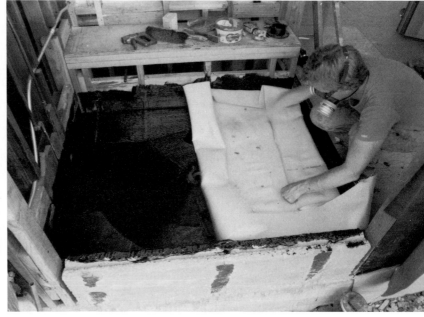

After coating the blocking, floor and curb with cold-patch roofing asphalt, I unfolded the bundled pan into position on the floor (top right). I smoothed the air bubbles out, folded the corners so that the triangular-shaped tabs ended up against the blocking (top left), worked the curb into place (above), and stapled around the top edge of the pan.

Next I rolled the prefolded pan into a bundle and positioned it over the shower floor. Starting at the drain, I smoothed the air bubbles out toward the walls and pressed the material into the corners, leaving no voids under or behind the pan. To flatten the folds in the corners, I first primed the contact portions of the fold with xylene and wiped off the excess with a lint-free rag. Then I drizzled some Nobleweld 100 adhesive onto the CPE, made the fold and held it in place for about 15 seconds until the adhesive had dried. When I was satisfied that the pan was snug, I stapled the top of the pan to the blocking every 1 in. to 2 in. along the top edge, making sure not to position any staples below the finished height of the curb. Then I covered the staples with asphalt. At the threshold I cut and folded the pan over the curb, and covered the resulting gap in the pan with a preformed corner patch. These patches can be purchased from the manufacturer or made from scrap and attached with solvent.

To put the drain halves together, I felt around for the bolts and pressed the CPE down over the head of each with one hand. With the other hand, I used a utility knife to cut small holes in the pan so it would slip over the bolts (I was careful not to cut any more pan material than was necessary). Then I stretched the CPE over each bolt, unscrewed them, and positioned the top half of the drain over its mate. I didn't put any caulk under the top half of the drain, since this could clog the weep holes. Once I had reinserted the bolts, I tightened them evenly with a socket wrench, rotating them a little bit at a time until they were snug. Finally, I cut away the disc of CPE covering the drain hole.

Before going any further in the installation, I needed to test the pan for leaks. To do this, I plugged the drainpipe with an expandable stopper (you can borrow one from your plumber, or buy one at a plumbing supplier) and filled the pan with water nearly to the top of the curb. I marked the level of the water and then let the pan sit undisturbed for 24 hours. The next day, I checked the water level; had it been possible, I also would have gotten under the floor with a flashlight to look for any sign of leaks. Fortunately, the pan looked very tight.

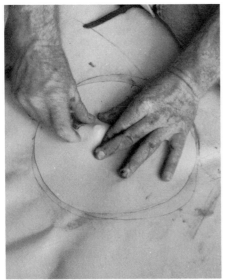
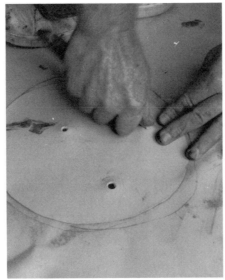
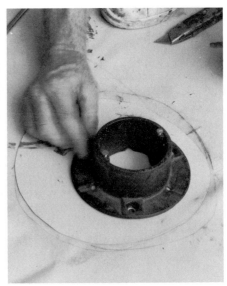

With the pan in position, I located by feel the bolts in the lower half of the subdrain and cut holes for them with my utility knife, making sure not to cut any more pan material than necessary. Then I bolted the two halves of the subdrain together and cut away the CPE over the drain hole.

If you find that the water has drained partway out of the pan, the leak may be around an errant staple near the top of the pan, or it may be behind one of the envelope folds. (Though it may seem as if the folds would be an unlikely culprit, from experience I've occasionally found this to be the case.) Once you've located the source of the leak, glue a 3-in.-dia. scrap of CPE or a manufactured accessory piece over the puncture with solvent—sort of like a tire patch. (Drain some water out of the pan and dry the area to be patched before making the repair.) If you find that the water has completely drained from the pan overnight, the leak probably occurred around the drain. Either the drain wasn't tightened enough, or it was tightened too much and the pan was cut. This latter problem is a common one for beginners, so do be careful. Whatever the cause of the leak, after you've made the appropriate repairs, test the pan again before proceeding with the installation.

Installing the membrane and reinforcing wire mesh

With the plumbing roughed in, all the blocking in place, and the pan installed and tested, a crew came in to install the drywall, which can be nailed or screwed to the wall studs. Make sure to protect the pan with scrap cardboard—a stray nail ground in by a boot heel would almost certainly result in a leak. The crew didn't bother filling the nail dimples or taping the joints of the drywall, except for those that would fall outside the field of tiles.

The curing/waterproofing membrane on the walls was to be made of overlapping, horizontal bands of tar paper, which would be laid out shingle-fashion over the drywall and the built-in seat. Because tar paper buckles between any anchoring staples when it comes in contact with freshly floated mortar, I spread cold-patch roofing asphalt over the drywall with a ⅛-in. V-notched trowel, which minimized the number of staples I needed. The thin layer of asphalt also seals around each staple as it enters the wall and provides a bit of insurance against any breaks in the membrane that may go unnoticed.

As I installed the bands of tar paper, I let them run wild at the edges, waiting until they were all in position to cut them to length.

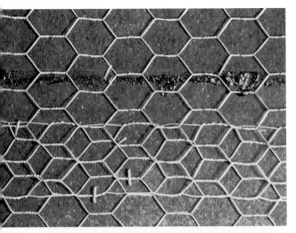

To provide the mortar with the greatest amount of support, this type of reinforcing wire mesh should be installed with the wire twists running parallel to the floor (top). I forced the wire mesh into the corners to make it neatly hug the walls (center). Wherever the mesh recalcitrantly bulged from the curb, I threaded short strips of CPE through it and glued the strips down to the shower pan (bottom).

Because the point at which the tar paper and the top of the shower pan would meet would be a potential spot for leaks, I wanted the 36-in. wide tar paper to overlap the pan by 3 in. So with a level and a pencil, I marked a horizontal line on the drywall 33 in. above the pan. Then I proceeded to comb the asphalt on the area below the line, extending the asphalt down over the top 3 in. of the shower pan. At the point where the pan and drywall met, I added enough asphalt to make up the difference in thickness between the two materials. This extra amount of asphalt would plug any tears that might develop in the tar paper as it passed from the drywall to the pan. I also applied tar paper to the seat, wrapping the framing like a birthday gift and slipping an edge under the tar paper on the walls. To ensure crisp corners and edges, I creased the paper before bedding it in the roofing asphalt. Each band of tar paper should be a continuous row around the shower. Creasing the corners of the paper ahead of time helps make the material lie flat in the corners of the shower. (Make sure that the tar paper is at room temperature before creasing it, since it can easily crack if folded when it's cold.)

As I applied the tar paper, I smoothed out any air pockets that developed behind it. When I had worked my way to a corner, I tucked the paper into the corner with the blade of a straightedge, making sure that the fit was snug. At one point I accidentally slit the paper in doing this, so I sealed the slit with a daub of asphalt. Then, when I had wrapped all the walls with this band, I stapled the lower edge of the paper to the top of the pan with ½-in. staples 6 in. on center, being careful not to staple below the top inch of the pan.

Once the curing/waterproofing membrane was in place, the reinforcing wire mesh followed. There are conflicting opinions about the kind of wire mesh that should be used. Many setters, however, use what's locally available, which, in most cases, means 20-gauge, 1-in. by 1-in., galvanized mesh, otherwise known as chicken wire or poultry netting. I've used chicken wire for thousands of installations above the waterline and have found that it always gave excellent service. If you're floating a mortar bed for an installation below the waterline, particularly for a tub or fountain, heavier-duty reinforcing is called for because the project must hold the weight of water, which is considerable. In this case, I switch to galvanized expanded metal.

On this job, the mesh I used contained strands of wire twisted together. This type of mesh should always be installed so that the twists run parallel to the floor to provide the mud with the most support. I fastened the bands of mesh to the drywall with 9/16-in. staples (if the substrate is plywood, as it was on the bench, the staples need only be ½ in. long) every 4 in. to 6 in., overlapping each band by 2 in. I positioned the first band of mesh to sit 1 in. off the floor of the shower (overlapping the pan). When placing both the tar paper and the mesh, I sometimes just cover over the brass fitting in the wall to which the shower arm is attached (it's called a drop-ear elbow). Later, once everything is in place, I feel through the paper for the location of the elbow and cut a neat hole just big enough to slip the shower arm through.

To cover the curb, I doubled up a piece of mesh and prefolded it, slightly exaggerating the fold, so that it would hug the inside, top and outside faces of the curb. While I couldn't use staples on the top of the curb, or below the top of the curb's inside face, I stapled it as needed on the outside face, where leaks were less likely to be a problem. Where the wire refused to lie flat on the top or inside face of the curb, I glued small strips of CPE in band-aid fashion to eliminate the bulges.

Preparing to float mortar walls

There are three distinct areas to be floated in a mortar-bed shower: the walls, the floor and the curb. The walls and curb should be floated first, and then the mortar floor can be addressed. That way you don't end up stomping over the mortar floor while you're doing the walls. The steps described below for floating walls apply to floating any vertical surface in a shower, whether a wall, the front of a seat, the face of a shower curb or the riser on a step. The procedure for floating floors is explained in full on p. 147 and in abbreviated form on p. 176 in this chapter. (For a summary discussion of the procedure for floating a mortar bed, see p. 86.)

Before mixing the wall mud, I sized up the situation and decided how I would place the float strips. In this case, the strips on the jambs of the window, those at the outer edge of the side walls and that on the outer face of the seat needed to be nailed to ensure that the mortar bed would be a precise thickness in these locations. When nailing the float strips, I kept the nails as close as possible to the mortar-bed side of the strip so that the resulting nail holes would eventually be covered by the trim tiles. The remaining float strips would be seated in columns of mud in order to plumb up the walls.

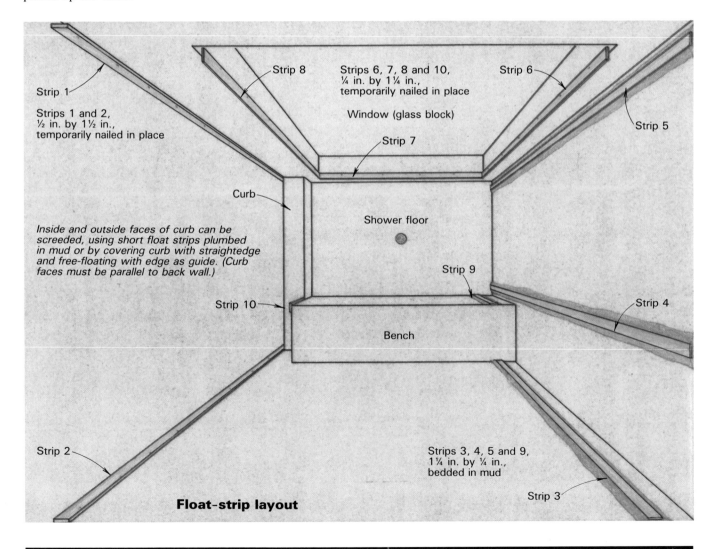

Strip 8

Strips 6, 7, 8 and 10, ¼ in. by 1¼ in., temporarily nailed in place

Strip 6

Strip 1

Strips 1 and 2, ½ in. by 1½ in., temporarily nailed in place

Window (glass block)

Strip 5

Strip 7

Curb

Shower floor

Inside and outside faces of curb can be screeded, using short float strips plumbed in mud or by covering curb with straightedge and free-floating with edge as guide. (Curb faces must be parallel to back wall.)

Strip 9

Strip 10

Strip 4

Bench

Strip 2

Strips 3, 4, 5 and 9, 1¼ in. by ¼ in., bedded in mud

Strip 3

Float-strip layout

After nailing the strips in place, I set up a plywood mortar board as a staging area between the box and the hawk. Then I gathered and arranged nearby everything else I needed for floating: a hawk, flat trowel, margin trowel, hammer, set of nesting straightedges, levels, bucket, sponge and the remaining float strips to be positioned. With all the tools at the ready, I mixed the wall mud.

Mixing wall mud   I follow the same procedure for mixing the dry ingredients for wall mud as I do for deck mud (see p. 145). But when the liquid and dry ingredients are to be combined, the procedure changes because wall mud must have a more spreadable consistency than deck mud in order to contend with gravity and adhere to the wall. Wall mud thus requires more liquid than deck mud, yet adding too much liquid can cause the floated bed to shrink excessively as it dries and it will crack. The question, of course, is how much liquid is enough? The answer, which depends on a number of factors, from the weather to the kind of sand used, becomes clear only in the actual process of mixing. Here's the way I always mix the wet and dry ingredients for wall mud.

I pile the mixed and chopped dry ingredients at the deep end of the mixing box and pour about 75% of the liquid needed into the shallow end of the box. Then I very slowly begin pulling the dry stuff into the liquid with small chops of the hoe. I go through the same mixing cycles as for combining the dry ingredients, and after each cycle I check to see if I need to add more liquid and, if so, I add it very gradually. As each mixing cycle is carried out, the mix will begin to homogenize to the proper consistency. What I'm aiming for is a smooth but spreadable mixture that is neither so wet that it runs nor so stiff that it's difficult to spread. I know that the mixture is right when it reminds me of peanut butter mixed with sand. It shouldn't be crumbly.

After getting the mixture to this point, I repeat the mixing cycle twice more to thin out the mud just a little. In other words, I slightly overmix the mortar so that it's a little wetter than it should be. This gives me a head start on the job—in the 10 or 15 minutes it takes me to get ready to float the wall, the mortar will have dried out to just the right consistency.

Using a flat trowel and hawk   For efficiently floating a mortar wall, a flat trowel and hawk are crucial pieces of equipment. The novice may find them a bit awkward to use at first, but a little practice is all that's needed. Here's how to use these tools.

After you've mixed the mortar, moisten the face of the hawk with a dampened sponge. Then prime the hawk by laying its edge on the edge of the mortar board and pressing a thin layer of mud onto its face with the flat trowel. Press hard! Then, with the flat trowel, push about a gallon's worth of mud onto the hawk. Lift the hawk up from the mud board and cut away the excess mud from the edges with the side of the trowel. The hawk is now loaded.

To get the mud off the hawk and onto the trowel for placement on the wall, tip the hawk toward the trowel and at the same time stick the trowel's edge into the mud. With an upward motion, scrape a trowelful of mud off the hawk. Then bring the hawk level before the remaining mud slides off. Using the trowel, spread the mortar on the wall. Throughout the process, the hawk will always be in one hand, and the trowel in the other. When you've loaded the wall with a hawkful of mud, go back to the mortar board for another helping.

I moved mortar from the mortar board to the wall by loading small amounts onto the hawk with the flat trowel.

Plumbing float strips   I first plumbed the two float strips on the back wall with the shower head, locating each 6 in. to 8 in. from a corner. Then I threaded a 6-in. pipe nipple into the wall fitting from which the shower elbow would eventually extend to help keep mortar out of the fitting.

To form the vertical columns of mortar that would anchor these float strips, I first pressed into the mesh a thin layer of mud the width of the trowel, applying it from floor to ceiling. This layer needed to be only thick enough to cover the wire—no more. I then built up additional layers of mud, ¼ in. at a time, until the column was about ½ in. to ⅝ in. thick.

I pushed each strip into its column of mud and, with the level held against it, plumbed each one so that the mortar was approximately ½ in. thick. Due to the vagaries of wood framing, the actual thickness of the mortar varied across the wall. But the mud allowed me to make up for these framing inaccuracies, and, with the help of the float strips as screeding guides, create plumb walls and later, parallel rows of tiles that didn't have to be tapered. This is the beauty of mortar-bed installations.

The section of the side wall nearest the back wall needed to be plumb so that when tiled the corner would not appear tapered from top to bottom. Along the outside edge of the wall, where the trim tiles would meet the drywall in an outside corner, however, the bed had to be a consistent ½ in. thick—even if the wall was out of plumb (thus the reason for the ½-in.-thick float strip tacked directly to the wall here). Otherwise, the grout joint between the trim tiles and drywall would be tapered and unsightly.

Floating mortar walls

Mortar is applied to walls in stages. With the float strips in place, I started on the back wall and pressed a thin coat of mud firmly into the wire exposed between the float strips. This coat ensured that the entire bed would be keyed into the wire. To apply this coat, I used the flat trowel held at a 15° to 20° angle to the wall to force the mud against the wire. Then, holding the trowel at about a 35° angle, I began to apply filler layers of mud, about ¼ in. thick at a time, to build the wall out to the desired thickness.

Building up the wall may take dozens of trips to the mortar board and can be hard work, but when I'm working with a sweet batch of mud, it becomes a pleasure. When I had sufficiently built up the wall, I held the trowel at about a 10° angle and ran it over the entire bed to flatten out the high spots and compact the mortar. I was careful not to press too hard, since the mortar would just squeeze out from under the trowel. With this done, I was ready to screed the bed.

Screeding both cuts away the excess mortar on the wall and reveals any depressions in the bed that need to be filled. I used a straightedge just long enough to overlap the float strips by a few inches. Facing the wall, I eased the straightedge onto the float strips at the bottom of the wall and held it lightly against them. (The float strips are to act as a guide, not supports, and too much pressure on them can push them out of place.) Then I simultaneously moved the straightedge upward and from side to side in a slight sawing motion, always keeping contact with both float strips. With each sawing motion, I moved the straightedge about 3 in. sideways and about ½ in. upward. I continued this back-and-forth movement until the straightedge filled with mortar. Then, to get the straightedge off the wall, I moved in one continuous motion from side to side, up and away from the bed. It's important not to stop and simply pull the loaded straightedge away from the wall. Good mortar has a tenacious grip, and a straightedge pulled directly away from the wall may tear chunks of mud from the float and may cause the screeded mortar to peel away from the wall.

Once I had built up the column of mud to the appropriate thickness, I positioned the float strips in the mud and plumbed them with the level (top). Then beginning at the bottom of the wall, I screeded away the excess mortar with a straightedge lightly held against the float strips and moved simultaneously upward and side to side (bottom).

After completing the center of each wall, I floated and screeded the areas beyond the float strips, then removed the strips and filled and screeded the channels they had left.

When a wall has a lot of excess mortar to be removed, the straightedge may not even touch the strips on the first pass or two. Be patient. Screeding too quickly usually tears mortar from the float, leaving holes that have to be packed full and rescreeded. Conversely, however, screeding too slowly may agitate the bed enough to loosen the particles of sand and cement in the mortar and cause the bed to slump. The bed may also slump if the mortar has been mixed too wet, in which case the mud should sit a while before it's screeded, and it may additionally need to be mixed with more dry ingredients to make it the right consistency. On the other hand, if the mortar is mixed too dry, it can be very difficult to screed and may push the float strips out of position. (For information on mixing mortar to the right consistency, see p. 146.)

After I had screeded the bed flat, I found that there were some marble-sized voids in the surface of the bed, but I waited until the mud had had a chance to set up before filling them in. Working fresh mortar too much with the tools can cause the mud to slump away from the wall. After I had filled in the center section of the wall, I floated and screeded the narrow areas beyond each float strip.

Once I had floated and screeded all sections of the three walls (the third one included the small areas to be tiled above and below the window), I removed the float strips that I had bedded in columns of mud (the nailed strips would be removed a little later). To do this without pulling mud off the wall, I took the margin trowel and ran the blade along both sides of each strip. Then I pried the strip away from the bed with the trowel, grabbed the strip with my free hand and pulled it away from the bed. Each strip left behind an empty channel that needed to be backfilled with mortar. To do this, I flattened the mud on the hawk until it was about 1 in. thick. Then I cut a strip of mud about 1½ in. to 2 in. wide and about 1 ft. long and forcefully troweled it into the channel. When the channel was filled, I ran the trowel over it from top to bottom to force as much mud into it as possible. I left the channels alone for 30 minutes or so to give the mortar a chance to set up before cutting away any excess mud with a wood float.

Finishing the mortar bed After about an hour, the walls had set up firmly enough for me to finish the bed, for which I needed to use a wood float. Wood floats can sometimes be confounding tools. My favorite one is twisted like a pretzel when it's dry, but after soaking for a few minutes, it begins to warp itself straight! The first thing I do with any wood float before using it is let it soak in a bucket of water for 10 minutes or so. This keeps the float from sucking any moisture from the mortar bed. A brand-new wood float is just about useless and must be dressed before it can be used. To do this, soak it for about 10 to 15 minutes. If the tool is going to warp at all, it will do so within this period of time. Then place a piece of 80-grit wet sandpaper on a flat surface, grit side up, and work the face of the wet float into the paper until the face is completely flat. Next hold the float at a 45° angle to the sandpaper and sand a ¹⁄₁₆-in.- to ⅛-in.-wide bevel on the bottom edge of all four sides. With the edges beveled, the float is less likely to dig into the mortar bed. Finally, smooth the face slightly on a piece of 100- to 120-grit sandpaper, and the tool should be ready to use.

I began finishing the bed by rubbing the entire surface with the wood float to cut down the high spots. Then I set the float aside, loaded up the hawk with a 1-in.-thick layer of mud and went back over the surface, filling any low spots with the margin trowel. Occasionally, I had to rough up the surface of the these low spots to get the fresh mortar to stick. After filling in these depressions, I rubbed the entire surface again with the wood float. To clean up the inside corners, I moved the float vertically, holding its edge at about a 35° angle to the corner. When I had trouble cleaning up an inside corner, I used the tip of the margin trowel to sharpen it up.

The final step in finishing the mortar bed was to remove the float strips that had been nailed in place. I gradually pried each strip off the wall, lifting it away first from the top or bottom. Once the nails began to back out, I could get at them with a nail puller or the claws of my hammer.

When the bed is finished, the setter can choose either to set tile immediately or to wait until the bed has hardened. I was taught to begin setting tile right away, but now I prefer to wait overnight before tiling. There are several reasons for this. First, the reinforcing mesh is already supporting the considerable weight of the mortar. Adding the weight of the tiles to that of the mortar courts disaster at this point. When the mortar has hardened somewhat, it will support itself. Second, mortar shrinks slightly as it dries, with about 95% of the shrinkage occurring within 10 to 12 hours after floating. Setting tiles over a wet bed that is shrinking may later produce cracked or loosened tiles. At one time the only way to get tiles to stick properly to a bed was to set them on the wet mortar. Nowadays, however, with the advent of modern thinset adhesives, setting tile on a wet bed is unnecessary and, I think, unwise. Finally, apart from these purely technical reasons, I like to concentrate on making a mortar bed as true as possible, and for this reason I approach setting the tiles as a separate and distinct operation. On this job, the client was planning to do his own setting, and I therefore didn't need to worry at all about that part of the process.

Floating the window jambs and curb

Floating the jambs on a window can be problematic, since most are barely wider than a float strip. The job is easier if you're working with a helper, but you can nonetheless float a jamb alone. The trick is to float the area around the jamb first. Then when the mud has set up, plumb a straightedge at the corner of the jamb and, if you haven't a helper to hold it, tack it to the mortar bed with a few small-gauge nails. Next float mortar on the jamb and cut away the excess with the blade of the margin trowel. You could use an adjustable square, guided by the wall, and screed off the excess mortar with the blade of the square, but with a little patience, you can do an acceptable job by simply eyeballing the float. With the straightedge still in place, finish the jamb with the wood float.

To remove the straightedge, I hold it against the wall and push up until its contact with the mud is broken. Then I lift it away from the bed. After the jamb has had a chance to set up—20 to 30 minutes is about right—I'll check the angle of the float with an adjustable square to see if the jamb needs to be pared down or filled in so that it's square to the walls. You can use essentially the same techniques to float the window sill and the top of the curb.

The curb's inside and outside faces should be floated with wall mud as if they were small walls, and the top of the curb, like a floor, should be floated with deck mud. A straightedge again provides a guide for floating the mortar, and a carpenter's square can be used as a screed. On this job, I floated both faces of the curb and then waited to float its top when I floated the shower floor.

To float the curb, I troweled mud over the wire mesh and then screeded it with the body of a carpenter's square held against the floor.

Floating the floor

On this project, I decided to float the floor and the top of the curb after the client had set tiles on the walls, but this needn't be the order of things. In any case, I floated both the floor and the curb top with deck mud. The floated floor had two requirements: its entire perimeter had to be level, and it had to maintain the plywood's slope toward the drain. There are two ways to float an even layer of mortar over a sloped floor, either freehand or using float strips. In either case, a piece of reinforcing mesh must be placed midway in the bed to keep it from cracking.

Floating a sloped floor freehand, the method used for this project, works well on floors less than 4 ft. square. I floated the floor in two steps so as to install the reinforcing wire mesh midway in the bed. First, I spread enough mud on the floor to build up about half the 2-in. thickness of the finished bed (that thickness will vary according to the height of the subdrain's top portion and the thickness of the tile). To allow water to flow freely into the drain's weep holes, I surrounded the bolting flange with plastic tile spacers (you could also use pea gravel). Then I placed the mesh over the first layer of mud and dumped on another layer of mud. I leveled the perimeter of the bed by gauging the bed's height against the nearest horizontal grout line.

To float the shower floor, I first built up half the thickness of the floor, placing tile spacers around the bolting flange to allow any water that entered the floor to flow freely around the weep holes (above). Then I covered the first layer of mortar with reinforcing mesh (right).

The mortar had to match the subfloor's slope toward the drain, and with a level I could easily duplicate this mild slope. It may seem a little odd to use a level to help make the mortar out-of-level, but there's a quick way to do it. Before I floated the first layer of mortar, I laid the level on the sloping plywood floor of the shower. Naturally, the bubble in the leveling vial was slightly off-center. I marked its position with a small bit of tape placed on the vial at one edge of the bubble, and thereafter all I had to do was align the bubble with the tape—the level would have a slope to match the floor.

As I troweled on additional mortar over the mesh, I compacted it thoroughly by pressing it into the floor with a wood float, and used the same float to pare away excess material. Periodically, I'd check the work with my temporarily out-of-level level. I usually use two wood floats for this type of work: a 14-in. float for moving the bulk of the mud, and a 10-in. float for the final forming and finishing. As I worked the mortar near the drain, I pared away material until the mud was below the drain by the thickness of a floor tile and a layer of thinset (allow about 1/16 in. for the thinset). It's important not to let the top surface of the tile end up *below* the surface of the drain, but it's okay for it to be slightly above.

Once I had the floor about the way I wanted it, I placed a straightedge on the floor from drain to wall to see if the mortar bed humped or dished, and made any needed adjustments. If the bed has been compacted properly, it's easy to carve away excess mortar with the wood float. I finished the bed with a wood float, too, just as I had done with the floated walls. If the area around the drain had been particularly narrow, I could have used short 2x4 blocks as makeshift floats.

I sloped the second layer of the floor with the wood float, using the base of the wall tiles and the top of the subdrain as my guides and checking the slope with the level as I worked.

Floating a sloped mortar shower floor

The floor of a shower stall must, of course, be sloped toward the drain. To do this, you can either build a sloping plywood subfloor (two methods are described in this chapter), or float a sloped bed of mortar on top of a standard subfloor. The latter method is particularly useful when you need to correct a subfloor that's uneven or out of level, and I'd like to sketch out the procedure for that method here, using a small shower with a square floor plan as the example.

Cut a hole for the subdrain in the center of the subfloor, or as near the center as you can (you may have to dodge floor joists or beams). Install the lower half of the subdrain, connecting it to the rough plumbing. The outer flange of this half should rest on top of the subfloor.

Measure from the center of the subdrain to the farthest point of the shower enclosure, and figure out how much slope will be needed over that distance. Any surface that's designed to drain water should slope at a rate of about ¼ in. per foot, so if you measure 4 ft., the farthest point of the shower will have to be 1 in. higher than the drain (4 x ¼ in. = 1 in.). Add enough to this measurement to account for the height that the subdrain flange sticks up above the subfloor.

Cut wood float strips to the height developed above, and nail them in continuous lengths to the floor around the perimeter of the shower. Unlike the float strips used on mortar walls, these strips need not be removed later on; instead they will become a permanent part of the floor.

Staple 15-lb. tar paper to the subfloor over combed-out asphalt, and staple a layer of reinforcing wire mesh over the paper. Then mix up a batch of deck mud. I use Laticrete 3701 (see the Resource Guide) instead of water to mix with the dry ingredients. This deck mud should be on the crumbly, dry side of mortar mixes. I dump it on the floor, pack it with a trowel and screed away the excess, using the drain flange and wood strips around the perimeter of the floor as screeding guides. You may not be able to maneuver a full-length screed in the confined spaces of a shower stall, but you can sometimes use short lengths of straightedge to do part of the job, and then finish off the rest by eye with a wood float. After waiting overnight for the deck mud to harden, you're ready to install the CPE shower pan.

First run two beads of butyl caulk along the lower flange (one inside the bolt circle and one outside). Then cut the CPE pan to size (see p. 166 for instructions on how to do this), and slide it into place on the sloped shower floor. You can comb out cold-patch roofing asphalt and bed the CPE in it, but this isn't necessary. Once the shower pan is in place, feel for the bolts in the lower half of the subdrain and knife a small hole over each one. Bed the CPE in the caulk to seal it tight, then remove the bolts. Now you can bolt the top half of the subdrain in place over the CPE. The remainder of the mortar floor, and the rest of the job, will proceed exactly as did the floor in this chapter.

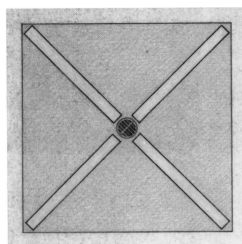

Positioning float strips for floating a sloped shower floor

Outside ends of strips should be level regardless of position of drain. This allows first row of base trim or wall tiles to be set level.

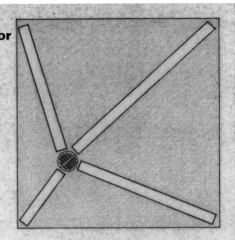

For sloped floors larger than 4 ft. square, I find it helpful to use float strips to get the desired pitch. These strips should extend from the drain to the corners of the shower floor. As with floating the floor freehand, I would begin by floating half the thickness of the desired bed and covering this with wire mesh. Then I would trowel four elongated piles of deck mud over the mesh, each pile running from the drain to a corner of the shower. A float strip would be tapped into each pile, then I'd check them for the proper slope by using the tape-and-level technique just described, making sure that the ends of the strips were at the same elevation. When all four were positioned, I would fill the areas surrounding the strips with deck mud and pack them with a trowel. Next I would place the level in the mud along each wall and tap it down to create a slender plateau connecting the ends of the four strips around the perimeter of the floor. Beginning at this flattened area and using the strips as a visual guide, I'd pare down the excess mud with the wood float, gauging the thickness of the mortar between strips by eye. Screeding with a straightedge accomplishes the same thing, of course, but in the confined space of a shower there isn't much room to maneuver one.

Once I had finished shaping the floor, I'd remove the float strips, fill the resulting channels with mud, pack them down and remove the excess with the wood float. The surface could then be finished with the wood float. □

Layout sketch

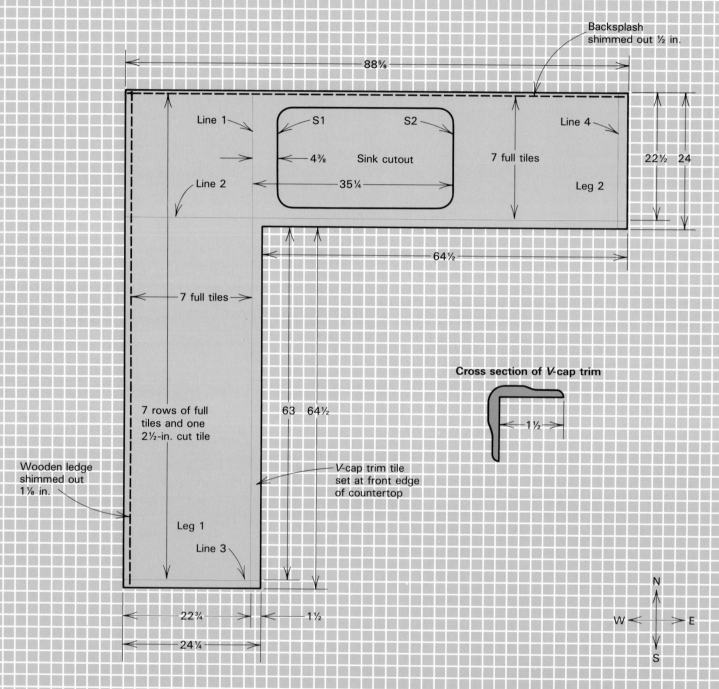

Backsplash shimmed out ½ in.

88⅝

Line 1

S1   S2

Line 4

4⅜   Sink cutout

7 full tiles

Line 2   35¼

Leg 2

22½   24

64½

7 full tiles

Cross section of _V_-cap trim

7 rows of full tiles and one 2½-in. cut tile

63   64½

1½

Wooden ledge shimmed out 1⅛ in.

_V_-cap trim tile set at front edge of countertop

Leg 1

Line 3

N
W ← → E
S

22¾   1½

24¼

(All dimensions are given in inches, unless otherwise noted.)

Thinset Countertop

T he owner of this house was an accomplished woodworker who planned to remodel his entire kitchen in his spare time. He had begun by moving a few walls to enlarge the kitchen and had built and installed new cabinets. He next wanted to tile the countertops, but realized that he needed help after making the rounds of the local tile shops. Each of the shops had given him conflicting information on how to proceed with the installation, and he called me in the hope that I could sort out the confusion and offer up some sound counsel.

Sizing up the job

When I visited the client's home, I found that only a portion of the kitchen was in fact ready for tiling. The owner explained that he wanted to finish the job in stages over a period of time and asked if I would be willing to tile the first countertop, with him acting as helper. This way he would learn how to tackle the other countertops himself. I liked his initiative and enthusiasm and agreed to the plan. As it turned out, we completed the entire first counter from cutting the backer board to grouting the tiles in about six hours.

The countertop we tiled together was on an *L*-shaped section of cabinets in the corner of the kitchen, and held a sink. The client had chosen vitreous, 3-in.-square tiles (about $\frac{3}{16}$ in. thick) with a glossy black glaze for the countertop. They were mounted in 12-tile sheets, and the grout joint was therefore predetermined at $\frac{1}{8}$ in. For the backsplash, he had picked lipstick-red 3-in. by 6-in. tiles that were $\frac{1}{2}$ in. thick. These tiles would be set in a single "soldier course" row—that is, standing upright instead of horizontally. Although the finished job would be stunning, I immediately discovered a serious problem with the countertop tiles: they scratched very easily. The client assured me that this counter would receive very little wear and that he planned to make cutting boards to protect the tiles when using the top. He insisted that he had always wanted a black countertop, and that was that.

With regard to the specifics of the job, I needed to use an installation method that the owner could duplicate by himself on the other countertops. I decided to set the tile on backer board, since it makes an excellent setting bed and is relatively easy to install. As well, the client had already covered the tops of the cabinets with a layer of ¾-in. AC exterior plywood, unwittingly accommodating the requirement that backer board used for floors and countertops should be laminated to a plywood substrate at least ½ in. thick. The backer board would need to be laminated to the substrate with either a latex or an epoxy thinset and further secured with 1½-in. roofing nails or 1½-in. screws. But since not all latex thinsets can be used on plywood, I opted to go with the epoxy for laminating the backer board. Because the countertop would see limited service, I decided that no waterproofing membrane was needed. Had this been a heavily used countertop, however, a waterproofing membrane would have been mandatory.

The sink the client had purchased was of the self-rimming variety, meaning that it was designed to be installed on top of the tiled counter. Although this type of sink makes life easy for the tilesetter, I think it proves a real nuisance for the owner, as food particles often get jammed beneath the sink's lip during cleaning. For this reason, I suggested that the sink be installed *under* the tiles to produce a neatly finished, sanitary edge. To do this, the top of the sink would need to be kept nearly flush with the top of the backer board.

Estimating materials

The customer had taken advantage of a sale at a local tile store and had ordered more than enough tiles for all the kitchen countertops, including trim pieces. I began the job by determining the exact dimensions of the tiles and making up a tile/grout-joint list.

Ordinarily when I compile a tile/grout-joint list, I determine the width of the basic tile-and-grout-joint unit and then calculate the total number of tiles needed to cover the job (see p. 111). Because the black tiles were sheet-mounted, however, the list had to include not only the combined width of a single tile and grout joint but also the combined width of an entire sheet and grout joint. I could, of course, have just done a list that included enough single tiles to stretch the longest length of the countertop. But after you've been in this business for a while, you learn some shortcuts. Doing a list for full sheets was like taking giant steps down the length of the counter, rather than the many tiny steps of a single tile width. In figuring the amount of tile that would fit, I consulted the first list to discover how many full sheets would fit down the length of the countertop, then found out how many single tiles would fill in the remainder of the countertop by looking at the single-tile list. For the width of the countertop, I used my single-tile list. I added to the end of the list the interior depth of the V-cap trim that would finish off the front edge of the countertop (see drawing, p. 180). Each sheet of tiles was approximately 12⅜ in. square.

With this information, I'll usually proceed to doing a trial tile layout on paper. One of the reasons for this is to suggest changes in the structure of the job, such as making the run of cabinets a little bit longer or shorter to accommodate full tiles. That's possible when cabinet construction has not yet begun, but in this case the cabinets were already built and in place and there wasn't anything to change about them. I therefore skipped the paper layout, and instead waited until the backer board was in to do an actual full-size layout.

Figuring the amount of backer board we would need wasn't difficult, but because the material isn't particularly cheap, I wanted to minimize any waste. I had a stock of 3-ft. by 4-ft. sheets already on hand, so I decided to use these. Cutting them lengthwise and carefully using the offcuts, I found that three full sheets would be sufficient. It's perfectly fine to use small, scrap pieces of backer board to fill in small areas (as long as you don't overdo it). Sometimes this saves having to buy an additional sheet, and it's often just easier to do. Had I cut a large, sink-sized hole in a single sheet of backer board, the sheet would have been too fragile to handle. So instead, I cut the backer board for the large open areas on either side of the sink, then cut smaller pieces to fit the narrow areas just in front of and behind the sink.

With regard to the amount of setting materials needed, I checked the coverage tables I keep in my notebook. In order to laminate the backer board to the plywood substrate and backsplash area, I would need enough epoxy thinset to cover about 22 sq. ft. of countertop with a ¼-in. square-notched trowel, that is, roughly ½ gallon of epoxy liquid and about 2 gallons of filler powder. While the same epoxy thinset could be used to set the tiles, I would switch, for economy's sake, to a latex thinset. Since I planned to use the same-size trowel to apply the latex thinset, the amount needed of this adhesive was the same as for the epoxy.

To calculate the amount of grout needed, I consulted the grout tables in my notebook and figured that the job would require a 10-lb. sack of dry grout. Before mixing any grout, I would set aside two cups of dry grout for the owner for any future repairs, wrapping up this grout in a plastic bag taped tightly shut to keep moisture out. Two cups will more than suffice if a few tiles have to be replaced later on. Then I would mix up the remaining ingredients, which might yield a pound or two more grout than I would actually need on the job. But it's always better to err on the high side, because coming up short in the midst of a job is a real nuisance.

Because the grout joint is the place where moisture can penetrate the installation and reach the other layers of the tile sandwich, I always mix an additive with grout to increase its effectiveness against water seepage. On this job, I would need between one and two quarts of additive for the 10 lb. of grout.

Preparing and installing the backer board

To make sure that all the backer board fit the job, I cut all the pieces and positioned them on the plywood substrate before laminating any of them. With the backer board in place, but not laminated to the substrate, I dropped the sink into the hole, let it rest on the backer board and with a pencil traced on the board the outline of the sink and the position of the reinforcing bars under its lip. I then removed the sink and the backer board and cut a groove for the reinforcing bars with a dry-cutting diamond blade. (If you don't have a diamond blade, use a ¼-in. carbide router bit.) The groove had to be deep enough to allow the lip of the sink to sit directly on the backer board, yet not so deep that it cut entirely through.

Before I mixed any thinset for laminating the backer board to the plywood, I wanted to make sure that the cabinets themselves wouldn't become casualties of the process. So I draped an apron of sheet plastic over the faces and ends of the cabinets, and taped it in place. Working with thinset—or any tile adhesive, for that matter—is messy business, and a few moments spent preparing for the worst will keep you from having to clean up the worst later on. It's a good idea to protect anything within splash, drip or splatter range with plastic sheet, a canvas tarp or kraft paper.

I used the dry-cutting diamond blade to cut the backer board to size and to create the groove for the sink. To control the depth of the groove, I shimmed up the blade with a scrap piece of backer board.

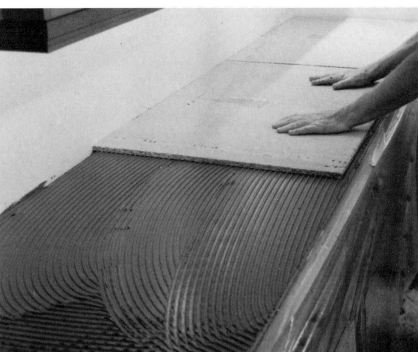

The first step in laminating the backer board to the plywood substrate was to spread and comb epoxy thinset on the plywood (above left). Next I positioned the board in the adhesive (above), "beat" it in with a hammer and beating block, and secured it with nails.

I positioned the backer board surrounding the sink in the adhesive, but waited to nail it until I had dropped the sink in place and made sure that the reinforcing bars on the sink's underside rode correctly in the grooves.

Working on one leg of the countertop at a time, after mixing the epoxy thinset I spread and combed it on the plywood with a ¼-in. square-notched trowel. Then I positioned each piece of backer board. To bed the backer board firmly in the epoxy, I used a hammer and an 8-in. square of ¾-in. plywood to "beat" each piece into the adhesive. Then I secured the board to the plywood with 1½-in. roofing nails spaced 8 in. on center.

To laminate the boards with the sink groove, I tentatively placed them in the adhesive and then slipped the sink into position to make sure that it was accurately seated before nailing any of the boards in place. Once I had nailed the grooved sections, I removed the sink, buttered the underside of its lip with epoxy and put it back in place. Buttering the lip would prevent the sink from moving around underneath the tiles.

The bottom edges of the backsplash boards would rest directly on the backer board of the countertop. While backer board used for walls need not be laminated but only nailed to the studs, it was easy enough to laminate the narrow strips for the backsplash anyway. When doing this, it's much simpler to apply and comb the thinset directly on the strips rather than on the wall. In this case, I used 2-in.-long nails to secure the strips because the nails had to penetrate the backer board and the drywall to reach the studs.

Once all the backer board had been nailed in place, I covered the joints with fiberglass-mesh reinforcing tape and forced thinset through the tape into the joints to edge-glue the sections of backer board. I treated all the joints this way and ran tape around the front edge of the boards so that it lapped over the edge of the plywood top as well—this helps to hold the thinset in place.

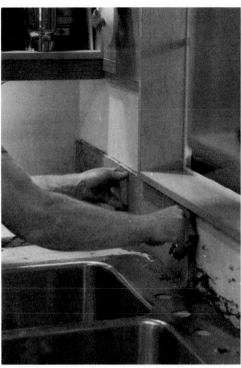

I combed thinset directly on the backer-board strips for the backsplash (left) and laminated them to the wall before nailing them to the studs behind the drywall (above).

Once the backer board was laminated, I taped all the joints with fiberglass-mesh tape (left) and edge-glued the boards with thinset adhesive to prevent any movement in the substrate from telegraphing through the joints and cracking the tile. For the same reason, I also taped and edge-glued the countertop's front edge (above).

Because the countertop was small, I needed layout lines only around its front edge for the grout joint between the V-cap trim tiles and the field tiles.

I began setting the tile on the L-shaped countertop at the inside corner of the L.

Doing the layout on the backer board

Because this countertop was relatively small, I needed to snap only the four layout lines representing the ones I had marked on the layout sketch (see p. 180). Corresponding to the grout joint between the V-cap trim tiles and the field tiles, these lines were placed 1½ in. from and parallel to the front and side edges of the countertop. But rather than confine the lines to the V-cap area, I ran them into the space for the field tiles at the back corner of the cabinets. Here they would help align the tiles on both legs.

My solution to the layout problems in this project involved some compromises, but that's not uncommon when you're faced with fitting tiles to an existing surface. Layout began at the intersection of *lines 1* and *2*. The distance from that point to the rear of the countertop on the west wall was 22¾ in. This gave me enough room for seven rows of full tiles, with a ⅞-in. space left over. But a cut this narrow would not look attractive. The usual thing to do in this case would be to adjust the layout to put cuts larger than half-size at the front and the back of the counter. This would lend some symmetry to the cuts, but it would also mean that a cut edge of field tile would be next to the V-cap, and this should be avoided wherever possible. Because tiles often have a rounded, or "cushioned," edge, the cut edge of a tile is higher than the edges of other tiles, and is prone to damage. So we decided that the solution to this layout problem was to shim out the backsplash with a layer of backer board. With a layer of thinset behind it, the ½-in.-thick backer board would reduce the width of the counter by about ⅝ in., and once the ½-in.-thick backsplash tiles were set, that awkward little ⅞-in. cut would no longer be needed. On the other leg of the countertop, the distance from *line 2* to the north wall was 22½ in. This gave me enough room to set seven rows of full tiles with a ½-in. space left over. Once again, we decided to absorb that space by installing backer board at the backsplash. The extra thickness of the backsplash would actually be an advantage, since the client wanted to cap the red tiles with a wooden ledge to hold spice jars.

Along the length of the cabinets, I found that I could set 20 full tiles with a 2-in. cut against the V-cap at the south end of *leg 1*. I didn't like it, but there wasn't much I could do. The counter couldn't be shortened or lengthened, and shifting the layout to the north would result in cuts all along the front of *leg 2*. I'd just have to live with the cut tiles here. A similar compromise was necessary on the other end of the countertop.

The next thing to check was the position of the sink in relation to the tiles. To see how the tiles would fall, I measured the distance from the sink edges (*S1* and *S2*) to *line 1*. Consulting the tile/grout-joint list, I saw that I would need a 1¼-in. cut tile on the left side of the sink and a 2⅛-in. cut tile on the right (I planned to use surface-bullnose tiles all around the sink). I didn't like the visual imbalance of the cuts, but on the whole the layout was a good one. Nothing was glaringly out of place, and the thickness of the backer-board backsplash would make the spice ledge a bit more stable.

Setting the tiles

Because it would take much longer to set the tiles than it did to laminate the backer board, I mixed only half the latex thinset needed. Since I planned to begin setting against the layout line at the inside corner of the L and work my way down the first leg, I would apply the first batch of thinset to this leg only. In order to keep from leaning on the V-cap trim tiles as I positioned the field tiles, I left setting the V-caps on both legs until last. After I had finished the first leg, I next set the tiles around the sink and finally addressed the balance of field tiles on the second leg.

Sheet-mounted tiles often need a little more coaxing than individual tiles to line up straight, in part because the additional expanse of tile has more grip than a single tile does. Another reason is that every sheet-mounted tile isn't always perfectly aligned with its neighbors, and the occasional black sheep must be prodded and pushed to conform, which, of course, is resisted by the backing. Using a straightedge or even the straight side of the notched trowel makes the alignment process considerably easier. If you wait about five minutes after initially positioning the sheet in the thinset, the backing will often lose its grip on the tiles and allow the offending tile to be easily repositioned. If you're in a hurry, of course, you can always cut through the backing with a utility knife and move the tile.

When I had finished setting field tiles on the first leg, I moved on to trimming out the sink, where surface-bullnose tiles would overlap the metal lip by about ¼ in. To make sure that these tiles adhered, I back-buttered each piece before positioning it in the adhesive on the setting bed. Instead of wiping off the excess adhesive that squeezed out between these trim tiles, I waited until the adhesive had set up and then cut it away with a knife—I didn't want to risk disturbing the tiles until the adhesive had set up somewhat. But I did want to make sure that any globs of thinset were cleared from the joints.

To keep the grout joints of the surface bullnose consistently sized across the front and rear edges of the sink, I checked the position of the tiles against the tile/grout-joint list. The novice setter might find it helpful instead to strike layout lines to identify the positions of the bullnose tiles around the sink. At each corner of the sink, the surface-bullnose tiles were cut to a 45° angle as a decorative solution to the problem of turning the corner while keeping a bullnose edge toward the sink. This kind of cut is easiest on the wet saw, but, with practice, it can also be made with the snap cutter. It's important to remember that the width of the angled grout joint between the corner tiles has to be the same as that used elsewhere. This thickness must be allowed for when the cuts are made.

Once I had set the countertop field and bullnose tiles, I combed thinset over the backsplash and positioned the red tiles. I made sure to align their joints with those on the countertop, and I inserted a spacing wedge under each tile to hold it in place until the adhesive had set up. Backsplash tiles shouldn't rest directly on the countertop tiles; instead, they should be raised above the countertop by the thickness of a grout joint and the gap later filled with caulk. Once the thinset on the backsplash had begun to set up, I cleaned the excess thinset out of the joints.

Having set the countertop and backsplash tiles and cleaned the joints, I no longer needed to lean over the counter and could begin setting the V-caps. These trim tiles needed to be bedded in thinset on both the top and the edge of the counter. To cover both surfaces, I spread thinset with the notched trowel on the countertop, and back-buttered the inside lower portion of each V-cap.

Trim tiles like surface bullnose and V-cap often tend to be slightly smaller or larger than the field tiles they accompany, probably because trim and field tiles are usually fired separately. Whenever I find that the trim tiles I'm using in an installation are different in size from the field tiles, I simply center the trim piece in relation to the field tile. This means that the grout joints between trim tiles may run a little wider than those between field tiles, but the slight difference usually isn't apparent to the casual observer.

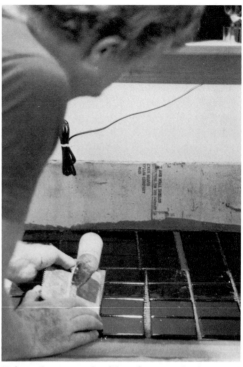

Using the smooth side of a notched trowel as a short straightedge lessened some of the difficulty of properly aligning the sheet-mounted tile.

Applying adhesive for setting V-cap trim tiles

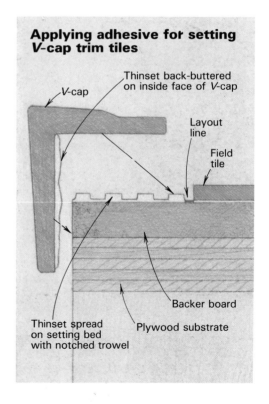

V-cap

Thinset back-buttered on inside face of V-cap

Layout line

Field tile

Thinset spread on setting bed with notched trowel

Backer board

Plywood substrate

On this job, factory-made, V-cap outside corners were available, but I had to miter two standard V-cap tiles to produce the inside corners. While it's possible to create these miters with the biters, it's more practical to use the wet saw. The latter does the job quickly and produces a smooth cut whose edge can be rounded over with a rubbing stone. To hold the V-caps up straight against the miter gauge of the wet saw and ensure an accurate cut, I supported the V-cap with a small wooden block.

Because V-caps often come out of the kiln slightly distorted, I always take time after setting each section of trim to sight along the top and front faces of the V-caps to see that they're aligned. Once I had set all the V-caps, I went over all the tiles again, looking for any that were out of place and checking to see that all the excess thinset had been cleaned off the tiles and from the joints.

Grouting the tiles

The customer's choice of white grout was no accident. He wanted to *see* the tiles, and there is no greater contrast than between black and white. A grouting situation like this, however, calls for precise work. If the grout is not evenly and thoroughly mixed to begin with, or if the joints are not uniformly filled, inconsistencies will be very apparent against the backdrop of black tiles.

Usually I can spread quite a bit of grout before I have to go back and begin cleaning up. With slick, black tiles like these, though, whose surface scratched easily, I had to work and clean up a small area at a time to keep the residual grout from hardening on the surface of the tiles and requiring heavy scrubbing. I used my regular technique for cleaning up the excess grout, but paid particular attention to uniformly shaping the joints with the sponge. Occasionally, I found that I had wiped away too much grout with the sponge and then had to repack these spots with fresh grout, making sure in each case to reshape the joint before the grout hardened.

While factory-made V-cap outside corners were available, I had to create V-cap inside corners by mitering cuts on the wet saw.

White grout used with the black and red tile produced a handsome effect, but the stark contrast in colors meant that I had to use extra care in grouting, and work and clean up a very small area at a time.

Grouting below the skirt of the *V*-cap tiles, which extended about ½ in. beneath the front edge of the plywood, was a little tricky. Because packing this area with grout would have been a little impratical with the grout trowel alone, I used my rubber-gloved hand as a second grouting tool, as I often do to grout an awkwardly positioned joint. In this case, I backed up the rear of the joint with one hand (using my thumb as a "fence" to keep grout within the joint) and packed the joint with the grout trowel held in the other hand.

Once I had cleaned off the grout residue and the grout had begun to set up, I went back over the entire surface looking for sloppy joints. There always seems to be a high or low spot here and there that was missed the first time around. The time to make any last-minute adjustments in the joints is while the grout is firm but not yet hard.

Finally, I used the margin trowel to square up the ends of the grout joints intersecting the sink (the ones between the bullnose trim tiles). I also squared up the joint between the backsplash and the countertop tiles. These two joints, which would be prone to cracking, also needed to be covered with a bead of white silicone caulk (matching the color of the grout) to keep water out. To save me an extra trip, the owner agreed to caulk the joint himself after giving the grout a couple of days to dry out. I also suggested that he wait at least 48 hours before installing the plumbing fixtures. After the effort spent setting the tiles, neither one of us wanted to risk damaging them by wrenching on the fixtures before the thinset was solid.

One thing to keep in mind as you're designing a tile job is the amount and visibility of any caulking that will be required. Caulk looks best when invisible, that is, when it matches the color of the grout joints or tile. If you're planning a job that will need to be caulked in conspicuous locations—for example, around a sink or shower surround—consider the color of available caulks when you're deciding on the color of the grout. Caulk generally comes in black, white, brown, tan or clear, and sometimes in gray.   □

Layout sketch

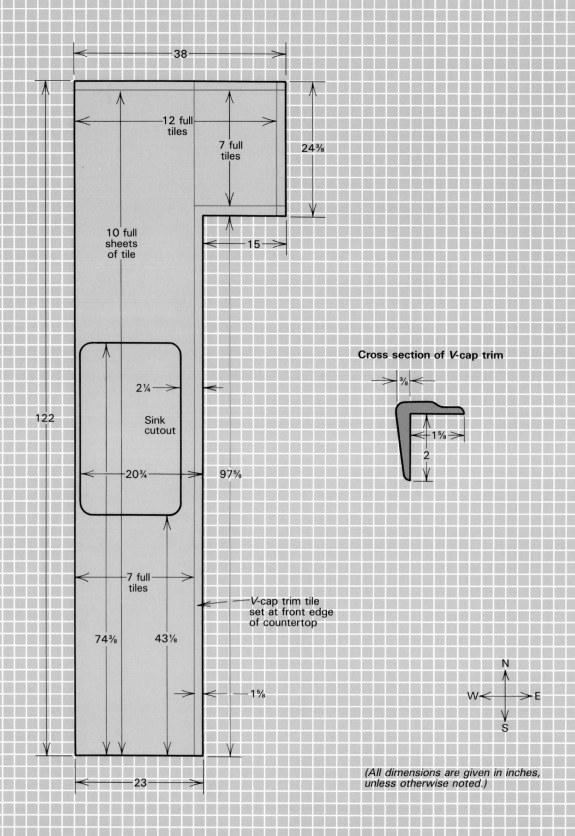

38

12 full tiles

7 full tiles

24³⁄₈

10 full sheets of tile

15

2¹⁄₄

Sink cutout

122

20³⁄₄

97⁵⁄₈

7 full tiles

V-cap trim tile set at front edge of countertop

74³⁄₈   43¹⁄₈

1⁵⁄₈

23

Cross section of *V*-cap trim

³⁄₈

1⁵⁄₈

2

N
W ← → E
S

(All dimensions are given in inches, unless otherwise noted.)

Mortar-Bed Countertop

U sually it's the homeowner who approaches me for a tile installation, but in this case the call came from a cabinetmaker with whom I had
worked on a number of other jobs. He was planning a kitchen remodeling
job and asked if I would do the tilework. The cabinets had to be made, and
I knew that this cabinetmaker would want only full tiles atop them. I wel-
comed the rare job on which the tiles would dictate the builder's design,
and immediately agreed to help out.

The countertop was to be *L*-shaped. The short leg would be a peninsula
work surface, and the long leg, bordered on its west and south sides by
walls, would hold a sink. The kitchen was large enough so that the countertop's size could, I hoped, be adjusted to hold full tiles. There were three
limitations on the countertop's size: Given the room's configuration, the long
leg had to be as close to 10 ft. long as possible, and the short leg could be no
more than 40 in. long. As well, the cabinets needed to be 22½ in. deep,
which meant that the countertop itself needed to be at least that width.

The customer had picked sheet-mounted, vitreous tiles for the job. Each
sheet was back-mounted with plastic netting, held 16 tiles, and measured
11⅞ in. square overall, or, with the ⅛-in. grout joint, 12 in. square. An
individual tile measured 2⅞ in. square, or, with the grout joint, 3 in.
square. Because of the even numbers involved, I didn't need to compile
my usual tile/grout-joint list, but I did need to do a bit of planning before I
could tell the cabinetmaker the size the countertop needed to be.

Planning the installation

Before doing any calculations, let me quickly identify two elements of a
mortar-bed countertop that are not found in mortar floors or walls. Just as
with any mud job, a mortar-bed countertop uses a curing membrane to
separate the mortar from the substrate, and wire mesh to reinforce the
bed. But unlike floors and walls, a countertop generally requires a strip of
metal, called sink metal, anchored around its front edge before it is floated. (If wood trim is used to finish off the countertop, the sink metal is

Materials list

Substrate:
¾-in. AC exterior plywood

Curing membrane:
15-lb. tar paper

Mortar-bed reinforcement:
20-gauge, 1-in. mesh poultry netting
and 9-gauge galvanized wire

Sink metal:
Prepunched countertop reinforcing
metal, 1½ in. by ¼ in. in 5-ft. lengths

Mortar bed:
3 parts mason's sand and 1 part
portland cement, mixed with ¼ part
lime and 1 part liquid latex mortar
additive for wall mud and slightly less
than 1 part liquid latex mortar
additive for deck mud

Adhesive:
Thinset powder, mixed with liquid
latex thinset additive

Tile:
Vitreous, 2⅞ in. square,
sheet-mounted

Grout:
Ivory sanded, mixed with liquid latex
mortar additive

optional, but an alternative method of reinforcing the front edge of the bed is then required, as explained on p. 217.) Second, because a counter-top mortar bed has several weak spots that are subject to cracking (for example, where it narrows around the sink), it needs extra reinforcement in addition to the wire mesh atop the curing membrane.

Sink metal Sink metal serves two functions: it helps the setter gauge the height or thickness of the bed, and it reinforces the front edge of the countertop. This strip of galvanized metal is pierced every 3 in. by an elongated slot, and between these slots are a series of ⅝-in.-dia. holes. The slots enable the setter to attach the strip to the plywood substrate with nails or screws, and the holes allow the trim tiles to contact the mortar and bond with the bed. There are two types of sink metal, as shown in the drawing below: C-shaped strips, for use with V-cap trim tiles, and L-shaped strips, for use with surface-bullnose trim tiles or wood trim.

In the case of C-shaped sink metal, which was what I used on this job, once the plywood substrate is prepared and the sink metal is attached to it, wall mud is floated on the face of the sink metal and will squeeze through the holes. The countertop itself is then floated with deck mud, which surrounds and locks into the slugs of wall mud penetrating the sink metal. (For a discussion of wall and deck mud, see p. 86.)

In the case of L-shaped sink metal used with surface-bullnose tiles, no wall mud is floated on the face of the metal strips. Instead, the deck of the countertop alone is floated and packed tightly against the metal (hold a margin trowel against the face of the sink metal as you compact the deck mud). The excess mud is trimmed off the face of the metal, and once the bed has dried, the bullnose tile is thinset directly to the face of the metal. (For the special requirements of installing wood trim over sink metal, see p. 217.)

The mortar bed for a floated countertop should be at least ¾ in. thick, and its height is controlled by the top of the sink metal. In calculating the exact thickness of the bed—and hence the height at which to position the top of the sink metal—the setter must add to the minimum thickness of the bed the thickness of any fixture, such as a sink, to be installed below the tiles, and that of the trim tiles. (I heartily recommend that fixtures be

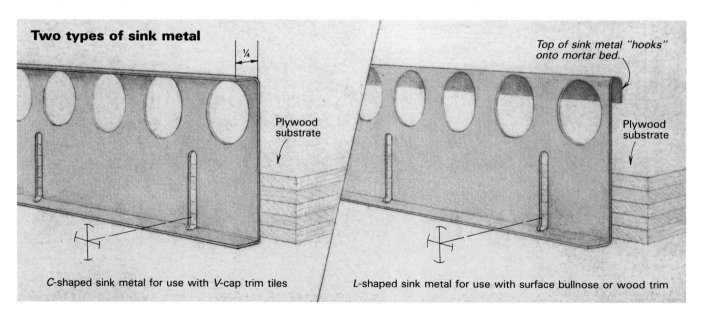

Two types of sink metal

¼

Plywood substrate

Top of sink metal "hooks" onto mortar bed.

Plywood substrate

C-shaped sink metal for use with V-cap trim tiles

L-shaped sink metal for use with surface bullnose or wood trim installed below the tiles, since this makes them easier to clean than surface-mounted, self-rimming fixtures, but if you choose the latter, they need not be considered in these calculations.) The drawing at right shows the relationship of the different parts on this countertop. Finally, the sink metal's ¼-in. thickness must be figured in when determining the size of the plywood substrate and the layout of the tiles.

Mortar-bed reinforcement In addition to the reinforcing wire mesh needed with any mortar bed to prevent cracking, a countertop bed requires extra strength at several vulnerable points: where the bed narrows around a sink or another built-in fixture, at inside corners, and along the length of a tiled peninsula. To reinforce these weak spots in the bed, I use 9-gauge galvanized wire. This wire, which is available at most masonry supply houses and is sold both in 100-lb. rolls and occasionally by the foot, is about ⅛ in. in diameter and can be cut to length with a pair of heavy-duty wire cutters. (If you can't find 9-gauge wire locally, a light-gauge rebar, called pencil rod, can be used.) I cut a long enough piece of wire so that, in the case of a narrow section of the bed or an inside corner, I can position the wire in the center of the weak spot and extend each end into the main areas of the bed. For a tiled peninsula, I snake the wire along the length of the countertop. Sometimes if I don't have any 9-gauge wire handy, I use a bent, galvanized nail to reinforce an inside corner or a sink corner trimmed with quarter-rounds.

Determining the size of the countertop When designing an *L*-shaped countertop, I start with the long leg and move to the short leg. Once I've figured out the dimensions for each, I can locate the position of the sink and other fixtures.

On this job, the long leg needed to be as close to 10 ft. as possible, but could run a tad over. This meant that I could fit 10 full sheets, which measured exactly 10 ft. (120 in.), on this leg. To that figure, I added ¼ in. for the thickness of the backsplash tile on the south wall, ⅛ in. for the grout joint between the backsplash and field tiles, and 1⅝ in. for the inside dimension of the *V*-cap at the north edge of the counter (see drawing, p. 190), making the overall length of this leg 122 in. Since the sink metal would be attached to the north end of the counter, it would add ¼ in. to the plywood, meaning that the actual length of the cabinetmaker's plywood substrate would need to be only 121¾ in.

On the peninsula counter, which was not to exceed 40 in. in length, 12 full tiles could be used. I added together 36 in. for 12 tiles, ¼ in. for the thickness of the backsplash tile, ⅛ in. for the grout joint between the backsplash and field tiles, and 1⅝ in. for the *V*-cap, for an overall countertop length of 38 in. Subtracting ¼ in. for the sink metal gave me a length of 37¾ in. for the plywood substrate.

Both legs of the countertop were to sit atop 22½-in.-deep cabinets, which meant that each could accommodate seven full tiles. To figure the width of the plywood substrate on the long leg, I added together 21 in. for the tiles, ¼ in. for the thickness of the backsplash tile, ⅛ in. for the grout joint between the backsplash and field tiles, and 1⅝ in. for the *V*-cap, for a total of 23 in. From this, I subtracted ¼ in. for the sink metal, for an overall width of 22¾ in. for the plywood. This meant that, with the sink metal installed and the ⅜-in.-thick *V*-cap tiles set, the front edge of the tiled countertop would overhang the cabinet by ⅞ in. The counter should, in fact, overhang the cabinet by at least the thickness of the face of the *V*-cap, but this extra ½ in. would not be enough to get in the way of the drawers.

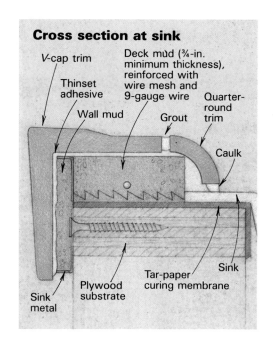

Cross section at sink

V-cap trim

Thinset adhesive

Wall mud

Deck mud (¾-in. minimum thickness), reinforced with wire mesh and 9-gauge wire

Grout

Quarter-round trim

Caulk

Sink

Tar-paper curing membrane

Plywood substrate

Sink metal

To figure out the overall width of the peninsula countertop, I added together 21 in. for seven full tiles, 3¼ in. for the two *V*-cap trim tiles and ⅛ in. for the grout joint between one of the *V*-caps and the field tile, for a total of 24⅜ in. Then, to determine the width of the plywood substrate, I subtracted ½ in. from this figure for the sink metal on both sides of the peninsula, which gave me 23⅞ in. Next I calculated the amount of countertop overhang, and when I added ¾ in. for the thickness of the two *V*-cap tiles on either side of the counter to the 1⅞-in. difference between the width of the cabinets and the countertop, I realized that the 2⅝-in. overhang might make fishing around in the drawers on the south side of the peninsula awkward. I therefore positioned this overhang on the north side of the countertop.

The remaining dimensions could be deduced by simple arithmetic, and, with this completed, I turned my attention to figuring out the position of the sink.

Locating the sink cutout   Sinks come in a variety of sizes, but I was unable to find one sized so that I wouldn't need to cut any of the field tiles on the countertop. The sink I chose measured 32¾ in. by 20 in. overall. With this size, I could trim the sink with quarter-rounds set against the *V*-cap in the front of the sink and full tiles at either side. At the rear of the sink, the quarter-rounds would have to be set against ⅞-in. cut pieces. I didn't like having to use cuts, but located at the rear and partially hidden by the faucet, they wouldn't be very noticeable. The important thing was that along the front and the two sides of the sink, I could preserve the factory edge of the tiles.

I like to trim out the perimeter of a sink with quarter-rounds rather than with surface- or radius-bullnose trim tiles because they make any future repairs to the sink easier. In the event that the sink gets chipped and needs replacing, the quarter-rounds can usually be removed without breaking, and the sink can be taken out without disturbing the field tiles.

Since the sink was made of cast iron and was quite heavy, it needed solid support. To cut the hole in the plywood top, the cabinetmaker used the template that came with the sink, which provided a ¾-in. supporting lip all around for the sink. This meant that the actual cutout for the sink had to measure 31¼ in. by 18½ in. (Had no template been available, he could have flipped the sink over, traced its outline on the plywood and then scribed a cutting line ¾ in. in from the tracing line.) I would have preferred a wider supporting lip (on some small sinks a narrower lip may be called for), but the shape of this particular sink wouldn't allow for one.

I determined the position of the hole by the layout of the tiles. Working from the south wall toward the cutout, I knew that 14 full tiles would take up 42 in. To this figure I added ¼ in. for the backsplash tile, ⅛ in. for the grout joint between the backsplash tiles and the field tiles, and the ¾-in. allowance for the supporting lip below the sink, which put the south side of the sink cutout at 43⅛ in. from the south wall. Since the hole was to measure 31¼ in. wide, the north end of the cutout would fall at 74⅜ in. from the south wall. To figure out where to place the east end of the cutout from the front edge of the tiled countertop, I added together 1⅜ in. for the interior depth of the *V*-cap tile (1⅝ in. minus ¼ in. for the sink metal), ⅛ in. for the grout joint and ¾ in. for the supporting lip, for a total of 2¼ in. Adding 18½ in. to this, I determined that the west end of the cutout would fall 20¾ in. from the counter's front edge.

Preparing the countertop

Once the cabinets were installed and the plywood substrate screwed in place, I could begin the tilework. To prevent damaging the new cabinets during tiling, I taped kraft paper over the front of them and stapled the top edge of it to the plywood substrate. (I made sure to carefully fold the edge of the paper so that it wouldn't get in the way of the sink metal when I installed it.) I then dropped the sink into its cutout and shimmed it up with scrap pieces of tar paper so that I could determine the proper height of the sink metal. After installing the sink metal, I would pull the sink out again to lay down the actual tar-paper curing membrane.

Leveling the sink metal Regardless of the type of tile used to trim a sink, the mortar bed floated on a countertop should be at least ¾ in. thick. This means that sinks being trimmed with surface bullnose or with thin quarter-rounds may need to be shimmed up with mortar to arrive at the minimum thickness for the bed (see p. 198 for information on how to do this). On this job, the quarter-rounds had an inside height of ½ in., the rim of the sink atop the scrap tar paper measured ¼ in. thick, and the grout joint between the quarter-rounds and the sink rim was to be ⅛ in., which meant that the bed would be ⅞ in. thick.

I wanted to start leveling the sink metal near the sink, since the quarter-round trim tile positioned over the sink's rim would determine the height of the mortar bed and sink metal. I lightly drove a 1½-in. drywall screw into the end of one strip to anchor it against the edge of the plywood in front of the sink. With a tape measure, I positioned the top of the metal exactly ⅞ in. from the top of the plywood, checked the position by holding a piece of quarter-round trim just over the rim of the sink, and tightened the screw. Then I lightly screwed in the opposite end of the metal, adjusted it with a level and tightened the screw. With this done, I installed screws through the other slots in the metal. As I worked, I kept the level on the sink metal to make sure that it remained straight, and held the metal tightly with one hand while driving the screws home to prevent the rotation of the screws as they were cinched down from moving the metal. I could have nailed, rather than screwed, the metal in place—it's certainly easier—but screws hold the metal better than nails do.

I lightly screwed the sink metal into the plywood substrate (left), checked and adjusted its height against a piece of quarter-round trim held over the rim of the sink (above), and then drove the screws home.

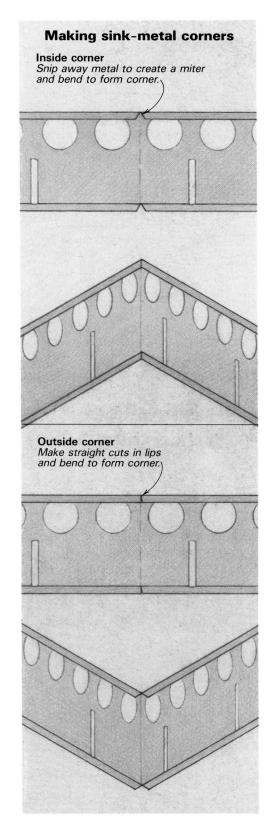

Making sink-metal corners

Inside corner
Snip away metal to create a miter and bend to form corner.

Outside corner
Make straight cuts in lips and bend to form corner.

I continued to anchor and level the remaining pieces of sink metal. To bend the metal around corners, I used tin snips to cut both lips, making mitered cuts for inside corners and simple, straight cuts for outside corners, as shown in the drawing at left. Wherever necessary, I used a hammer to sharply bend the corners.

If you're tiling a countertop that has cutouts for built-in fixtures that won't be in place when the mortar bed is floated, you should stop after installing the sink metal to work with these holes. Line each opening with pine lattice, ¼ in. by 2½ in., as shown in the drawing below, to create "dams" so that you can tightly pack the deck mud around the perimeter of the opening. Level the top of the lattice against the sink metal and surround the cutouts with 9-gauge wire to strengthen these potentially weak spots in the bed. The wire should be anchored with furring nails and positioned an inch or two away from each opening. Its two ends can be twisted together to complete the circle around the opening.

After all the sink metal was installed, I spread a layer of cold-patch roofing asphalt over the countertop with a ⅛-in. notched trowel and stapled the tar-paper membrane on top of it. Since water frequently leaks between the backsplash and the rear of a countertop, I cut the tar paper large enough to sharply crease it at the back wall, box-fold the inside corner and lap the paper up the walls about 3 in. to 4 in. Once the countertop had been floated and the deck tiles set, I would trim the paper to about ½ in. to ¾ in. above the deck and set the backsplash tiles. The combination of the backsplash tiles overlapping the tar paper would provide an effective watershed, as shown in the top drawing on the facing page.

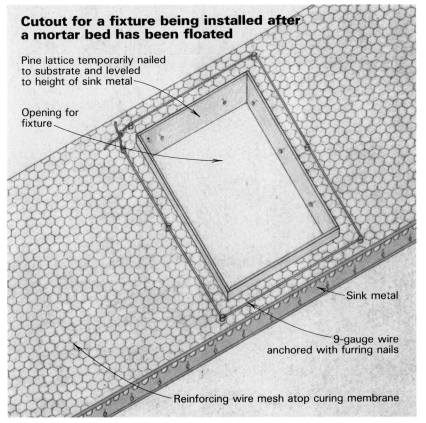

Cutout for a fixture being installed after a mortar bed has been floated

Pine lattice temporarily nailed to substrate and leveled to height of sink metal

Opening for fixture

Sink metal

9-gauge wire anchored with furring nails

Reinforcing wire mesh atop curing membrane

Another potentially leaky spot was the edge of the sink. To prevent water from seeping under the sink rim, which would cause the edge of the plywood supporting lip to swell and pop tiles loose, I covered this edge with asphalt, lapped tar paper over it and stapled the paper to the edge.

Installing the reinforcing metal   After installing the curing membrane, I positioned the sink over its hole. (Had the sink needed to be shimmed up with mortar, I would, of course, have had to mix the mud before positioning the sink.) Next I completely covered the tar-paper curing membrane with reinforcing wire mesh, stapling the mesh to the bed. With this done, I added lengths of 9-gauge galvanized wire at the narrow sections of the bed—around the sink, at the inside corner and along the length of the peninsula counter. For this wire to add any strength to the mortar, it needed to be located more or less in the middle of the bed. To position the wire in mid-bed, I attached it with the ½-in. furring nails commonly used for stucco jobs. I keep a bunch of these nails soaking in a small can of polyurethane sealer. The paper furring disc on each nail soaks up the polyurethane, which prevents it from swelling when the nails come in contact with the wet deck mud.

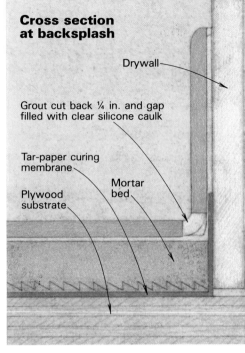

Cross section at backsplash

Drywall

Grout cut back ¼ in. and gap filled with clear silicone caulk

Tar-paper curing membrane

Plywood substrate

Mortar bed

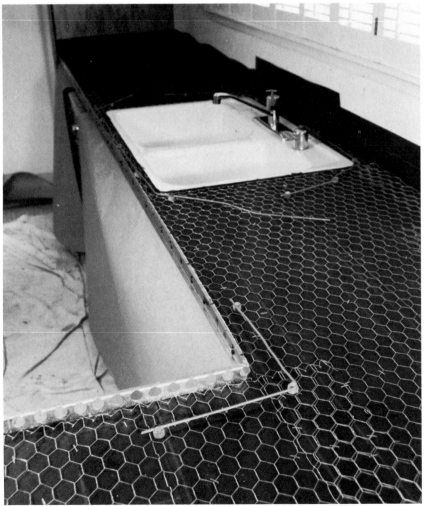

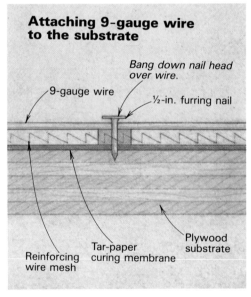

Attaching 9-gauge wire to the substrate

Bang down nail head over wire.

9-gauge wire

½-in. furring nail

Reinforcing wire mesh

Tar-paper curing membrane

Plywood substrate

After stapling reinforcing wire mesh over the curing membrane, I installed lengths of 9-gauge wire in the weak spots in the bed, positioning it so that it encircled the sink, turned the inside corner of the countertop and snaked down the peninsula counter. I anchored the wire with furring nails to lift it into what would become the center of the mortar bed, where it would provide the greatest strength to the bed.

Floating the countertop

Only three float strips were needed to float the deck of the countertop, and since the sink metal was set at the height of the bed, positioning the float strips was quite easy. I first mixed up some deck mud (see p. 145) and then, across the width of the countertop, laid down three columns of mortar, which were about 1 in. to 2 in. higher than the sink metal. Next I positioned a float strip on top of each column. To level each strip with a level, one end of which was positioned over the sink metal, I pressed on the tool until it contacted the top of the sink metal and then tapped it to evenly adjust the float strip.

I started floating the countertop by filling the sink metal with wall mud, which, since I wanted it to set up quickly, I had mixed slightly drier than regular fat mud. (For instructions on mixing wall mud, see p. 172.) After loading the trowel with enough mortar to overfill the metal and make it squeeze through the holes, I gently worked the mud into the sink metal so that the mortar slugs protruding on the countertop did not break off. When I had completely filled the sink metal, I cut the excess off the front of the strip by running the steel trowel along its two lips. With this done, I let the mud set up for about an hour.

(Had the sink needed shimming with mud, I would have done this before filling the sink metal. To shim up the sink, I would have laid down a strip of fat mud about 1 in. high around the perimeter of the sink cutout. Then I would have slowly positioned the sink over the mud, aligning it parallel to the sink metal and allowing enough room for the trim tiles in front of the sink. Finally, I would have placed a level on the top of the sink and tapped it into position, checking its height against the sink metal.)

With the float strips leveled, I dumped a bucket of deck mud on the countertop and began to pack it down with a wood float. I packed, screeded and finished off each section of the bed just as I would a mortar floor (see Chapter 7). To prevent the mud floated on the sink metal from being

I leveled each float strip in a column of mud, with one end of the level placed on the sink metal to gauge the height of the strip (above). Then I troweled wall mud onto the face of the sink metal (right), forcing it through the holes in the metal. These protruding slugs of mortar would give the deck mud floated on the countertop something to lock into.

forced out as I packed the countertop mud, I backed up the face of the metal with the steel trowel. If any mud fell out of the sink metal, I left it on the floor and replaced it with fresh fat mud once I had screeded off the deck mud on the countertop.

To screed the area to the left of the sink, I rode the straightedge on the left and middle float strips. For the sink area, I sat the straightedge on the middle and right float strips. For the area to the right of the sink, I used the float strip on the right and the sink metal at the right edge of the countertop, and for the peninsula countertop, the sink metal rails on both sides of the leg. Whenever using the sink metal, I screeded with a light touch—the sink-metal rails tend to vibrate under the movement of the straightedge, and working the straightedge too vigorously can shake mud loose from the face of the metal.

Shaping the mortar at the perimeter of the sink to accept the quarter-rounds is, at best, a tedious job. Instead of taking time to do this, I cut the mortar away at the point where the full tiles and the V-cap tiles would end. After setting all the other countertop tiles, I would set the quarter-rounds in a bed of grout. Once the bed was completely floated, I let it set up overnight before laying out the countertop and setting any tiles.

For a countertop this size, I needed only to snap lines representing the center of the grout joint between the V-cap and field tiles. I positioned these lines 1⅝ in. (the depth of the V-caps) from the front edge of the countertop. Since there would be 1/16 in. of thinset between the face of the counter and the V-caps, these lines were effectively snapped at what would become the center of the grout joint.

As I packed the countertop mortar (left), I held the trowel against the face of the sink metal to keep the wall mud from being forced out. Because the sink-metal rails vibrated when used to support the screed, I worked carefully to keep from losing mud from the face of the sink metal (above). Some mud inevitably dropped out, however, and had to be replaced with fresh material.

Setting and grouting the tiles

After mixing the thinset adhesive, I spread and combed it with a 3/16-in. notched trowel, as the tiles were not quite 1/4 in. thick. I began setting the field tiles at the left side of the long leg of counter, working toward the sink. (To keep from leaning on the V-caps as I set the field tiles, I would set all the V-caps later.) After I had set the first few field tiles, I stopped to check the adhesive's coverage (see photos, p. 59).

Once I had set the last row of field tiles on the left of the sink, I measured the distance covered from the south wall to make sure that I wasn't getting ahead of myself. Then I checked the field tiles for square, holding a carpenter's square against the tiles and layout line, and repositioned any that had gone astray.

To make sure that the tiles to be set behind and to the right of the sink would be spaced accurately, I marked a point on the layout line 33 1/8 in. from the last row of field tiles to the left of the sink, which represented the beginning of the first row of field tiles to the right of the sink. I then penciled a line from this point onto the mortar bed, using a carpenter's square held against the layout line. As for the 7/8-in. cuts to be set behind the sink, I would check their spacing with the tape measure.

I next spread thinset on the area to the right of the sink and continued setting sheets of tile. But when I had reached the north end of the counter, something was wrong—the tiles fell short of the estimated location of the joint between the field tile and V-caps by 7/16 in. I stopped to measure the dimensions of the sheets and found that those taken from the second box of tiles were all undersized. This is not uncommon with some sheet-mounted tiles. The problem occurs during manufacturing when the netting sprayed onto the backs of the tiles bunches up while the plastic is still hot. Unless the plastic is straightened out before cooling, the sheets remain undersized. The solution to the problem was simple: I simply took a utility knife, slit through the netting and repositioned the tiles with a straightedge.

When I had set all the field tiles, I stepped back from the counter and looked over the tiles to see if any were out of place. For several that needed repositioning, I cut the netting and coaxed them back into alignment.

Setting the trim and backsplash tiles Because of their basic shape, V-cap tiles often leave the kiln slightly distorted. I back-buttered the distorted tiles I found with a 1/4-in.-thick coat of thinset to supplement the adhesive on the setting bed. I then lined up the V-caps with the field tile. Next I cut mitered pieces on the wet saw for the inside corners (factory pieces were available for outside corners), allowing for a full grout joint between two pieces. When I had set all the V-caps in place, I sighted down the edge of the countertop to make sure that they were all aligned.

With the V-caps set, I was ready to install the quarter-rounds around the sink. I would set the butterfly corners first and then the full quarter-rounds. I first spread a thin layer of thinset (about 1/32 in. thick) on the back of each quarter-round and then back-buttered the piece with a generous helping of the same grout used to fill the joints of the tiles (I mixed this grout a little stiffer than that used for the field tiles). Then I spread a thin coat of thinset on the mortar bed, pressed the quarter-round into position and held it in place for a couple of seconds until the grout began to set up. Since I had cut off the excess mortar from the edge of the sink rather than fashioning a curved edge, the idea now was to shim out the tiles by applying more grout to them than was actually needed. Next the quarter-rounds had to be cut to fit against the butterfly corners. Once the cuts were made, I rounded the cut edge with a rubbing stone to soften it.

Since I had simply cut away the mortar at the edge of the sink, I shimmed out the quarter-round trim tiles with a thin layer of thinset and a generous helping of grout.

After an hour, I used my utility knife to undercut the grout between the quarter-rounds and the sink by about ⅛ in. I would later fill this undercut with clear silicone caulk, which would seal the edge of the sink.

Before setting the backsplash tiles, I trimmed the tar-paper curing membrane running up the wall to about ½ in. to ¾ in. above the deck tiles. Then I back-buttered each piece of surface bullnose and aligned it with the deck tiles. I used tapered tile shims to hold these tiles in place until the thinset had hardened.

I waited overnight before grouting the tiles and began, as usual, by cleaning out the joints and vacuuming away the dust from the surface of the tiles. Because these were vitreous tiles, I didn't need to mist or wet down the surface of the tiles before grouting.

I followed my normal grouting procedure for the field, backsplash and quarter-round tiles (see p. 62). But when grouting the *V*-cap tiles, I used my rubber-gloved hands instead of the grout trowel. I did this by scooping up a handful of grout, curving my hand to conform to the shape of the caps and pressing the grout in place.

After cleaning up the tiles, I squared the grout at the junction of the deck and backsplash tiles. Three days later, once the grout had fully dried, I returned and covered this joint and the sink joint with clear silicone caulk. □

Special Installations/Repairs CHAPTER 12

I f you're new to tilesetting, you'll probably consider every installation a special one, and in a real sense, you'll be right. No two residential tile jobs are ever exactly alike. Each has its own set of unique characteristics and problems, and each requires its own individual strategy and layout. Nonetheless, with several installations under your belt, you'll begin to realize that the fundamental principles of tilesetting remain the same from job to job, and that most tile jobs fall into several generic categories: floors, walls and countertops, set in either thick-bed or thinset installations. These are the examples found in Chapters 6 through 11, and I'd bet that 99% of the tile jobs in or around the home will be some variation of these.

If your tilesetting plans are a bit more exotic, or if you just haven't found a detail or two you need for a particular project, you should find it here. This chapter serves as a catchall for special installation information that ranges from how to put in a soap dish to how to set slate and other paving stones. In some cases, what distinguishes the installation from an "ordinary" job may be only a couple of special requirements—for example, the need for extra heavy-duty waterproofing protection or a heat-resistant adhesive—with the balance of the tiling procedure the same as for a similar wet or dry job on a comparable setting bed. But whatever the extent of the discussion, carefully note the special techniques or materials prescribed, since they are crucial to the success of the job.

Built-in chopping block

A chopping block built into a tiled countertop is a real convenience in a kitchen, provided it's properly installed. To produce a handsome and serviceable installation, I suggest that you first buy a block larger than desired and cut it down to fit between full tiles.

To prevent damage to the tiles if the block gets wet and swells, leave a ⅛-in. gap between it and the tiles. This gap also allows for easy removal of the block, should it need replacing. To keep the gap from getting clogged with food particles, fill it with silicone caulk after the grout has dried.

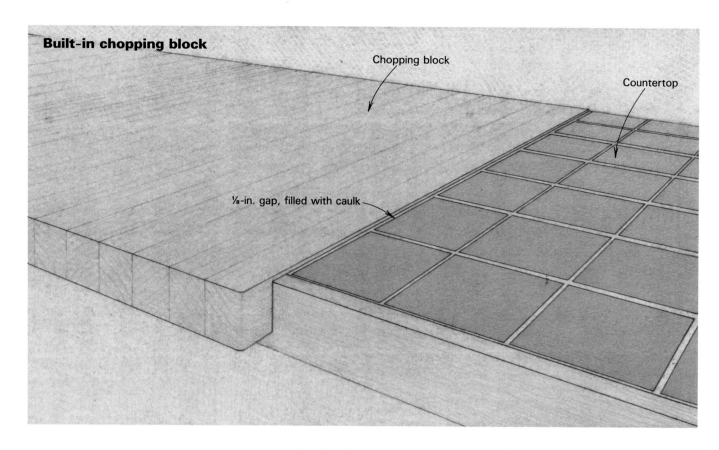

Built-in chopping block

Chopping block

Countertop

⅛-in. gap, filled with caulk

Finally, I recommend mounting the block so its top sits about ⅛-in. above the surface of the tiles. This will help prevent knife blades from coming in contact with the tiles and scratching them. When possible, you should also position the block so that its front edge protrudes slightly beyond the edge of the counter. This will make it easier to keep the block clean.

Mosaic tile

As with any back-mounted tile, the backing material on mosaic tile can interfere with the bond of the adhesive. If the tiles are dot-mounted, that is, joined on the back side by rubber or plastic dots mounted between the joints, an oily residue left on the backs of the tiles during manufacturing may cause additional bonding problems. Be sure when purchasing dot-mounted tile to check the back of several sheets in two or three boxes before taking the tile from the store. If you can wipe oil from the back of the sheets with a paper towel, ask for another lot of the tile, or consider choosing different tile altogether. If you've already bought the tile and find oil on the sheets, try exchanging it. If you can't, clean the backs of the sheets with a mild detergent and water (wiping the backs "clean" with a rag won't suffice). Then allow the tile to fully dry before setting it.

Whatever the type of backing material, its interference with the adhesive is a particular problem with 1-in. mosaic tiles. With the already small surface area of the individual tiles largely covered by the backing material, the issue is how to apply enough adhesive to firmly bond each tile to the setting bed and at the same time avoid the next-to-impossible cleanup of adhesive that will ooze up into all the grout joints. Most setters quickly clean as much adhesive as possible from the surface of the tiles and the

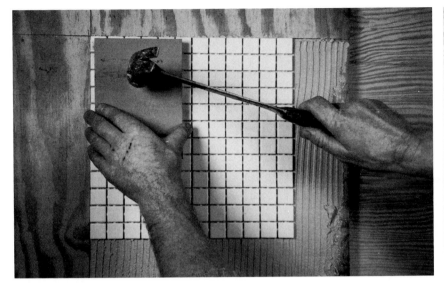

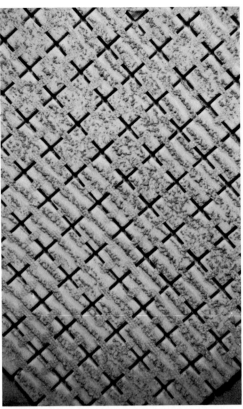

tops of the grout joints and then simply use a white grout over white adhesive or a gray grout over gray adhesive. This approach can reduce the mottling that sometimes occurs in colored grouts at the thin spots that lie over globs of adhesive. But the drawback to this system is that the color of the grout and adhesive may not be identical, and with time both may change and still produce a mottled effect. As well, the setter has only two grout colors to choose from.

To avoid these problems, I draw upon the thick-bed setting method used by the ancient Romans (see p. 2) and combine their approach with modern materials. Nowadays when I install mosaic tiles, I make a combination adhesive-and-grout by mixing the liquid component of an epoxy thinset adhesive with a sanded grout, and allow the material to ooze up between the tiles as I'm setting them. This mixture provides the extra-strong grip needed to adhere the tiles to the bed, eliminates the separate step of grouting, and resolves the problem of differing shades of grout and adhesive. As well, by using a colored grout as the filler for this mixture, I expand the possible palette of "grouts" for the job.

I begin the installation by making sure that the setting bed is completely flat, since even the slightest depression or high spot becomes glaring when covered with small mosaic tiles. Then, with a ⅛-in. square-notched trowel, I spread and comb the thinset/grout mixture on a small area of the bed and also back-butter the back of a sample sheet with it. After setting the sheet on the bed, I force it into the thinset/grout with a beating block and hammer.

To check the coverage, I remove the test sheet and examine the back. There should be a distinct impression of the sheet in the thinset/grout, and the back of the sheet should still be fully covered. If the coverage is inadequate, I switch to a ¼-in. square-notched trowel and recomb the adhesive/grout. Then I bed a new sheet of tiles with the beating block and carefully check the coverage. Though many setters feel that the bond is sufficient with 75% coverage of the tiles, I disagree. In my experience, if the job gets normal wear, a lot of the tiles will eventually break or become loose unless they're fully bedded in the adhesive/grout. To achieve the full coverage shown on the sample sheet in the bottom photo at right, I switched to an even larger trowel with notches ¼ in. wide by ⅜ in. deep.

At the outset of a mosaic-tile job, I always set a sample sheet of tiles to check the adhesive's coverage. After setting and beating in the sheet (top left), I remove it to look at the back. Here, my adhesive/grout combination combed with a ⅛-in. square-notched trowel provided insufficient coverage (top right). After first trying a ¼-in. square-notched trowel, I finally got full coverage with a ¼-in. by ⅜-in. notched trowel (above).

When I actually begin setting the sheets, I beat them level with their neighbors and check all the joints to see that they're filled. If I find any voids, I fill them with a fingerful of thinset/grout. Then I begin cleaning up the tiles, using my regular method (see p. 65).

It's especially crucial with this setting technique to use as little water as possible when cleaning the tiles. Too much water can wash away the epoxy resin in the adhesive/grout at the top of the joint, weakening it. After initially cleaning off the surface of the tiles, I check all the sheets to see if any need slight repositioning. Then I shape the joints and do the final cleanup. It's important to do a thorough job of cleaning the tiles, as hardened epoxy resins are extremely difficult to remove.

How to install CPE membranes

As explained in full in Chapter 4 (see p. 91), chlorinated polyethylene (CPE) in sheet form makes an excellent waterproofing or isolation membrane. Any surface that's prepared for tiling can be covered with a CPE membrane, provided that surface is compatible with the adhesive used. Although a number of adhesive manufacturers state that their products can be used to laminate CPE membranes, I recommend sticking with a latex or acrylic thinset or an epoxy thinset. The same adhesive can be used for setting the tiles.

1. Preparing the substrate   Prepare the substrate so that it's flat, plumb or level, and square. After thoroughly cleaning the surface, knock down any raised nail heads. Finally, wipe any lingering dust from the substrate with a damp sponge.

2. Cutting the membrane   For small, simply shaped jobs, measure and transfer the dimensions of the substrate to the CPE. Be sure to position the membrane with the curve from the roll facing down to counteract its tendency to curl upward at the edges. Then cut the CPE with a sharp utility knife. For large substrates or those complex in shape, cut a piece of CPE about 1 ft. longer than the substrate's longest dimension, position the piece directly on the surface and cut it to fit. If a membrane wider than the CPE sheet is needed, additional pieces of CPE can be cut and bonded to cover the surface (see *step 4* below). If the membrane will be composed of several parts, cut and install the largest pieces first. Any cut pieces should overlap the larger CPE sheet by 2 in. at the seams.

When the CPE is to serve as a waterproofing membrane, it should be carefully fit to the job. If the job contains an expansion joint (see p. 95), the membrane should run down into the joint and out again in one continuous piece. If the CPE is to function simply as an isolation membrane, however, it needn't fit the job with such precision.

3. Laminating the membrane   To laminate the membrane for a small floor (about 16 sq. ft. or less), comb thinset over the floor with no less than a ¼-in. notched trowel, and position the CPE. You may need to pull it a bit here and there to work it into place.

Installing a membrane on a larger floor is a bit trickier. Leave the membrane in place after cutting it on the substrate and fold back a large portion. Then spread adhesive on the uncovered substrate, flop the CPE into place, and smooth the air bubbles out with a roller or a short straightedge (*don't* use your hands alone because you're liable to miss some bubbles), working from the center outward. Then check the position of the entire membrane. On a small project, you may not have to walk or lean on freshly laminated CPE; on large jobs, though, avoiding this is often impossible. Newly laminated CPE can easily be deformed, so protect it with plywood pads that will distribute your weight.

After checking the position of the entire membrane, pull back a corner of the laminated CPE to check the bond of the adhesive. You should find an even layer of thinset on both the floor *and* the membrane. If you don't, pull up the entire laminated section, apply more thinset and comb it with a trowel with larger notches.

With the initial section laminated, roll back the remainder of the membrane, exposing a little of the thinset below the first section. Then spread more adhesive and unroll and smooth out a new portion of the membrane. Adding more protective plywood squares as the work advances, continue in this fashion until the full membrane has been laminated.

4. Bonding pieces of membrane   To bond two pieces of CPE at a seam, first pull up the overlapping edges, clean away stray thinset with a sponge and let the inside facing surfaces dry. (If the CPE is a product like Noble-Seal whose surface is covered with fibers, you'll need to pull away these fibers, as shown in the photo at right below, in order to bond the seam. To do this, first spray the edge with a solvent—such as xylene or a similar product offered by the CPE manufacturer. Then, with a utility knife, lightly score a line 2 in. from the edge of the CPE to cut the ends of the fibers, and pull them away with your fingers. If you're working with a piece that still retains a "selvage" factory edge on which the manufacturer has eliminated the fibers, of course, you needn't worry about this.)

Wearing a charcoal-filter mask and making sure that the room is well ventilated, now prime the facing sides of the seam with the solvent, which also serves as the adhesive. Apply a second coat of solvent/adhesive, press the seam together and smooth it out with a roller. Work slowly to ensure that the seam is thoroughly bonded.

5. Making corners   The tricky areas of any CPE installation are the outside and inside corners. Using a heat gun or a hair dryer to soften the material, prefold all corners before bedding the CPE in the adhesive. When cool, the CPE will retain the creases.

After spreading thinset adhesive on a sample area of the surface being covered with a CPE membrane, pull back a corner of the membrane to check the coverage (left). The thinset should amply cover both membrane and substrate. If the edge of the CPE is covered with fibers (above), remove them before bonding a seam between two pieces of the membrane.

If the CPE puckers out from an inside corner, push a stick of wood tightly into the corner and nail it in place overnight. After the thinset has dried, remove the wood and plug the nail holes with butyl caulk. If the membrane falls away from an outside corner, either refold the membrane's corner to be less than 90° (which should make the CPE hug the corner), or nail 1x's to each side of the corner and repeat the counsel above.

6. Tiling and making repairs to a membrane For best results, wait overnight before installing tile over a CPE membrane. If the membrane's primary purpose is to provide waterproofing, apply a generous bead of butyl caulk to the joint between the membrane and the shower pan or bathtub. (Use enough caulk to make a watertight seal but not so much that it overflows into the area being tiled.) Flatten the joint with a margin trowel and let the caulk harden. Remove any caulk smears around the seam.

If you come across a bubbled or loose section of membrane while setting tiles, don't despair. For a small area, no larger than 50 sq. in., cut around three sides of the unbonded section with a utility knife and peel back the flap. Cover the setting bed with a 1/16-in.-thick layer of butyl caulk and use a roller or a straightedge to smooth the flap back down. If you find a large, unbonded area, be suspicious about the condition of the rest of the membrane, and look closely for any conditions that would impair a good bond between the membrane and substrate. You may be able to peel up the affected sections and reapply thinset adhesive (after removing the thinset already there), but if you're in doubt as to the effectiveness of this approach, you'll just have to remove all the CPE and figure out what went wrong.

Patios

Tile set outdoors, as for a patio, should have a concrete slab as its setting bed. I recommend floating this slab with enough of a crown to allow water to drain from the surface of the tile. Choose only vitreous tiles for this installation to prevent freeze-thaw damage and use additives with both the thinset adhesive and the grout.

Tiles exposed to heat

Setting tile around fireplaces and woodstoves (and sometimes around ranges) involves some special considerations, the foremost of which is heat. Fireplaces and stoves can generate enough heat to destroy the bond of many adhesives. Organic mastics, for example, should never be used for these installations, and even some thinset adhesives should be avoided. Choose instead a heat-resistant adhesive, such as Laticrete 100 AAR-II-HT (see the Resource Guide). This particular adhesive can withstand sustained temperatures of up to 400°F. Heat-resistant adhesives are generally a little more expensive than epoxy thinsets.

Before proceeding to install tile near any appliance that generates lots of heat, however, you *must* consult your local building inspector for installation details. Local codes vary, but some are very strict about such things. Depending on the circumstances of the job and your local codes, you may have to incorporate an airspace or some fire-resistant material between the tilework and any combustible walls. Whatever the method, choose a high-heat-resistant adhesive for setting the tile.

If you must incorporate an air channel behind the tilework—maybe you're tiling a woodstove surround—the task isn't too difficult. The idea is to build up a slender wall of noncombustible material, set the tile on that, then separate this assembly from any combustible wall with noncombustible

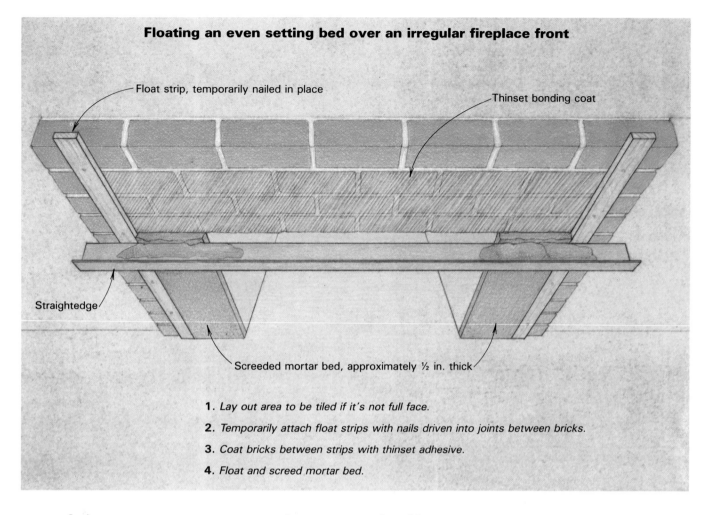

Floating an even setting bed over an irregular fireplace front

Float strip, temporarily nailed in place

Thinset bonding coat

Straightedge

Screeded mortar bed, approximately ½ in. thick

1. *Lay out area to be tiled if it's not full face.*

2. *Temporarily attach float strips with nails driven into joints between bricks.*

3. *Coat bricks between strips with thinset adhesive.*

4. *Float and screed mortar bed.*

spacers. Let's assume you want to put your woodstove near a combustible wall (standard drywall, by the way, fits into this category). One noncombustible spacer that's easy to work with is called "hat channel." It's just a light-gauge sheet-metal track about ⅞ in. deep, which in cross section resembles, well, a fedora. First, snip the hat channel into lengths appropriate for the size of surround you want and screw them to the wall (and into the studs) through their "brim." Next fasten at least two layers of backer board to the "crown" of the hat channel with drywall screws. Then simply set tile on the backer board using a heat-resistant adhesive. The resulting installation will use air to carry heat away before it can reach the combustible wall. Be sure, though, to use enough hat channel to give the backer board adequate support. And don't figure on saving money by using 2x4s as spacers instead of hat channel—remember, they're combustible, and I wouldn't want to bet *my* house on their suitability.

The face of a fireplace requires preparation before tiling. Scrupulously clean off all traces of soot, which would prevent the adhesive from properly bonding. Also check to make sure that the surface is reasonably smooth and flat. If not, knock down the high spots with a masonry rubbing stone. If the front of the fireplace is composed of bricks and their surface is too irregular for setting tiles, clean the bricks, coat them with a thin layer of thinset and float a mortar bed on the surface, as shown in the drawing above.

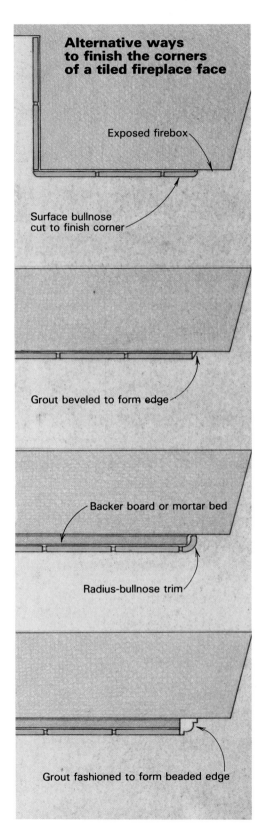

Alternative ways to finish the corners of a tiled fireplace face

Exposed firebox

Surface bullnose cut to finish corner

Grout beveled to form edge

Backer board or mortar bed

Radius-bullnose trim

Grout fashioned to form beaded edge

If the fireplace has a metal face, like those on some "zero-clearance" fireplaces, do *not* set tires directly on this surface. Most of these faces are too flimsy to properly support the weight of tiles. Instead, I recommend laminating backer board to the surface. Before laminating the board, grind or sand off any paint and then use a high-heat resistant epoxy adhesive for both lamination and tilesetting. Be sure not to tile over any intake or exhaust vents. After the face tiles have been set, the inside edge between the tiles and the firebox can be trimmed in one of several ways, as shown in the drawing at left. To support the tiles until the adhesive sets up, either tape them in place or use a bridge like the one shown in the drawing below. The bridge is simply propped in place—it's not necessary to fasten it.

If you're tiling only the hearth of a fireplace, the major concern is not so much heat damage as it is the pounding that most hearths have to endure. Even if you're horrified at the idea of using your hearth as a chopping block for wood, it will take a beating from logs that get dropped on it and fireplace tools that fall out of their rack. For this reason, you need to provide a setting bed for the tiles that's at least 1 in. thick. Since I'm a fan of mortar beds, I'd suggest floating a 1-in.-thick bed over the hearth, but you could also laminate a couple of pieces of backer board together with thinset to achieve this thickness. The hearth will get its share of heat, so a heat-resistant thinset wouldn't be a bad idea. Consult your local building inspector, though. If the hearth borders wood flooring (whether finished or subflooring), leave a 1/8-in. gap between the tiles and the wood, and caulk the joint with silicone caulk to prevent seasonal expansion from destroying either surface.

Using a wooden bridge to hold tiles in place until the adhesive sets up

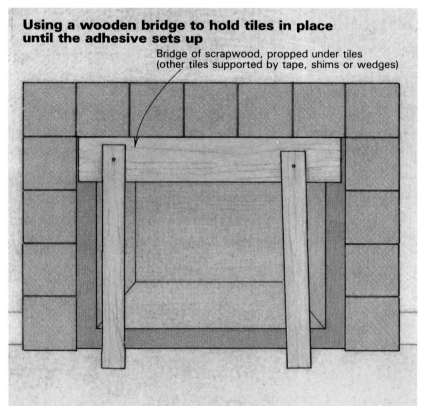

Bridge of scrapwood, propped under tiles (other tiles supported by tape, shims or wedges)

Fountains and swimming pools

For installations where the tile will be continuously submerged in water, choose only vitreous tile. And because such installations tend to expand when filled with water because of the added weight, I strongly recommend using only thinset adhesives and grouts to which a latex additive has been added. While many of the details of tiling swimming pools and fountains will be familiar to anyone who has studied earlier chapters, many others are unusual, and beyond the scope of this book. I'd suggest that you contact one of the tile trade associations (see the Resource Guide) for their technical publications on the subject.

Paving stones

As much as I like ceramic tile, I am easily seduced by the natural beauty of paving stone, and I thoroughly enjoy the challenge of its installation. Stone is usually purchased in gauged form, that is, cut to a uniform thickness and dimension, but some is available in cleft form, meaning that it has been split rather than sawn from large chunks of stone. Gauged stone is set more or less like regular ceramic tile (see p. 18 for basic information on working with gauged stone), while the very irregular shapes and sizes of cleft stone require that it be set quite differently. Before exploring how to install cleft tile, let's look at one kind of gauged tile that has a few of its own special setting requirements.

Gauged onyx tile All stone tiles require a sturdy setting bed, but this is especially important for onyx tiles because of this stone's delicate internal structure. I suggest limiting your choice of setting bed for an onyx floor to either a concrete slab or a 1½-in.-thick mortar bed floated over a ¾-in.-thick plywood subfloor. If you're obliged to work with another type of setting bed, call in a structural engineer or an architect. Either can arrange a test to determine the deflection rate of the bed, that is, how much it will flex in use. The test is not particularly complicated (it takes me about 20 minutes to do), but it does require some special equipment.

If onyx tile is to be installed on a wall or countertop, it will bear less weight than it would on a floor, and minimizing deflection in the setting bed is less of a problem. By pushing on the wall or countertop, you'll see if the surface flexes noticeably. If it does, it needs reinforcement to serve as a setting bed for this tile.

When setting onyx tiles, use only an epoxy thinset as the adhesive and combine it with a latex additive. Choose a white epoxy to keep it from showing through any transparent spots in the stone. In addition to spreading adhesive on the setting bed, back-butter each of the tiles as it is set. Be sure to clean the joints afterwards.

If you find that the tiles have small pits in the surface, a problem introduced in the manufacturing process and common to many types of stone tiles, the cavities can be filled after the tile is set. To create the filler, mix clear-colored epoxy glue (the kind sold in tubes in a hardware store) with some onyx dust sanded from a tile. Pack the paste into the pits and let it harden. Then sand the surface smooth with 200-grit and progressively finer wet-or-dry sandpaper, and finally polish the tiles with stone polishing compound (see the Resource Guide). Do *not* use steel wool to sand the tiles—steel-wool fragments can get trapped in the epoxy.

When grouting this or any other stone tile, combine a latex additive with the grout. Also be sure to clean up the grout quickly, and at all costs avoid using an acid cleaner for the grout haze, as this spells disaster on stone tiles.

Cleft paving stones Because of the highly irregular shape and size of cleft stone, installing it is like working a jigsaw puzzle: each piece is contoured to fit its neighbor. Let's look at the special procedures for installing cleft stone in the context of an entryway I recently set with slate from mainland China.

Cleft slate should be set only on a bed of mortar or concrete, twice as thick as the average thickness of the slate being set (in this case, the thickness ranged from ¼ in. to almost 3 in.). In no case, however, should the setting bed be less than 1 in. thick.

If you're floating a bed of mortar, I recommend using a latex additive with the deck mud to prevent efflorescence. If the bed is concrete, waiting the full 28-day period concrete needs to cure should prevent this problem. In both cases, the bed should be allowed to harden before any of the stones are actually installed.

The organizing principle in setting a cleft-stone floor is to position the largest and thickest pieces first and then build the rest of the floor around these anchoring stones—a procedure that needs to be done in overlapping stages. I began this job, as I always do when working with cleft stone, by grouping the stones in piles according to size. Once I had arranged all the pieces of slate into about a dozen piles, I was ready to begin the first round of setting. After first installing the largest pieces, distributing them evenly throughout the entryway, I would set progressively smaller sizes of stones until the entire area had been covered. At the point when the stones began to touch or overlap one another, I would have to begin trimming them to make them fit together. To do this, I would slip a new stone into the fresh mortar supporting one already set and then scribe a trimming line on the new stone to guide me in chipping it to shape with a mason's hammer. While this may sound like a tedious way to proceed, this setting pattern actually saves a lot of work. If I had simply started in one corner of the entryway and worked my way across the floor, I would have needed to trim almost every piece of stone to fit its neighbor.

After grouping the cleft stones according to size, I distributed the largest ones throughout the entryway (below left). Then I set the slate, progressing from the largest to the smallest sizes and placing the pieces randomly about the foyer. When the stones being set overlapped one another, I marked trimming lines on them and chipped them to shape with a mason's hammer (below right).

To set the stones, I used a combination of thinset adhesive and a slightly wet mixture of deck mud. I applied a thin layer of the adhesive to both the setting bed and the back of the slate, and then troweled deck mud over the thinset on the setting bed to shim up the stone and make its top surface level with that of its neighbor. To ensure accuracy and to speed up the lengthy procedure of leveling the large stones set first, I made a height gauge, like that shown in the drawing below, from a couple of scraps of 2x4s.

After positioning each of these large pieces of slate in the mortar, I placed the gauge over each stone and tapped it with a hammer until the gauge's "legs" made contact with the setting bed. I then removed the gauge and cut away the mud that had oozed beyond the edge of the slate. By repeating this procedure with each new piece of slate, I ensured that it was set at the correct height.

Once I had set the largest stones randomly over about a third of the entryway, I no longer needed the height gauge. Instead, I could gauge the height of each new stone with a straightedge bridging two pieces of slate already set in mortar. When I had gotten the largest pieces of slate set, I stopped to let the mortar supporting the slate set up overnight.

I set the remaining stones just as I had the larger pieces of slate, using a straightedge leveled on the surface of neighboring stones to adjust the height of each new piece. When I had set a "community" of stones, I raked the deck mud from between them with the tip of a narrow margin trowel, cutting the mud down to a depth of about ½ in. to leave room for the grout. Then I cleaned off the surface of the slate with a damp sponge.

The process for grouting cleft stone is about the same as that for ceramic tile. More care, however, must be taken to clean up the grout and to do it quickly, since the uneven surface of the stone can easily trap the grout.

While grout joints up to 1 in. wide are not uncommon on informal slate floors, I chose ¼-in.-wide joints for this formal foyer, which meant many hours of chipping with the mason's hammer to produce these narrow joints.

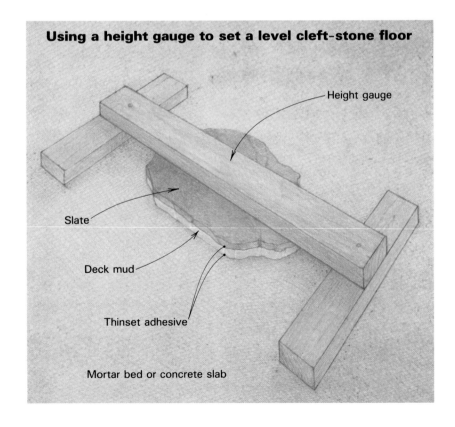

Using a height gauge to set a level cleft-stone floor

Height gauge

Slate

Deck mud

Thinset adhesive

Mortar bed or concrete slab

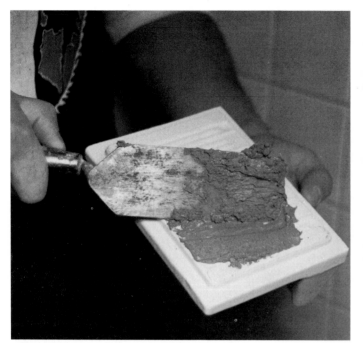

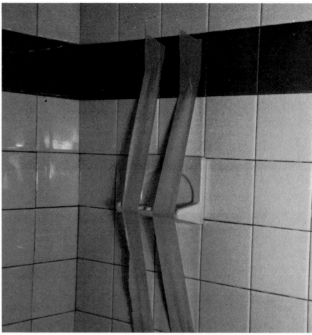

After applying adhesive to the setting bed and the back of the soap dish (above left), position the dish, shimming it with tile chips, and secure it with masking tape until the thinset has dried (above right).

Soap dishes and grab bars

Both metal and ceramic-tile soap dishes can be installed in showers. I don't care for metal soap dishes because they're difficult to keep clean and because installing them requires cutting a hole in the setting bed and the waterproofing membrane. Instead, I always urge customers to choose ceramic-tile soap dishes, which come in two types: one that's mounted to the setting bed like a regular tile and protrudes out from the wall, and one that's recessed into the wall.

While these two types of soap dishes are installed differently, they should both be positioned *after* the rest of the tile has been set on the wall or backsplash. This, of course, means that as you're setting the main field of tile, you'll need to omit or cut tiles to accommodate the dish. As well, despite the fact that many manufacturers of soap dishes say in their installation instructions that the dishes can be installed with grout, they should be adhered with a thinset adhesive—*not* grout and certainly *not* an organic mastic.

The surface-mounted dish is bonded directly to the setting bed. There's usually a mounting pad on the back side that spaces the dish slightly away from the wall. Depending on the size of the dish, this allows it to be inset either with a grout joint surrounding it, or to partially or completely overlap the surrounding tiles, eclipsing one or more grout joints.

Installing a surface-mounted soap dish is simple. Cover both the setting bed and the mounting pad with a layer of thinset about ¼ in. thick, and firmly press the dish into position. If your soap dish and field tiles are different sizes (as were mine in the photos above), you may want to use tile wedges or chips of tile to shim up the dish and support its weight until the adhesive sets up. Clean off any thinset that oozes out of the joints and temporarily anchor the dish in position with a couple of strips of masking tape. Allow the thinset to harden overnight before grouting the joint.

If you prefer the look of a recessed soap dish, be ready to tackle a more complex job. Whether you plan a thick-bed or a thinset installation, fasten 2x blocking to the framing to create support around the approximate mounting position of the dish. The space within the blocked area should be about 6 in. wider and higher than the actual size of the dish. Next install the substrate and the waterproofing or curing membrane, cutting a hole in the membrane corresponding to the position of the dish. Seal the membrane to the blocking with cold-patch roofing asphalt. Then fashion a small "pocket" out of membrane material, using the box-fold technique described in making a shower pan (see p. 166) to fit into the recess created by the blocking. Around the wall opening, spread cold-patch roofing asphalt (if you're floating a mortar bed) or thinset adhesive (if you're doing a thinset installation), then press the pocket into place and seal its folds and the flaps overlapping the wall membrane with asphalt or adhesive, respectively. Next, if you're using a mortar setting bed, float the wall up to and around the opening and let the float harden. For both thick-bed and thinset jobs, set the wall tiles up to the opening and let them sit overnight. Then lightly coat the recessed membrane pocket with thinset and stuff it with wall mud, shaping it approximately to fit the back of the soap dish. Once this has dried, coat its surface and the mounting sides of the dish with a ¼-in.-thick layer of thinset and press the dish into place. Clean off any excess thinset and allow the adhesive to harden before grouting.

Soap dishes often have a handle molded into the body of the dish. Since the dish is designed to hold soap, not the weight of a person, *never use this handle as a grab bar!* You risk serious injury, or, at the very least, you're liable to break the dish or pull it away from the wall. If you want a grab bar on your tiled wall, buy hardware specially designed for this purpose, and fasten it securely to the wall framing behind the tile.

Steamrooms

Steam heat is notorious for the cracks it causes in mortar beds, and when those beds are covered with tiles, they, too, are likely to be affected. Steamrooms are usually built in a shower stall and, depending on how often they're used, may require extra heavy-duty waterproofing to combat the excessive heat and steam. If they're used once a week or less, the shower's regular waterproofing membrane and shower pan should suffice.

There are two different methods of waterproofing a steamroom that gets frequent use. The first method is to laminate CPE to the walls and ceiling, using the same material used for the shower pan. But if you're floating a mortar-bed substrate, the reinforcing wire mesh needed for the job would have to be attached through the membrane to solid material behind, thereby puncturing the membrane.

The second method, and the one I prefer for mortar-bed substrates, is to add a waterproofing membrane to the surface of the bed. This membrane supplements rather than replaces the shower pan on the floor and the curing membrane beneath the bed, both of which are still required. You can use either CPE material for this membrane, bonding it to the floor and walls with a latex or acrylic thinset, or a trowel-applied membrane (I like Laticrete 9235). Both the CPE and trowel-applied membranes will accommodate the differing rates at which the tiles and mortar expand from the heat of the steam and prevent the installation from cracking. In both cases, the membrane should be continuous from pan to walls to ceiling (for instructions on installing a CPE membrane, see pp. 166 and 206). As well, the joints between abutting planes of tile within the shower should be caulked with silicone or butyl caulk.

Trim—nonceramic alternatives to trim tiles

If ceramic trim tiles are not available to accompany the tiles you're setting, you may want to consider some alternatives to ceramic trim. Any
number of materials can be used. Wood is probably the most common
alternative, but I've fashioned trim out of everything from sculptured marble and stone to old decorative bricks, glass wine bottles, broken pieces of
pottery, shells, and even ceramic drainpipe (cut lengthwise into four
pieces to create a massive quarter-round).

Plastic trim Another substitute for ceramic trim, when the job calls just
for surface bullnose, is one of the plastic strips made especially to finish
off glazed tile installations. One such product called TILETRIM is made by
the Homelux Company and is available from Q.E.P. Company (see the Resource Guide). This strip comes in a variety of colors and in two sizes, one
for ¼-in.-thick tiles and another for ⅜-in.-thick tiles. The strips are held in
place with regular thinset adhesive. There are other, similar products, and
your local tile store would be the place to ask about them.

This type of trim has several limitations. The material itself is not as
durable as most ceramic tiles. When used where it will be subject to lots of
wear (to trim the step of a tiled stairway, for example), the strip will wear
out. Unless the plastic is immediately replaced when it begins to show
signs of wear, the edges of the tiles on the steps may in turn get damaged.
Replacing this strip is difficult, however, since the trim is embedded in the
adhesive anchoring the neighboring tiles. For these reasons, I suggest reserving this trim for locations where it will receive minimal wear.

Wood trim Wood is increasingly popular for trimming off tile installations. The only problem with using wood trim is that it expands when it
gets wet and tile does not, and the resulting gaps aren't exactly attractive.
In some instances, the expanding wood may even damage the tile. Even if
the planned installation will not get wet, the wood trim will nonetheless
expand and contract with seasonal changes in humidity. Therefore I recommend completely sealing the wood used for trim, firmly attaching it
with screws, and isolating it from the tiles and the setting bed.

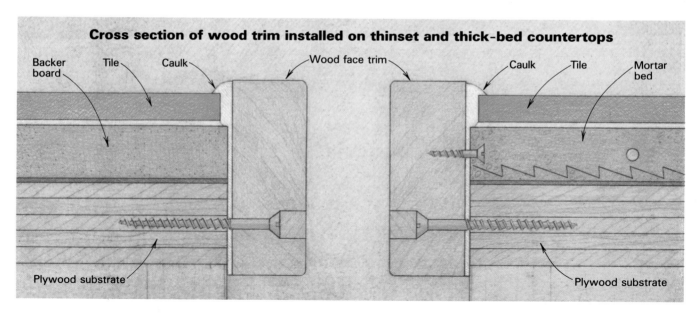

Cross section of wood trim installed on thinset and thick-bed countertops

Backer board — Tile — Caulk — Wood face trim — Caulk — Tile — Mortar bed

Plywood substrate

Plywood substrate

When installing wood trim, screw it to something solid, like a stud or a plywood substrate. The trim should be positioned about ⅛ in. away from the tiles and setting bed to allow for expansion and contraction in both the bed and the wood. Use silicone or another waterproof caulk to fill this gap.

Wooden stair nosing is often used to trim off tiled steps. Even though it's usually nailed in place, I think the nosing should be glued and screwed in position. Although water isn't usually a problem here, the nosing should nonetheless be given at least two coats of sealer before being installed.

On most kitchen countertops, water is a constant problem. Before attaching any trim to a countertop, I recommend sealing the front of the trim and giving the back two or more extra coats of sealer. While wood trim can be installed flush with the surface of the tiles, I prefer to set it 1⁄16 in. to ⅛ in. higher than the tiles to create a lip that will keep spills on the countertop. The trim should be drilled and counterbored every 6 in. to 8 in. to accept screws. Be sure to bore the holes deep enough so that you'll be able to cover the head of the screw with a plug. In addition to the regular counsel on attaching the trim and isolating it from the tiles, I like to fill the joint between the tiles and trim with a marine-grade caulk.

On a thinset countertop, the sealed wood trim should be bedded in caulk and attached to the plywood with screws long enough to offer secure attachment to the plywood. Again keep the tiles ⅛ in. from the trim.

If the trim is to finish off a thick-bed countertop, I suggest attaching it before floating any mortar. The trim can be attached with or without the sink metal usually installed at the front edge of a floated countertop (see p. 192). If you choose not to use the sink metal, prepare and install the trim as explained above. Then run short screws partway into the back side of the trim, so that the protruding screw heads will key into the mortar when it's floated and lock the trim into place. Without the sink metal, the front edge of the countertop needs to be reinforced when it's floated. I like to run lengths of 9-gauge wire or pencil rod 1 in. to 1½ in. from and parallel to the front edge. The wire should be installed in mid-bed.

If you want to use sink metal to float the countertop, choose the *L*-shaped variety and install it before attaching the wood trim. After counterboring the trim every 3 in. to coincide with the elongated slots in the sink metal, caulk the back of the trim, press it into position on the lip of the sink metal and screw it into the slots (with wood trim, you don't need to float wall mud, as you ordinarily would, on the face of the sink metal). Whether or not you use sink metal on the countertop, when tiling the deck, keep the tiles ⅛ in. away from the trim and fill the gap with caulk.

Once the installation is in use, keep an eye out for any dark streaking on the trim, which would indicate water penetrating the wood. The amount of maintenance required for the sealer will depend on how much wear the installation receives. But you can expect the need for a periodic touch-up.

Repairing and maintaining installations

Tiles can be damaged in many ways. Improper installation, insufficient backing or water damage in the substrate are the most common culprits, but falling objects and normal wear and tear can also do tile harm. Before making any repairs, you need to determine whether the damage is being caused by internal forces within the setting bed or by external forces.

Damage caused by external forces—usually falling objects—is generally confined to one or two tiles, which can be replaced without needing any repair to the setting bed. Damage caused by internal forces requires that the setting bed or substrate be repaired before any tiles are replaced. In some cases, this may mean replacing the entire installation.

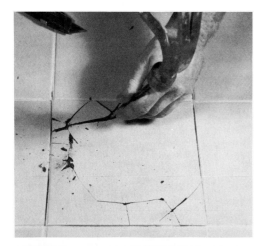

Whether you're removing a single tile or an entire field, *always* wear safety glasses. And when taking out an entire field, I recommend wearing gloves, too, since it's easy to get cut. As well, whenever removing an entire field of tile, always begin the job by disconnecting any tub spouts, shower heads or plumbing valves present, and protecting tubs, preformed shower floors, carpeting or other finished surfaces with tarps.

Removing a single tile The first step in removing a single tile (or only a few tiles) is to remove the grout from the joints surrounding the tile. This prevents the hammer blows to the problem tile from "jumping" through the grout and damaging neighboring tiles. (If you're replacing several tiles, you need only remove grout from the perimeter of the area being repaired.) Do this with a short piece of hacksaw blade, a utility knife, a grout saw, or, if the joints are wide enough, a dry-cutting diamond blade.

Once the grout has been removed, deliver a sharp blow to the offending tile with a relatively light hammer, or with a hammer and punch or cold chisel. Some tiles may shatter throughout with only one blow; others may require several hits. But whatever the number, the blows should be short and sharp rather than earth-shaking. The idea is to be able to remove the tile in small chunks. If you use a punch, try alternately holding it perpendicular to the tile when you hammer it and then at an angle. The latter position may enable you to "wedge" the punch under the tile and pry sections away from the substrate.

Next, with a utility knife, a putty knife or a margin trowel, remove any traces of tile adhesive left on the setting bed. After scraping away all the adhesive, remove any grout remaining on the edges of the adjacent tiles and vacuum away the chips and dust. If all the original adhesive is not removed, the replacement tile will sit higher than the surrounding tiles.

With this done, the replacement tile can be set. You'll get the best results by using the same adhesive as that used to attach the original tiles. If you don't know what that was, at least use the same type of adhesive—that is, organic mastic or a thinset adhesive. Apply adhesive both to the

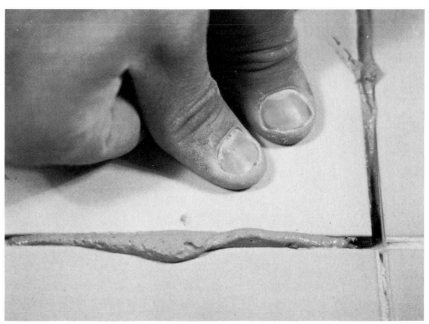

To remove a single tile, first remove the grout surrounding it and then crack the tile with a hammer and punch (top). After removing the chunks of tile, scrape off the adhesive on the setting bed (center and bottom). With fresh adhesive applied to the bed and the back of the new tile, firmly press the tile into place and clean up the excess adhesive (right).

setting bed and to the back of the tile, then firmly press the tile into place and clean up the adhesive that oozes up through the joints. If you're replacing a tile on a vertical surface, tape it in place until the adhesive has dried. Finally, grout the tile in the regular fashion, making sure to dampen the area being grouted so that the setting bed doesn't suck moisture out of the grout.

Removing a field of tiles set over drywall   To protect the surrounding walls, first use a utility knife or a drywall saw to cut through the drywall around the field of tiles. Be sure to cut only through the drywall—any deeper and you might cut through plumbing or wiring behind. Then punch through the tiles with a hammer to create a hole, and grab the edge of the hole with both hands. Give it a few sharp jerks, wiggling the tile and drywall away from the studs. Unless the drywall has been badly damaged by water, the entire installation should come out in moderately large sections. (Some of the sections may be quite large, so it's a good idea to have some help nearby.) Use a pry bar if necessary to get leverage, but be sure not to put a strain on the surrounding walls. After the sections of tiled drywall have been removed, pull out all the nails from the studs before installing a new substrate for the tiles.

Removing a field of tiles set over plywood   There are two ways to remove tiles set over a plywood or particleboard substrate—one at a time or in sections. Try ripping out a couple of individual tiles to see how good the original adhesive's bond is and whether, if it's plywood, the substrate can be reused. If the substrate is particleboard, it should be ripped out and replaced. If the grip of the adhesive is weak and the plywood substrate appears in good condition, you may want to remove the field tile by tile. You may find it difficult to scrape away the old adhesive from the setting bed, however, in which case I'd suggest writing off the substrate and removing the tile and substrate in sections. Compared to the effort of salvaging marginal substrate, the cost of new material is minimal.

When all the tiles have been removed, scrape the adhesive away from the bed with a margin trowel or a putty knife, or power-sand it off using 50- or 80-grit sandpaper. Try not to gouge the plywood too much as you work, and make sure to pound all nail heads level with the surface.

If you decide to remove the tiles and substrate together, first cut through both layers around the perimeter of the installation with either a carborundum or a dry-cutting diamond blade. Then make a second cut, parallel to and about 3 ft. to 4 ft. away from the perimeter cut. Next make perpendicular cuts every 4 ft. to 5 ft. to connect the first two cuts. Pound the hook of a pry bar into one of the cuts and lift out one of the sections of tile and substrate. Once the perimeter of the tile and substrate has been removed, the remainder of the installation may be able to be removed with the pry bar alone.

Removing a field of tiles set over a concrete slab   Before removing any tiles set on a slab, determine if the tiles actually have to be removed. If they're being removed solely for aesthetic reasons, and not to correct structural problems, you'll save yourself a lot of work by simply setting the new tiles over the old ones. If not, grab your hammer and punch and have at it. Once the tiles have been removed, scrape or sand away the remaining adhesive. If the tiles were set with an organic mastic, avoid using chemical strippers to remove the residue, as this could interfere with bonding the new tiles.

Removing a field of tiles set over a mortar bed As with concrete slabs, removing a field of tiles set over a mortar bed is tough work. For this reason, I again suggest considering setting tile over an existing thick-bed installation, unless, of course, there's structural damage in the substrate and framing. If you want to remove the tiles, don't expect to be able to reuse the mortar setting bed. You'll have to rip up the bed, too.

You can remove the tiles in one of two ways. First, you can attack the wall, floor or countertop with a hammer, punch and pry bar. I recommend that you start hammering along the full length or width of the installation at its midpoint and then follow up with more blows to crumble the underlaying mortar. Then cut through the reinforcing mesh with wire snips and use the pry bar to remove portions of the tile and bed.

An alternative method, and the one I find easier, is to use a carborundum or dry-cutting diamond blade to make a grid of cuts in the installation, spaced 12 in. apart. Adjust the depth of the blade to cut through, but no deeper than, the thickness of the tile and bed. Then insert the tip of the pry bar into the sawkerf (enlarge the kerf with the sawblade if necessary) and pry away each section. Once the debris has been cleared away, you can float a new bed in place of the old.

Regrouting an installation Sometimes it isn't the tiles themselves in an installation that evidence damage but the grout joints. Cracked or crumbling grout joints are often the first sign of internal or structural problems, though they sometimes signal nothing more than the fact that the grout itself was improperly mixed, contained too much water or lacked an additive. If the installation is a wet one, the problems may be caused by leaks within the walls or floors. If the installation is dry, the cracks may be produced by seasonal movement within the setting bed. In either case, regrouting may only temporarily resolve the problem, and the first task is therefore to diagnose the trouble as best you can.

If you're faced with a leaking shower stall, begin by checking the obvious sources of the leaks. Make sure that all the seams in the enclosure are properly caulked. The shower floor, whether tiled or of prefabricated fiberglass, should get a careful bead of silicone where it intersects the walls and the enclosure. Also check the packing behind the faucet valve covers and shower head. These should be filled with putty to prevent the passage of water. If all of these areas are in order and the shower still leaks, make sure that the walls supporting the tiles are sound and that the tiles themselves are firmly attached. If you find a loose tile, lift it off and check to see whether the installation includes a waterproofing membrane. If it doesn't, or if the setting bed appears "spongy" when you push on the tiled wall, there's likely to be trouble behind the tilework, which will require ripping out the tiles for repair work.

In a dry installation, check to see if there are other signs of seasonal movement or of settling in new construction. Are any walls cracked or do any doors no longer hang properly? If the answer is yes, the problem may be an improperly prepared setting bed. But before hastily deciding to rip out the tile to repair the setting bed or, alternatively, to add an isolation membrane to protect against the stress of seasonal movement (see p. 94), I suggest regrouting the offending joints—or the full installation if it's not large—and waiting a while to see if properly mixed and applied grout solves the problem.

If you've resolved the problems without ripping out the tiles and are ready to regrout, assess the size and condition of the cracks. If they're relatively small and clean, you can leave the old grout in place and press fresh grout into them with your finger. If the cracks are large or dirty, remove all the grout from the joints with a grout saw, cutting right to the bottom of each joint (try not to cut into the substrate).

Where some of the old grout is to remain in place, you'll of course want to match the new grout with the old. If you're unable to find out the exact type and color of grout originally used, borrow a sample grout card from your local tile store, take it home and pick the closest match. It's unlikely that you'll be able to exactly duplicate the original shade, but unless the color difference is glaring, it will probably go unnoticed. When mixing up a sample color, always wait three or four days for the test grout to dry thoroughly before deciding how well it matches, since the residual moisture in damp grout will slightly alter its hue. A final, and very important, word on mixing the new batch of grout: Always use a latex additive with the grout. The additive will both help waterproof the grout and increase its resistance to cracking.

Once you've cleaned out and vacuumed the grout joints, disassemble, remove and clean any elements in the installation that should be kept clean of grout (a shower head and faucets, for example). Then clean the tiles with a 10% to 20% dilution of muriatic acid or a proprietary cleaner for removing dirt, oil or any soap scum (see the Resource Guide). After mixing the new batch of grout, you're ready to regrout the installation, using the steps outlined in Chapter 3.

Maintaining an installation To clean a tile installation, I recommend using a solution of one cup vinegar to a gallon of water. Although there are many good products on the market specifically designed to clean tile, this mildly acidic solution works well to cut through light oil and dirt, leaves no residue on the tile, and is inexpensive. If you find that the grout joints in an installation routinely get very dirty, give them a thorough cleaning with one of the special tile-cleaning products, let them dry for a full three to four days, and apply a silicone tile sealer on the entire surface of the installation (a tile sealer should not be used on a countertop on which food is prepared). This sealer will occasionally need to be reapplied as it's worn away with use. □

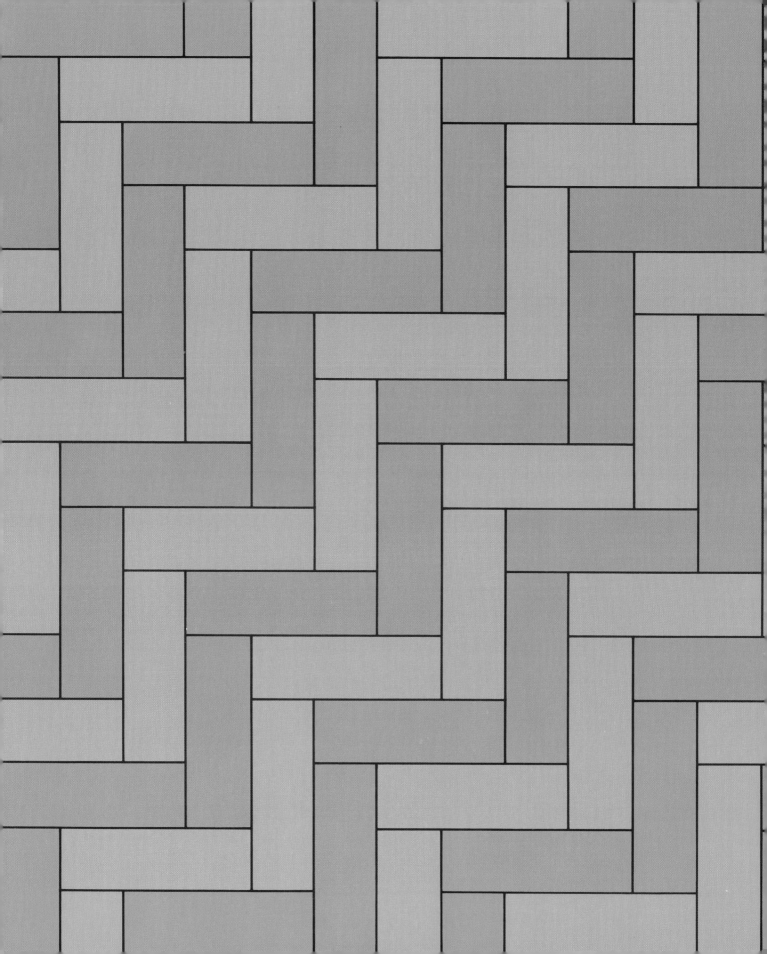

Sources of supply

This listing is intended to help you make your way through the vast array of tiles and tilesetting products that are currently available. While I like best the setting materials used in the projects in Chapters 6 through 11, which I've indicated below, there are many other good products from which to choose. I've included here only those companies whose tilesetting products are endorsed by the Tile Council of America or the Ceramic Tile Institute.

In addition to tile manufacturers found in this listing, there are thousands of artisans around the country producing custom tiles in small shops. If you want really distinctive tiles, I suggest that you seek out one of these craftspeople. You might start by inquiring at the nearest pottery studio or at the art department of the local college or university.

Tile manufacturers

American Olean Tile Company
1000 Cannon Ave., PO Box 271
Lansdale, PA 19446
(215) 855-1111

Art Tile Co.
Etruria Tile Works
Garner St.
Etruria, Stoke-on-Kent
England ST4 7SB
782-29892
(Carries a line of reproduction tiles and makes custom reproduction tiles.)

Buchtal USA
Suite 450
5780 Peachtree Dunwoody Rd., N.E.
Atlanta, GA 30342
(404) 256-0999

Color Tile Supermart, Inc.
515 Houston St.
Forth Worth, TX 76102
(817) 870-9400

Elon, Inc.
642 Saw Mill River Rd.
Ardsley, NY 10502
(914) 693-8000

Epro, Inc.
156 Broadway
Westerville, OH 43081
(614) 882-6990

Florida Tile Division
Sikes Corporation
PO Box 447
Lakeland, FL 33802
(813) 687-7171

Heath Ceramics, Inc.
400 Gate 5 Rd.
Sausalito, CA 94965
(415) 332-3732

Huntington/Pacific Ceramics, Inc.
PO Box 1149
Corona, CA 91718
(714) 371-5320

Impo Glaztile
A Division of Diastone U.S.A. Corporation
PO Box 0207
2852 W. 167th St.
Markham, IL 60426
(312) 333-1800

International American Ceramics, Inc.
PO Box 6600
4942 E. 66th St. North
Tulsa, OK 74156
1-800-331-3651

Italian Tile Center
Division of Italian Trade Commission
499 Park Ave.
New York, NY 10022
(212) 980-8866
(Provides information on the numerous Italian tile manufacturers.)

Marazzi USA, Inc.
Sunnyvale
Dallas, TX 75182
(214) 226-01110

Metropolitan Ceramics
Division of Metropolitan Industries, Inc.
PO Box 9240
Canton, OH 44711
(216) 484-4871

Mid-State Tile
A Mannington Company
PO Box 1777
Lexington, NC 27292
(704) 249-3931

Ro.Tile, Inc.
1615 S. Stockton St.
PO Box 410
Lodi, CA 95241
(209) 334-1380

Summitville Tiles, Inc.
PO Box 73
Summitville, OH 43962
(216) 223-1511

United States Ceramic Tile Company
10233 Sandyville Rd., S.E.
East Sparta, OH 44626
(216) 866-5531

Villeroy & Boch (USA), Inc.
Interstate 80 at New Maple Ave.
Pine Brook, NJ 07058
(201) 575-0550

Wenczel Tile Company
200 Enterprise Ave.
PO Box 5308
Trenton, NJ 08638
(609) 599-4503

Setting tools

American Olean Tile Company
1000 Cannon Ave., PO Box 271
Lansdale, PA 19446
(215) 855-1111
(Full line of setting tools)

Bottini Enterprises
3383 Melendy Dr.
San Carlos, CA 94070
(415) 595-1992
(Straightedges)

Color Tile Supermart, Inc.
515 Houston St.
Forth Worth, TX 76102
(817) 870-9400
(Complete line of tools)

L.S. Starrett
Athole, MA
(617) 249-3551
(Measuring tools)

Los Angeles Diamond Tools, Inc.
13425 Pumice St.
Norwalk, CA 90650
(213) 802-1003
(Distributor of diamond blades)

MK Diamond Products, Inc.
12600 Chadron Ave.
Hawthorne, CA 90250
1-800-421-5830
(Wet saws)

Q.E.P. Company, Inc.
520 W. Nyack Rd.
W. Nyack, NY 10994
(914) 358-4134
(Complete line of tools and supplies)

Risso Machine Shop
8310 Amelia St.
Oakland, CA 94621
(415) 569-2145
(Wet saws)

Rubi Tile Cutters
c/o Arting Spanish Trade, Inc.
7924 N.W. 66th St.
Miami, FL 33166
(305) 591-8669
(Tile cutters)

Superior Tile Cutter, Inc.
1556 W. 134th St.
Gardena, CA 90249
(213) 324-3771
(Tile cutters, biters and other installation tools)

Target Products Division
Federal Mogul Corp.
4320 Clary Blvd.
Kansas City, MO 64130
(816) 923-5040
(Wet saws)

Walton Tool Company
517 W. 17th St.
Long Beach, CA 90813
1-800-421-7562
(Full line of tools)

Safety equipment

AM/SAFE Industrial
Division of Gateway Safety Products
4722 Spring Rd.
Brooklyn Heights, OH 44131
1-800-822-5347
(Full line of safety equipment)

American Optical Corporation
Safety Products Division
14 Mechanic
Southbridge, MA 01550
(617) 765-9711
(Safety glasses)

Fisher Scientific Company
711 Forbes Ave.
Pittsburgh, PA 15219
(412) 562-8300
(Safety glasses, hearing protectors)

Mine Safety Appliances Co.
PO Box 426
Pittsburgh, PA 15230
(412) 273-5000
(Safety glasses, respirators, gloves)

3M Company
Occupational Health and Safety Division
3M Center
St. Paul, MN 55101
(612) 733-1110
(Respirators)

Backer board

Laticrete International, Inc.
1 Laticrete Park North
Bethany, CT 06525
1-800-243-4788
(Latapanel)

Modulars, Inc.
PO Box 216
Hamilton, OH 45012
(513) 868-7300
(Wonder-board)

U.S. Gypsum Industries, Inc.
101 S. Wacker Dr.
Chicago, IL 60606
(312) 358-9500
(Duroc, used in projects in chapters 8 and 10; Imperial Type P fiberglass reinforcing mesh, used in chapters 8 and 10)

Membranes and sealers

Applied Polymers of America
PO Box 2129
Wayne, NJ 07470
(201) 633-1130
(Tile-Tite trowel-applied membrane)

Bostik Construction Products
Division of Emhart (UPCO)
County Line and New Rds.
Huntingdon Valley, PA 19006
(215) 674-5600
(Bostik 2000 butyl caulk)

Compotite Corp.
878 N.E. 160 Terrace
N. Miami Beach, FL 33162
(305) 947-2098
(Composeal, a PVC membrane 20-mil, 30-mil or 40-mil thick)

Laticrete International, Inc.
1 Laticrete Park North
Bethany, CT 06525
1-800-243-4788
(Laticrete 301/335 and Laticrete 9235 trowel-applied membranes)

The Noble Company
614 Monroe St.
PO Box 332
Grand Haven, MI 49417
(616) 842-7844
(Chloraloy 240 and Nobleweld 100, used in project in Chapter 9; NobleSeal T/S)

W.W. Henry Co.
5608 Soto St.
Huntington Park, CA 90255
(213) 583-4961
(Cold-patch roofing asphalt sealers)

Adhesives and grouts

Boiardi Products Corporation
453 Main St.
Little Falls, NJ 07424
(201) 256-1100

Bostik Construction Products
Division of Emhart (UPCO)
County Line and New Roads
Huntingdon Valley, PA 19006
(215) 674-5600
(Hydroment sanded grout, used in projects in Chapters 8, 9 and 10)

Cambridge General
9461 Le Saint Dr.
Fairfield, OH 45014
(513) 874-5980

Color Tile Supermart, Inc.
515 Houston St.
Forth Worth, TX 76102
(817) 870-9400

Custom Building Products
6511 Salt Lake Ave.
Bell, CA 90201
(213) 582-0846
(Type S sanded grout, used in project in
Chapter 11)

Garland-White and Co.
PO Box 365
Union City, CA 94587
(415) 471-5666
(Bon-Don, used as thinset powder for
adhesive in projects in chapters 8, 10
and 11)

H.B. Fuller Co.
Building Products Division
315 S. Hicks Rd.
Palatine, IL 60067
1-800-323-7407

Jamo, Inc.
8850 N.W. 79th Ave.
Miami, FL 33166
(305) 885-3444

L & M Surco Mfg., Inc.
PO Box 105
South River, NJ 08882
(201) 254-4830

Laticrete International, Inc.
1 Laticrete Park North
Bethany, CT 06525
1-800-243-4788
(Laticrete Drybond mixed with Laticrete
333, used as adhesive in project in
Chapter 6; Laticrete 4237, used as liquid
latex additive for adhesive in projects in
Chapters 7, 8, 9, 10 and 11; Laticrete
3701 used as liquid latex additive in
mortar in projects in Chapters 7, 9 and
11, and in grout in projects in Chapters 6,
7, 8, 9, 10 and 11; Latapoxy 210 used as
adhesive for ceiling tiles in project in
Chapter 9 and as laminating adhesive for
backer board in project in Chapter 10)

Les-K Products Division
Western Industrial Mineral Products, Inc.
5004 E. 59th Pl.
Maywood, CA 90270
(213) 560-1673

Miracle Adhesives Corporation
250 Petit Ave.
Bellmore, NY 11710
(516) 221-0950

Southern Grouts & Mortars, Inc.
1502 S.W. 2nd Pl.
Pompano Beach, FL 33060
1-800-641-9247
(Southcrete 900 Type 1 grout, used in
project in Chapter 7)

Stone Mountain Manufacturing Co., Inc.
5750 Chesapeake Blvd.
Norfolk, VA 23513
(804) 853-7451

Summitville Tiles, Inc.
PO Box 73
Summitville, OH 43962
(216) 223-1511

The Syracuse Adhesives Company
14500 Darley Ave.
Cleveland, OH 44110
(216) 851-6065

U.S. Gypsum Industries, Inc.
Durabond Division
101 S. Wacker Dr.
Chicago, IL 60606
(312) 321-4000

W.R. Bonsal Company
PO Box 241148
Charlotte, NC 28224
(704) 525-1621

West Indian Products Corporation
Box 4427
San Juan, Puerto Rico 00936
(Complete line of setting materials)

Tile and grout sealers and cleaners

American Olean Tile Company
1000 Cannon Ave., PO Box 271
Lansdale, PA 19446
(215) 855-1111
(Full line of tilesetting products)

General Electric Company
Silicone Products Division
RTV Products Department
Bldg. 80-87
Waterford, NY 12188
(518) 237-3330
(Silicone caulks)

H.B. Fuller Co.
Building Products Division
315 S. Hicks Rd.
Palatine, IL 60067
1-800-323-7407
(BANISH Grout Cleanup Concentrate,
nonacidic cleaner, as well as other tile
and grout cleaners and sealers)

Laticrete International, Inc.
1 Laticrete Park North
Bethany, CT 06525
1-800-243-4788
(TC-500 and TC-50, mild tile and grout
cleaners)

Mapei Corporation
2900 Francis Hughes
Laval, Quebec
Canada H7L 3J5
(Cottaseal, penetrating sealer for stone
and porous terra-cotta tiles)

Pacific Research Company
1825 E. Flauson Ave.
Los Angeles, CA 90058
(213) 582-6117
(Dresslate, sealer for slate and other stone
tiles)

Southern Grouts & Mortars, Inc.
1502 S.W. 2nd Pl.
Pompano Beach, FL 33060
1-800-641-9247
(Penetrating Sealer, sealer for stone tiles)

The Flecto Company, Inc.
1000 45th St.
Oakland, CA 94608
415-655-2470
(Flecto urethane penetrating oil)

Watco-Dennis Corporation
19610 Rancho Way
Rancho Dominguez, CA 90220
(213) 635-2778
(Watco oil)

Appendices
Resource Guide

Miscellaneous supplies

Atlantis Manufacturing
3605 Arundell Circle
Ventura, CA 93003
(805) 644-9507
(Sink metal)

General Plumbing & Supply
PO Box 4666
Walnut Creek, CA 94596
(415) 939-4622
(E-Z Test Shower Drain, used in
chapter 9)

Multi Seal Pacific Corp.
616 Marengo Ave.
Alhambra, CA 91803
1-800-222-6915
(Multi Seal marble and stone-tile sealer
and polish)

Q.E.P. Company, Inc.
520 W. Nyack Rd.
W. Nyack, NY 10994
(914) 358-4134
(TILETRIM)

Foreign companies making a full line of setting materials

**Australian Master Builders Co.
Pty., Ltd.**
Head Office:
79 Victoria Ave.
Chatswood, N.S.W. 2067
Australia

Axulejos Orion, S.A.
Apartado 500
Monterrey, N.L.
Mexico

Dow Chemical GMBH Werkstade
PO Box 1120
D-2160 Butzfleth
West Germany

L & M Ceramo
Box 578
60 Cassidy St.
Kingston, Ontario
Canada K7L 4X1

Mapei Corporation
2900 Francis Hughes
Laval, Quebec
Canada H7L 3J5

Oy Partek AB Building Chemicals
SF-21600 Pargas
Finland

Organizations

American National Standards Institute
1430 Broadway
New York, NY 10018
(212) 354-3300
(Promotes knowledge and voluntary use
of approved standards for industry,
engineering and safety design in all
industries, including the tile industry.)

**American Society for Testing
and Materials**
1916 Race St.
Philadelphia, PA 19103
(215) 299-5400
(Sets tile materials specifications.)

Art Hazards Information Center
5 Beekman St.
New York, NY 10038
(212) 227-6220
(Addresses issues of health and
occupational safety in all the arts and
crafts.)

**Association of Tile, Terrazzo, Marble
Contractors & Affiliates**
PO Box 13629
Jackson, MI 39236
(601) 939-2071
(Serves every level of the tile industry
with publications, seminars and technical
assistance.)

Ceramic Tile Distributors Association
15 Salt Creek Lane, Suite 422
Hinsdale, IL 60521
(312) 655-3270
(Serves as the marketing arm of the tile
industry.)

Ceramic Tile Institute of America
700 N. Virgil Ave.
Los Angeles, CA 90029
(213) 660-1911
(Provides technical services and
information, and also publishes *Tile
Industry News*.)

**Materials and Methods
Standards Association**
315 S. Hicks Rd.
Palatine, IL 60067
(312) 358-9500
(Shares nonsecret, technical tilesetting
data and encourages the free exchange of
information on tiling problems and
solutions.)

**National Association of
Home Builders of the U.S.**
15th and M Streets, N.W.
Washington, DC 20005
(202) 822-0200
(Disseminates information on all phases of
homebuilding, including tilesetting.)

Tile Council of America
PO Box 326
Princeton, NJ 08542
(609) 921-7050
(Composed of members from various
companies involved in producing ceramic
tile and related products, this group is
dedicated to maintaining a high standard
of quality for tile installations.)

Bibliography

Tile and tile history

Most tile manufacturers provide pamphlets about their products, which include
information about the size, weight, appropriate uses and any special setting
requirements for each line of tile. If these
pamphlets are not available at your local
tile retailer, write directly to the manufacturer for them. One of the most
informative of these booklets is produced
by American Olean Tile Company. *Ceramic Tile Trim* (booklet no. 182)
presents this company's complete line of
trim tile, showing more than 1,000 pieces
of trim and their various uses in a series of
clear line drawings. Whether or not you're
using American Olean tile, this booklet
will give you ideas for trimming off an installation and will also provide helpful
information for ordering trim pieces from
any manufacturer, since the drawings
identify the pieces by their standard industry numbers.

American National Standards Institute. *Standard Specifications for Ceramic Tile* (ANSI A137.1-1980). New York, 1980. (Lists and defines types, sizes, physical properties and industry grading procedures for ceramic tile.)

Austwick, Jill and Brian Austwick. *The Decorated Tile: An Illustrated History of English Tile-making and Design.* New York: Charles Scribner's Sons, 1981.

Berendsen, Anne. *Tiles, A General History.* New York: The Viking Press, 1967.

Catleugh, Jon. *William de Morgan Tiles.* New York: Van Nostrand Reinhold Co., Inc., 1983.

de Solà-Morales, Ignasi. *Gaudí.* New York: Rizzoli International Publications, Inc., 1983.

Descharnes, Robert and Clovis Prévost. *Gaudí: The Visionary.* New York: Viking Penguin, Inc., 1982.

Gonzalez-Palacios, Alvar and Steffi Röttgen. *The Art of Mosaics.* Catalogue with essays by Steffi Röttgen and Claudia Pryzyborowski. Los Angeles: Los Angeles County Museum of Art, 1982.

Haswell, J. Mellentin. *Van Nostrand Reinhold Manual of Mosaic.* New York: Van Nostrand Reinhold Co., Inc., 1973.

Hutton, Helen. *Mosaic Making Techniques.* New York: Charles Scribner's Sons, 1977.

Schaap, Ella, with Robert L.H. Chambers, Marjorie Lee Hendrix and Joan Pierpoline. *Dutch Tiles in the Philadelphia Museum of Art.* Catalogue with essays and technical notes. Philadelphia: Philadelphia Museum of Art, 1984.

Sherman, Anthony C. *The Gilbert Mosaic Collection.* West Haven, Conn.: Pendulum Press, Inc., 1971.

Tile installation

For tips on installing or working with particular materials, for example, backer board, CPE membranes or thinset adhesives, write the product's manufacturer for the relevant brochure.

American National Standards Institute. *Standard Specifications for the Installation of Ceramic Tile* (ANSI A108-1985). New York, 1985. (Lists and defines setting materials and installations.)

Ceramic Tile Institute of America. *Ceramic Tile Manual.* 2nd edition. Los Angeles, 1986. (Lists tools and setting specifications, and recommends solutions for problem installations.)

Materials and Methods Standards Association. *MMSA Bulletin.* Palatine, Ill., 1984. (Provides specific recommendations for problem installations.)

Tile Council of America. *1986 Handbook for Ceramic Tile Installation.* Princeton, N.J., 1986. (Describes various setting materials and installation methods.)

Tile tools and health and safety

American National Standards Institute. *Practice for Occupational and Educational Eye and Face Protection* (ANSI Z87.1-1968). New York, 1968.

———. *Practices for Respiratory Protection* (ANSI Z88.2-1969). New York, 1969.

———. *Safety Requirements for Ceramic Tile, Terrazzo and Marble Work* (ANSI A-10.20-1977). New York, 1977.

Jackson, Albert and David Day. *Tools and How to Use Them.* New York: Alfred A. Knopf, Inc., 1981.

McCann, Michael. *Artist Beware.* New York: Watson-Guptill Publications, 1979.

Power Tool Institute, Inc. *Safety Is Specific.* Arlington Heights, Ill., n.d. (Pamphlet available from Power Tool Institute, Inc., 501 W. Algonquin Rd., Arlington Heights, IL 60005.)

General carpentry and home maintenance

Better Homes and Gardens. *Step-by-Step Basic Plumbing.* Des Moines, Iowa: Meredith Corporation, 1981.

Feirer, John R. and Gilbert Hutchings. *Carpentry and Building Construction.* Peoria, Ill.: Glencoe Publishing Co., 1986.

Safford, Edward L., Jr. *Electrical Wiring Handbook.* Blue Ridge Summit, Penn.: Tab Books, Inc., 1980.

Sunset Editors. *Basic Home Wiring.* Menlo Park, Calif.: Lane Publishing Co., 1977.

———. *Basic Plumbing.* Menlo Park, Calif.: Lane Publishing Co., 1983.

Wagner, Willis H. *Modern Carpentry.* South Holland, Ill.: The Goodheart-Wilcox Company, Inc., 1984.

Periodicals

Tile and Decorative Surfaces. Magazine published ten times a year by Tile and Decorative Surfaces Publishing, Inc. (17901 Ventura Blvd., Suite D, Encino, CA 91316) for any interested reader.

Tile Industry News. Newsletter published bimonthly by Ceramic Tile Institute of America (see listing of organizations on p. 226) for industry employees.

Tileletter. Newsletter published monthly by Association of Tile, Terrazzo, Marble Contractors & Affiliates (see listing of organizations on p. 226) for industry employees.

acrylic thinset adhesive   See *latex thinset adhesive.*

ANSI   American National Standards Institute. This organization was established in 1918 to promote knowledge and voluntary use of approved standards in industry, including engineering and safety design.

back-butter   To apply adhesive on the back of a tile to supplement the adhesive spread on the setting bed. All button-backed tiles, sheet-mounted mosaic tiles, small cut tiles and any tile with an uneven back require back-buttering to ensure a strong bond between them and the setting bed.

back-mounted tile   Tile packaged in sheet format, with the mounting material applied to the back of the tile.

bisque   The refined mixture of clay, water and additives that has been shaped into the body of a tile.

bond strength   A tile adhesive's ability to resist separating from the tile and setting bed after curing (see *grip*).

brick-veneer tile   Tile produced by several methods that simulates the appearance of real brick.

button-backed tile   Tile manufactured with raised dots or squares on the back, which serve to separate the individual tiles when they are stacked in the kiln and ensure that heat circulates uniformly among them.

caulk   A soft, putty-like, flexible and waterproof material used in tiling primarily to seal seams around plumbing valves and faucets and to cap off expansion joints.

cement-bodied tile   Tile made of mortar rather than clay. This tile has the appearance of stone or paver tile, is very durable and is less expensive than ceramic tile.

chlorinated polyethylene (CPE) membrane   A covering made of chlorinated polyethylene in sheet form, which is applied to a setting bed or substrate to serve as a waterproofing, curing or isolation membrane.

cleft stone   Stone tile split, rather than sawn, from a large block of stone and consequently uneven in thickness and dimensions.

cold joint   A poorly bonded joint formed in a mortar surface when one area of mortar hardens before the next batch is placed against it.

compressive strength   A tile adhesive's ability to withstand a heavy load without fracturing.

cove trim   Trim tile with one concave edge that serves to form the juncture between a floor or countertop and a wall.

CTI   Ceramic Tile Institute of America. Established in 1954, this organization works to upgrade installation standards and test new materials.

curing membrane   A covering applied to a substrate over which a mortar setting bed is to be floated in order to prevent the substrate from sucking moisture from the mortar and causing it to cure prematurely.

deck mud   See *mortar, mud.*

dot-mounted tile   Tile packaged in sheet format and held together by plastic or rubber dots between the joints.

down angle   Trim tile with two rounded or curved edges that serves to finish off an outside corner.

efflorescence   The whitish deposit of soluble salts on the surface of grout or mortar. Carried to the surface by moisture that evaporates, the salts can come from the water used to mix the grout or mortar, the bisque of the tiles, or any salt-bearing water that enters the installation from an outside source.

embossed-back tile   Tile whose back is embossed with marks to identify manufacturing specifications for a particular production run.

epoxy thinset adhesive   One of the three types of sand-and-cement-based, thinset tile adhesives, which must be mixed with liquid epoxy resin before use. See also *thinset adhesive.*

expansion joint   An intentional interruption in a field of tile to prevent damage to the tiles from seasonal movement in the setting bed.

extruded tile   Tile formed when green bisque is pressed through a die and cut to specified lengths.

face-mounted tile   Tile packaged in sheet format, with the mounting paper applied to the face of the tile.

fat mud   See *mortar, mud.*

field tile   Tile set in the main field of an installation.

float strips   Wooden strips used in pairs when floating a mortar bed to gauge the depth of the bed and provide a guide for screeding away the excess mortar on the surface. Sometimes called screeds.

floated bed   A bed of mortar applied to a floor, wall or countertop to serve as the setting surface for tile.

freeze-thaw stability   The ability of a tile installed outdoors to withstand, without cracking, the cycle of freezing and thawing in colder climates. Porous, nonvitreous tiles, which readily absorb water, are less freeze-thaw stable than nonporous, vitreous tiles.

gauged stone   Stone tile cut to uniform thickness and dimensions and sometimes polished.

glaze   The protective, decorative coating, usually made of lead silicates and pigment, that is fired on the face (and sometimes edges) of many tiles.

green bisque   The unfired bisque, or body, of a tile.

grip   A tile adhesive's ability to hold a tile in place once the adhesive has cured (see *bond strength*).

grout   A sand-and-cement-based powder, mixed with a liquid before use, that serves to fill in the joints between tiles and finish off an installation.

grout, plain and sanded   Cement-based material used to fill in the joints between tiles. Plain grout is used for joints less than $\frac{1}{16}$ in. wide, while grout to which sand has been added for strength is used for wider joints.

hang A tile adhesive's ability to hold a tile in place on a vertical surface before the adhesive has cured.

hot-mopped pan An old-fashioned type of shower pan made of alternating layers of hot asphalt and tar paper.

impervious tile An extremely dense-bodied tile that, by comparison with nonvitreous tile, is fired at a very high temperature for a long period of time. The bisque of this tile contains less than 0.5% air pockets, is therefore almost waterproof and is freeze-thaw stable. Some impervious tiles have high compressive strength, while others are very fragile.

inside corner The joint at the internal angle of two intersecting surfaces.

isolation membrane A covering used on top of a setting bed to prevent seasonal movement in the bed from cracking the tiles.

jury stick (story pole) A measuring stick created for a particular tile installation whose unit of measure, rather than inches or centimeters, is the width of a single tile and grout joint used for that job. This tool gives the setter a quick, efficient means of determining how many tiles will fit in a given area and where to position layout lines.

latex or acrylic thinset adhesive One of the three types of sand-and-cement-based, thinset tile adhesives, which must be mixed with a liquid latex or acrylic additive before use. See also *thinset adhesive.*

layout lines Lines chalked on a setting bed to guide in accurately setting tile.

leather-hardened tile Bisque ready for firing in a kiln, which has dried sufficiently to lose its pliability.

level (1) A surface or line with all points at the same elevation. (2) Horizontally straight.

margin The perimeter of an installation. In the case of a floated mortar bed, the margin refers both to the bed's entire outside edge and also to the narrow side areas of the bed falling beyond the farthest float strips (see drawing, p. 87).

mesh See *sand.*

mortar The mixture of sand, cement and water used for floating mortar beds, often referred to as mud by professional tilesetters. Mortar is prepared either as deck mud or as wall mud. Used on floors and countertops, deck mud is a stiff mixture that can support heavy loads when dry. Wall mud, also called fat mud, is a thinner, more spreadable mixture to which lime has been added to make it sticky so that it will cling to walls.

mosaic tile Glass or vitreous porcelain or clay tiles that are 2 in. square or smaller, usually unglazed and generally packaged in sheet-mounted format.

mud The term professional tilesetters often use for the mortar floated over a floor, wall or countertop as a setting bed for tile. See also *mortar.*

nonvitreous tile A soft-bodied, very porous tile that, by comparison with vitreous tile, is fired at a low temperature for a short period of time. With about 7% of its bisque made of air pockets, nonvitreous tile is very absorbent and hence not freeze-thaw stable.

open time The time exposed adhesive spread on a surface takes to begin to "skin over," or lose its bonding ability.

organic mastic A ready-to-use petroleum- or latex-based tilesetting adhesive, which, by comparison with any of the thinset adhesives, has less bond and compressive strength, is more readily damaged by water, and is less flexible when cured.

outside corner The joint at the external angle of two intersecting surfaces.

paver tile Clay, shale or porcelain tile, either formed in frames by hand or mechanically rammed into a die, which is usually at least ½ in. thick, occasionally glazed and principally used on floors. Most paver tiles are produced in Mexico and in the Mediterranean countries.

penetrating oil A type of sealer used to protect the surface of unglazed tile, which penetrates the bisque of the tile.

penny rounds Small mosaic tiles shaped like thick pennies.

perimeter joint An expansion joint placed at the margin of an interior floor between 16 ft. square and 24 ft. square or a wall 12 ft. to 24 ft. long. This joint allows for seasonal expansion in the floor or wall while preventing damage to the tiles.

plumb A surface or line perpendicular to a level surface or line (see *level*).

quarry tile Extruded, unglazed, vitreous or semi-vitreous clay tile, usually ½ in. to ¾ in. thick, which, because of its density, is often used on floors.

radius trim (radius bullnose) Curved tile used to border and complete a field of tile installed on a raised setting bed.

reference lines A pair of lines chalked on a setting bed that intersect at a 90° angle and establish the starting point for plotting a grid of layout lines to guide in accurately setting tile.

reinforcing mesh Wire mesh used over a mortar substrate being floated or at midpoint in a mortar bed to strengthen the bed.

retarder additive An ingredient found in adhesive and grout additives that slows down the evaporation of liquid from the setting material, retarding the rate at which the setting material cures and enabling it to achieve a higher bond strength.

ridge-backed tile Tile manufactured with a series of ridges on the back, which increase the surface area contacting the tile adhesive and thus improve the adhesive's grip.

sand The fine aggregate used to increase the strength of mortar and concrete and reduce shrinkage tendencies. The grade, or size, of sand particles is determined by passing the sand through various mesh materials called sieves, which are given a designation based on the number of holes per inch in the material.

screed (noun and verb) The straightedged tool used to straddle a pair of float strips and cut away, or screed, the excess mud on the surface of a floated bed of mortar.

semi-vitreous tile Somewhat porous tile fired at approximately the same temperature as nonvitreous tile but for a slightly longer time. Because air pockets make up from 3% to 7% of its bisque, this tile is absorbent and not particularly freeze-thaw stable.

set-up time The time adhesive spread on a surface takes to begin curing, or hardening.

setting bed The surface on which tile is set.

shower and tub pan A heavy-duty type of waterproofing membrane used on installations below the waterline, for example, shower floors and tubs, which is installed below the setting bed and which must be able to hold water.

slake In tilesetting, to allow the mixture of mortar, thinset adhesive or grout to "rest" for a brief period after its ingredients have been thoroughly combined and before the final mixing occurs. Slaking enables the moisture in the mix to penetrate any lumps in the dry components, making it easier to complete the mixing procedure.

spacer See *tile spacer.*

spacing lugs Built-in projections on the edges of a tile that, like tile spacers, enable the setter to install tiles with a consistently sized grout joint.

speed-cap trim Two-piece trim tile that, like *V*-cap trim, is used on the front edge of a countertop and has a top surface curved slightly upward to prevent water from running onto the floor.

spots Small, glazed paver tiles used as accent tiles with larger pavers.

square Having corners that are 90°.

story pole See *jury stick.*

subfloor A rough floor, whether plywood or boards, which is laid over joists and on which an underlayment, or substrate, is installed.

substrate The backing to which another material is applied or attached.

surface trim (surface bullnose) Field tile with one rounded edge used to border and complete an installation.

TCA Tile Council of America. Established in 1945 and composed of companies producing tile and related products, this organization promotes the industry and sets installation specifications.

thick-bed installation An installation using a floated bed of mortar as its setting bed.

thin-bed, or thinset, installation An installation using a nonmortar setting bed, which may or may not use a thinset adhesive.

thinset adhesive One of three types of powdered, cement-based tilesetting adhesives that must be mixed with a liquid before use. Whether a water-mixed thinset, a latex or acrylic thinset, or an epoxy thinset, this type of adhesive, by comparison with an organic mastic, has greater bond and compressive strength, sets up more quickly, is more flexible when dry, and is more water- and heat-resistant.

thinset installation See *thin-bed installation.*

thinset mortar The generic term tilesetters use to refer to mortar-based tilesetting adhesives.

3-4-5 triangle A triangle with sides in the proportion of 3:4:5, which produces one 90° corner. Plotting a 3-4-5 triangle is a method many tilesetters use to establish a pair of square reference lines on a large surface. These lines can be used both to determine if the installation site is square and to create a grid of layout lines for setting tile.

tile spacer A plastic device sold in various shapes and widths that is used to ensure a consistently sized grout joint when setting tile.

tolerance limits Acceptable deviations in the level, plumb and square conditions of the framing whose effect on a tile installation will be negligible. The TCA guidelines, for example, state that walls no more than ⅛ in. out of square in 10 ft. can be tiled with minor adjustments in the layout.

top-coat sealer A product that seals and protects the surface of unglazed tile.

trim tile Tile glazed on one or more edges and produced in a variety of shapes to border and finish off the main field of an installation.

trowel-applied membrane A three-part waterproofing membrane applied on top of the setting bed and consisting of a layer of fabric sandwiched between two layers of liquid latex.

tub pan See *shower and tub pan.*

underlayment On floors, a smooth surface applied over a subfloor, on which tile is set.

up angle Trim tile with one rounded or curved corner that serves to finish off an inside corner.

V-cap trim *V*-shaped trim tile used on the front edge of a countertop. The tile's top surface is gently curved upward at the front edge to prevent water from running onto the floor.

vitreous tile Dense-bodied, nonporous tile that, by comparison with nonvitreous tile, is fired at a high temperature for a long period of time. Because the ingredients in the resulting bisque have fused together like glass, this tile contains only from 0.5% to 3% air pockets, absorbs very little water, is freeze-thaw stable and has a high compressive strength.

wall mud See *mortar, mud.*

water-mixed thinset adhesive One of the three types of sand-and-cement-based, thinset tile adhesives, which must be mixed with water before use. See also *thinset adhesive.*

waterproofing membrane A covering applied to a substrate or on top of the setting bed before tiling to protect the substrate and framing beneath from damage by water that may penetrate the installation.